SILICON VALLEY BANK

This book provides a firsthand account of the founding, ascent, and dissolution of Silicon Valley Bank (SVB), a tech community bank founded in 1982 with US$5 million that became the nation's 13th largest bank and tech industry's lender and bank. In this pathbreaking work, which challenges conventional understanding of risky tech lending by showing how an independent community bank became the go-to bank for the tech industry in the United States, Xuan-Thao Nguyen includes interviews with key players, ranging from the original founders and early employees to the final CEO of SVB. Chapters explore how the relationship between the venture capital (VC) industry and SVB transformed the way commercial banks comply with banking regulators while lending and nurturing young tech clients. The book demonstrates why the relationships between investors, startups, bankers, lenders, experts, lawyers, regulators, and community leaders are key ingredients for ongoing innovation in the tech industry. The book concludes with the sobering dissection of SVB's sudden death by $142 billion cuts inflicted by tech bros, social media, and the Federal Reserve Bank's successive interest rate hikes to squash the overheated economy.

XUAN-THAO NGUYEN is the Pendleton Miller Endowed Chair in Law at the University of Washington in Seattle. She has authored numerous books, treatises, and law review articles in the areas of intellectual property, finance, business, and taxation. She also serves as a senior consultant to the World Bank Group IFC.

Silicon Valley Bank

THE RISE AND FALL OF A COMMUNITY BANK FOR TECH

XUAN-THAO NGUYEN

University of Washington

CAMBRIDGE
UNIVERSITY PRESS

CAMBRIDGE
UNIVERSITY PRESS

Shaftesbury Road, Cambridge CB2 8EA, United Kingdom

One Liberty Plaza, 20th Floor, New York, NY 10006, USA

477 Williamstown Road, Port Melbourne, VIC 3207, Australia

314–321, 3rd Floor, Plot 3, Splendor Forum, Jasola District Centre, New Delhi – 110025, India

103 Penang Road, #05–06/07, Visioncrest Commercial, Singapore 238467

Cambridge University Press is part of Cambridge University Press & Assessment, a department of the University of Cambridge.

We share the University's mission to contribute to society through the pursuit of education, learning and research at the highest international levels of excellence.

www.cambridge.org
Information on this title: www.cambridge.org/9781009416177

DOI: 10.1017/9781009416153

First published 2024

A catalogue record for this publication is available from the British Library

Library of Congress Cataloging-in-Publication Data
NAMES: Nguyen, Xuan-Thao N., author.
TITLE: Silicon Valley Bank : the rise and fall of a community bank for tech / Xuan-Thao Nguyen, University of Washington.
DESCRIPTION: Cambridge, United Kingdom ; New York, NY : Cambridge University Press, 2024. | Includes bibliographical references and index.
IDENTIFIERS: LCCN 2023041700 | ISBN 9781009416177 (hardback) | ISBN 9781009416160 (paperback) | ISBN 9781009416153 (ebook)
SUBJECTS: LCSH: Silicon Valley Bank–History. | Community banks–Law and legislation–California–Santa Clara Valley (Santa Clara County) | Banking law–California–Santa Clara Valley (Santa Clara County) | Financial institutions–Law and legislation–Santa Clara Valley (Santa Clara County) | Bank failures–Law and legislation–California–Santa Clara Valley (Santa Clara County)
CLASSIFICATION: LCC KFC250 .N48 2024 | DDC 332.1/2240979473–dc23/eng/20231003
LC record available at https://lccn.loc.gov/2023041700

ISBN 978-1-009-41617-7 Hardback
ISBN 978-1-009-41616-0 Paperback

Contents

Figures

Tables

1

The Bank for the Innovation Economy

Banks know that customers hate them. That is the headline from a CNN Business report from a survey of banking executives.[1] The financial crisis of 2008 engraved stains on banks that more than 80 percent of managers at banks, brokerages, and other financial services firms believe continue to have a negative impact on their companies. JPMorgan Chase, Bank of America, and Citigroup saw their biggest fall in reputation. Their names stayed in the headlines for settlements with the regulators reaching billions. Regulators imposed hefty fines against banks in 2021: Capital One, $390 million; Deutsche Bank, $130 million; Julius Baer, $79 million; Apple Bank for Savings, $12.5 million.[2] The total fines against big banks in the United States in 2020 escalated to more than $11 billion, including the largest single fine issued against Goldman Sachs ($3.9 billion) and the second largest against Wells Fargo ($3 billion).[3]

In recent years, shareholders have voiced their opposition to executive pay and voted to reject pay plans at the world's biggest banks.[4] The excessively large bonuses, lawsuits, and big fines tied to bad practices fuel the public resentment toward banks.

[1] Paul R. La Monica, "Banks Know That Customers Hate Them," *CNNBusiness*, June 17, 2014, available at: https://money.cnn.com/2014/06/17/investing/banks-crisis-reputation [https://perma .cc/RMH3-NRZK] (last accessed September 18, 2023).

[2] Ian Henderson, "Lessons from the Seven Largest AML Bank Fines in 2021," *Forbes*, March 24, 2022, available at: www.forbes.com/sites/forbestechcouncil/2022/03/24/lessons-from-the-seven-largest-aml-bank-fines-in-2021/?sh=374fccd88ced [https://perma.cc/2W9L-45E4] (last accessed September 18, 2023).

[3] "Banks Worldwide Amass $15B in Fines in 2020, U.S. Banks Account for 73%," *Corporate Compliance Insights (CCI)*, January 11, 2021, available at: www.corporatecomplianceinsights .com/banks-15b-in-fines-in-2020/ [https://perma.cc/HF7A-ECZ8] (last accessed September 18, 2023).

[4] Steve Slater, "Shareholder Anger Simmers Worldwide over Bankers' Pay," *Reuters*, May 29, 2014, available at: www.reuters.com/article/banks-salary-shareholders-agm/shareholder-anger-simmers-world wide-over-bankers-pay-idINL6N0O74Tl20140529 [https://perma.cc/MSS5-REKG] (last accessed September 18, 2023).

Banks have a reputation score of 342, compared to retail at 515 and automotive at 570.[5] Wells Fargo ranked the worst on both the 2019 and 2020 Harris Poll Reputation Quotient Rankings.

One site named Wells Fargo, TD, Commerce Bank, Bank of America, Fifth Third, Citibank, and Capital One amongst the banks receiving the most common customer complaints.[6] Another site surveyed and listed the most hated banks in every US state.[7] According to this site, Wells Fargo is most despised in Alaska, Colorado, Idaho, Montana, Nevada, New Mexico, North Carolina, South Carolina, and Virginia. Bank of America is the most loathed in nine states: California, Connecticut, Florida, Kansas, Maryland, Massachusetts, Oklahoma, Texas, and Washington. Chase Bank is the most detested in five states: Arizona, Illinois, Indiana, Louisiana, and New York. Credit One Bank is the most reviled in five different states: Hawaii, Maine, Michigan, North Dakota, and Wyoming. At all times and in all places, the public are ready to name a bank that they dislike. It rests true that customers abhor banks and banks are fully aware of it.

The idea of writing a good story about a bank invites ridicule; yet it seems right. This is because the story is about an independent, community bank that nurtured many startups in the tech community during its path of survival and growth to become the bank for the innovation economy.

The grey building, a modest two levels in height with a prominent ocean blue chevron, right arrow logo perched above the entrance door signaled you were approaching another value, a relative forward direction, a morphism in category theory, a material implication in logic, a pathway of a chemical reaction in a chemical equation, and a notation of Conway chained arrows for very large integers. The logo could very well be a bird with spread wings on its flight path, a boomerang moving toward its destination, or a road sign showing a dangerous curve in the road to keep drivers safe. Pick any of those meanings that the logo teases in your knowledge and subconscious, and you arrive at the unassuming headquarters of the former Silicon Valley Bank (SVB), also known as the Bank for the innovation economy before its sudden demise on March 10, 2023.

The Bank boasted 50 percent of all venture capital-backed tech and science companies in the United States as its clients. The Bank cultivated tech enterprises at all stages, from startups to mid-growth, late-growth, and initial public offering phases.

---

5   Tom Groenfeldt, "Banks Have Got a Reputation, but They Can Improve It," *Forbes*, June 14, 2019, available at: www.forbes.com/sites/tomgroenfeldt/2019/06/14/banks-have-got-a-reputation-but-they-can-improve-it/?sh=70688388247d [https://perma.cc/8KVN-UKBE] (last accessed September 18, 2023).

6   Katherine Muniz, "10 Most Common Bank Customer Complaints," *MyBankTracker*, June 28, 2022, available at: www.mybanktracker.com/news/customer-banking-complaints [https://perma.cc/C6WQ-XSG7] (last accessed September 18, 2023).

7   "These Are the Most Hated Banks in Every U.S. State," *Fairshake*, available at: https://fairshake.com/consumer-guides/most-hated-banks-us/ [https://perma.cc/BE25-QEYB] (last accessed September 1, 2022).

Of all the US venture capital-backed companies that went public by the end of December 31, 2022, the Bank claimed about 55 percent of them as its clients. In tech lending, SVB carefully evaluated and executed loans to fast-growth enterprises of the innovation economy. Without growth, companies will soon wither and die, and the Bank held key factors to make its assessment of a company's financial health in determining a credit line or loan amount. The Bank dedicated 2 percent of its loan portfolio to fledgling enterprises; startups with less than $5 million in revenue. The remaining 98 percent of the loan portfolio were concentrated on venture capital (VC)-backed tech companies at different growth phases and with revenues above $5 million.

Airbnb, Fitbit, Pinterest, and Uber are some of the tens of thousands of tech companies the Bank courted as startup clients. Known as a part lender, part consultant, part cheerleader, and part investor, the Bank helped sustain tech companies in the early stage when their ideas for disruption and world domination were far-fetched. Airbnb founders used technology to persuade strangers to sleep in one another's homes worldwide in arrangements where the host can make extra income while the overnight guests pay less than they would have at a conventional lodging establishment. Maximizing use of the extra room in a house, an apartment, or a residence became a $31 billion company when Airbnb launched its initial public offering (IPO). James Park, the CEO of Fitbit, was inspired in 2006 by his Nintendo Wii, purchased at Best Buy, because the combination of hardware, sensors, and software brought a holistic experience that transforms gaming into an active, fun, and positive activity. A few months later he started Fitbit, leveraging wireless-enabled wearable technology to motivate people to get off their chairs and couches, take steps and get moving, stay active, and become healthier by furnishing them key data, guidance, and inspiration. Fitness enthusiasts adore Fitbit wearable products, and the company has morphed into an American digital health and fitness brand. Before the age of Pinterest, people clipped and pinned their favorite images in scrapbooks and on boards. On Thanksgiving Day in 2009 Ben Silbermann conceived the idea of a site where people post, repost, and share their recipes and beautiful décor images. His now-wife named it "Pinterest." Through word of mouth, eleven million new people visited the site in its first seven months. Pinterest joined the lexicon meaning for sharing photos, just as Twitter had for sharing messages and Facebook for finding friends. Young entrepreneur Travis Kalanick met Greg Becker, CEO of Silicon Valley Bank, with a global plan to connect passengers with ordinary drivers who use their own vehicles without taxi medallions to hire out for ride sharing. Strangers get into other strangers' cars, blissfully disregarding warnings from parents of prior generations that you should never get a ride from a stranger. The world then opened up to the idea of ride sharing as Uber, and riders have no problem with climbing into strangers' cars.

By banking and lending to startup clients for the last forty years, the Bank rose from obscurity to one of the top fifteen largest banks in 2022. From its humble origin as a community, independent bank with one location in the isolated industrial area of northern San Jose in 1983, the Bank amassed assets totaling $208.58 billion. This large sum propelled the Bank forward eight spots from number 22 to 14, joining the group of the largest fifteen banks in the United States during the COVID-19 pandemic. Forbes listed SVB in its prestigious "America's Best Banks 2022." SVB was also on the "List of 100 Best Companies to Work For." Shareholders enjoyed seeing the Bank's net interest income on a fully taxable equivalent basis and noninterest income for 2021, which reached $3.2 billion and $2.7 billion, respectively.[8] At the end of Q1 2022, SVB's assets of $220 billion placed the Bank as the thirteenth largest bank in the United States. These national rankings were astounding because SVB was the only bank in the country, and perhaps the world, with 100% of its business devoted to serving the tech sectors.

Back in 2002, 1,019 full-time employees were working at the Bank's twenty-seven regional offices in innovation centers across the United States. The number of total full-time employees reached 8,000 in 2023. The latest number is even more significant when contrasting it to the original thirteen people crammed into an office in northern San Jose when the Bank first opened its doors in October 1983 with $5 million from 100 investors. The early employees, led by a fearless leader with the mindset of a startup stalwart, all shared a conviction of devoting a third of their business to serving the burgeoning new tech sectors in Silicon Valley.

In the forty years of its existence, witnessing and weathering the 1990s real estate crisis, the 2000s internet bubble, the 2008 Great Recession, and the COVID-19 pandemic in 2020–2022, the Bank faced challenges head-on and transformed itself along the way. Among these challenges, the Bank had to navigate operating in the tech community marred with scandals of sexual harassment and discrimination. But the Bank failed to withstand the herd mentality unleashed by the tech bro culture and social media risks of 2023. The Bank died within the tech sector it operated. But let's not get ahead of ourselves about the Bank's demise. We should first look at the tech culture it once lived within.[9]

The tech culture is rooted in welcoming new ideas, breaking down barriers, and encouraging creative collaboration. However, the same tech culture also enables sexual harassment and misconduct.[10] At the annual Foo Camp, an "unconference" annual tech event, attendees "bounce around the space and ideas and conversations,

---

[8] SVB 2022 10K Filing.

[9] The tech #MeToo is from the author's prior works, see Xuan-Thao Nguyen, #MeToo Innovators: Disrupting the Race and Gender Code by Asian Americans in the Tech Industry, 28 *Asian American Law Journal* (2021): 17–56; Xuan-Thao Nguyen, Disrupting Adhesion Contracts with #MeToo Innovators, Virginia J. of Social Policy & Law, 26 (2019): 165–199.

[10] Katie Benner, "Women in Tech Speak Frankly on Culture of Harassment," *The New York Times*, June 30, 2017, available at: www.nytimes.com/2017/06/30/technology/women-entrepre neurs-speak-out-sexual-harassment.html (last accessed September 18, 2023); Sara O'Brien and Laurie Segall, "Sexual Harassment in Tech: Women Tell Their Stories," *CNN Tech*, July 2017, available at: https://money.cnn.com/technology/sexual-harassment-tech/ [https://perma.cc/ UA5A-FYCC] (last accessed November 28, 2019); John Pletz, "1 in 4 Women Report Harassment at Tech Conferences: Study," *Crain's Chicago Business*, March 12, 2019, 2:04 P.M., available at: www.chicagobusiness.com/john-pletz-technology/1-4-women-report-harassme nt-tech-conferences-study (last accessed September 18, 2023).

and so many of the normal social distances break down into collaboration," but the hidden reality is that at the same conference, female attendees frequently face sexually explicit questions from creators of tech companies during their presentations.[11] During the evening, the Foo Camp unconference shifts to a casual vibe for different activities, as recalled by attendees. The drinking, and the pressure to drink, has reportedly led to male attendees continuing to pour drinks for drunk female attendees, creating an uncomfortable environment. At the Foo Camp and Startup Riot conference, a powerful technology evangelist openly sexually assaulted female attendees by putting his hands on their breasts and bottoms when others introduced him to them in public spaces. From Foo Camp to Startup Riot to Dent Conference, predators roamed and assaulted women in tech even after the women had reported the misconduct to the organizers.[12]

[11] Caitlin Mullen, "Where Tech Conferences Get It Wrong for Women," *Bizjournals*, March 26, 2019, 9:59 A.M. EDT; updated: March 27, 2019, 12:32 P.M. EDT, available at: www.bizjournals .com/bizwomen/news/latest-news/2019/03/where-tech-conferences-get-it-wrong-for-women.htm l?page=all [https://perma.cc/UM8J-CDYC] (last accessed September 18, 2023) ("From sexist comments to robot strippers, tech conferences – and the industry itself – often have an atmosphere that doesn't exactly convey gender equality in the field."). Quinn Norton, "Robert Scoble and Me," *Medium*, October 19, 2017, available at: https://medium.com/@quinnnorton/robert-scoble-and-me-9b14ee92fffb [https://perma.cc/5QYV-TA86] (last accessed September 18, 2023). Additionally, female attendees face sexual harassment and assaults at tech camps and conferences. Davey Alba, "A Multimillion-Dollar Startup Hid a Sexual Harassment Incident by Its CEO: Then a Community of Outsiders Dragged It into the Light," *Buzzfeed News*, May 13, 2019, 9:30 A.M., available at: www.buzzfeednews.com/article/daveyalba/datacamp-sexual-harassment-metoo-tech-startup [https://perma.cc/ZJK3–9539] (last accessed September 18, 2023) ("One evening that week at an after-hours bar with a live band playing, DataCamp CEO Jonathan Cornelissen groped 27-year-old Kara Woo, a DataCamp curriculum lead. According to Woo, as other DataCamp employees milled about, a drunken Cornelissen pressed his crotch into Woo's behind, fondling her hips and thighs."); Gaby Del Valle, "A WeWork Employee Says She Was Fired after Reporting Sexual Assault. The Company Says Her Claims Are Meritless. A New Lawsuit Claims the Company Spent More on Parties than on Sexual Harassment Training," *Vox*, updated October 12, 2018, 6:05 P.M., available at: www.vox.com/the-goods/2018/10/12/ 17969190/wework-lawsuit-sexual-assault-harassment-retaliation [https://perma.cc/E7BG-TZZ2] (last accessed September 18, 2023) ("The complaint, which was filed on Thursday in the Manhattan Supreme Court, details former employee Ruby Anaya's allegations against the company. Anaya, who began working at WeWork in 2014, says she was groped by two different employees at two company-wide events where attendance was mandatory and alcohol was readily available. . . . The first alleged incident occurred in August 2017 at an annual company event called Summer Camp; on Facebook, the company described Summer Camp as a "festival-esque getaway" for employees and their guests. Anaya claims that a male co-worker "grabbed [her] from behind in a sexual manner," and that when that employee was questioned by human resources, he said he didn't remember the event because he was "black-out drunk."); O'Brien & Segall, *supra*, note 9 (reporting that at a tech conference in 2014, Pavel Curda propositioned to Gesche Haas with an email that read, "I will not leave Berlin without having sex with you. Deal?").

[12] Alyssa Newcomb, "#MeToo: Sexual Harassment Rallying Cry Hits Silicon Valley," *NBC News*, October 23, 2017 12:30 P.M. PDT updated October 23, 2017, 12:30 P.M. PDT, available at: www.nbcnews.com/tech/tech-news/metoo-sexual-harassment-rallying-cry-hits-silicon-valley-n813271 [https://perma.cc/G578-QXJM] (last accessed September 28, 2023) ("Sarah Kunst, founder of Proday Media, tweeted she had reported Scoble's bad behavior to organizers of the Dent Conference, yet he still continued to attend.").

Meanwhile, the same behavior goes on in the ordinary workplace at Uber. Susan Fowler, a former engineer at Uber, recounts experiencing a culture of sexual harassment daily.[13] Beginning on her first official day on the Site Reliability Engineer team, the team manager asked her to have sex with him in a string of messages over the company's chat platform. She immediately took screenshots and reported him to Human Resources (HR). HR and upper management at Uber informed her that, because it was the first time the manager had committed sexual harassment and he was a "high performer" at the Company, they would not take any action beyond talking to him. HR also ordered that Fowler choose either transferring to a different team or staying with the same team and receiving a negative review from the manager. HR explained to Fowler that the negative review would not be viewed as retaliation because she was given the option to transfer. Fowler subsequently transferred to a different team. During her one-year tenure at Uber, Fowler also documented other sexist emails and chat records and sent them to HR. Instead of working to fix the problems, the HR representative accused Fowler of initiating the incidents and blamed her for saving the emails and chat records. Her new manager then threatened to fire her if she reported him to HR. Fowler reported the threat to HR and the Chief Technology Officer. Though they admitted to her that the threat was illegal, they once again did nothing because the manager was a "high performer."

Fowler soon learned that other female engineers at Uber had similar experiences. They, too, had reported to HR to no avail. Together, Fowler and the female engineers requested a meeting with HR about the manager's sexual harassment, but the HR representative insisted that the manager "had never been reported before."[14] Later, around the same time these women left Uber, the company's female workforce dropped from 25 percent women to less than 6 percent.[15]

Sexual harassment and misconduct are an "open secret" in the tech industry.[16] The pervasiveness of the open secret occurs beyond the campfires, conferences, unconferences, and team projects. Harassment has even occurred during the initial interviews for jobs at tech companies. For example, the cofounder and former CEO

---

[13] Susan Fowler, "Reflecting on One Very, Very Strange Year at Uber," *Susan Fowler Blog*, February 19, 2017, available at: www.susanjfowler.com/blog/2017/2/19/reflecting-on-one-very-strange-year-at-uber [https://perma.cc/8QH7-VBK6] (last accessed September 28, 2023).

[14] Ibid.

[15] Ibid.

[16] Alyssa Newcomb, "#MeToo," *supra*, note 11 ("Much like Hollywood and the Harvey Weinstein story, a culture of sexual harassment and misconduct being perpetrated by some of the most powerful men in Silicon Valley had long been whispered about. The technology industry's shameful open secret was publicly aired earlier this year when female founders began coming forward to share stories of male investors crossing the line.").

of a startup accelerator told a potential female hire, "I was getting confused figuring out whether to hire you or hit on you."[17]

Very few women dare to speak out about this harassment for fear of destroying both their careers and personal lives. For example, entrepreneur Cheryl Yeoh did not speak out after Dan McClure pushed himself against her in a corner because she "had to preserve" her business relationship with him to ensure a contract was signed that same week.[18] The few female founders in the industry have received lurid texts, groping, and unwanted sexual propositions. Female founders Niniane Wang, Susan Ho, and Leiti Hsu all described their dealings with a partner at a VC firm.[19] Wielding their economic prowess, venture capitalists have attempted to use their companies' funding to silence the female founders.[20]

Tech companies go after "talent," which, in reality, means just male talent. That translates into rewarding male tech workers who are deemed "high performers" with a slap on the wrist when women report sexual harassment.[21] Tech companies protect high-performing men by driving women out of the workplace. They do this by refusing to grant transfers, giving them negative reviews, and threatening to fire them. But forcing women out of the industry is not the only way that the tech companies protect perpetrators of sexual misconduct.

Tech companies have also paid powerful predators attractive exit packages. A survey by Blind reported that 33.05 percent of respondents stated that their companies have paid "high dollar exit packages" to employees accused of sexual

---

[17] Alyssa Newcomb, "Silicon Valley Grapples with How to Fix a Sexist Culture," *NBC News*, July 26, 2017, 3:15 P.M., available at: www.nbcnews.com/tech/tech-news/silicon-valley-grapples-how-fix-sexist-culture-n776906 [https://perma.cc/F8E3-LE6R] (last accessed September 28, 2023).

[18] Cheryl Y. Sew Hoy, "Shedding Light on the 'Black Box of Inappropriateness'," *Cheryl: Breadcrumbs: A Series of Connected Events*, July 3, 2017, available at: https://cherylyeoh.com/2017/07/03/shedding-light-on-the-black-box-of-inappropriateness/ [https://perma.cc/GX8C-PJPC] (last accessed September 2, 2022).

[19] Sarah Lacy, "Binary Capital's Justin Calbeck Accused of Unwanted Sexual Advances towards Female Founders. Where's the Outrage?," *PANDO*, June 22, 2017, available at: https://pandodaily.com/2017/06/22/binary-capitals-justin-caldbeck-accused-unwanted-sexual-advances-towards-female-founders-wheres-outrage [https://perma.cc/W9TH-CCU3] (last accessed September 2, 2022). See also Laura Sydell, "How a Female Engineer Built a Public Case against a Sexual Harasser in Silicon Valley," *NPR*, December 13, 2017, 1:17 P.M., available at: www.npr.org/sections/alltechconsidered/2017/12/13/568455103/how-a-woman-engineer-built-a-public-case-against-a-sexual-harasser-in-sil icon-va [https://perma.cc/82XN-F8WM] (last accessed September 28, 2023).

[20] Sarah Lacy, "Founder: Days before Scandal Broke, Binary's Justice Caldbeck 'Tried to Use Funding to Shut Me Up'," *PANDO*, June 24, 2017, available at: https://pandodaily.com/2017/06/25/niniane-wang-days-scandal-broke-binarys-justin-caldbeck-tried-use-funding-shut-me [https://perma.cc/P3AZ-8QVP] (last accessed September 2, 2022).

[21] Marianne Cooper, "The 3 Things That Make Organizations More Prone to Sexual Harassment," *The Atlantic*, November 27, 2017, available at: www.theatlantic.com/business/archive/2017/11/organizations-sexual-harassment/546707/ [https://perma.cc/XP9Y-U24V] (last accessed September 18, 2023) (reporting that Amazon's CEO Jeff Bezos' silence after Roy Price, head of Amazon Studios resigned amid sexual harassment allegations, "continues a pattern of inaction by the company").

misconduct.[22] These companies include Google, Intel, Booking.com, Uber, Microsoft, Cisco, Overall, Oracle, Amazon, Apple, LinkedIn, and Facebook. For example, Google paid Android founder Andy Rubin almost $100 million amid employees accusing him of sexual harassment. Google also paid $15 million to Amit Singhal, also accused of sexual harassment.[23]

There is yet another way the tech sector has been enabling sexual misconduct: the tech culture fails to punish powerful male employees or employers who have sexually harassed women, even encouraging rivals to hire them or prompting investors to fund them. A long list of examples illustrates this. Google paid Amit Singhal to leave the company, but Uber immediately hired him, allowing him to collect $15 million from Google and enjoy new power at Uber.[24] Eyal Gutentag, Uber's LA general manager, left the company after multiple employees reported him for groping female subordinates. Four months later, Gutentag had a new powerful position as Chief Operations Officer at HopSkipDrive, a competitor of Uber.[25] He subsequently joined ZipRecruiter, a tech unicorn valued at more than a

---

[22] Kyle McCarthy, "1/3 of Tech Employees: My Company Has Given Generous Exit Packages to Employees Accused of Sexual Misconduct," *BLIND BLOG*, November 13, 2018, available at: www.teamblind.com/blog/index.php/2018/11/13/one-third-of-tech-employees-my-company-has-given-generous-exit-packages-to-employees-accused-of-sexual-misconduct [https://perma.cc/7K FH-2D3A] (last accessed September 2, 2022).

[23] Nate Swanner, "Sexual Harassment Payouts in Tech: Here Are the Worst Offenders," *Dice*, November 15, 2018, available at: https://insights.dice.com/2018/11/15/sexual-harassment-payouts-tech-companies/ [https://perma.cc/A2XU-WR8A] (last accessed September 19, 2023); *see also* Jillian D'Onfro, "Google's Approval of $135 Million Payout to Execs Accused of Sexual Misconduct Sparks Fresh Employee Backlash," *Forbes*, March 12, 2019, available at: www.forbes .com/sites/jilliandonfro/2019/03/12/googles-approval-of-135-million-payout-to-execs-accused-of-sex ual-misconduct-sparks-fresh-employee-backlash/#6dea10e23cf3 [https://perma.cc/CLZ6-D2SZ] (last accessed September 19, 2023).

[24] Shannon Liao, "Google Confirms It Agreed to Pay $135 Million to Two Execs Accused of Sexual Harassment," *THE VERGE*, March 11, 2019, 8:35 P.M. EDT, available at: www.theverge.com/2019/3/11/18260712/google-amit-singhal-andy-rubin-payout-lawsuit-accused-sexual-harassment [https://perma.cc/T7ZL-T8Z7] (last accessed September 19, 2023) (reporting that Google first offered to pay Amit Singhal $45 million but then reduced to $15 million because he joined Uber, a rival company); Gabrielle Canon, "Google Gave Top Executive $90m Payoff but Kept Sexual Misconduct Claim Quiet: Report," *The Guardian*, October 25, 2018, 6:42 P.M., available at: www .theguardian.com/technology/2018/oct/25/google-andy-rubin-android-creator-payoff-sexual-mis conduct-report [https://perma.cc/TR79-WGV5] (last accessed September 19, 2023) ("[E]xecutives had relationships and extramarital affairs with subordinate employees, including David Drummond, Alphabet's chief legal officer," with Jennifer Blakely, who "was then transferred to another department, before leaving a year later, having been asked to sign paperwork saying she had departed voluntarily. Drummond's career, meanwhile, accelerated."); Mike Isaac & Daisuke Wakabayashi, "Amit Singhal, Uber Executive Linked to Old Harassment Claim, Resigns," *The New York Times*, February 27, 2017, available at: www.nytimes.com/2017/02/27/technology/uber-sexual-harassment-amit-singhal-resign.html (last accessed September 19, 2023).

[25] Ryan Mac & Davey Alba, "These Tech Execs Faced #MeToo Allegations. They All Have New Jobs," *BuzzFeedNews*, April 16, 2019, 8:00 A.M., available at: www.buzzfeednews.com/article/ryanmac/

billion dollars, as Chief Marketing Officer.[26] Likewise, Mike Cagney, the former
CEO of Social Finance, left the company after a series of reports of sexual misconduct. He then founded a new startup with fresh funding of $120 million.[27] In another
incident, Steve Jurvetson left Draper Fisher Jurvetson after the firm's internal
investigation about his sexual misconduct and, two months later, he debuted
Future Ventures with $200 million in new funding.[28]

Deeply embedded in the tech community is tech bro culture.[29] Beyond their tech
uniforms of hoodies and power vests, tech bros value power, finance, marketing, and
business, in addition to tech. Caleb Williams, a former venture development
specialist, wrote in Quora that the "tech bro is the latest cultural evolution of the
Alpha Male super breed."[30] Tech bros today include both professionals in "VC and
Tech, manifesting in the form of VC's, Product Managers, and family-funded
startup founders, almost entirely localized to the Bay Area."[31] Williams distinguishes
the "tech bro" from the "tech nerd" based on physical appearance, "because the
nerd is far too interested in technology to waste time making himself look good."[32]
Unlike tech nerds, tech bros possess more power, finance, marketing, and business
backgrounds. Outsiders of the tech industry offer similar observations about tech
bros. For example, explicit definitions of common tech bro expressions help society
understand their "language."[33]

tech-men-accused-sexual-misconduct-new-jobs-metoo [https://perma.cc/X32W-WB5W] (last
accessed September 19, 2023).

[26] Ibid.

[27] Ibid.

[28] Ibid.

[29] Jennifer S. Fan, "Innovating Inclusion: The Impact of Women on Private Company Boards,"
Florida State University Law Review 46 (2019): 345, 385. (noting how the bro culture has led to
the rampant sexual harassment and sexist conduct in the tech industry).

[30] Caleb Williams, "What Is a Tech Bro?," *QUORA*, January 17, 2020, available at: www.quora
.com/What-is-a-tech-bro [https://perma.cc/Z6BH-KHC7] (last accessed September 19, 2023).

[31] Ibid.

[32] Ibid.

[33] See, e.g., Julia Carrie Wong & Matthew Cantor, "How to Speak Silicon Valley: 53 Essential
Tech-Bro Terms Explained," *The Guardian*, June 27, 2019, available at: www.theguardian
.com/us-news/2019/jun/26/how-to-speak-silicon-valley-decoding-tech-bros-from-microdosing-to-
privacy [https://perma.cc/84B8-GWVC] (last accessed September 19, 2023) (caricaturizing the
culture of tech bros). *The Guardian* defines "tech bro" as a "US-born, college-educated,
Patagonia-clad male whose entry level salary at one of the FAANG companies was at least
$125,000 and who frequently insists that his female co-workers give him high-fives. Typically
works in product management or marketing. Had he been born 10 years earlier, he would have
been a finance bro instead." Ibid.; see also, Ginny Hogan, "11 Tips for Dating a Tech Bro,"
Medium: The Bold Italic, August 19, 2019, available at: https://thebolditalic.com/eleven-tips-for-
dating-a-tech-bro-4c9fba6552bf [https://perma.cc/X4TT-7TSD] (last accessed September 19,
2023); Kyler Sumter, "What We Mean When We Say 'Bro Culture'," *USA Today*, June 7,
2017, available at: www.usatoday.com/story/college/2017/06/07/what-we-mean-when-we-say-bro-
culture/37432805 [https://perma.cc/42AX-VPTT] (last accessed September 19, 2023) (discussing
the bro culture in the tech industry).

As tech bros ascend in power in tech firms and companies that fund tech entrepreneurs, the bro culture allows men to abuse women in tech systematically. The #MeToo movement reveals the ugly side of tech bros. Over 40 percent of women in the tech industry have reported being harassed by a boss or an investor.[34]

Numerous examples plague the VC sector. Justin Caldbeck, cofounder of venture capital fund Binary Capital, was accused of using his position of power in exchange for sexual gain. Caldbeck targeted female tech entrepreneurs, and six women came forward with allegations against him.[35] Likewise, Chris Sacca, a well-known venture capitalist, an early investor in startups like Twitter, Uber, and Instagram, and a Shark Tank judge, was accused of sexually harassing a female entrepreneur at a tech gathering and admitted to "helping make tech hostile to women."[36] Tom Frangione, COO at Greylock Partners, one of the oldest venture firms with $3.5 billion under management, stepped down after accusations he engaged in an inappropriate relationship with an employee.[37] Dave McClure of venture fund 500 Startups admitted making "inappropriate advances" on "multiple women" and a job candidate.[38]

Women received no relief outside the VC sector either. Tech evangelists with enormous influence like Robert Scoble have faced allegations from several women

[34] Courtney Connley, "Over 40% of Women in Tech Say They've Been Harassed by a Boss or Investor, According to a New Report," *CNBC*, December 17, 2020, 4:00 P.M., available at: www .cnbc.com/2020/12/16/40percent-of-women-in-tech-say-theyve-been-harassed-by-boss-or-investor .html [https://perma.cc/8MAC-BBEP] (last accessed September 19, 2023).

[35] Nathan Vardi, "Founders of Silicon Valley Firm That Imploded Amid Sex Harassment Allegations Are Now Fighting Each Other," *Forbes*, February 28, 2019, available at: www .forbes.com/sites/nathanvardi/2019/02/28/founders-of-silicon-valley-firm-that-imploded-amid-sex-ha rassment-allegations-are-now-fighting-each-other/#475f336a357f [https://perma.cc/3U4W-RQBC] (last accessed September 19, 2023) (reporting that Caldbeck faced allegations he had sexually harassed female tech entrepreneurs who sought funding and that six women came forward to accuse Caldbeck of sexual wrongdoing).

[36] Alex Konrad, "How Super Angel Chris Sacca Made Billions, Burned Bridges and Crafted the Best Seed Portfolio Ever," *Forbes*, April 12, 2015, available at: www.forbes.com/sites/alexkonrad/ 2015/03/25/how-venture-cowboy-chris-sacca-made-billions/?sh=6cdoffcf6597 [https://perma.cc/ NG94-DQHK] (last accessed September 19, 2023); Becky Peterson, "'Shark Tank' Judge Chris Sacca Apologizes for Helping Make Tech Hostile to Women: After Being Accused of Inappropriately Touching a Female Investor," *Business Insider*, June 30, 2017, 3:38 P.M., available at: www.businessinsider.com/chris-sacca-apologizes-after-accusation-of-inappropriate- touching-2017-6 [https://perma.cc/L65Q-JXDV] (last accessed September 19, 2023) (reporting on Sacca's apology for "behaving in ways that made women feel uncomfortable" and *The New York Times*' report that he had inappropriately touched a female entrepreneur).

[37] Cromwell Schubarth, "Greylock Partners COO Left Firm after 'Lapse of Judgment'," *Silicon Valley Business Journal*, August 3, 2017, 7:04 A.M., available at: www.bizjournals.com/sanjose/ news/2017/08/02/greylock-partners-coo-left-firm-after-lapse.html [https://perma.cc/WG5Z-23NH] (last accessed September 19, 2023).

[38] Jonathan Shieber, "500 Startups' Dave McClure Apologizes for 'Multiple' Advances toward Women and Being a 'Creep'," *TechCrunch*, July 1, 2017, available at: https://techcrunch.com/ 2017/07/01/500-startups-dave-mcclure-apologizes-for-multiple-advances-toward-women-and-being- a-creep [https://perma.cc/Z378-B6T4] (last accessed September 19, 2023).

for groping them at tech conferences.[39] Roy Price, Head of Amazon Studios, allegedly made unwanted sexual remarks to a female employee and others.[40] Price "lewdly and repeatedly propositioned" an executive producer of one of Amazon's popular shows.[41]

From tech workplaces and camps to official VC firm parties, tech bro culture parades power and domination through sex and objectification of women. For instance, Steve Jurvetson, a founder of a top-tier VC firm Draper Fisher Jurvetson, hosted an alleged "sex party" with "rampant sex and drug use" following the firm's annual conference in 2017.[42] In a lawsuit, a former WeWork employee alleged that she was fired in retaliation for reporting sexual assault and that the company spent more on parties than on sexual harassment training.[43] Another woman sent a fifty-page document to the company laying out claims of illegal drug use, sexual harassment, and pay discrimination at WeWork.[44] A subsequent investigation discovered instances of managers sleeping with subordinates.[45]

---

[39] Doree Shafrir, "Another Woman Has Accused Robert Scoble of Sexual Harassment," *BuzzFeedNews*, October 19, 2017, 11:56 P.M., available at: www.buzzfeednews.com/article/doree/woman-accuses-robert-scoble-of-sexual-harassment [https://perma.cc/VKD9–68B4] (last accessed September 19, 2023) (reporting Robert Scoble's sexual harassment at O'Reilly Media's Foo Camp event).

[40] Laura Bradley, "Roy Price Stands Accused of Sexual Harassment, Nepotism, and Bad TV Taste," *Vanity Fair*, October 18, 2017, available at: www.vanityfair.com/hollywood/2017/10/roy-price-amazon-sexual-harassment-allegations-big-little-lies [https://perma.cc/LCT2–2FA6] (last accessed September 19, 2023).

[41] John Koblin, "Roy Price Quits Amazon Studios after Sexual Harassment Claim," *The New York Times*, October 17, 2017, available at: www.nytimes.com/2017/10/17/business/media/roy-price-amazon-studios.html [https://perma.cc/2XLR-XQBX] (last accessed September 19, 2023) (reporting on Price's resignation days after the producer publicly accused him of sexual harassment).

[42] Theodore Schleifer, "DFJ Has Apologized for the Reported 'Sex Party' Event at Steve Jurvetson's Home," *Vox*, January 11, 2018, 5:55 P.M., available at: www.vox.com/2018/1/11/16880806/dfj-steve-jurvetson-sex-party-apology [https://perma.cc/S3UF-U6ZC] (last accessed September 19, 2023); see generally, Emily Chang, 'Oh My God, This Is So F—ed Up': Inside Silicon Valley's Secretive, Orgiastic Dark Side," *Vanity Fair*, January 2, 2018, available at: www.vanityfair.com/news/2018/01/brotopia-silicon-valley-secretive-orgiastic-inner-sanctum [https://perma.cc/M9S2-Y5HE] (last accessed September 19, 2023) (reporting on the prevalence of secretive sex parties hosted throughout Silicon Valley and describing Juvertson's party specifically, but anonymously); Erin Griffith, "'Sex Party' or 'Nerds on a Couch'? A Night in Silicon Valley," *Wired*, January 11, 2018, 5:31 P.M., available at: www.wired.com/story/sex-party-or-nerds-on-a-couch-a-night-in-silicon-valley [https://perma.cc/E2BA-2CZN] (last accessed September 19, 2023) (confirming that one of the parties described in Chang's Vanity Fair piece was Juvertson's).

[43] Del Valle, "A WeWork Employee," *supra*, note 10 (describing the claims alleged in former WeWork employee's lawsuit).

[44] Meghan Morris, "Bosses Frequently Slept with Subordinates at WeWork," *Business Insider*, February 22, 2020, available at: www.businessinsider.com/office-relationships-and-sex-abounded-at-wework-under-adam-neumann-2020-2 [https://perma.cc/QM9D-ACJK] (last accessed September 19, 2023).

[45] Del Valle, "A WeWork Employee," *supra*, note 10 (describing the claims alleged in former WeWork employee's lawsuit).

At Uber, a toxic culture of sexual harassment and ineffective HR responses has allegedly existed for years.[46] Under the helm of CEO Travis Kalanick, Uber ignored allegations of rampant sexual harassment and misconduct. Kalanick's "reputation for ruthlessness and machismo" fostered Uber's insider culture, filled "with persistent stories about organisational sexism."[47] Amit Singhal, Uber's Vice President of Engineering, and Ed Baker, Uber's Vice President of Product, resigned over allegations of sexual harassment.[48] Emil Michael, Uber's Senior Vice President, was implicated in an escort–karaoke scandal.[49] The toxic culture drove female innovators away from Uber.[50]

The tech bros seem to share the same superiority belief as billionaire Michael Moritz. As chair and partner at the prestigious venture capitalist firm, Sequoia Capital, Moritz once said that women simply are not as superior as men and that the firm would not "lower our standards" to hire a woman.[51] Other premier VC

---

[46] *See* Johana Bhuiyan, "How Uber Got into This Human Resources Mess," *Vox*, February 21, 2017, 3:25 P.M., available at: www.vox.com/2017/2/21/14673658/uber-travis-kalanick-susan-fowler-diversity-sexual-harassment [https://perma.cc/8AGK-K8CW] (last accessed September 19, 2023) (chronicling Uber's human resources team's slow and delayed development).

[47] Zoe Kleinman, "Uber: The Scandals That Drove Travis Kalanick Out," *BBC*, June 21, 2017, available at: www.bbc.com/news/technology-40352868 [https://perma.cc/K2GY-G8Y6] (last accessed September 19, 2023) (noting Kalanick's resignation came after a series of scandals about sexual harassment, macho culture, and the departure of senior executives).

[48] Vincent Lanaria, "Uber Loses Product and Growth VP Ed Baker amid Company Issues: The Odd Timing of His Resignation," *Tech Times*, March 3, 2017, 11:03 P.M., available at: www.techtimes.com/articles/200181/20170303/uber-loses-product-and-growth-vp-ed-baker-amid-company-issues-the-odd-timing-of-his-resignation.htm [https://perma.cc/7AQM-X75B] (last accessed September 19, 2023); Carl Velsco, "Uber Executive Told to Resign over Undisclosed Sexual Harassment Allegations During Stint at Google," *Tech Times*, February 28, 2017, 02:02 A.M., available at: www.techtimes.com/articles/199535/20170228/uber-executive-told-to-resign-over-undisclosed-sexual-harassment-allegations-during-stint-at-google.htm [https://perma.cc/7KTZ-8TNU] (last accessed September 19, 2023).

[49] Michael J. Coren, "Sexual Harassers in Silicon Valley Have No Idea How to Redeem Themselves," *QUARTZ*, January 13, 2018, available at: https://qz.com/1166153/silicon-valley-sexual-harrasers-are-trying-to-redeem-their-reputations-at-the-expense-of-their-victims [https://perma.cc/WE84-R7C2] (last accessed September 19, 2023).

[50] Christina Cauterucci, "The Sexism Described in Uber Employee's Report Is Why Women Leave Tech: Or Don't Enter at All," *SLATE*, February 21, 2017, 2:03 P.M., available at: https://slate.com/human-interest/2017/02/the-sexism-in-uber-employees-report-is-why-women-leave-tech-or-dont-enter-at-all.html [https://perma.cc/7MZE-ZS7L] (last accessed September 19, 2023).

[51] Noah Kulwin, "One of Silicon Valley's Top VC Firms Finally Hired a Woman Investor," *VICE*, October 20, 2016, 11:00 P.M., available at: www.vice.com/en_us/article/43qg9p/one-of-silicon-valleys-top-vc-firms-finally-hired-a-woman [https://perma.cc/X9CM-7U92] (last accessed September 19, 2023); see also, Liza Mundy, "Why Is Silicon Valley So Awful to Women?" *The Atlantic*, April 2017, available at: www.theatlantic.com/magazine/archive/2017/04/why-is-silicon-valley-so-awful-to-women/517788 [https://perma.cc/2LW8-LZFM] (last accessed September 19, 2023) (reporting on Moritz's statement about not lowering standards at Sequoia Capital to hire more women). Mortiz is an influential venture capitalist who was ranked 49th on Forbes's list of most top tech investors in 2021. #49 Michael Moritz, *Forbes*, available at: www.forbes.com/profile/michael-moritz/?sh=63ab8af96439 [https://perma.cc/8LVK-FRFK] (last accessed August 7, 2021).

firms like Accel Partners and Redpoint Ventures have only recently started hiring women to join their investment teams.[52] In fact, as recently as 2019, less than a third of VC firms employed even a single woman in their business and investment practice.[53]

Some male engineers in Silicon Valley enforce Moritz's belief using biological essentialism and determinism. For example, James Damore, a former senior software engineer at Google with a master's degree in Systems Biology from Harvard, penned a manifesto explaining why women are the minority in the tech industry.[54] He asserted that women have more neuroticism and lower "stress tolerance" than men, and that men maintain a "higher drive for status" than women.[55] He posted the manifesto on the company's forum for employees to read.[56]

Scandals of all nature plague the innovation economy. Facebook faced lawsuits over the Cambridge Analytica data scandal in the aftermath of the 2016 presidential election. Another whistleblower renewed scrutiny of how Facebook deceived the public and its investors about its ability to address hate speech and misinformation on its platform.[57] Google faced criticism of tax avoidance, misuse and manipulation of search results, data breach, intellectual property theft, and illegally spying on workers, in addition to having 20,000 employees and contractors protest the Company's sexual harassment problems by participating in global walkouts.[58] Antics from the CEO of Tesla regularly rocked the public. WeWork's colossal IPO failure was "an implosion unlike any other in the history of startups" noted

[52] Ibid.

[53] See, Pam Kostka, "More Women Became VC Partners Than Ever before in 2019 but 65% of Venture Firms Still Have Zero Female Partners," *Medium – All Raise*, February 7, 2020, available at: https://medium.com/allraise/more-women-became-vc-partners-than-ever-before-in-2019-39cc6cb86955 [https://perma.cc/GFD7-LZW2] (last accessed September 19, 2023).

[54] Aja Romano, "Google Has Fired the Engineer Whose Anti-Diversity Memo Reflects a Divided Tech Culture," *Vox*, August 8, 2017, 8:50 A.M., available at: www.vox.com/identities/2017/8/8/16106728/google-fired-engineer-anti-diversity-memo [https://perma.cc/LD2U-ANX8] (last accessed September 19, 2023) (explaining how biological essentialism and determinism have long been discredited).

[55] James Damore, "Google's Ideological Echo Chamber," July 4–5, 2017 (unpublished memo), available at: https://s3.documentcloud.org/documents/3914586/Googles-Ideological-Echo-Chamber.pdf [https://perma.cc/F7RW-JUCM] (last accessed September 19, 2023).

[56] Elizabeth Chuck and James Damore, "Google Engineer Fired for Writing Manifesto on Women's 'Neuroticism,' Sues Company," *NBC News*, January 8, 2018, available at: www.nbcnews.com/news/us-news/google-engineer-fired-writing-manifesto-women-s-neuroticism-sues-company-n835836 [https://perma.cc/QZ2E-3JJW] (last accessed September 19, 2023).

[57] Jacklyn Diaz, "Facebook's New Whistleblower Is Renewing Scrutiny of the Social Media Giant," *National Public Radio*, October 4, 2021, available at: www.npr.org/2021/10/04/1042921981/facebook-whistleblower-renewing-scrutiny-of-social-media-giant [https://perma.cc/92F8-UA6A] (last accessed September 19, 2023).

[58] Zoe Schiffer, "Google Illegally Spied on Workers before Firing Them, US Labor Board Alleges," *THE VERGE*, December 2, 2020, available at: www.theverge.com/2020/12/2/22047383/google-spied-workers-before-firing-labor-complaint [https://perma.cc/YG9Z-5UVX] (last accessed September 19, 2023).

by *The New York Times*.[59] Theranos founder acted like the female version of Steve Jobs and lied to investors by saying that, with a few drops of blood, its Edison test could magically detect conditions such as cancer and diabetes quickly but failed to convince a jury armed with prosecutor's evidence.[60]

The controversial gig economy and the downfall of mostly powerful men in tech during the #MeToo era burnished Big Tech's reputation. SVB, however, stood tall. The Bank did not face any scandal, but the scandal hit its clients across the United States. The Bank later took concrete and meaningful steps to address inequity faced by women and minorities in the tech community.[61]

The Bank stayed focused on its growth in the tech community. Wherever clients expanded into different subsectors of tech and science or ventured into new geographical locations, the Bank mapped itself organically on the innovation trails. The Bank followed the money.

With its marquee reputation as the Bank for the innovation economy, entrepreneurs and their enterprises poured their deposits into accounts at the Bank. In total, the Bank held $397 billion in deposits from tech companies. In 2021, the economy was overheated, and more money flooded into the tech sector, resulting in bigger deposit sums at the Bank. Ironically, because tech companies didn't borrow too much money and the Bank was also prudent in its tech lending approach, the total loans reached only $69 billion. Since 2001, the Bank had leveraged deep connections and knowledge in the VC ecosystem to make shrewd investments including SVB Capital, the Bank's investment banking subsidiary, which brought in the fees. Overall, the Bank's stock performance in the last five years brought a 124.81 percent return to shareholders.

Like any commercial bank, SVB provided banking and lending services and sought to receive prompt payments on loans and interest from clients. However, unlike traditional banks, stepping inside the SVB's entrance, you won't find a fancy lobby adorned with marble hauled from Italy. Their building and offices were at the center of innovation. Proximity to entrepreneurs was what really mattered because SVB was the only bank in the country with deep relationships with the VC and private equity (PE) firms, investors' portfolio companies, leading law firms, and influencers through its four decades of tech lending. SVB bankers claimed they knew everyone in the VC ecosystem.

---

[59] Amy Chozick, "Adam Neumann and the Art of Failing Up," *The New York Times*, November 2, 2019, updated May 18, 2020, available at: www.nytimes.com/2019/11/02/business/adam-neumann-wework-exit-package.html (last accessed September 19, 2023).

[60] Avery Hartmans, Sarah Jackson, and Áine Cain, "The Rise and Fall of Elizabeth Holmes, the Former Theranos CEO Found Guilty of Wire Fraud and Conspiracy, Who's Now Asking a Judge to Toss Out Her Conviction," *Business Insider*, July 7, 2022, available at: www.businessinsider.com/theranos-founder-ceo-elizabeth-holmes-life-story-bio-2018-4 [https://perma.cc/3X5K-H2QE] (last accessed September 19, 2023).

[61] See Chapter 11, *infra*, for the frustrations expressed by female and minority founders in the aftermath of SVB's demise.

Intel Museum can be found just a short drive away from the Banks' headquarters. If you go west of the Bank within a five-mile radius, numerous tech conglomerates' offices dot the area: Facebook, Google, Amazon, Baidu USA, Juniper Networks, Finisar, Cepheid, PACCAR Innovation Center, Barefoot Networks, DigiLens, Turntide Technologies, ViaBot, Silk Road Medical; and, just a few steps from the parking lot, GoDaddy, Astera Labs, and Aviatrix Systems are the immediate neighbors.

The Bank's Menlo Park office on Sand Hill Road, a two-story grey building with a hint of beige tucked in a gentle slope of a park-like setting, prided itself on being within walking distance to luminary VC firms like Sequoia Capital, Kleiner Perkins, New Enterprise Associates, Mayfield, Andreessen Horowitz, and Greylock Partners. Standing outside the office, the bankers regaled other VC firms like Lightspeed Venture Partners, Trinity Ventures, Shasta Ventures, Felicis Ventures, and DCM, within a one-mile radius. Besides the VC firms, SLAC National Accelerator Laboratory, a US Department of Energy National Laboratory operated by Stanford University, is across Sand Hill Road. Stanford and its incubator hub of entrepreneurs are nearby. The Bank's Menlo Park office anchored its deep roots in the fertile soil of Silicon Valley for startups.

The Bank itself was once a startup, and its history and growth are a startup story. Understanding the Bank's journey requires first understanding startups.

From innovation centers across the nation to state capitols and the halls of Congress, startups are known to be the engine for jobs. Startups have historically created 11 percent of all private sector jobs, added 10 percent of total US sales, and contributed 21 percent of US GDP.[62] Startups in technology-based industries contribute a higher employment share than startups in other fields.[63]

Still, startups are very risky. The lucky few startups may receive outside capital to grow. Everyone in the tech industry knows that scaling a startup is incredibly hard. Everyone is aware and afraid of a death valley curve, the fearsome period of time from initial capital infusion to when the enterprise can generate revenue. The risk of failure is very real because in pursuit of growth the startup burns so much cash by paying numerous expenses – renting office space, payroll, insurance, marketing, research and development – before it can generate any revenue. The longer a company spends on its death valley curve, the higher the risk it will fail prematurely. If the company survives its death valley period and is able to rapidly scale, the

[62] Money Market Fund Reform; Amendments to Form PF, Release No. IC-30551; File No. 57-03-13, Letter from Joe Morgan, Chief Innovation Officer, Silicon Valley Bank, to Elizabeth M. Murphy, Securities and Exchange Commission, available at: www.sec.gov/comments/s7-03-13/s70313-153.pdf [https://perma.cc/9GJY-NXG5] (last accessed September 19, 2023).

[63] See John Wu & Robert D. Atkinson, "How Technology-Based Start-Ups Support U.S. Economic Growth," *Information Technology & Innovation Foundation*, November 28, 2017, available at: https://itif.org/publications/2017/11/28/how-technology-based-start-ups-support-us-economic-growth [https://perma.cc/BT3F-PWTK] (last accessed September 19, 2023).

rewards are handsome to the investors and the entrepreneurs. High risks, high growth, and high rewards are common features associated with tech and life science startup sectors. These are the same features pushing banks away from accepting startups as potentially attractive customers for lending.

Conventional banking practices dictate banks make loans to legacy and established companies with real, physical, and tangible assets. Banks require borrowers to produce positive cash flow and long credit histories. Banks eagerly compete against each other for active participation in real estate lending transactions, from commercial to residential. Banks ignore innovators in the tech and life science sectors, avoiding startups and high-growth companies that don't generate profits.

Born in one of the industrial parks of Silicon Valley, SVB rejected conventional banking practices. It dared to provide banking and lending services to the unbanked innovators in the early 1980s. Banking for the innovators compelled SVB itself to be innovative in meeting local innovators' needs. The new approach required SVB to embrace intellectual property assets, cultivate networks of experts to assist innovators, and behave not like bankers but more like their entrepreneurial clients. SVB's model of banking innovators means that the Bank must understand the VC ecosystem and leverage the ecosystem's network effects to assist innovators. The network includes investors, technical experts, founders, entrepreneurs, business and community leaders, and politicians. Utilizing the network effects, the Bank could seek investments, enhance publicity, vet new ideas proposed by innovators, and connect innovators to members of the network. In the ecosystem, the SVB bankers assisted in incubating and nurturing innovators, building companies in different growth stages, in addition to providing pivotal banking and lending services to startup clients and their investors.

SVB carved its presence where innovation centers spring up from north to south along the serpentine shape of California. Because entrepreneurs in the tech industry do not limit themselves to a particular location, the Bank followed the entrepreneurial paths to different states and countries. The independent, community bank, that once had only one office in the industrial part of northern San Jose, enlarged its footprints for new roots and grew its influence in innovation centers, first in California and then along Route 128 in Massachusetts. It added offices in Portland to serve new innovation centers in the Pacific Northwest, ventured to Colorado and Texas, and later included Arizona, Florida, Georgia, Illinois, Minnesota, New York, North Carolina, Pennsylvania, Utah, and Virginia on its roster of banking expansion locales serving the dynamic ecosystems created by the US tech community.

Innovation is both local and global. The Bank's VC and investor clients expanded their investments with inquisitive and insatiable attention to growing companies in new innovation centers overseas. The Bank supported investors and their portfolio companies in the United Kingdom, Israel, China, Canada, Denmark, and Germany. Where tech growth occurred was where the Bank located its new home to assist innovators, enterprises, and investors to reach their next milestones around the world. This meant the Bank had to keep its eyes and ears attuned to new trends and constantly nurture VC/PE relationships for new business. Lots of hard and smart work was required.

Expansion of offices into new innovation centers in the United States or overseas was an organic process for the Bank. SVB had no set goals, but it flowed with the tech currents and grew with the tech waves. The aggressively adaptive nature of the Bank allowed its practices to evolve, expand, contrast, and dominate while serving clients in different innovation sectors: Hardware & Frontier Tech, Software & Internet, Science & Healthcare, Fintech, Climate Technology & Sustainability, VC/PE Investors, and Premium Wine. Banking is a relationship business and the Bank's expansion was the direct result of its carefully cultivated relationships in tech sectors throughout its existence.

Fundamentally, SVB operated differently than other banks. Asking former employees of the Bank about their experience, the answers uniformly revealed that SVB was very different and was not a typical commercial bank. No retail services, no fancy lobbies and offices, no advertising expenses, no suits and ties, and no sitting at the offices waiting for clients to walk through the door. Former employees proudly asserted that the Bank's relationships in the tech ecosystem were so deep that "we know everyone" appeared as both a badge of honor and a bragging right.

For the Startup Division, the Bank encompassed a team of more than seventy-five bankers with expertise in helping unseasoned entrepreneurs through the maze of fundraising, introducing them to investors, and offering useful critique and advice. The Bank built a special platform called SVB GO specifically for founders so they can easily use the platform's features while remaining focused on their projects. Time is too precious to waste when startups are in the fragile early stage.

If the client enterprises were in science, the Bank provided the CipherBio Science Digital Platform, a free global database that connected companies with investors, VCs, and accelerators, and kept founders informed of the latest news and insights related to the industry. By providing founder-focused services, the Bank went beyond the traditional modern banking products marketed by other commer- cial banks that have only a small segment of the entire banking business devoted to tech industry clients.

As a startup advanced and received its first round of VC funding, its revenue was in the range of $5–$75 million. The Bank built a robust roster of 300 tech banking and growth experts in the Venture-Funded Division to serve the VC-backed enter- prises. These experts were often referred to as Relationship Managers because they worked closely with both the investors and the VC-backed companies by leveraging the Bank's vast connections, expertise, and resources in the VC ecosystem to enable these companies to accelerate in the grueling path of rapid scaling.

The Bank understood that, at this new stage, the enterprise must be able to scale rapidly in order to advance to subsequent rounds of funding or exit at a later, more mature, robust stage. Accordingly, the Bank met the enterprise's needs by providing both banking services and business strategy support. Ideally, the Bank aimed to partner with the enterprise for a long-term relationship as the enterprise grows through different stages. The Bank offered its financial and banking services to help the enterprise raise capital, protect equity, manage cash flows, and access global markets through the Bank's extensive network of partners. One of SVB's key products was venture debt.

Venture debt is a line of credit or loan that enables entrepreneurs to fuel their high-growth, VC-backed company a little longer, so they can reach the next funding milestone to realize a better valuation. By exploring the potential of a debt solution and obtaining the debt, the venture-backed company gained the time it needed and the resources it must have for reaching the milestone. In so doing the company was not diluting its equity because the debt requires repayment in cash not in equity. The Bank was a known expert in venture debt because it was the only bank besides Bank of America in the early 1980s that provided this type of loan to VC-backed companies. When Bank of America exited the tech lending segment, SVB became the default number one go-to bank for venture debt. Through venture debt offerings, the Bank staked its position as the long-term partner of the majority of VC-backed companies and their investors across the country. In fact, in 2021, 63 percent of VC-backed companies that went public were SVB's clients. In providing venture loans to VC-backed companies, the Bank gained both interest payments and warrants or rights to purchase shares in the companies.

One example of how the warrants worked is a warrant given to the Bank by Coinbase in 2014 in which the Bank stood to gain $152 million.[64] The warrant gave the Bank the right to purchase more than 400,000 shares of Coinbase's Class B common stock. The warrant was scheduled to expire in June 2024. Coinbase issued the warrant to the Bank in connection with the Bank's ACH Origination Services. According to Coinbase's prospectus for IPO, Class B common shares are identical to Class A common shares but have more voting rights. Class B shares are convertible to Class A shares at any time. If SVB exercised its right on November 9, 2021, the stock price was at $357. It could have gained a very handsome amount. But if SVB wanted to keep the warrant for a later time, it had until June 2024 to exercise its right whenever it wished. As reported in September 2021, the Bank held 3,000 warrant positions in tech startups, an enviable role that separated and distinguished SVB from bank and non-bank lenders in the tech industry.[65]

---

[64] Bram Berkowitz, Silicon Valley Bank's Stake in Coinbase Could Be Worth $152 Million, *Fool. com*, February 26, 2021, available at: www.fool.com/investing/2021/02/26/silicon-valley-banks-stake-in-coinbase-could-be-wo/ (last accessed September 19, 2023).

[65] Mark Calvey, "Here's Why Odeon Capital's Dick Bove is Bullish on SVB, Even after Its Stock Has Soared 46% This Year," *Silicon Valley Business Journal*, September 1, 2021, available at: www.bizjournals.com/sanjose/news/2021/09/01/heres-why-analyst-bullish-on-svb-after-stock-jump.html (last accessed September 19, 2023)

As the enterprises in the late-growth stage are infused with capital, the Bank turned its attention to serving VC/PE professionals and founders and management teams of companies. SVB Private Banking and Wealth Advisory group assisted these entrepreneurs in how to unlock their liquidity and advised them about how to build tax-efficient investment strategies for their newly found wealth. SVB made loans for their home acquisitions, aircraft, vineyards, and whatever their taste desired.

Having VC-backed companies who were scaling to the next phases as clients presented both opportunities and challenges in helping to nurture and shape these new enterprises in the #MeToo and DEI (diversity, equity, and inclusion) era. The Bank demonstrated its awareness of gender parity issues and turned its awareness into action. The Bank connected its high-growth clients to an online talent market-place called the Boardlist to change the ratio in the boardroom. The Boardlist assisted both private and public companies in seeking qualified corporate board directors with diverse backgrounds and experiences in shifting the gender gap from the top. Concerning Black professionals, the Bank added Valence, a novel platform enabling companies to recruit, retain, and promote Black talent in the tech industry. Simply, no other bank serving the tech industry confronted gender and race dispar-ity in the early phase of VC-backed companies. SVB was its own class of pioneers. Whether these connections alter the actual numbers of executives and board members at VC-backed companies who were SVB clients remains to be seen. Meanwhile, SVB exhibited that it was on the right path by working directly with the relevant solutions-based platforms and identifying them on the SVB's webpages.

Also, for high-growth enterprises, the Bank assisted with their needs for recruiting and hiring executive and management talent by providing access to SVB's network of partners who possess expertise and connections to the executive talent market-place. Specifically, SVB worked with Bolster, a company with an extensive database to assist companies scale their CEOs, Executive Teams, and Boards. Bolster's platform matches on-demand executives with high-growth companies based on their specific criteria of needs. Whether the need is a fractional executive, a part-time general counsel, or the right coach for the enterprise, Bolster meets the unique demands of VC-backed companies in hiring top talent immediately. Overall, SVB carved out a comprehensive suite of services and connections in positioning itself as an innovative and relationship-driven bank for the innovation economy.

Another interesting characteristic in the age of multimedia is SVB's storytelling on its site. The Bank frequently featured personal narratives and stories from founders and entrepreneurs who overcame challenges and navigated their business complexities to share their insights with the new crop of founders and entrepreneurs. Survival tips, radical course correction, and the uncomfortable truth of executing successful pivots are available from those who had experienced them now and can tell their sides so those in the room who can summon the courage can switch gears, abandon the old plans, and morph into a new identity. For instance, Gigya, one of the Bank's clients, was a software startup that sold solutions to customers who used them to enhance their MySpace and Friendster pages. Gigya met its revenue targets with ease. But Facebook quickly changed the social media scene, forcing first-generation social networks like MySpace and Friendster into oblivion. That meant Gigya had to replace its business plan with a pivot strategy if it had any hope of survival. The founding team shifted resources into building something new. Gigya started producing a beta of a new social infrastructure product for businesses. They had to lay off some of the salespeople who were used to pitching ads for a consumer product but failed to transition to sell the new product to businesses. In the end, Gigya was able to pivot and exited at a much higher valuation. Gigya offered a lesson that success today does not guarantee success tomorrow. The Bank asked Gigya's former CEO to share his insights into the painful period of pivoting. In many ways, the Bank demonstrated that it too empathized with many young tech clients and the difficulties they face in doing what is right for their business.

The hard truth about a startup's financial health must be seen in numbers and metrics. The Bank understood there are times the clients must confront and address the hard truth in order to survive and thrive. The Bank gathered insightful comments from veteran analysts who share top metrics for evaluating a startup's financial health. Startups must focus on key performance indicators (KPIs) like revenue, cost of goods, gross margins, marketing, and EBITDA.[66] These KPIs help determine the company's underlying contribution margin. In a simplistic sense, contribution margin means gross margin (revenue minus the cost of sales, such as parts and factory labor) minus sales and marketing costs. The contribution margin must exceed basic costs like executive salaries, taxes, and administrative costs for functions like payroll and IT. Otherwise, the enterprise will not generate an operating profit. By understanding the company's financial health, the entrepreneurs can calculate projections for the future that are grounded on historical trends.[67] Such insights assist the clients in obtaining an overall picture of the financial health of their enterprises.

The startup clients the Bank frequently showcased hinted at inspiring stories of the innovation economy like Irving Fain, the CEO and cofounder of Bowery Farming, an urban farming startup. Who would imagine that farms are warehouses located less than 10 miles from the company offices in Manhattan? Who would believe that technology and the innovation economy would automate agriculture? Fain did. He developed his proprietary software to collect plant data to grow better and healthier crops in space-challenged environments. At his warehouse, greens are cultivated at a 100-times greater speed than those grown on outdoor farms for the same amount of space! He uses precision farming techniques, data analytics, and

---

[66] EBITDA: Earnings before interest, taxes, depreciation, and amortization (EBITDA) is a business analysis metric.

[67] "Top Metrics for Evaluating Startup Health," *Silicon Valley Bank*, available at: www.svb.com/startup-insights/startup-growth/top-startup-metrics-evaluate-health [https://perma.cc/KL65-X2CZ] (last accessed September 2, 2022).

automation to produce greens without the use of pesticides and with only 5 percent of the water typically required in traditional farming. Fain also reduces the distribution distance because his farms are closer to his clients.

Ring and its entrepreneurial inventor Jamie Siminoff ignited the modern day's garage into a global success story that we used to hear about from the founders of Apple, Google, and the like. The serial entrepreneur Siminoff produces and saves his new inventive ideas on his mobile phone. He likes to tinker with technology because he sees problems that either need fixing or require new solutions. Siminoff invented a doorbell with Wi-Fi enabled to send alerts to cell phones while he worked in his garage on a different concept. He went to ABC's Shark Tank trying to raise both his company's profile and cash. He rejected their offer, but Ring sales shot up from the show's publicity. Despite the Shark Tank investor's prediction of doom to his company on live TV, top VCs showed strong interest in Ring. VCs invested in Ring, and the company has raised $209 million since 2014. Ring products are now sold on Amazon and in retail stores in 100 countries.

Shivani Siroya is a fearless romantic who believes that successful entrepreneurs must possess the drive of putting oneself out there and allow one's heart to be broken. Through her observations while working for the UN Population Fund, she learned that microentrepreneurs and small business owners in emerging economies face difficult hurdles in gaining access to credit. Consequently, these individuals hold no credit history, but they may be creditworthy for small loans. Siroya solved the problem by launching a tech startup with a mobile app that would provide a credit scoring system and lending tool. Her company, Tala, allows customers from Kenya to obtain loans to start their small businesses. Tala is in a very early stage; it received a seed round of money which it deposited at SVB.

In a highly competitive online job search market, ZipRecruiter stands above the rest. The company bootstrapped itself and grew without VC funds for five years. Ian Siegel, the cofounder of ZipRecruiter, remembered the frustration of receiving numerous resumes in his inbox. His team refines their algorithms to seize the right job and present it to the right job candidates. ZipRecruiter has matched more than one million people with jobs via relentless improvements of their algorithms and targeted email job alerts, mobile apps, and posts on hundreds of online job boards. For a new job posted, ZipRecruiter can pick the top 100 job candidates from its vast database of millions of resumes and alert those candidates that there is a "perfect job" available, just waiting for them to apply. The company has generated more than eight million job postings and connected employers to more than 10 million active job seekers. In the Series A round of funding, ZipRecruiter raised $63 million!

These startup stories all have one thing in common: SVB *was* their bank. To them, SVB functioned as a partner and a networking tool; it was simply not *just* a bank.

For large and publicly traded companies with revenue above $75 million, SVB's Corporate Banking Division served this group of clients. Based on PitchBook and

NVCA data, 67 percent of US venture capital-backed companies with an IPO in 2020 were SVB clients. Based on Pitchbook data as of February 14, 2022, more than 700 publicly traded technology and healthcare companies were SVB's long-term financial partner. These corporate clients demanded different types of services and attention in the Bank's partnership with the enterprises.

These clients may need debt and equity financing to fuel their growth, acquisitions, global expansion, or balance sheet optimization. SVB understood that growth means survival and thriving in all companies, and innovation means both scaled and fast-paced for these clients. The Bank furnished global banking and credit and capital solutions to these clients. More specifically, the Bank segmented the practice into target groups like "Leveraged & Sponsor Finance," "Project Finance," "Venture Capital & Investing," and "Investment Banking," tailoring solutions to these clients within the tech industry ecosystem.

SVB provided leveraged finance that focused on the corporate clients and private equity investors in both small-cap and large-cap markets. For project finance, SVB leaned on its network of project owners, sponsors, and investors to provide financing to large cleantech and sustainability resource projects. Here, SVB distinguished itself as a bank with expertise in proposing financing solutions to address climate change challenges and making a positive influence on environmental change. The Bank supported a broad spectrum of clients and climate change innovation projects. For instance, in the Sunrun Mars project, a 195 MW residential solar portfolio, SVB was the coordinating lead arranger, administrative agent, and hedge provider of the $265 million term loan and letter of credit facilities. In the financing deal of a portfolio of 92.9 MW fuel cell projects for Daroga, SVB served as the sole coordinating lead arranger, sole book runner, and administrative agent for the $133.9 million term loan and letter of credit facilities.

Some tech executives at large private and public companies are visionaries in technologies that would disrupt existing industries in sciences, health care, fintech, frontier tech, enterprise software, consumer internet, and cleantech. SVB supported these executives as clients by serving as their financial partner through leveraging the Bank's VC/PE connections and industry expertise. After all, SVB demonstrated that it always lived technology and breathed sciences and heatlh care. The Bank's business faced no competition among commercial banks in the United States, and SVB was second to none in its position of serving all facets of the tech industry.

In the last twenty years, the Bank expanded its reach with the creation of SVB Capital, opening new doors for large corporate clients and private equity investors to make their venture investments in tech companies and venture funds. SVB Capital offered its clients access to investments in the innovation economy by utilizing SVB's long history and relationships with tech companies and VC/PE sectors, including more than 50 percent of all VC-backed companies in the United States and funds and corporations in different countries with innovation centers. SVB Capital funds were pooled investment vehicles, including direct venture funds that invest in tech companies, funds that focus on other venture capital funds, and debt funds that engage in lending and provide financial solutions. Through its expertise and services, SVB Capital generated handsome income from investment returns which carried interest and management fees, enriching third-party limited partner investors and the Bank's shareholders. SVB Capital invested in more than 700 unicorns across its fund strategies. SVB Capital managed $7.5 billion in assets.

On the expansion trajectory, SVB Securities emerged as a wholly owned subsidiary of the Bank's Holding Company with a sole focus on the innovation economy. As new bold ideas and technologies in heatlh care grew rapidly, SVB Securities extended investment banking services in Biopharma, Digital Health, and HealthTech, Healthcare Services, Medical Devices, and Tools and Diagnostics. In 2021, SVB Securities initiated Technology investment banking that cornered the tech subsectors like Consumer Internet, Commerce Enablement and Marketing Software, Digital Infrastructure and Tech-Enabled Services, Education Technology, Enterprise Software, Industrial Technology, and FinTech. As SVB Securities continued to expand, it amassed equity research coverage with the acquisition of MoffettNathanson LLC in 2021. By 2022, SVB Securities solidified its positions in four main areas: Capital Raising, M&A Advisory, Equity Research, and Sales and Trading. Consequently, with SVB Securities, the Bank prevented other big bank competitors from seizing large deals in the Healthcare and Technology subsectors.

Unlike conventional banks, SVB hosted numerous networking events and summits to bring innovators and their peers together, introduce innovators to investors, and connect innovators, investors, and industry icons at special events. The Bank hosted SVB Fintech Open House for both existing clients and the general fintech public. The Open House covered venture debt for fintech founders, warehouse lending practice, payments enablement, and the corporate venture capital ("CVC") in the fintech landscape. Likewise, the Bank partnered with top-tier VCs to create a series of "Meet the Investors" events to introduce Early Stage companies to potential investors. The Bank's webinars covered topics from "Why Gender Is Just the Tip of the Diversity Iceberg," "Racial Equality: Hiring Diverse Talent into Your Company," "US Expansion & Fundraising," "SVB's State of the Markets 2021," to "In Conversation with Atomico: What's Next for European Tech in 2022." These contents conveyed a sense that SVB was trying to be a modern bank for the innovation economy. The Bank feared being complacent.

In the digital era, data holds the key to investments in VC. Gathering vast data and generating relevant insight through its network of clients, investors, and partners throughout innovation centers in the United States and worldwide, SVB produced quarterly reports pertaining to investments in private equity and VC markets. The Family Offices report was based on SVB's own surveys and interviews with family offices to ascertain investments in VC activity, staffing and compensation, portfolio investment trends, perspectives, and generational priorities. In the investment context, family offices refer to private companies that focus on the management of investment and wealth of ultra-high-net-worth families to effectively grow and strategically transfer generational wealth.

In the 2022 Q2 report from SVB's *Global Fund Banking Outlook Report*, SVB identified fund activities in the US market and highlighted global capital distributed by fund types like venture capital, PE growth, and PE buyout. *The Report*, as expected with the SVB brand name, focused on IPO and M&A markets and competition for capital from limited partners, cross-border deals, and hedging transaction growth. To be both current and relevant, *The Report* featured four experts discussing cybersecurity essentials for fund and portfolio companies.

Likewise, SVB displayed its data and insights prowess in healthcare venture funding. SVB's *Healthcare Investments and Exits Annual 2022 Report* covered data on venture funding in healthcare sectors like biopharma, healthtech, dx/tools, and devices. It revealed that venture funding in these sectors increased 30 percent in the United States and Europe compared to the previous year's data. The increase was not an isolated event, but it was part of a pattern showing healthcare venture investments have doubled every two years since 2017, from $16 billion to $34 billion to $80 billion in 2021. Further, forty-two healthtech companies with valuations of $1 billion or higher, generally referred to as "unicorns," emerged in the new year. Dissecting the data at a more granular level, the Report showed that startups at Seed and Series A funding stages obtained large seed investments of $10–$20 million from mostly institutional investors. Also, investments in early stage companies like Nano Cures and Pardes Biosciences in the anti-infective sector increased reflecting investors' focus on technology to prevent infectious diseases, epidemics, and pandemics. Deals in computational bio and Dx analytics were included in *The Report* with historical trends. Post-pandemic, innovators of non-invasive monitoring devices to monitor patients outside a hospital setting received an infusion of over $1 billion in early-stage device investment. These reports, along with the *State of the Markets Report*, cemented SVB as the only bank possessing a vantage point through its relationships with top science and healthcare entrepreneurs and investors, demonstrating that the Bank's insights were the must-read resources.

In addition to the reports pertaining to trends, SVB published a series of Startup Insights, Industry Insights, Market Insights, Business Growth, Foreign Exchange Advisory, and Private Bank targeting different groups of clients with specific and relevant content. Overall, these insights cover topics across the innovation economy. For instance, SVB analyzed data from tech companies that went IPO between 2016 and 2019 for currency practices employed by these companies during their high-growth periods during the venture funding rounds based on their IPO filings. The data indicated that nine in ten companies reported global revenues, a third of the companies' total revenues originated outside of the United States, and revenues grew 50 percent faster outside the United States than within the United States, but nine in ten of the companies cited foreign currency exchange as a key risk factor.

A high-growth company without established overseas revenues would pay foreign operations in US dollars obtained through VC rounds of funding.

> [But] weakness in the USD makes foreign-denominated costs more expensive, aggravating the companies' cash burn and shortening their cash runways. Past research using SVB's proprietary data found that for one in four technology companies, a 25% adverse move in currencies could shorten runways by six months. A strong US dollar also can present challenges. Although a rising US dollar extends cash runways, it may cause revenues and profits denominated in foreign currencies to lose value in USD terms. In this scenario, valuations tied to revenue and profit multiples may be at risk.

By publishing these insights on foreign currency factors and other insight reports, SVB positioned to make itself indispensable to VC-backed, high-growth companies and their investors.

On the investors side, the Bank served clients in private equity (PE), venture capital (VC), and corporate venture (CV) fields. The Bank offered a wide range of products and services catered to Private Equity Chief Financial Officers. The Bank counted BainCapital, SilverLake, Primus, Trive, WynnChurch Capital, Insight Partners, and Frazier Healthcare Partners among their PE clients. For the VC community in the United States and worldwide, the Bank was known as the most experienced and leading provider to venture funds since its inception in 1983. Its VC clients were in the hundreds, including Andreessen Horowitz, Lightspeed, Venrock, Hyde Park, and Polaris Partners, among others. In corporate VCs where corporations dedicate innovation units to identify, discover, and evaluate tech and healthcare investments, SVB directed its attention to support corporate VCs by leveraging its client base and deep connections in the VC-backed tech and science sectors to provide support to corporations looking for new investments. Together, SVB served the investors and their portfolio companies in the tech industry ecosystem.

Woven intensely in the innovation economy, SVB worked with pioneers and witnessed disruption. Working with clients on the investors side, SVB did not limit itself to established funds and fund managers. SVB assisted new and growing funds across sectors and partners with emerging managers who want to change the VC landscape. SVB bankers who were former investors and operators knew very well that launching a new fund for the first time is an exciting journey fraught with unexpected challenges. The bankers brought their experience and insight to help emerging managers and offer critical advice and advocacy across funds, sectors, stages, and geographical regions. True to its word, the Bank included HomeBrew, Harlem Capital, Scribble Ventures, Pear, Mucker Capital, Matchstick Ventures, Halogen, Array VC, Basis Set Ventures, and Precursor Ventures among other emerging managers and funds as clients. Obviously, the Bank served both the emerging manager clients and their portfolio companies in the tech startup ecosystem. However, the Bank did not report specific data showing the results of its efforts in this area.

As part of its efforts to assist emerging managers of new funds, SVB gathered experienced managers to share lessons that they wish they had known when they were working on raising their first fund. The "Advice for New Fund Managers" built a new SVB community of emerging managers through experience. Also, the Bank produced videos on the role of a fund manager's main job in coaching founders, offering startups advice, guidance, and inspiration. In the three videos, the Bank invited Tim Connors of PivotNorth Capital, Shruti Gandhi of Array Ventures, and Richard Kerby and Rick Zullo of Equal Ventures to share their lessons with new fund managers. Essentially, through the "Emerging Fund Managers" program, the Bank was banking on new startup VCs, in addition to the established VCs.

The Bank harvested a handsome income by banking and lending to clients in the innovation economy in the United States and worldwide. Like any bank, SVB's total revenue included net interest income on a fully taxable equivalent basis and noninterest income. Unlike all banks, SVB's total revenue came solely from serving the tech industry. For 2021, SVB's net interest income was an astonishing $3.2 billion and noninterest income $2.7 billion, compared to the prior year's $2.17 billion net interest income and $1.84 billion noninterest income.[68] The Bank derived more than 90 percent of its revenue from US clients.

The Bank generated net interest income from the interest rate spread differences between the interest rates borrowers pay and depositors save in their accounts with the Bank. In bank parlance, the net interest income is the difference between the interest rates received on interest-earning assets like loans to clients and securities from fixed income securities portfolio and the interest rates paid by the Bank on interest-bearing liabilities like deposits and borrowings. In yearend 2021, the interest rates difference yielded the Bank $3.2 billion!

The noninterest income was from the Bank's fee-based services and gains from the Bank's investments and derivative securities. That meant the Bank generated fee-based financial services for its clients for global commercial and private banking. The Bank earned a fee-based income for services associated with client investment fees, wealth management and trustee fees, foreign exchange fees, credit card fees, deposit service charges, lending-related fees, letter of credit fees, and standby letters of credit fees. Through SVB Securities, the Bank garnered fees from investment banking, M&A advisory services, and commissions. The Bank also held a variety of marketable investment securities and gains from investments in privately held companies and funds. In addition, the Bank realized gains from warrants to acquire stock in client companies that the bankers secured in extending credit facilities and other services to clients. The noninterest income significantly contributed to the Bank's overall revenue in the last few years. In yearend 2021, that number was $2.7 billion, representing a 46.7 percent increase from the previous year.

---

[68] SVB 2022 and 2021 10K Filings.

In serving the innovation economy, SVB articulated its core values as including "start with empathy for others; take responsibility; embrace diverse perspectives; speak and act with integrity; and keep learning and improving."[69] The Bank asserted in its annual 10K filings that it believed the core values were key to attracting, retaining, and inspiring its employees and contributed to the success of both the Bank's business and the innovation economy more generally. SVB's core values were seen in its hiring of Tosh Ernest on June 14, 2022, as Head of *Access to Innovation*, SVB's signature initiative to advance women and Black and Latinx individuals to positions of influence in the innovation economy. Whether *Access to Innovation* would make concrete inroads to address the tech industry's notoriously clubby and closed circles of whites and males in leadership roles was too prematurely terminated when SVB collapsed in March 2023. But SVB did make a strategic step by creating the new program and hiring a Black woman to lead it.

Notably, some of the Bank's core values were reflected in its $11.2 billion, five-year Community Benefits Plan announced in 2021. The Bank tied the Plan to its proposed acquisition of Boston Private Bank. The Plan's five-year period from January 2022 through December 2026 aimed to provide financial support to low-and-moderate-income (LMI) communities in California and Massachusetts, allocating $5 billion in small business loans of $1 million or less, $4.8 billion in Community Reinvestment Act's community development loans and investments, $1.3 billion in residential mortgages to LMI borrowers and in LMI census tracts, and $75 million in charitable contributions. SVB was to create a community advisory council and work with representatives from the California Reinvestment Coalition, The Greenlining Institute, the Massachusetts Affordable Housing Alliance, and the Massachusetts Association of Community Development Corporations toward the Plan's goals. The impact of the Plan was to be revealed by 2026 and beyond.

For comparison purposes, First Citizens Bank allocated $16 billion to a five-year Community Benefits Plan that would reinvest in LMI communities and communities of color throughout the United States without geographical restrictions. First Citizen Banks would support lending and invest in LMI communities following the competition of its proposed merger with the CIT Group. Similarly, US Bank announced its $100 billion Community Benefits Plan for a five-year period when it planned to merge with MUFG Union Bank. PNC launched a $88 billion Community Benefits Plan when it acquired BBVA US. These Community Plans are a reactive move to advance proposed bank merger deals and serve as strategic tactics to win the support of regulators. Banks attempt to address social equity in the communities and geography where they plan to expand. Interestingly, First Citizens Bank is significantly smaller than SVB but allocated 45 percent or $5 billion more than SVB in the Community Benefits Plan.

---

[69] SVB 2022 10K Filings.

Likewise, the Bank launched Nasdaq Private Market with Nasdaq, Citi, Goldman Sachs, and Morgan Stanley in 2021. Essentially, the private market platform will be an independent entity, a centralized secondary trading venue; it is a spin-out of Nasdaq's 2014 Private Market for institutional trading of private company stock. SVB played the role of the big bank, together with the notable established big banks of Citi, Goldman Sachs, and Morgan Stanley, making strategic investments in the joint venture platform that would continue to enable brokers and investors to access, manage, and trade private company stock via a global marketplace and technology solutions. At the time of the announcement, the platform facilitated 477 private company transactions for 59,000 shareholders and executed over $30 billion in volume for private companies. In other words, this joint venture platform revealed that SVB kept reinventing itself by crafting new solutions to existing and new clients.

As a commercial bank like any other commercial bank, SVB bank was subject to stringent federal and state banking regulations. After all, depositors are the owners of the money held by the Bank, and they are protected under the banking regulations. The Federal Reserve and state banking regulators impose supervision and examinations over the Bank. Also, the Bank's consumer banking activities are subject to regulation and supervision by the Consumer Financial Protection Bureau. Like many financial holding companies of banks, SVB Financial (the holding company) had to be well-capitalized and well-managed under Federal Reserve's Regulation Y. Because the Bank's assets had enlarged and it became a big bank, SVB Financial was subject to enhanced prudential standards. The Bank was also subject to Community Reinvestment Act examination. It was no surprise that, under the new Community Benefits Plan announced in 2021, the Bank's CRA examination earned its first "outstanding" rating.

For the non-bank subsidiaries, they were primarily subject to SEC and FINRA regulations.

As the Bank occupied offices in other countries in Europe, Asia, and Canada, these offices had to comply with the regulatory regimes in these jurisdictions. As it turned out, among all the foreign jurisdictions, India's regulations posted severe roadblocks to the Bank's efforts to serve the tech sector there; Indian regulators insisted that the Bank served the rural sector, but the Bank possessed no such expertise. The Bank understood its limitations and pulled out of India. As the UK Branch opened in 2012, the Bank found its rhythm as its office in the Alphabeta building nestled between London's Old Street Roundabout and the City, serving some of the most innovative businesses in the United Kingdom and Europe. The Bank touted that the UK Branch was "the only local bank in the United Kingdom focused on the Innovation Economy." The UK Branch was bustling with growth and the hiring posts on Twitter exulted excitement. Plans were in place for the Bank's UK Branch to become a subsidiary. Indeed, the regulatory approval occurred in August 2022 and the UK Branch achieved its status as a standalone bank within the United Kingdom, not just a branch but a new legal entity, wholly owned subsidiary of the Bank with a new name, SVBUK Ltd.

Before its demise, SVB served the US and UK banking needs of investors and entrepreneurs from many different parts of the world. As emerging global centers constantly change the landscape of banking the innovation economy, SVB leveraged its knowledge and relationships to follow new money trails whether they were in Brazil, Mexico, Argentina, Russia, India, Turkey, or Australia. This brought both opportunities and challenges for a big bank like SVB, with 8,000 employees, to keep its core values and culture coherent.

The leadership at the Bank is reflected in a picture of eleven men and one woman. It is an image of white people in a financial and innovation economy possessing all the authority and power. The image is reflective of Silicon Valley itself and the innovation sectors in general. The networks and circles of the innovation sectors are exclusionary despite the belief of meritocracy preached to many. Perhaps the new Diversity, Equity, and Inclusion (DEI) initiatives embraced by the Bank may change the face of the leadership in the tech ecosystem in the future. The occurrence of such a change was determined by the same people whose pictures are on the leadership roster. The image of the leadership at the Bank before its collapse is not much different from when it began forty years ago when women and people of color were not included.

The undeniable truth is that the community independent bank transformed into a big bank, a very special big bank with relationships that dominated venture banking and lending throughout the United States. With its vast connections and expertise, how did the community independent bank founded in 1983 survive and excel to be the Bank of the innovation community in the United States and overseas? How did the Bank shine in the tech and science sectors avoided by conventional banks? How did the Bank begin? This book looks at the conception of the Bank, dispels myths regarding its creation, and provides a picture of an entrepreneurial bank that dared to tread where other banks declined to venture by banking for and lending to high-tech companies forty years ago.

This book is an American story of a bank's rags to riches, of an underdog in the banking industry, of founders' heartbreak, and strong conviction. It is a feel-good story amidst justifiably hateful sentiments against banks in the United States and worldwide.

This book is also a tragic story about the last chapter of an innovative bank destroyed by the very innovators who the Bank encouraged, who used social media to burn down their own bank through an unprecedented bank run.

2

The Origin of the Idea

A myth started several years ago and still floats around concerning the origin of Silicon Valley Bank (SVB). The myth goes that the idea of the Bank popped up at a poker game where important men in the Valley got together during one of their outings to play their favorite game. Like a good poker game, the story was told with a straight face. And, as in any good poker game, someone is bluffing. A bluff is a hand that is not the best hand but possesses the power to induce at least one opponent with a better hand to fold first. The poker game origin of SVB is a good bluff perpetuated by SVB's video clips posted on YouTube.[1]

The idea of having a bank to serve entrepreneurs in the "high tech" sector actually originated with Stanford students in a Construction Management class.

IT'S CONSTRUCTION!

The decade was the 1970s. California's natural beauty, ample sun, and youthful fun attracted creative imagination. The students came from different states. They arrived at Stanford through an admission process that asked about students' height and weight, a practice inherited from military procedures, and that only admitted 31 percent of applicants.[2] Like other campuses in the 1970s, Stanford experienced social and political movements, reaching their peak with protests, demonstrations, and sit-ins where students clashed with the university administration and police on

---

[1] "Silicon Valley Bank: The Founders' Story: Bill Biggerstaff, Co-Founder," *SVB*, October 7, 2013, available at: www.youtube.com/watch?v=ktSQZP_vYug (last accessed September 12, 2022).

[2] George Anders, "What if Stanford Admitted 31%? A Journey Back to the 1970s," *Forbes*, April 3, 2015, available at: www.forbes.com/sites/georgeanders/2015/04/03/what-if-stanford-admitted-31-a-journey-back-to-the-1970s/?sh=5e7b83c583do [https://perma.cc/8SNY-TF7F] (last accessed September 12, 2022).

campus.[3] The gay liberation and women's liberation movements forced new changes at Stanford. The Gay Peoples Union, which was later renamed the Lesbian, Gay, and Bisexual Community Center, operated in the Old Fir Truck House in 1970. On February 10, 1971, students held a rally in Dinkelspiel Auditorium and White Plaza and marched to the Computation Center against the US invasion of Laos. The demonstration at the Computation Center resulted in twelve hours of confrontation and violence. Twelve people were arrested.

In January 1972, fifty-four members of the Stanford Native American community signed a petition to the university ombudsman denouncing the use of the Indian caricature by the Stanford Athletic Teams on posters, flyers, and buttons as part of the university's marketing efforts to promote events.[4]

On March 2, 1972, Stanford voted to officially discontinue the use of the mascot that had been used by the university since the 1930s. This action shows that Stanford was ahead of its time in response to the racist depiction of Native Americans in branding and marketing materials. Not until 2018 did the Cleveland Indians, a Major League Baseball team, retire the Chief Wahoo logo, changing their name to Guardians in 2021. After several decades of opposition from Native American advocacy groups and their disappointment with the Supreme Court's decision to decline to hear the challenge of the Redskins' trademark in *Harjo v. Pro-Football, Inc.*,[5] the groups witnessed the Washington Redskins finally changing their name to Commanders in 2020.[6]

Title IX required the university abolish preset targets for male-to-female ratios among undergraduates in 1972 and "afford equal facilities and give equal advantages in the university to both sexes."[7] In 1974 the Organization of Stanford Women Athletes (OSWA) was formed and actively voiced their unequal treatment in sports programs. Under President Lyman's Administration the university merged men's and women's sports programs into the new Department of Athletics, Physical Education, and Recreation, attempting to comply with Title IX.[8]

---

[3] "Student Demonstration at the Computation Center, February 10, 1971," *Stanford Stories from the Archives*, 1970s, available at: https://exhibits.stanford.edu/stanford-stories/feature/1970s [https://perma.cc/ZR8R-S7B4] (last accessed September 12, 2022).

[4] "Petition Presented to the Ombudsman of Stanford University, January 1972"; "'Once an Indian Always an Indian' button, circa 1970s," ibid.

[5] *Harjo v. Pro-Football, Inc.*, 558 US 1025 (2009).

[6] Emma Bowman, "For Many Native Americans, the Washington Commanders' New Name Offers Some Closure," NPR, February 6, 2022, available at: www.npr.org/2022/02/06/1078571919/washington-commanders-name-change-native-americans [https://perma.cc/EL39-2MYN] (last accessed August 31, 2023); Frank James, "Supreme Court Declines to Hear Redskins Name Lawsuit," NPR, November 16, 2009, available at: www.npr.org/sections/thetwo-way/2009/11/supreme_court_declines_to_hear.html [https://perma.cc/6EQF-ZT6A] (last accessed August 31, 2023).

[7] "Stanford in Turmoil: Campus Unrest, 1966–1972" (2009), *Stanford Stories from the Archives*, 1970s, *supra*, note 3.

[8] "Women's Sports at Stanford: 40 Years of Title IX" (2012), *Stanford Stories from the Archives*, 1970s, *supra*, note 3.

Stanford saw the largest gathering of students in their civil disobedience action in the sit-in at Old Union on May 9–10, 1977, demanding the the Board of Trustees divest its interests in South Africa.[9] The anti-apartheid disinvestment movement began first at Stanford on the West Coast and Michigan State University in the Midwest in 1977 before it spread to other university campuses across the nation.

During the 1970s some graduate students also came to Stanford to learn about Construction Management through the famed Engineering Program.

John Igoe earned his Civil Engineering undergraduate degree from Villanova in Pennsylvania but came to Stanford for his master's degree in Civil Engineering with a concentration in Construction Management.[10] Igoe enrolled in the class where some classmates kept pestering the professor about sources of financing for entrepreneurs. The students really wanted to know where entrepreneurs could obtain financing to support their new ideas. Construction projects need capital. Construction projects and other business projects need loans. Where could new entrepreneurs get financing? Why did banks refuse to lend to new entrepreneurs? Were there alternative lending sources?

The students also came from other countries. Japan sent students with engineering interests to study at Stanford; among them, Kazuo Hirai in Mechanical Engineering, Katsuhiko Okubo in Electrical Engineering, Yoichiro Nakagawa in Material Science, Eiichiro Suhara in Engineering-Economic Systems, and Takeo Obayashi in Civil Engineering. Obayashi also took the Construction Management class in the late 1970s. Like many Stanford students at this time, he raised questions with his professor about where entrepreneurs could turn to for finance for new projects.

The Construction Management class brought the graduate students and their dreams and questions to their professor, Robert "Bob" Medearis, whose teaching affiliation at Stanford could not have existed without his former professor, Clark Oglesby.[11]

CLARK OGLESBY

Stanford's Construction program started with Clark Oglesby. Born in Clarksville, Missouri, and raised in Arizona, with an associate degree from Phoenix Junior

[9] "Old Union Sit-In Protesting Apartheid, May 9–10, 1977," *Stanford Stories from the Archives, 1970s, supra,* note 3.

[10] Sharon Simonson, "Google Names General Contractors for NASA Campus," *The Registry,* August 1, 2012, available at: https://news.theregistrysf.com/google-names-general-contractors-for-nasa-campus/ [https://perma.cc/2KJ4–4K5B] (last accessed August 31, 2023); "John Igoe, Director of Campus Development, Google," *NASA,* www.nasa.gov/centers/ames/research park/lecture/speaker_igoe.html [https://perma.cc/KM5X-ZQEP] (last accessed September 12, 2022).

[11] "Clarkson H. Oglesby," *CII* (1991), available at: www.construction-institute.org/awards/leader ship-awards/caroll-h-dunn-excellence/clarkson-h-oglesby [https://perma.cc/VLV9-K2MZ] (last accessed September 12, 2022).

College, Oglesby worked for the Arizona Highway Department for ten years as a field draftsman for a survey crew. Evidently, he was hungry for more; he wanted to be an engineer. Learning from a reliable source about two top engineering programs in California, Oglesby enrolled in the 1920s in Civil Engineering at Stanford, choosing it over University of Southern California (USC)'s engineering program. He returned to the Arizona Highway Department with his newly minted civil engineering degree and became a structure designer with the bridge division.

Two years later, in 1934, Oglesby became restless. He realized he wanted to learn more about engineering at the graduate level. He returned to Stanford for graduate studies in engineering and graduated with distinction. However, he went back to Arizona again for a job as a construction engineer for the Arizona state government and later for a private construction company.

Still, Oglesby loved Stanford. He missed the energy and excitement of Stanford's engineering students. He would return to Stanford for good and pitched an irresistible offer of teaching two Construction Engineering courses for no pay. During that time at Stanford, no serious academics thought much about construction education. Vocational schools were the place for construction courses, not university engineering programs. Based on his decades of real-world experience in construction and his extensive engineering knowledge, Oglesby thought differently, and he believed that he knew what students really wanted and needed from engineering education in postwar America. He designed two courses, Construction Estimating and Construction Engineering and Methods, and, to Stanford's surprise, seventy students registered for the courses!

Oglesby was ambitious. He saw an opportunity for Stanford to distinguish itself from other universities and attract graduate students in construction engineering. He dreamed of updating Stanford's construction program to the graduate level and offering an advanced degree program for construction engineering. He was convinced that engineers from other states would come to Stanford for advanced degrees. Eugene Grant, the chair of the civil engineering department and Oglesby's mentor, did not need much persuasion and agreed with Oglesby about the new graduate program for construction engineering. After all, Oglesby was Grant's former graduate research assistant back in the 1930s. Grant sold the idea to Frederick Terman, the Dean of Engineering, who was later recognized as "the Father of Silicon Valley." Terman extended his support and Construction gained full legitimacy as a field for both undergraduate and graduate studies.

Stanford was the only university in postwar America to offer a Construction graduate program. Oglesby's courses taught students engineering construction techniques, safety, management, and human behavior, in addition to knowledge about the construction business. His students multiplied his programs through their own creation of construction graduate programs at other universities throughout the United States. Oglesby mentored many students and followed their careers.

Oglesby's mentees included Bob Medearis. Like Oglesby, Medearis paid close attention to the students in his Construction Management class at Stanford. The students kept asking him about financing sources for entrepreneurs. John Igoe and Takeo Obayashi particularly stood out.[12]

TAKEO OBAYASHI

Takeo enrolled in Medearis' Construction Management class because construction ran through the young man's blood. His great-grandfather, Yoshigoro Obayashi, founded his first construction company in January 1892 in Osaka, Japan.[13] As a civil engineer and building contractor, Yoshigoro embraced the excitement of modernization initiated by the Meiji Restoration, and his company was involved in the construction of new offices and plants, and in infrastructure construction projects for ports and railroads throughout Japan. Cementing his name in the construction business at the national level, Yoshigoro changed the company name to Obayashi Corporation in 1904 and placed his son, Yoshio, a 22-year-old student at Waseda University, in charge of the company.[14]

In its first decade under the Obayashi name, the company successfully designed and built the iconic Tokyo Central Station (which is now called Tokyo Station), the Hanshin Koshien Stadium, and the Main Tower of Osaka Castle. The name Obayashi soon became synonymous with marvelous modern construction. Everyone took note after the Great Kanto Earthquake in 1923, as Tokyo Station was one of the few structures that survived, a testament to the Obayashi Corporation's engineering feat. Earthquake-resistant and fireproof modern buildings were in high demand as Japan rapidly developed and expanded its power, and clients looked to the Obayashi Corporation for their construction expertise.

After World War II, the Obayashi Corporation focused on construction projects throughout Japan to rebuild the nation. Government offices, schools, and hospitals became the focal point of the rebuilding efforts. The nation needed electricity and the Obayashi Corporation delivered by engaging in several dam construction projects for hydroelectric power. The company constructed the Nukabira Dam Power Generation Development, Yoyogi National Stadium 2nd Gymnasium, the Japan World Exposition theme pavilion, and the Minato Bridge on Hanshin Expressway Route 5 Bayshore Line, among its notable projects in the decades of postwar Japan.

[12] Hernan Martinez was not one of the students in Construction Management contributing to the new bank, Silicon Valley Bank, idea. See *Interview with Hernan Martinez* conducted on May 13, 2022 (on file with the author). Medearis later consulted with Martinez after the Bank was already in operation. Ibid.
[13] "Company History," *Obayashi*, available at: www.obayashi.co.jp/en/company/history.html [https://perma.cc/TST3-HNR4] (last accessed September 12, 2022).
[14] "Ohbayashi Corporation," *Encyclopedia.com*, available at: www.encyclopedia.com/books/politics-and-business-magazines/ohbayashi-corporation [https://perma.cc/V7RS-TD9N] (last accessed September 12, 2022).

As Japan's car manufacturing, petrochemical, and synthetic fiber industries began to take off at a feverish pace in the postwar period, innovations in new materials, engineering, and construction methods unfolded in the construction industry. New exciting developments arrived from overseas. Innovation and reputation carried the Obayashi name beyond Japan to land the Obayashi Corporation's first overseas project in Indonesia in 1965.

During the war, Yoshio Obayashi came to rely more on his son-in-law, Toshiro Obayashi, who adopted the family name in accordance with tradition where there is no direct male descendant, to run the business. In 1946, Toshiro succeeded as head of the Obayashi conglomerate in the construction and real estate business.

Toshiro Obayashi and his wife welcomed the birth of their son, Takeo, in 1954. Takeo earned his undergraduate degree at Keio University and went to Stanford's Civil Engineering School for his master's degree. In the late 1970s, Takeo arrived at the Stanford campus. Studying in California was a natural move for an Obayashi offspring because by the mid-1970s the Obayashi Corporation had already expanded into the US market with the acquisition of 50 percent ownership in the San Francisco Bay Area's James E. Roberts construction company. In 1979, the same year Takeo Obayashi took graduate courses, including Medearis' Construction Management class, the Obayashi Corporation won a major US contract to build a sewer system for the City of San Francisco.

Three years after Takeo earned his graduate degree from Stanford in 1980, the Obayashi Corporation gained full ownership of James E. Roberts and changed the name to the James E. Roberts–Obayashi Corporation. The Obayashi name continued to make inroads in the US construction market with notable projects, including the 1985 Toyota automobile plant in Kentucky. Obayashi made a subsequent acquisition of E. W. Howell, another US construction company in the midwestern and northern regions of the United States, and led many new construction initiatives.

Growing up in the tradition of design-built iconic structures across the world, Takeo exhibited a passion for construction with a strong focus on architecture. From architecture, Takeo later reached out to contemporary arts with many sculptural art pieces and became a serious arts collector. Merging construction, architecture, and contemporary arts, Takeo commissioned a Tadao Ando-designed space where the residential building itself is artwork and the house is the home for his arts collection. Interestingly, Takeo continues to keep an imprint in California; he consequently donated funds for the creation of the Japanese Friends Room in the San Francisco Museum of Modern Art (SFMOMA).[15]

[15] Yidi Tsao, "Collector Takeo Obayashi: The Many Paths to Art Patronage," COBOSOCIAL, available at: www.cobosocial.com/dossiers/the-many-paths-to-arts-patronage-collector-takeo-obayashi/ [https://perma.cc/9SRF-ENWW] (last accessed September 12, 2022); The Obayashi Foundation, available at: www.obayashifoundation.org/english/about/ (last accessed August 31, 2023).

Thirty-four years after he graduated from Stanford, Meaderis still fondly remembered his student, Takeo. Construction Management and a curiosity about where entrepreneurs can acquire loans to start their new business ideas came together in the class where Meaderis taught and where his students raised questions. Some questions proved so fundamental that Meaderis had no answers.

JOHN IGOE

Igoe became one of Meaderis' favorite students in his Construction Management class. Meaderis knew the young man, like other engineers from other states, came to Stanford for the special blend of real-world engineering. Igoe worked for a few years after obtaining his Civil Engineering degree from Villanova University in 1963. He wanted more. He had an interest in both engineering and business. Stanford was the best school with a graduate program in Civil Engineering with a concentration in Construction Management. Igoe graduated from Stanford's graduate engineering program in 1970 and then pursued his MBA in Finance from Drexel University. With the two credentials, he would soon become one of the leaders in corporate real estate and the construction industry.

Deep in innovative ideas for construction and real estate, Igoe worked with tech corporations, from Palm, Peoplesoft, 3Com, Octel, to NeXT, in the Bay Area for fifteen years. Corporate real estate became his specialty. His calling involved building a new tech campus where workspaces and happy healthy innovators all correlated. Steve Jobs recruited Igoe to work at NeXT.[16] At Octel, Igoe's team built the corporate campus from scratch.

Construction and design were part of Igoe's DNA. Fun and joy must be associated with a corporate office building for the innovators who spend long hours inside the buildings and on campus. The office space provides both an environment to stimulate creative thinking and a building to adhere to environmental sustainability. Corporate office buildings must also both represent and embrace the corporate culture. According to his peers, Igoe possesses the ideas and the ability to execute his vision. Igoe has been serving as Google's Director of Design and Construction for more than ten years. He oversees Google's construction projects around the world. He counts the complex, large-scale, domed offices at Google campus as his visionary ideas.

Construction Management brought Igoe to Stanford, and Medearis remembered his student years later. In that class, for almost ten years in the 1970s and into the early 1980s, many students asked about where young entrepreneurs could obtain

---

[16] "2019 Distinguished Leaders Circle Inductees Announced," *CoreNet Global*, 2019, available at: www.corenetglobal.org/files/CNG/PDF/distinguished-leader-2019-final-v2.pdf [https://perma.cc/FX7R-QAZN] (last accessed September 12, 2022); Igoe, *supra*, note 10.

financing. They wanted to know why banks kept saying "no" to young entrepreneurs. Medearis mulled over their questions for many years thereafter.

Perhaps there ought to be a bank saying "yes" to young entrepreneurs, staving off the relentless force of banks' unlimited "no power."

BANKS WITH UNLIMITED "NO POWER"

Medearis' students and other entrepreneurs heard the ready "no" answers from bank loan officers. With a new business idea in search of a startup or new business loan, entering a bank, the entrepreneur would hear a resounding "no" from the loan officers. The dejected entrepreneurs would walk away empty handed. "No" and "no" were the mantra from banks. So much so that, as one bank executive later recalled, at Wells Fargo, "everyone ... has unlimited 'no power'" to dole out at new entrepreneurs hesitantly walking through the door at any time.[17] Loan professionals at banks across the United States, both then and now, seem to lack the creativity to identify ways to provide new products to emerging new entrepreneurs in different emerging tech areas.[18] Banks see new entrepreneurs as having "high risk of losses" etched on their foreheads. They are afraid, rightly so, to make loans to new unproven, profit-missing businesses. It is simply too risky because losses often encountered by new startups are in real red ink, and banks fail to see growth potentials from the losses.[19] In the late 1970s, a few bankers at Wells Fargo became frustrated with the "no" mantra and the "no" culture and were restless for an opportunity at a new independent bank that would incorporate in its mission a commitment to serve new entrepreneurs.

Bank of America, Wells Fargo, Bank of the West, and others concentrated substantially in the real estate sector. The money was good. Construction was booming in California in the 1970s. The government pumped lots of money into defense projects. People from other states moved to California. Los Angeles flourished as the epicenter of aeronautics in the Cold War years, occupying 108 million square feet of new industrial space in the 1970s. Industrial construction reigned supreme.[20]

From the 1940s to 1970s, California witnessed its population grow 242 percent faster than the national figure but the median home value grew only 16 percent

---

[17] Computer History Museum, "Silicon Valley Bank Oral History Panel Robert 'Bob' Medearis and Roger Smith," 1–41, 13, November 11, 2014, available at: https://archive.computerhistory.org/resources/access/text/2015/07/102739977-05-01-acc.pdf [https://perma.cc/C6BW-S6XD] (last accessed August 31, 2023).

[18] Ibid.

[19] Ibid., at 15.

[20] "How L.A. Keeps Coming Back: An 80-Year Overview of Real Estate Development," *Commercial Cafe*, August 11, 2020, available at: www.commercialcafe.com/blog/history-los-angeles-real-estate-development/ [https://perma.cc/UC3M-6CVS] (last accessed August 31, 2023).

faster than the national number. Soon, the housing bubble frenzy unfolded. There were not enough houses to meet the demand in the 1970s, as land use restrictions limited zoning to only single-family houses or to height restrictions of two-stories, and environmental concerns limited new housing development and community involvement. The restrictions only gave the then-existing residents a voice in land use decisions, depriving future residents of the same opportunity.[21] California has long been known to have caused its own housing crisis, and the roots can be traced back to the 1950s when developers invented a new "municipal technology" to form concentric circles of the city around old urban centers to insulate suburban home-owners with all the comforts within their incorporated limits and prevent the so-called big city ills from encroaching on their comforts.[22]

The real estate market in California ballooned from 1970 to 1980 to a giant bubble where an average house price in West Los Angeles rose 600 percent and houses in Malibu doubled in value every year in the late 1970s. A starter home in a remote desert suburb demanded $200,000 at the end of the decade. A house in Pacific Palisades priced at $29,000 in the early 1950s commanded a price tag of $1.7 million in 1980.[23] Real estate agents touted that the house value would keep going up. Banks made loans at mortgage rates lower than the rising house price rates. Everyone wanted a house and took out first and second mortgages.[24] Overall, the median price of a house in California was $23,210 in 1968, which had shot up to $99,550 by 1980.[25] A tiny house of 960 sq. ft. in Palo Alto had already fetched $40,000 in the 1970s.[26] Construction was everywhere. In Orange County, the number of houses built in the 1960s was up 76 percent from the prior decade. In the 1970s the number continued to climb.[27]

[21] Issi Romem, "California's Housing Prices Need to Come Down," *Bloomberg*, March 28, 2018 11:54 A.M., available at: www.bloomberg.com/news/articles/2018-03-28/california-s-housing-laws-should-be-under-state-control [https://perma.cc/L8TZ-BZBC] (last accessed August 31, 2023).

[22] Benjamin Schneider, "How to Make a Housing Crisis," *Bloomberg*, February 21, 2020 11:10 A.M. PST, available at: www.bloomberg.com/news/articles/2020-02-21/a-brief-history-of-california-s-housing-crisis [https://perma.cc/DFQ9-GRX8] (last accessed August 31, 2023).

[23] Benjamin J. Stein, "Housing Boom Goes Bust in Los Angeles," *The New York Times*, August 17, 1981, available at: www.nytimes.com/1981/08/17/opinion/housing-boom-goes-bust-in-los-angeles.html (last accessed August 31, 2023).

[24] Ibid.

[25] "California Real Estate Median Prices of Existing Homes since 1968," *Real Estate ABC*, available at: www.realestateabc.com/graphs/calmedian.html [https://perma.cc/B8RM-4T2Y] (last accessed September 12, 2022).

[26] Anna Marie Erwert, "Tiny Palo Alto Pad Was Just $40K in the 70s. Now, It's $2.5M," *SFGate*, June 30, 2018, available at: www.sfgate.com/realestate/article/235-webster-st-palo-alto-2-5M-13040216.php [https://perma.cc/VA66-G94L] (last accessed August 31, 2023).

[27] Susan Christian, "Real O.C. Boom Was in the '60s: Growth: The Number of Houses Built in the Decade Was Up 76% to 232,379 from 132,193 Units Constructed in the 1950s," *The Los Angeles Times*, May 11, 1992 12 A.M. PT, available at: www.latimes.com/archives/la-xpm-1992-05-11-fi-1315-story.html (last accessed August 31, 2023).

Banks do what they know best: real estate. They can see the land, touch the buildings, feel the houses, and survey the construction. Valuation experts could quickly provide the comps. The insurance industry stands by ready to issue policies. The underwriters know what to do with real estate loans. Banks stick to what they are familiar with every day for so long. The real estate boom in California, where easy money could be made from writing mortgages to meet the feverish demand, affirmed bankers' belief in concentrating loan activity in the real estate sector. Loan professionals did not need to leave their desks looking for borrowers in new sectors, particularly the burgeoning new tech sector in the Santa Clara Valley, when real estate is a rock-solid business for banks. The lenders could continue to stay in the office, where phones would ring and borrowers would stream in for new real estate loans. Lending in the old real estate business has long been established to be good for bankers, if they can, of course, drive through the bust after the boom years.[28]

It is easy to say "no" to anything that is new. "No" was, and still is, an unlimited power for loan officers at local and national banks to say to new entrepreneurs who don't own land, building, or construction sites, whose new business possesses no physical and hard assets, and whose ideas are untested. Banks chased after the real estate industry for the immediate and foreseeable big bucks while ignoring the new business model of growth inhabited by entrepreneurs in the new tech sector in the 1970s.

Construction was what brought Medearis to Stanford. Construction was what brought his students from Japan and the east coast and the Midwest to Stanford. But it was the construction boom in industrial and residential real estate sectors that allowed banks to shun his students and entrepreneurs for loans. In searching for an answer to his students' query about where to obtain financing in light of bank rejections, Medearis would later both embrace and reject the obsession of lending in the construction real estate sector by banks. He and his two cofounders forged their vision of an independent, community bank solution to disrupt banking norms. However, construction or real estate lending was also what brought their new bank financial trouble in the last year of the first decade of its existence. But that story will be told in later chapters.

---

[28] Paragon Real Estate Group, "3 Recessions, 2 Bubbles and a Baby (Recovery)!," August 2012 Market Report (documenting the past 30 years of real estate market boom and bust cycles in San Francisco 5-County Metro area).

3

Bank Atrophy and Outliers

Medearis and his two cofounders of Silicon Valley Bank wished to tackle the antiquated banking practices that led to a massive reduction in the number of banks, the disappearance of community banks, and the mergers of Big Banks. Bank regulations and culture prevent banks from embracing tech startups and entrepreneurs as lending clients. The SVB founders knew about Bank of America's abandonment of its early tech lending, missed opportunities, and bank failures to capture tech startups and entrepreneurs. The old, conservative banking environment during the early days of the tech sector presented the founders with an opportunity.

* * *

Each day, new startups with new ideas are born.[1] Without access to financing, brilliant founders simply cannot bring their most promising enterprises into existence. Upstart entrepreneurs, possessing dreams of innovation, know all too well that banks in the cities and towns where they live shun them as potential lending customers. Their startups have no positive cash flow. Some are months, if not years, from generating revenue. Some are still trying to establish their niche; they are trying to grow and hopefully rapidly scale. Their growth model does not yield any profit and will most likely not be generating a profit any time soon. Their most valuable assets are soft assets, ranging from trade secrets, patent applications, patents, and copyrights, to mobile apps,

---

[1] The background studies on startups, outlier banks and IP venture lending are from the author's prior works. See Xuan-Thao Nguyen, "Lending Innovation," Brooklyn Law Review 86 (2020):135–178; Xuan-Thao Nguyen, "Banking the Unbanked Innovators," Journal of Corporation Law 45 (2020): 715–742; Xuan-Thao Nguyen and Erik Hille, "The Puzzle in Financing with Trademark Collateral," Houston Law Review 56 (2018): 365–400; Xuan-Thao Nguyen and Erik Hille, "Disruptive Lending for Innovation: Signaling Model and Banks Selection of Startups," University of Pennsylvania Journal of Business Law 21 (2018): 200–234; Xuan-Thao Nguyen and Erik Hille, "Patent Aversion: An Empirical Study of Patents Collateral in Bank Lending, 1980–2016," University of California Irvine Law Review 9 (2018): 141–176.

software, and data analytics. Their trademark is unknown in the marketplace because their enterprise is still too new, and the goodwill has attached only to new products that the enterprise is still struggling to roll out beyond the beta testing phase.[2]

Consequently, banks reject startup technology as collateral for a business loan because there is too much uncertainty. To banks, startups and their intangibles are too risky and most likely cannot pay back the loans. In the end, banks sit on the sideline of innovations. Only a few outlier banks, a small group led by SVB, served startups and growing tech companies.

BANK RISES AND DECLINES

The dual federal and state system of governance, in addition to economic, geopolitical, and other conditions, greatly affects the rises and declines of banks in the United States. While the federal government possesses the sole authority on issuing currency and imposing taxes on interstate banking, states exert their control by permitting charters, taxing, and regulating banks on their capital, deposits, dividends, profits, and franchises.

On December 14, 1790, Alexander Hamilton submitted *The Report on a National Bank*, urging Congress to establish a central bank. Congress utilized its authority under the Constitution and passed the Bank Bill of 1791, which gave birth to the First Bank of the United States. The bank received a twenty-year charter. In 1811, the First Bank's charter expired because Congress decided not to renew it. Stephen Girard stepped in and purchased the First Bank's stock, building, and furnishings, and reopened it as a private bank named after himself, Girard Bank. Five years after Congress allowed the First Bank's charter to expire, it issued the new charter of the Second Bank of the United States in 1816. The second federally authorized Hamiltonian national bank was allowed to lapse its charter in January 1836. Nationwide, however, the number of private banks reached 788 in 1837.

Less than three decades later, the number of total banks had risen to 1,643 in 1865, the same year the National Banking Act of 1864 became effective. The Act created the Office of the Comptroller of the Currency ("OCC") which oversees banks with national charters. Congress imposed a 10 percent tax on all non-national bank notes, forcing most banks at that time to join the national banking system. However, the control and limitations imposed on banks under federal banking law both restricted banking services and failed to meet the needs of many expanding communities in new states and territories.

---

[2] Xuan-Thao Nguyen, "Lending Innovation," *Brooklyn Law Review* 86 (2020): 135–178; Xuan-Thao Nguyen, "Banking the Unbanked Innovators," *Journal of Corporation Law* 45 (2020): 715–742; Xuan-Thao Nguyen and Erik Hille, "The Puzzle in Financing with Trademark Collateral," *Houston Law Review* 56 (2018): 365–400; Xuan-Thao Nguyen and Erik Hille, "Disruptive Lending for Innovation: Signaling Model and Banks Selection of Startups," *University of Pennsylvania Journal of Business Law* 21 (2018): 200–234; Xuan-Thao Nguyen and Erik Hille, "Patent Aversion: An Empirical Study of Patents Collateral in Bank Lending, 1980–2016," *University of California Irvine Law Review* 9 (2018): 141–176.

The demand for banking services opened the door for states to pass laws in the 1880s and 1890s making it easier for banks to obtain their charters. The competition between federal and state charters thus began; the federal OCC system desired to implement branching but state regulators resisted such poaching into their jurisdictions. Federal and state regulators openly competed against each other for chartering of banks. That led to the explosion of banking charters. By 1890, there were 10,382 commercial banks, and that number reached a historic peak of 30,312 in 1921.

The Great Depression began with the stock market crash in October 1929 and lasted until 1939. The United States suffered the worst economic downturn in history. The banking system failed during the Great Depression. The banking crisis of 1930–1933 wiped out many banks. By 1933, there were 14,146 banks still in operation, less than 50 percent than at the historic peak. To restore public trust in the banking system after its spectacular failure, the federal government established the Federal Deposit Insurance Corporation in 1934 which extends some measure of protection to depositors.

From 1934 to 1985, the number of banks was relatively steady, with some small declines and gains, and the total number of banks ranged between 13,114 and 14,496. The Savings and Loan (S&L) Crisis of 1986 sent banks into a new adjustment. The banks saw a small decline of 45 banks in 1984 but soon witnessed 621 banks fail in 1988.

Banks continued to decline due to bank failures, mergers, and interstate banking. As early as 1978, the State of Maine became the first state that welcomed interstate banking. Other states then followed by allowing banks to acquire out-of-state banks. Since the 1990s, the banking sector has been experiencing a gradual decline in the number of banks. In the decade between 1994 and 2004, the sector witnessed a 29.2 percent decline in bank charters, as seen in the bank downfall from 12,589 in 1994 to 8,918 in 2004. The mergers and acquisitions of banks across states, encouraged by the enactment of the Riegle-Neal Interstate Banking and Branching Efficiency Act in 1994, accelerated the drop in bank charters. Advances in technology and online banking also contributed to the decline in bank branch networks. Payment apps have replaced the need to have a bank account associated with fees that people loathe to pay.

In 2000, there were 8,315 FDIC-insured commercial banks in the United States. Two decades later, by the end of 2021, this number had plunged to 4,236.[3] As the number of banks dwindled, the American's dislike of banks rose.

* * *

COMMERCIAL BANK, COMMUNITY BANK UNIT BANK:
INDEPENDENT BANK

Banks in the United States are chartered either as state or national banks. A "national bank" or "federal savings bank," as the names denote, can operate across the United States

---

[3] "Number of FDIC-Insured Commercial Banks in the U.S. 2000–2021," *Statista Research Department*, May 24, 2022, available at: www.statista.com/statistics/184536/number-of-fdic-insured-us-commercial-bank-institutions/ [https://perma.cc/U9FQ-JQTW] (last accessed September 19, 2023).

under the federal bank charter system. The Office of the Comptroller of the Currency has the authority to charter and regulate national banks and federal savings institutions.

Under the dual banking system, the counterpart of federal banking is state banking. That means a state-chartered bank does not carry "national" or "federal" in its name and has permission to conduct banking services only within a particular state. Every state has a specific agency to charter and regulate state-chartered banks. Because some state banks are members of the Federal Reserve, they are also subject to the Federal Reserve's regulations. The remainder, nonmember state banks, are under the regulations of the Federal Deposit Insurance Corporation.[4]

In addition, "commercial banks" and "community banks" are frequent names for banks based on their activities. Commercial banks typically provide national banking operations, possess large cash reserves to make large business loans, tolerate greater risks associated with the loans, offer corporate clients comprehensive banking services, and employ technology to enhance their services. Community banks are standalone and small banks, serving local community needs for cash safe loans to small businesses and farmers and mortgages for local housing. Community banks represent 92 percent of FDIC-insured institutions. Despite having only 14 percent of the banking industry's assets, community banks provide 43 percent of the industry's small loans to businesses and farmers. Community banks are also referred to as "unit banks" or banks operated as single-branch entities. In 1935, the United States typically conducted banking services at unit banks. In fact, more than 94 percent of banks in 1935 functioned as unit banks.[5]

Most banks today operate within a parent holding structure. Banks have become subsidiaries, and the parent companies own many different subsidiaries. For example, SVB Financial Group was a diversified financial services company, as well as a bank holding company and a financial holding company. SVBFG offered commercial and banking products and services through its subsidiary, Silicon Valley Bank. The parent company also owned two other subsidiaries: SVB Capital, the venture capital and credit investment arm, with a focus on funds management, and SVB Securities, an investment bank in Healthcare and Technology sectors, with a focus on Capital Raising, M&A Advisory, Equity Research, and Sales & Trading.

The 2008 financial crisis, some argued, traced the financial instability to the "Too Big to Fail" problems percolating from the holding company of giant financial institutions. The Great Recession witnessed bank failures, decimating 507 bank charters between 2008 and 2014. "Too Big to Fail" and the subprime mortgage crisis

4 "2022–2026 Strategic Plan: Supervision Program," *Federal Department Insurance Corporation*, updated February 8, 2022, available at: www.fdic.gov/about/strategic-plans/strategic/supervision .html#:~:text=Program%20Description,of%20the%20Federal%20Reserve%20System [https://perma .cc/R6CM-VNT2] (last accessed September 19, 2023).

5 Stephen Matteo Miller, Vera Soliman, and Joe Brunk, "On the Historical Rise and (Recent) Decline in the Number of Banks: A Series on Bank Size and Concentration," *Mercatus Policy Digest*, available at: www.mercatus.org/bridge/commentary/historical-rise-and-recent-decline- number-banks [https://perma.cc/A2AP-D2Z2] (last accessed September 19, 2023).

hastened the deaths of many financial institutions in an industry that is too old to learn, adapt, and evolve.

BANKS AND LENDING PRACTICES

Based on assets, there are two groups of small and large banks. At the end of 2020, there were 4,899 banks with less than $10 billion in assets and 151 banks with more than $10 billion.[6] On March 31, 2022, there were 2,130 insured US-charted commercial banks with consolidated assets of $300 million or more.[7] SVB was in the top fifteen largest banks in the United States as of September 2022.[8] Together, the fifteen largest banks held a combined total of $13.44 trillion in assets.

Banks are subject to capital adequacy guidelines issued by the Federal Reserve Board of Governors. Banks must meet the minimum ratio of total capital to total assets set forth in the banking regulations.[9] For instance, a bank may be subject to the minimum capital requirement of 8 percent of assets and certain off-balance sheet items weighted by risk. The regulations may permit at least half of the 8 percent ratio to consist of common equity, including retained earnings, and the remainder may include subordinated debt, cumulative preferred stock, or a limited amount of loan loss reserves. Interestingly, depending on the types of assets the bank holds, different levels of risk category, and an associated minimum ratio are required. Assets like cash and government securities are in the 0 percent risk category. Home mortgage loans are in the 50 percent risk category requiring a 4 percent ratio, and commercial loans are in the 100 percent risk category requiring an 8 percent ratio.[10] An entrepreneur may wonder how tech loans can be categorized? Certainly, they must be in the 100 percent risk category like "commercial loans" or perhaps even higher as banks are known to stay away from them.

Banks exist to take in deposits, turn the deposits into loans, harvest the difference in loans and deposit interests, and make some investments, in addition to collecting fees generated from a host of services. A bank's net income is the difference between income (interest and noninterest) and expense (interest expense, noninterest

---

[6] Marc Labonte and David W. Perkins, "Over the Line: Asset Thresholds in Bank Regulation," *Congressional Research Service*, May 3, 2021, available at: https://sgp.fas.org/crs/misc/R46779 .pdf [https://perma.cc/Z2C4-FN6W] (last accessed September 19, 2023).

[7] "Federal Reserve Statistical Release: Large Commercial Banks," *Federal Reserve*, June 30, 2022, available at: www.federalreserve.gov/releases/lbr/current/ [https://perma.cc/FJ2D-EC7G] (last accessed September 19, 2023) (Insured U.S.-Chartered Commercial Banks That Have Consolidated Assets of $300 Million or More, Ranked by Consolidated Assets).

[8] Matthew Goldberg, "The 15 Largest Banks in the US," *Bankrate*, September 8, 2022, available at: www.bankrate.com/banking/biggest-banks-in-america/ [https://perma.cc/2EHT-WVDH] (last accessed September 19, 2023).

[9] 12 Code of Federal Regulations § 3.10: Minimum capital requirements, www.ecfr.gov/current/ title-12/chapter-I/part-3/subpart-B/section-3.10 [https://perma.cc/WL4S-SL6J] (last accessed September 19, 2023).

[10] *1989 Annual Report* 18 (Silicon Valley Bancshare, 1989).

expenses, income tax expense, and provision for loan losses). The bank's growth in earning assets is primarily concentrated in its loan portfolio. The bank's lending practices are subject to statutes and regulations with respect to lending limits, loans to insiders, involuntary tying arrangements involving loans, and usury. Lending limits restrict the total amount of loans to any one person at any one time. The limits force banks to diversify their loans to different borrowers and to increase access to banking services.

With respect to loan administration, for instance at SVB in its first decade, the Board of Directors was responsible for the loan policy. The Board exercised the initial approval and periodic review of the Bank's loan policy. The Board delegated the authority to supervise loan activities to the Directors' Loan Committee which is comprised of five outside Directors and one inside Director. Under Silicon Valley Bank's loan policy, no individual loan officer possessed the sole lending authority. That meant all loan requests must be decided by the Bank's Internal Loan Committee which consisted of the Senior Credit Officer, President, and four Senior Vice Presidents. If a loan request exceeded the Internal Loan Committee's authority, the request would be submitted to the Directors' Loan Committee for its review and approval. Such internal processes were designed to reduce nonperforming loans. Not all banks share the same internal approval path, but all do implement mechanisms to review and approve loan requests.

Under the generally applicable lending limits, how much a bank can lend to a borrower depends on whether the loan is fully secured by *readily marketable collateral*. If the loan does not satisfy the collateral requirement, the applicable limit is the basic 15 percent of the bank's unimpaired capital and surplus. If the loan satisfies the collateral requirement, the applicable limit is an additional 10 percent of the bank's unimpaired capital and surplus, separate and additional to the basic 15 percent limit. That means the bank can make loans up to the 25 percent limit.[11]

Illustratively, a hypothetical commercial bank holds a total unimpaired capital and surplus of $10,000,000. The bank finds a borrower who has no outstanding loans or credit with the bank. The borrower possesses assets that are readily marketable collateral to fully secure loans. That means the bank can lend that borrower $1,500,000 (15 percent basic limit) plus $1,000,000 (the additional 10 percent limit), for a total of $2,500,000. If the borrower does not qualify for the additional 10 percent limit, the bank can provide loans and extensions to the borrower that would not, in the aggregate, exceed $1,500,000.

Some loans secured by certain types of collateral, including bills of lading or warehouse receipts covering readily marketable staples, documents covering livestock, and discounts of installment consumer paper, encompass lending limits pursuant to federal banking regulations. The term "readily marketable staple" is

---

[11] 12 Code of Federal Regulations § 32.3: Lending Limits, available at: www.ecfr.gov/current/title-12/chapter-I/part-32 [https://perma.cc/SM85–9QJZ] (last accessed September 19, 2023).

defined as an article of commerce, agriculture, or industry, such as wheat and other grains, cotton, wool, and basic metals such as tin, copper, and lead, in the form of standardized interchangeable units that are easy to sell in a market with sufficiently frequent price quotations.[12] Moreover, the banking regulations defined that *readily marketable collateral* means financial instruments and bullion that are salable under ordinary market conditions with reasonable promptness at a fair market value determined by quotations based upon actual transactions on an auction or similarly available daily bid and asking price market.[13] Financial instruments are further defined as stocks, notes, bonds, and debentures traded on a national securities exchange, commercial paper, negotiable certificates of deposit, bankers' acceptances, and shares in the money market and mutual funds.

States may impose different legal lending limits.[14] For instance, Section 103 of New York Banking Law imposes lending limits on New York-chartered banks restricting the extension of credit to one borrower to 15 percent of the bank's capital stock, surplus fund, and undivided profits (CUPS) but permitting the limit to increase to 25 percent of CUPS if the additional 10 percent is secured by collateral that has "an ascertained market value or otherwise [has] a value as collateral as found in good faith by an officer of such bank or trust company" – that is, an "ascertained market value" or "good faith value."

These legal definitions greatly restrict what banks can accept as potential borrowers' assets and as collateral to secure a line of credit or loan. Unfortunately, the "readily marketable collateral" definition does not include the types of assets that startups in the technology sector typically possess. Thus, operating under federal and state lending limits, many banks decline to make loans to startups and growing tech companies. They fail to see how they could make tech loans. Saying "no" is much easier than attempting to identify ways to serve the tech industry.

BANKS SHUN STARTUPS AND GROWING TECH COMPANIES

From innovation centers across the nation to state capitols and the halls of Congress, startups are known to be the engine for jobs. Startups have historically created 11 percent of all private sector jobs, added 10 percent of total US sales, and contributed 21 percent of US GDP.[15] Startups in technology-based industries currently contribute a higher employment share than new businesses in other fields. High

---

[12] 12 Code of Federal Regulations § 32.2: Definitions, available at: www.ecfr.gov/current/title-12/chapter-I/part-32/section-32.2 [https://perma.cc/YJC2–938F] (last accessed September 19, 2023).

[13] Ibid.

[14] "Banking Interpretations: Lending Limit," *New York Department of Financial Services*, available at: www.dfs.ny.gov/legal/interpret/lo091214.htm [https://perma.cc/7RPZ-UE7K] (last accessed September 12, 2022).

[15] Letter from Joe Morgan, Chief Innovation Officer, Silicon Valley Bank, to Elizabeth M. Murphy, Securities and Exchange Commission, see, Chapter 1, note 61.

risks, high growth, and high rewards are common features associated with technology-based startups. These are the same features pushing banks away from accepting startups as potentially attractive customers.

Conventional banking practices both dictate and encourage banks to make loans to legacy and established companies with physical assets. Banks require borrowers to have positive cash flow and long credit histories. Banks are eager to participate in real estate, from commercial to residential, transactions, while ignoring innovators in the technology sector, avoiding startups and high-growth companies.

One of the common reasons for shunning startups and high-growth companies is that these companies lack hard assets. Their most valuable assets are intellectual property, including patents, trade secrets, trademarks, and copyrights. Banking regulations do not count intellectual property assets as readily marketable collateral, restricting the ability of banks to rely on these assets when calculating the legal lending limit.

As a young entrepreneur, Mark Zuckerberg filed his first patent application titled "Dynamically Generating a Privacy Summary" in July 2006. Zuckerberg later procured several more patents with his name listed as an inventor. Like most startups, Facebook generated very few patents. Patents are valuable to the company. As Facebook grew and later headed to an Initial Public Offering (IPO), Facebook acquired 750 software and networking patents from IBM for $83 million to fend off a lawsuit filed by Yahoo and 650 patents from Microsoft for $550 million by April 2012.

Patents are valuable as they are used both offensively and defensively by companies in the modern economy. Still, banks reject startup patents and other intellectual property assets as collateral and refuse to extend a credit line against these intangible assets.

Patents are issued by the United States Patents Office to those who invent or discover any new and useful process, machine, manufacture, or composition of matter, or any new and useful improvement thereof. The inventions must also be novel, in that the patent holder is the first to make the invention as claimed. If the claimed invention was known or used by others in the United States or patented or described in a printed publication in the United States or a foreign country before the invention date, such invention is disqualified from becoming a patent. The inventor's own conduct, such as a failure to file a patent application within one year of invention disclosure at a conference, in a scientific publication, or during an offer of sale of the invention, will bar the inventor from obtaining patent protection. In addition to the novelty requirement, the inventions must satisfy the "nonobviousness" requirement which measures, through a combination of references, whether the claimed invention is obvious to those of ordinary skill in the field of the invention. Enablement is another patentability requirement: that the claimed inventions enable a person of ordinary skill in the art to practice their full scope without undue experimentation. The enablement requirement also requires that the specification of the patent adequately disclose the claimed invention so as to enable a person skilled in the art to use and make the invention at the time the patent application was filed. If an invention satisfies all the patentability requirements, the invention will be granted a patent through a formal process called patent prosecution. The average time for patent prosecution is 16.9 months, according to a report released by the US Patent and Trademark Office (USPTO) in 2021.

Due to recent Supreme Court decisions on patentability, startups face a difficult battle to obtain patents on their inventions in software, personal medicines, and medical diagnosis.[16] Patents, if the startups can successfully procure them, are used to signal the industry that the company is innovative, separating itself from other competitors. A patent contains a legal life of twenty years from the date of filing. The company, as the patent holder, can assert infringement actions against others. The patent holder can also assign and license the patents to a third party and use patents to attract funding. Many established tech companies, from Google and Microsoft to Uber, hold large patent portfolios. Some tech companies like IBM and Qualcomm, instead of engaging in manufacturing new products based on their patent portfolios, license their patents to generate revenue as their primary business model.

Startups own trade secrets which cover all forms and types of financial, business, scientific, technical, economic, or engineering information, including patterns, plans, compilations, program devices, formulas, designs, prototypes, methods, techniques, processes, procedures, programs, or codes, whether tangible or intangible, and whether or how stored, compiled, or memorialized physically, electronically, graphically, photographically, or in writing. Trade secrets deserve protection because they (i) derive independent economic value, actual or potential, from not being generally known, and not being readily ascertainable by proper means, and (ii) are the subject of efforts that are reasonable under the circumstances to maintain its secrecy. Trade secrets are also referred to as know-how. Federal and state laws protect against the misappropriation of trade secrets by improper means such as theft, bribery, misrepresentation, breach or inducement of a breach of a duty to maintain secrecy, or espionage through electronic or other means.[17] A trade secret lasts as long as the holder maintains secrecy.

A notable trade secret theft case that rocked the startup world involved autonomous vehicle technology during the Uber–Waymo trade secret trial. Anthony Levandowski, a former Google engineer, faced eighteen months in prison after he pleaded guilty to stealing Google's trade secret. Levandowski was ordered to pay a $95,000 fine and $756,499.22 in restitution to Waymo, Google's self-driving car unit. Levandowski downloaded and copied files from Google onto his laptop before he resigned from the company. He subsequently used the trade secrets when founding

[16] See *Alice Corp. v. CLS Bank Int'l*, 573 U.S. 208 (2014); *Association for Molecular Pathology v. Myriad Genetics, Inc.*, 569 U.S. 576 (2013); *Mayo Collaborative Services v. Prometheus Laboratories, Inc.*, 566 U.S. 66 (2012).
[17] 18 U.S. Code § 1836: Civil Proceedings, available at: https://uscode.house.gov/view.xhtml?path=/prelim@title18/part1/chapter90&edition=prelim [https://perma.cc/4WA4-2WZ7] (last accessed September 19, 2023)..

the startup Otto, a self-driving truck company. Uber then acquired Otto. Uber and Waymo settled for $245 million.[18]

Despite trade secrets being important assets to startups, like patents, banks do not make loans against trade secrets. Under banking regulations, as explained before, trade secrets and patents are not covered in the definition of readily marketable collateral. Both banking regulations and industry norms shy away from accepting trade secrets and patents in the calculation of the borrower's base.

A copyright is a work of authorship, such as a song, poem, book, computer software, sound recording, painting, architectural plan, or movie, that is independently created by the author, fixed in a tangible medium of expression, and contains a modicum of creativity. Copyright protection begins immediately the work of authorship is complete. The author of copyright can be an individual or an entity employer under the works-made-for-hire doctrine. Copyright enjoys a term of the life of the author and 70 years thereafter. For works made for hire, the term is 95 years after publication or 120 years after creation.

Ownership of valid copyright confers five exclusive rights: the right to make copies of the work; the right to prepare derivative works; the right to distribute copies of the work; the right to perform the work publicly or by means of digital audio transmission (in the case of sound recordings); and the right to display the work publicly. Any violation of the exclusive rights committed by others without permission of the copyright owner constitutes a basis for a copyright infringement action. A copyright holder can assign and license any of the exclusive rights.

Because copyrights cover software, many startups in the tech industry are authors of copyrights. The proliferation of computers in the 1980s transformed the software industry, expanding from customized computer programs to application packages. Subsequently, software enables the growth and expansion of the network economy. As the Supreme Court restricted patent protections for software invention, startups turn to both copyright and trade secret laws for the protection of their software and valuable data. Unfortunately, like patent and trade secret assets, banking regulations and norms prevent them from being utilized as readily marketable collateral in lending.

Every startup has a name and seeks protection for the name under trademark law. A trademark is a word, phrase, logo, device, or design that functions as a source identifier of the goods or services on which the trademark is affixed. A trademark also distinguishes its associated goods or services from those of others. To be qualified as a protectable trademark under the federal Lanham Act, a trademark is either inherently distinctive or has acquired distinctiveness through use in commerce.[19]

---

[18] Aarian, Marshall, "Uber and Waymo Abruptly Settle For $245 Million," *Wired*, February 9, 2018 12:17 P.M., available at: www.wired.com/story/uber-waymo-lawsuit-settlement/ [https://perma.cc/D3RR-ER5G] (last accessed September 19, 2023)..

[19] Xuan-Thao Nguyen and Erik Hille, "The Puzzle in Financing with Trademark Collateral," *Houston Law Review* 56 (2018): 365–400, available at: https://digitalcommons.law.uw.edu/faculty-articles/865/ (last accessed September 19, 2023).

Examples of some trademarks that are common words used uncommonly, are APPLE (for computers) and AMAZON (for platform marketplace). There are fanciful trademarks which are words not found in a dictionary. Examples of such marks include EXXON (for gasoline), CLOROX (for laundry bleach), and FACEBOOK (for social media networking). There are suggestive trademarks that reflect a level of creativity, abstract thought and intuition, metaphorical resemblance, and sheer incongruity. They are, for example, PENGUIN (for refrigerators), CITIBANK (for banking services), GOLIATH (for large pencils), and ROACH MOTEL (for insect traps). On the other hand, there are descriptive trademarks that describe the quality or characteristics of the goods or services upon which they are affixed. For instance, SWEET (for certain candies), FISH-FRI (batter to fry fish), and COCA-COLA (for beverages made with cacao). Descriptive trademarks are entitled to protection only if the trademark holders have extensively used and advertised the trademarks so that consumers have recognized the trademarks as a source.

There is simply no shortage of evidence that trademarks are valuable and important to businesses. CEOs of companies readily defend their corporate name and image. Mark Zuckerberg had to endure days of preparation by handlers before testifying in Congress, and then days of apologizing, deflecting, and defending Facebook tactics in front of lawmakers from different committees to make sure that the brand would stay intact after the privacy scandal. Tim Cook seized the moment to reaffirm Apple's pristine image in contrast to Facebook's behavior of monetizing users' privacy as products. Kevin Johnson immediately addressed the controversy over the arrest of two black patrons in Starbucks' Philadelphia store by employing a sweeping and unusual action of closing more than 8,000 stores for all employees to attend racial-bias training, striving to maintain the "inclusivity" image of the Starbucks brand.

Trademarks are not random words or symbols; they are the embodiment of the company's product and culture. In monetary terms, the embodiment is expressed in the valuation, often in billions of dollars, assigned to top brands in various sectors. Marketers issue annual lists of brands and their associated valuations, commanding attention from all.

Businesses often pay extra care to the visibility of their trademarks in the marketplace. Some would devote resources to ascertain whether their trademarks are recognized in a particular niche through a brand awareness consumer survey. Many embark on strategic campaigns to identify and implement different strategies and methods to enhance trademark visibility. All know that being without a trademark presence in the marketplace mean no product, no service, and no corporate existence in the near future.

In addition to marketing efforts for trademark enhancements, trademarks are important for tax strategies. Indeed, many multistate companies maximize returns from their trademarks through tax avoidance schemes. Through assignment and license-back schemes, owners of many trademarks avoid paying state taxes on royalty income stemming from the licensing of trademarks between affiliated companies. Companies including Victoria's Secret, Nordstrom, and Sherwin-Williams have turned their trademark assets into effective tax tools to boost the corporation's overall value.

Assisting businesses in leveraging, protecting, and enforcing trademarks is an army of trademark practitioners. Trademark practitioners can provide plenty of evidence of valuable trademarks to private and public organizations through dockets of litigation involving trademark ownership, infringement, false advertisement, and unfair competition claims. Businesses use litigation to protect and enforce their trademark rights. Without enforcement, the trademark's associated goodwill may soon lessen in value in the marketplace due to unauthorized use by others. Worse, the trademarks may fail to distinguish the client's products from others' goods.

Also, trademark practitioners can rely on the annual increase in the number of trademark registrations granted by the USPTO as evidence of a trademark's value and importance. The high volume of trademark registrations explains that businesses need trademarks in daily operations and existence. They are willing to pay registration fees for each class of goods and services and submit necessary samples to secure the registrations.

In academic circles, scholars have elevated the importance of trademarks by devoting substantial time to numerous studies and publishing voluminous treatises, books, and law review articles on trademarks. Some may even argue that trademarks are perhaps more valuable than other types of intellectual property in some cases. Given the existing copious scholarship on trademarks and the continuous litigation involving trademarks, we do not anticipate that the scholarship will slow down in the foreseeable future.

Overall, the evidence suggests that trademarks are valuable corporate assets. Despite being valuable assets, are lenders willing to provide financing against trademarks? Suffering the same treatments encountered by patents, trade secrets and copyrights, bank regulations and practices do not calculate trademarks as readily marketable collateral.

Moreover, as startups are young companies without existing or established markets for their trademarked products, there is no goodwill or name recognition in their new trademarks. Accordingly, banks decline to court startups with intellectual property assets. That means banks stand on the sideline of the innovation economy.

INTELLECTUAL PROPERTY VALUATION PROBLEMS FOR STARTUPS

Broadly speaking, conventional experts on valuation advocate that there are three different methods of valuing intellectual property assets of a business: market-based, cost, and income approaches. None of these valuation methods for intellectual property are relevant for any banks attempting to lend to startups.

The market-based approach has other names: "the industry standards method" and the "comparable technology method."[20] As its names suggest, the approach requires that there are comparable assets and transactions for sellers and buyers to determine the likely price a buyer would pay for the intellectual property assets being valued. The question the valuator would seek to answer is: "What would be the value of the asset on the open market based on information from similar market transactions?"[21] Thus, the market approach is only relevant if there exists information for a specific transaction involving the specific property. In a startup situation, there simply are no comparables in existence for a market-based approach. Startups are in the innovation space; they are not in the legacy, established sectors, or, if they are, they are seeking to differentiate themselves and be industry disruptors, and thus no comparable exists. They do not deal in real estate, vessels, aircraft, or autos that can be easily compared in the marketplace.

Appraisers often prefer the income approach – also referred to as the discounted cash flow method – because it is more accurate than the other methods in approximating the value of an intellectual property and capturing the going concern value of the intellectual property. As the name of the valuation method denotes, the intellectual property must have been generating regular income for the appraisers to credibly project future income with some adjustment or discount made for perceived risks. If the company has no income or cash flow coming from its intellectual property assets, for instance, the licensing of the intellectual property at a certain royalty rate or the sales record of products based on the intellectual property assets, then the income approach is either inapplicable or the property's value is speculative. Consequently, the income approach is not suitable for valuing a startup's intellectual property, as startups have no income and are still working on perfecting their technology. Moreover, startups exist to disrupt and need lots of cash input in order to meet targets and scale. The income, if any, that they generate does not reflect the historic, regular, reliable cash flow that an established company typically generates for appraisers to predict the value of the intellectual property asset. In addition, when a company is not an established business with historic cash flow for traditional asset-based financing, experts in valuing intellectual property for traditional, asset-based lending purposes would estimate the value of the intellectual property for liquidation, not for "going concern value."

Finally, the cost approach is also not suitable because, under this approach, the intellectual property is assumed to be replaceable. It is not possible to ascertain the cost

[20] See generally, Ted Hagelin, "Valuation of Intellectual Property Assets: An Overview," *Syracuse Law Review* 52 (2002): 1133–1140.
[21] Krista F. Holt, Brian P. O'Shaughnessy, and Thomas B. Herman, "What's It Worth?: Principles of Patent Valuation," *American Bar Association*, September/October 2015, available at: www.americanbar.org/groups/intellectual_property_law/publications/landslide/2015-16/september-october/what-s-it-worth-principles-patent-valuation/ [https://perma.cc/667B-D5F6] (last accessed September 19, 2023).

to replace the intellectual property assets created by the startups. All the investments contributed by the founder, the founder's friends, and family members, angel investors, and by venture capital firms, in addition to the countless hours and efforts of all who work at the startup, do not accurately reflect the cost of replacing the intellectual property assets. Also, if the intellectual property has income-generating potential, the cost method does not capture that value. The method is, therefore, typically not used for financial transactions, but rather for accounting and bookkeeping.

In addition, the valuation of intellectual property assets is generally expensive and too costly for startups, particularly as it requires experts to conduct the valuation. Startups simply do not have the financial resources to pay for such experts, and the valuation cost would cause the overall loan price to increase to a degree that enterprises would prefer to avoid.

As the approaches are costly, unsuitable, and unreliable, banks do not lend against intellectual property assets owned by innovators. Even if any bank accepts intellectual property assets as security for a loan, there is no market for the bank to readily dispose of intellectual property assets when the borrower is in default. Moreover, many tech companies have no revenue. If they generate revenue, they still have no profits. Banks cannot lend to such companies out of fear that loans will not be paid. Across the United States today, banks still do not dare to lend to tech companies. In other words, tech companies are still largely unbanked today.

PROHIBITION AGAINST UNSAFE AND UNSOUND PRACTICES

Assuming that the valuations of intellectual property assets held by a startup are ascertainable, banks attempting to make loans or extend a credit line to the startup may encounter problems related to the legal lending limit. Applying the general limit requirements, technology companies will not be able to obtain loans for the 10 percent additional limit because they simply do not own "readily marketable collateral." Intellectual property assets do not fall within the definition of "readily marketable collateral," as the definition covers mainly financial instruments. That means banks will not blatantly violate the law by making loans or extending credit to technology companies for the additional 10 percent limit with intellectual property as collateral.

The next concern is whether banks are willing to lend to technology companies for the basic 15 percent limit. Though the law allows banks to make aggregate loans with or without collateral within the 15 percent limit of the bank's capital and surplus, banks are required to engage in banking practices that are not "unsafe or unsound." A banking practice is unsafe or unsound if the bank's action is "contrary to generally accepted standards of prudent operation and potentially exposes the bank to an abnormal risk of loss or harm contrary to prudent banking practices."[22]

---

[22] *Michael v. Federal Deposit Insurance Corporation*, 687 F.3d 337, 352 (7th Cir. 2012).

In other words, an unsafe or unsound practice is the type of practice that poses a "reasonably foreseeable undue risk to the institution."[23]

The law does not provide a list of unsafe or unsound banking practices. Court cases and FDIC Board decisions, however, provide numerous examples of unsafe or unsound banking practices. They include, for instance, lacking the necessary expertise and information to evaluate the transactions the bank enters into, extending credit without adequate documentation, making loans without credit analysis, violating the bank's loan policy, obtaining inadequate collateral, and failing to verify collateral being pledged and the double-pledging of the collateral.

In the riskier area of bank lending activities, such as lending for corporate acquisitions, developments, and construction projects, unsafe or unsound practices reflect concerns unique to those industries. They encompass, for example, generating loans that the bank lacks the capacity to underwrite adequately, relying on deficient or outdated appraisals, lending to a borrower without ensuring that the borrower will have sufficient funds to complete the project, and failing to perform sufficient analysis of the borrower and guarantor's finances in order to verify their ability to repay the loan.

Consequently, banks would be averse to making a loan or extending credit to technology companies with intellectual property as their key asset of the enterprise value for fear of falling into the unsafe or unsound practices category. First, most startup and technology companies are losing money because they are still in the growth stages. These companies often have cash flow problems. Second, these companies do not have an established credit history. Third, technology companies do not have tangible collateral to secure loans or credit lines. Fourth, even if a technology company does not have a cash flow problem, banks do not want to accept patents as collateral because banks have no expertise in conducting a patent valuation.

Overall, banking regulations and traditional lending practices prevent banks from making loans against intellectual property assets. Banks cannot rely on intellectual property assets as collateral to reduce the bank's estimates of expected losses in the case of default. That would have a direct impact on the bank's statutory capital requirements.

BANKS CONTINUE WITH TRADITIONAL PRACTICES

Today entrepreneurs know that if they walk into a bank asking for a business loan, the bank will typically scrutinize the company's history, business credit, revenues, balance sheet, and the entrepreneur's equity contribution. Most entrepreneurs simply cannot fulfill the bank's requirements because their enterprise is too young to generate revenue or possess a business history, business credit, and a balance

---

[23] *Landry v. Federal Deposit Insurance Corporation*, 204 F.3d 1125, 1138 (D.C. Cir. 2000).

sheet. The entrepreneur may not be personally wealthy enough to provide equity contributions to the enterprise that satisfy the bank's requirements for a loan. Moreover, as a typical startup in the innovation sector, the enterprise focuses on growth, not profit.

The entrepreneur may disclose to the bank that the enterprise owns some patents and copyrights, and that the entrepreneur strongly believes that the intellectual property assets are very valuable. Perhaps the entrepreneur insists that the intellectual property assets are worthy enough to serve as collateral in asset-based lending. After all, asset-based lending is a common practice where lenders provide a term loan or a line of credit at a percentage of the assets, and the assets serve as collateral for the primary source of repayment in the event of default.

But the typical assets that banks accept in asset-based lending are accounts receivable and inventory. That means the company must have an established product in the marketplace that is expected to generate revenue on a regular basis. That, in turn, means the company has customers who have already relied on and ordered the company's products, and that the customers will soon pay the company for the outstanding accounts receivable. The bank will then calculate a borrowing base, typically 65 percent of the book value of eligible inventory and up to 90 percent of eligible business-to-business accounts receivable. None of the asset-based lending with accounts receivable, however, is applicable to the entrepreneur's startup, as the young enterprise is still pre-revenue. Likewise, asset-based loans with inventory as collateral are not applicable to the entrepreneur's startup because it is still working on perfecting the technology. The startup has neither produced nor held inventory.

Banks are still very insistent on accounts receivable and inventory as the common assets for asset-based lending. Banks are generally not interested in accepting intellectual property assets as collateral. For example, Bank of America Merrill Lynch issued its white paper on asset-based lending and informed the public that it does not make loans against patents and copyrights, except for businesses the Bank views as higher quality companies.[24] In other words, patents, copyrights, and other intellectual property are simply not the assets that banks accept in asset-based lending. Trademarks, if they have matured and transformed into brands with equity, may be acceptable to banks in asset-based lending because the brands are able to generate specific income and purchasers recognize and trust the brands. This brand-dependent asset-based lending is of no use to startups, however, as they and their products, if they have any, are not known in the marketplace.

Moreover, if banks do accept the intellectual property as collateral, banks insist on having the intellectual property assets appraised by independent experts when calculating the borrowing base. But intellectual property valuation will not work for startups

---

[24] *Frequently Asked Questions about Asset-Based Lending* 5 (Bank of America Merrill Lynch, 2014), available at: www.ohiomfg.com/wp-content/uploads/01-13-17_lb_tax_FAQ-Asset-Based-Lending.pdf [https://perma.cc/54CR-CM64] (last accessed September 19, 2023).

because the young enterprise's technology is new and unproven, and the enterprise does not have an established market. In addition, the enterprise's trademark is unknown in the marketplace; the trademark is years from generating predictable income. Consequently, traditional banks reject startups' intellectual property as collateral in asset-based lending in the innovation-intensive sectors because there is too much uncertainty when valuing assets owned by startups without cash flow.

Worse still, even in the rare case where a startup actually has a stream of receivables and a positive cash flow, banks continue their reluctance to approve business loans to a startup that possesses no hard assets. In addition, the entrepreneurs at these companies know all too well that if they today approach a bank for a loan to purchase office equipment, they will encounter resistance. Banks may not flatly reject the equipment financing deal with the entrepreneurs; they instead move at "glacial speed" while the enterprise needs the loan much sooner.[25] Banks essentially discourage potential clients from seeking out typical business loans.

Peculiarly, on the one hand, banks decline to have startups in tech and innovation centers across the nation as clients by refusing to lend. On the other hand, banks themselves have been under assault due, in part, to the onslaught of online banking, payments by third-party and alternative lenders, and the rapidly shrinking number of banks. Yet banks continue to focus on the traditional real estate market, provide loans to established and mature companies, and finance asset-based deals backed only by inventory and accounts receivables.

This means only banks and bankers who embrace a disruptive mindset will search for potential solutions to the entrenched banking practices of shunning startup and growing tech companies.

✳ ✳ ✳

OUTLIER BANKS AND THEIR BUSINESS MODELS

Addressing Banks' Fear of Tech Lending

Banks operate within a heavily regulated industry under both federal and state regimes. Due to the regulatory constraints in banking, banks must be prudent in

---

[25] Sarah E. Needleman, "When Banks Won't Lend to Your Startup," *The Wall Street Journal*, March 8, 2014, available at: www.wsj.com/articles/when-banks-wont-lend-to-your-startup-1394328392 [https://perma.cc/YK5S-3389] (last accessed September 19, 2023); Shannon Henry, "Taking New Account of High-Tech Investment," *The Washington Post*, September 28, 1998, available at: www.washingtonpost.com/archive/business/1998/09/28/taking-new-account-of-high-tech-investment/1017c731-2c5d-4b85-8a1b-5dec2b33566a/?utm_term=.1b27b7a018ea [https://perma .cc/TX87-BRQ4] (last accessed September 19, 2023) (reporting that traditional banks ignore lending to tech companies when they desperately need loans to purchase equipment for their fast-growing companies).

their lending practices. Under lending regulations, banks feel justified in avoiding devoting part of their lending strategies to startups due to the high level of risk. As noted, what attracts startups to equity inventory is not what banks care to consider in attempting, if at all, to evaluate a startup for an equipment loan, a term loan, or a credit line against account receivables.

The few banks that do lend to startups cannot lend to just any startup. With startups that have procured a few patents, banks exhibit a strong aversion to lending against patents. Even with the fortunate few startups that have received VC funding, banks are still very cautious. The survival rate for startups between the Series A round of funding obtained from VCs to the next Series B round of funding is about 50 percent. That means, for banks to succeed in the venture lending niche, they need reliable or truth-telling signals to screen the startups that will be able to pay back the loans.[26]

Information Asymmetry Problem for Outlier Banks

Information asymmetry is a familiar problem banks encounter when they decide to lend to entrepreneurial firms.[27] In an information asymmetry situation, one party has all the information while the other party does not. In startup financing, the entrepreneurs have all the information about the startup's technologies, innovation, business operation, competition, and prospects. If banks want to lend to startups, banks are the uninformed party facing serious information asymmetry problems in screening startups while having no traditional means to reduce default risks compared to lending to established companies. Because banks can easily obtain information relating to an established company's cash flow, earnings, credit history, and tangible assets, among others, banks continue their traditional lending practices.[28] Startups simply cannot provide what banks require for a loan.

---

[26] Xuan-Thao Nguyen and Erik Hille, "Disruptive Lending for Innovation: Signaling Model and Banks Selection of Startups," *University of Pennsylvania Journal of Business Law* 21 (2018): 200–234, 230, available at: https://digitalcommons.law.uw.edu/faculty-articles/863/ (last accessed September 19, 2023).

[27] Abraham J. B. Cable, "Fending for Themselves: Why Securities Regulations Should Encourage Angel Groups," *University of Pennsylvania Journal of Business Law* 13 (2010): 107–172, 122 ("'Information asymmetry' refers to the concept that whatever information is available about the company's prospects at the time of the investment is 'soft' (not easily observable by an investor and difficult for an entrepreneur to communicate credibly).").

[28] Banks typically engage in cash-flow lending and asset-based lending. *See* Mark N. Berman and Jo Ann J. Brighton, *Handbook on Second Lien Loans & Intercreditor Agreements* 6 (American Bankruptcy Institute, 2009). Cash-flow lending is a type of debt financing typically associated with traditional bank debt financing. It is senior debt financing provided to a borrower based on a certain multiple of profitability of the borrower deemed sufficient to give the lender comfort that the borrower will have sufficient cash flow to satisfy its obligations to the lender. In this regard, the cash flow-lender with a lien on all of the borrower's assets is concerned with the overall enterprise value of the borrower as a function of its earnings. Asset-based lending, in contrast, is where the lender makes its credit decision on the basis of the appraised value of the

In broad strokes, banks with a desire to engage in lending to startups in the innovation-intensive sectors face information asymmetry problems similar to those faced by VC financing. But the solutions to VCs are different compared to banks, as banks are heavily regulated.

In the VC financing model, the informed entrepreneurs have all the information and the uninformed investors, including individuals and institutions, have none.[29] Yuk-See Chan solved the information asymmetry problem in his agency model by introducing VCs as the informed intermediaries based on their experience and expertise in the industry, enabling them to screen potential investments. Consequently, VCs finance high-quality projects, reject low-quality projects, and ensure the integrity and viability of the entrepreneur funding market. Building on the agency model, scholars developed new models to focus on the terms of the contract, illuminating further what VCs do to screen fledgling entrepreneurs in order to achieve good investment results.[30] For example, contract terms challenge entrepreneurs' projections and discourage entrepreneurs with low-quality projects from participating in the VC pool of potential capital investment seekers.[31] Contract terms relating to staged venture capital investment allow VCs to control when to release certain amounts of funding and when to discontinue. Also, contract terms force the entrepreneur to have skin in the game by tying compensation to specific milestones achieved by the firm, thus inducing the entrepreneur to reassess himself before seeking capital investment from VCs.[32]

In short, both the agency model and the terms of contract model literature for VC capital investment screenings are numerous and have been explained and summarized elsewhere. Can banks behave like VCs in screening borrowers who are startups?

Unlike VCs, banks conduct some due diligence in lending decisions but not at the same level. Conventional bankers do not spend much time outside the office with potential borrowers; they do not serve on a startup's board, connect startups with industry leaders, or advise on management. In other words, bankers are not the same

---

borrower's current assets (receivables, equipment, and inventory) and expects that, if the borrower defaults, the value of the assets even in liquidation will be sufficient to repay the loan.

[29] Yuk-Shee Chan, "On the Positive Role of Financial Intermediation in Allocation of Venture Capital in a Market with Imperfect Information," *The Journal of Finance* 38 (1983): 1543–1568, 1543.

[30] For a summary of the literature, see Michael Klausner and Kate Litvak, "What Economists Have Taught Us about Venture Capital Contracting," in *Bridging the Entrepreneurial Financing Gap: Linking Governance with Regulatory Policy* (Michael Whincop, ed., Ashgate 2001), available at: https://ssrn.com/abstract=280024 or http://dx.doi.org/10.2139/ssrn.280024 [https://perma.cc/FY2P-KWSS] (last accessed September 19, 2023).

[31] Mathias Dewatripont and Gerard Roland, "Soft Budget Constraints, Transition, and Financial System," *Journal of Institutional and Theoretical Economics (Jite)/Zeitschrift Fur Die Gesamte Staatswissenschaft* 156 (1999): 245–260, 252–253.

[32] Steven N. Kaplan and Per Stromberg, "Venture Capitalists as Principals: Contracting, Screening, and Monitoring," *The American Economic Review* 91 (2001): 426–430, 427.

type of financial intermediators as VCs.[33] Moreover, startups do not have hard assets for traditional bank loans, meaning there is not much for banks to conduct due diligence on for potential loans. Banks are less informed intermediaries compared to VCs. Banks are relatively uninformed parties in screening which startups to lend to.

On the other hand, banks have access to deposits and cheap capital.[34]

As a result, the cost of a loan from banks is significantly less than that from non-bank lenders. To minimize agency costs, banks take security interests in real and personal property owned by potential borrowers and impose many covenants to restrict an entrepreneur's discretion. Banks have long used contract terms to release loans in increments in accordance with the level of collateral availability, to retain the right to review new information about the borrower, and to allow banks flexibility to refuse requests to draw on a credit line or waive events of default. Even in the high risk of IP Venture Banking, banks provide loans to startups at about 1/40th (as a measure of dilution) of the cost of equity financing from a VC.

Overall, the agency model and terms of the contract model are not suitable for banks seeking a reliable device to screen startups. In order to maintain a lower cost in lending to startups in the IP Venture Banking niche and adhere to banking regulations, banks must acquire reliable signals about the health of potential startup clients. Because about half of the startups do not make it from Series A to Series B funding, it is imperative that banks have the most up-to-date information. Before banks make a loan to the startup, banks want to know whether the firm will be able to obtain the next round of VC funding so it can repay the loan. In other words, banks need a truth-telling signal. Consequently, only a few outlier banks could participate in IP Venture Lending. First, who are the outliers?

Identifying Outliers

While more than 99.9 percent of banks shun lending to startups and high-growth companies in the innovation-intensive sectors, there are outlier banks.[35] But only four such outlier banks – out of 6,000 banks – devote themselves exclusively to serving startups and high-growth companies in the tech industry.

An empirical study of all banks and their lending activities identified outlier banks.[36] The study focused on banks and credit facilities that have accepted and

---

[33] With respect to bank due diligence, Risk Management Association produced a white paper to explain what type of due diligence bankers must conduct in commercial lending. *Ethics and Commercial Lending: Understanding Due Diligence* (Risk Management Association, July 2014), available at: www.rmahq.org/ethics-and-commercial-lending-understanding-due-diligence/ [https://perma.cc/28F8-QRLF] (last accessed August 28, 2022).

[34] William A. Klein, "The Modern Business Organization: Bargaining under Constraints," *Yale Law Journal* 91 (1982): 1521–1564, 1556, n.126.

[35] Nguyen, "Lending Innovation," *supra*, note 1.

[36] See generally, Xuan-Thao Nguyen and Erik Hille, "Patent Aversion: An Empirical Study of Patents Collateral in Bank Lending, 1980–2016," *University of California Irvine Law Review* 9

TABLE 3.1 *Top banks and patent collateral*

Name	Patent collateral	Cumulative percent
JPMorgan Chase	180,598	22%
Bank of America	163,673	42%
Citibank	69,848	51%
Deutsche Bank	65,354	59%
Wells Fargo	54,174	65%
BNY Mellon	44,775	71%
U.S. Bank	38,315	75%
Silicon Valley Bank	28,019	79%
PNC Bank	21,071	81%
Barclays Bank	17,357	83%
ComericA Bank	11,938	85%
BankMO Harris	10,690	86%
City National RBC	7,601	88%
Goldman Sachs Bank	6,376	89%
HSBC Bank USA	6,360	90%

recorded patents as collateral for loans. As secured creditors, the banks that had accepted patents as collateral for their loans would file their security interests in the patent collateral with the US Patent and Trademark Office (USPTO). Also, the study relied on the USPTO patent assignments database to conduct searches for "security interest" in patents filed by banks from 1980 to 2016. The results were then aggregated for individual banks. Among all banks, those familiar names dominate 90 percent of the patent collateral. These banks are traditional banks with large asset sizes.

Table 3.1 shows the top banks that control 90 percent of the market of lending with patents as collateral, according to 1980–2016 USPTO data. These banks were also among the fifty largest banks in the United States in 2018.

Table 3.2 shows the ratio of patent collateral per deal for the top banks listed in Table 3.1 and the four outlier banks, according to 1980–2016 USPTO data.

In Table 3.2, Silicon Valley Bank, Comerica Bank, Pacific Western Bank/Square 1 Bank, and Western Alliance/Bridge Bank are the outliers. These banks lend to companies that have few patents per deal. That means they lend to startups; high-growth companies with ownership of a small number of patents. Other banks lend to established, legacy companies with substantially larger patent portfolios. We confirmed our findings with other publicly available information and publications. Overall, there are only a handful of outlier banks that dare to invest in technology lending. Their business operations and strategies are discussed next.

(2018): 141–176, 168–171, available at: https://digitalcommons.law.uw.edu/faculty-articles/864/ (last accessed September 19, 2023); Nguyen and Hille, "Disruptive Lending for Innovation," *supra*, note 25, at 230.

TABLE 3.2 *Top banks and patents per deal*

Name	Deals	Patents per deal
JPMorgan Chase	3,504	51.54
Bank of America	5,106	32.06
Citibank	404	172.89
Deutsche Bank	1,197	54.60
Wells Fargo	2,962	18.29
BNY Mellon	717	62.45
U.S. Bank	953	40.20
Silicon Valley Bank*	2590	10.82
PNC Bank	1,287	16.37
Barclays Bank	306	56.72
ComericA Bank*	1,493	8.00
Bank of Montreal	764	13.99
Scotiabank	207	45.86
City National RBC	255	29.81
Goldman Sachs Bank	133	47.94
HSBC Bank USA	291	21.86
PacWest/Square 1 Bank*	443	7.49
Western Alliance/BridgeBank*	272	6.54

* Outlier banks.

Mapping the Outlier's IP Venture Lending: Industries and Geography

One of the puzzling characteristics of outlier banks is that they are typical commercial banks chartered by states and are members of the Federal Reserve Bank. That means they are just like the other commercial banks; they are highly regulated at both state and federal banking levels. As commercial banks, they must be "99 percent right" in taking risks. While meeting all the stringent banking regulations, outlier banks have innovatively developed their core strategy to provide banking products and services to VCs and their portfolio companies. Specifically, the outlier banks lend to early-stage and late-growth-stage companies that have already received backing from venture capital firms. The outlier banks' lending decisions are based on the likelihood that the VC-backed companies will receive additional rounds of equity capital from investors. In addition, the outlier banks enjoy deposits from these companies. The outlier banks also target particular industries and focus their businesses geographically to facilitate lending within those industries. As noted above, there are four such outlier banks.

SVB AND OTHER OUTLIER BANKS IN THE VC ECOSYSTEM

As of 2018, the leader of this group of banks, Silicon Valley Bank (SVB), was known as *the* bank for startups. By 2018 SVB joined the list of the top fifty largest banks in the United States. SVB had distinguished itself since its inception as the go-to bank in the technology lending space and had served more than 40,000 startups. SVB dominated the innovation-intensive sectors by lending to ~50 percent of all VC-backed companies in the tech and life science sectors. It also counted two-thirds of tech and life science companies with an IPO in 2017 as clients. From Fitbit to Uber, SVB focused its businesses exclusively to serve entrepreneurs and their enterprises, nurturing them in the early-growth, growth, and late-growth stages before the initial public offering, as well as in post-IPO phases. As of the first quarter of 2020, SVB amassed $75 billion in assets, extending $36 billion in loans and holding $269 billion in deposits and investments. Ninety-four percent of SVB's loans went to high-growth and large companies and 6 percent to startups with revenue of less than five million dollars. In 2016, SVB's stock rose 70 percent, and 37 percent in 2017. During the Great Recession, it was the only bank that escaped the crisis and made profits.[37]

ComericA, a Texas bank, was among the top thirty-five largest US financial holding companies with total assets of $73.3 billion as of December 31, 2019. The bank is known for its Technology and Life Sciences group which has provided financial services to the "technology, life sciences and cleantech" industries for more than twenty years, and claims to understand the "unique challenges entrepreneurs face."[38] ComericA counts startups and high-growth companies in software, SaaS, social networking, business and IT services, cloud computing, mobile computing, digital media, and storage as its clients.

Square 1 Bank, a division of Pacific Western or PacWest, serves "entrepreneurs" located in various key innovation centers across the United States. After the merger, PacWest developed a "Venture Banking" division, concentrating on financial services to clients in Life Sciences and Technology.[39] Likewise, BridgeBank focused

---

[37] Scott Duke Harris, "Silicon Valley Bank Unscathed by Credit Crisis," *The Mercury News*, November 6, 2008, available at: www.mercurynews.com/2008/11/06/silicon-valley-bank-unscathed-by-credit-crisis/ [https://perma.cc/P9VP-EVEF] (last accessed September 19, 2023) (reporting that when SVB released its quarterly report in late 2008, the bank "showed itself to be unscathed by the credit crisis. Chief Executive Kenneth P. Wilcox sent an upbeat letter to about 11,000 clients, including many of the valley's tech and venture capital firms"); Nicholas Rossolillo, "Forget Goldman Sachs, SVB Financial is a Better Bank Stock," *The Motley Fool*, April 29, 2020, available at: www.fool.com/investing/2020/04/29/forget-goldman-sachs-svb-finan cial-is-a-better-ban.aspx [https://perma.cc/TPK9-CU49] (last accessed September 19, 2023) ("Even better than Goldman Sachs, though, was investment bank SVB Financial Group (NASDAQ:SIVB), better known as the parent of Silicon Valley Bank. Over the past decade, SVB's stock has roughly tripled, which includes a nearly 30% fall from recent highs this year. The regional institution is a top way to play investment banking in the tech- and start-up-rich San Francisco Bay Area, and a better bank stock in general than most of its larger peers.").

[38] "Technology and Life Sciences," *ComericA*, available at: www.comerica.com/business/industry-solutions/Archive/technology-life-sciences-archive.html [https://perma.cc/QN9F-7NSP] (last accessed June 27, 2020).

[39] "Venture Lending," *Pacific Western Bank*, available at: www.pacwest.com/lending-solutions/venture-lending [https://perma.cc/YPE5-DLPN] (last accessed June 27, 2020); "Life Sciences,"

on Life Sciences and Startup & Technology. As a division of Western Alliance, BridgeBank serviced its clients "located in technology-centric regions of the country."[40] BridgeBank understood that its potential clients "disrupt" existing business and technology norms and that Bridge Bank's bankers crafted "solutions geared to technology businesses at every stage of the growth cycle."[41]

Industry and Geographic Focus of Outlier Banks

The outlier banks attained extensive knowledge in four tech industries: software/internet, life science/health care, hardware/infrastructure, and energy/resource innovation. To serve these industries effectively, one of the outliers, SVB, had offices in fifteen states and twenty-eight major US technology centers. The strategically selected states with known technology centers, in alphabetical order, are Arizona, California, Colorado, Georgia, Illinois, Massachusetts, Minnesota, New York, North Carolina, Oregon, Pennsylvania, Texas, Utah, Virginia, and Washington. Unlike the typical commercial bank with branches for retail banking, SVB had no branches in fifteen of the sixteen states it served; SVB's offices devoted all of its operations to serving the tech industry.

Overall, the outlier banks cultivated unique relationships with VC firms and followed the VCs geographically to provide lending and banking services to both the VCs and their portfolio companies. Silicon Valley Bank, for example, followed the VCs by having bank offices in London, Beijing, Shanghai, Dublin, and Tel Aviv. Square 1 Bank/PacWest extended funding to venture capital and private equity firms through lending products and services that are flexible and delivered with speed. ComericA financial advisors touted that they "help plan, guide and consult tech businesses and venture capitalists on planning, projecting, growing and protecting their earnings, every step of the way."

Following the VC Deals

One of the key characteristics of outlier banks in IP Venture Banking is the relationship between the banks and their VC clients. In fact, the banks follow their VC clients for several important reasons. The banks rely on the VCs for knowledge,

---

Pacific Western Bank, available at: www.pacwest.com/lending-solutions-venture-lending/life-sciences-venture-lending [https://perma.cc/U7QZ-BVYG] (last accessed June 27, 2020); "Square 1 Bank Acquired by PacWest Bancorp," *Crunchbase*, available at: www.crunchbase.com/acquisition/pacwest-bancorp-acquires-square-1-bank–d7c4c984 [https://perma.cc/AB3P-J3U9] (last accessed June 27, 2020).

[40] "Client Types," *BridgeBank*, available at: www.westernalliancebancorporation.com/bridge-bank-home/client-types [https://perma.cc/5A79-Q6UJ] (last accessed June 27, 2020).

[41] "Services," *BridgeBank*, available at: www.westernalliancebancorporation.com/bridge-bank-home/about-us/company-overview [https://perma.cc/7ZXV-36LT] (last accessed June 27, 2020).

due diligence, networking, client development, and repayment of the loans made to the VC-backed companies.

Gaining VCs' Knowledge and Tapping into VC-Backed Clients

The VCs are firms that invest in a roster of portfolio companies, which the VCs nurture for scale and exit strategy. The outlier banks, by providing banking services to the VCs, learn the ecosystem inhabited by VCs and entrepreneurs at the portfolio companies. With that knowledge, and through the VC relationship, the outlier banks gain both the entrepreneurs and their startup business or high growth companies as clients. In addition to their connections to VCs, the outlier banks shaped relationships and partnerships with private equity, corporate ventures, and angel investors, and, through them, gain new clients who are the new enterprises in innovative tech and life science sectors. For example, on its website, SVB boasted its partnerships with private equity and venture capital firms:

> Succeeding in venture capital and private equity investing is more complex than ever. Competition for the best companies is fierce, and the entrepreneurial ecosystem is expanding globally. Private investment firms need a bank that knows their world intimately and can help them take a strategic approach to managing capital. SVB makes a natural partner for venture capital, private equity, corporate venture and angel investors. We offer a suite of financial services with one goal in mind – helping seize opportunities. We provide unique insights for firms and their portfolio companies. And, through SVB Capital, they can leverage our deep expertise to construct concentrated portfolios that help meet investment goals.[42]

Likewise, ComericA Bank advertised that its financial advisors had the expertise to assist both venture capitalists and companies in the tech sector. Bridge Bank formed the Equity Fund Resources group to serve as the "central hub" of the VC and private equity communities and provides services to "investment funds and their portfolio companies."[43] Similarly, Bridge Bank listed "Venture Capital & Private Equity" in addition to Startups & Technology, Life Sciences, and others it serves. BridgeBank claimed the motto "[t]he smarter banking choice for growing technology companies."[44]

---

[42] See, "Industries We Serve," *Silicon Valley Bank,* available at: www.svb.com/industries-we-serve/ [https://perma.cc/YBL2-AY52] (last accessed April 20, 2020). Likewise, Square 1 Bank (or PacWest's Venture Banking division) serves clients in technology, life sciences, and startups. The Bank's clients are diverse, ranging from CallRail, Invoca, MapAnything, to Credit Karma. Furthermore, Square 1 provides "nationwide focus on venture-backed companies and venture capital firms ... [in] a network of 80 branches."

[43] "Venture Capital and Private Equity," *Western Alliance Bancorporation,* available at: www .westernalliancebancorporation.com/our-expertise/venture-capital-privateequity [https://perma .cc/6FV3-B4WH] (last accessed April 20, 2020).

[44] "Startups & Technology," *BridgeBank,* available at: www.westernalliancebancorporation.com/ bridge-bank-home/client-types/startups-and-technology [https://perma.cc/LT8N-TJHX] (last accessed May 27, 2020).

Relying on VCs for Outliers' Due Diligence

As outlier banks are commercial banks regulated under strict banking laws and regulations, the banks must exercise extreme caution in selecting young tech companies as clients, in order to avoid running afoul of bank regulators. The outlier banks relied on the VCs, preferably the top-tier VCs, for their due diligence to filter out the startups. To fully understand how outlier banks depended on VCs in selecting startups as clients suggests a look at the funding statistics and VC due diligence is prudent.

Globally, the number of newly created businesses approximates 100 million annually. In the United States, there were 8,751,000 new startups in 2017. As of 2018, the total number of all small businesses operating in the United States is 30.2 million. Startups generally suffer large failure rates. For example, "of all businesses started in 2014, eighty percent made it to the second year," "70 percent" to the third year, "62 percent" to the fourth year, and "56 percent" to the fifth year.[45]

Without financing, startups wither. When an entrepreneur forms a startup, the first source of funding typically comes from the entrepreneur's personal savings and credit, family, and friends. For the startup to survive and advance, it must next obtain outside funds in the form of seed money from incubation funds or angel funding. The rare and fortunate few among startups can then attract funding from VC firms.

Startups' funding statistics are a sobering reminder of the competitive nature of obtaining funding. Of all the startups in 2013, only 0.05 percent received VC funding and 1 percent received angel funding. Angel investors invested in 61,900 companies, with the average amount of $74,955. But, for the fortunate few of all startups that received VC funds – a total of 3,700 companies in 2012 – the average investment by VCs was $5.94 million. In other words, angel investors write sixteen checks for every check VCs write, but the average amount from angel investors is extremely small compared to VC's funding rounds. Breaking down the VC-funded companies further, early-stage companies received an average of $2.6 million from VCs.[46]

The numbers above, though sobering, dovetail with the outlier banks' strategy: because the VCs have already conducted their due diligence in their own selection of worthy startups for funding – as seen by the mere 0.05 percent of startups selected to receive VC money – the banks reduce the risks of default by lending to only the VC-backed startups. Indeed, banks know that, while top-tier VCs tolerate higher levels of risk, they must still be very careful in their lending decisions. Only startups

[45] Matt Mansfield, "Startup Statistics: The Numbers You Need to Know," *Small Business Trends*, March 28, 2019, available at: https://smallbiztrends.com/2016/11/startup-statistics-small-business.html [https://perma.cc/NK6T-E9QG] (last accessed September 19, 2023).

[46] Laura Entis, "Where Startup Funding Really Comes From (Infographic)," *Entrepreneur*, November 20, 2013, available at: www.entrepreneur.com/article/230011 [https://perma.cc/K2Z2-HC7D] (last accessed September 19, 2023).

that represent potentially the most disruptive and best technology can secure pitch meetings with top-tier VCs. Out of 100 pitches, VCs select only ten startups for further scrutiny. Through intensive due diligence, VCs then narrow the ten investment opportunities even further, ultimately funding only one.[47]

VCs conduct a "thorough due diligence process on the entrepreneur or scientist, the technology and the potential market."[48] The due diligence focuses on minimizing risks by aiming to address questions such as, "Does the technology work? Is there a market for it? Is the market accessible? Who are the competitors? Does the entrepreneur have the skills to bring the concept to the market?" Moreover, for startups with technology in regulated industries, VCs focus on additional risks: "Can clinical trials be conducted? Will they be successful? Can regulatory approval be obtained?"[49]

The level of due diligence conducted by VCs is extensive and costly. Outlier banks can simply neither afford to conduct the same nor absorb the cost. Nor can the banks then pass the cost on to the startups or high-growth companies. That would make the total cost of the loan prohibitive for potential tech clients whose resources are concentrated on growth, not high loan costs and fees. To minimize the total cost of the loan, outlier banks leverage their unique relationship with VCs and depend on the VCs for their due diligence in selecting potential clients from among the startups that have already received VC funding.

Depending on VCs for the Next Round of Funding for Payments on Loans to Startups and High-Growth Companies

Outlier banks face the same concern as any commercial banks when they lend: the risk that their loans will not get repaid. But a tech startup's business model is about trying to perfect its technology and succeed at specific milestones for high growth. This means the startup is constantly in need of cash infusion and is not in the position to be paying back a loan even if it could obtain such a loan. The only way for outlier banks to lend to a startup is if there is a strong likelihood that the startup will pay back the loan. That can only happen if there is a strong likelihood that the startup will receive funding from outside investors. This is when the next round of VC funding comes in to provide the startup with the needed cash infusion and to pay back the loans to outlier banks.

Consequently, relying on the VCs for their due diligence alone is not sufficient to ascertain whether the startup, which has already received funding from the VCs, will

---

[47] For a discussion of the due diligence VCs must conduct in selecting startups for investment, see "Brief of Amici Curiae Venture Capital Firms Aberdare Ventures et al. in Support of Respondents" (No. 10-290), 2011 WL 1042210, March 18, 2011, at *12–*14, *Microsoft Corp. v. i4i Ltd.*, 564 U.S. 91 (2011).

[48] Ibid.

[49] Ibid.

pay back the loan, because the VCs may abandon the startup, or other VCs may not be interested in joining the original VCs to provide the startup with the next round of funding. In other words, to ensure the likelihood that outlier banks can get paid on loans to startups, the banks must have comfortable certainty that the startup that has just received Series A funding from VCs will be likely to receive Series B funding from the same VCs and, perhaps, additional VCs.

Startups that have received VC funding for Series A have only a 50 percent chance to survive to the next round of Series B funding. That means the outlier banks cannot lend to just any startups that have received Series A funding, as it is still too risky for default. There is information asymmetry that outlier banks face, because the startups and the VCs simply know more about the startup's situation than the outlier banks. To overcome the information asymmetry problem, the outliers must cultivate and build a uniquely strong relationship with the VCs, as well as a nurturing relationship with the startups. In *Disruptive Lending for Innovation*, Nguyen and Hille have identified quality signals banks can rely on to independently verify the likelihood that the VC-backed companies will secure the next round of VC funding.[50]

Connecting Startups to Networks of Experts

In a typical banking relationship, a bank may learn how well a client is doing by monitoring the client's banking activities with the bank. After all, the client has their deposit accounts and uses the bank to manage payments and finances. The bank is, therefore, informed in deciding whether it should make a loan to an existing client. The outlier banks in IP Venture Banking can acquire pertinent information about the startup's business and financial condition if the startup has become a client for a suite of banking activities with the outlier bank. Relying on the knowledge gained through client banking products, the outlier banks can evaluate whether to make a loan to their startup clients. However, that knowledge alone is still insufficient in IP Venture Banking because there remains a risk that the VCs will not fund the next round. In other words, the startup's past banking activities as seen on the bank's computer monitor within the comfort of the bank's office are not a guarantee that a cash infusion is around the corner. To mitigate risks, the outlier banks must be more than the typical banker sitting inside his or her office.

Consequently, in addition to serving the lender role, the outlier banks must also function as part cheerleaders, part mentors, and part counselors to the entrepreneurs in nurturing the startups to success. To do so, the outlier banks rely on the VCs for connections to networks of experts that are helpful to young tech enterprises. The bottom line is that, if the entrepreneurs are successful, their enterprises will meet their milestones, obtain the next round of VC funding, and pay the loans and

---

[50] See Nguyen and Hille, "Disruptive Lending for Innovation," *supra*, note 25, at 230.

associated costs to the outlier banks. In other words, it is in the outlier banks' best interest to develop and maintain networks of experts in assisting entrepreneurs. Through the uniquely strong relationship between the outlier banks and their VC clients, the outlier banks are exposed to the networks of experts who work with VCs or are within the various VC circles, and vice versa. The outlier banks can leverage their connection with the experts to introduce the entrepreneurs to the most relevant and helpful experts in fulfilling the outlier banks' efforts to act as cheerleaders, mentors, and counselors.[51]

In summary, looking beyond the assertions on the website of each outlier bank, the relationship between the outlier bank and VCs is uniquely intertwined with the funding cycle that ultimately results in the outlier banks receiving a handsome return. The outlier banks know the venture capitalists and firms. They gain knowledge about the technology sectors and industries and the ecosystem in which entrepreneurs and VCs exist. The outlier banks provide banking services to VC firms. They attend VC meetings and presentations. They network with experts, tech executives, mentors, and entrepreneurs. They follow their VC clients' trail. If a venture capitalist goes abroad for deals, they follow to make loans overseas and accept deposits from new clients in other countries. They have their offices in London, Beijing, Shanghai, Ireland, Israel, and wherever their VC clients form new ecosystems with new entrepreneurs.

Account Receivables as the IP Proxy

A company utilizes intellectual property assets or the byproduct of the IP assets in the form of account receivables to attract financing sources. The company may seek investors to exchange capital for equity in the business, but that may not be palatable because the company may not want new shareholders to dictate and control the company's business direction. Instead of equity financing, the company turns to debt financing. In debt financing, the company, of course, desires a lower cost for the loan. Two sources of debt are banks and nonbank financial institutions.

Loans from banks are typically cheaper than from nonbanks because bank money is from deposits and banks can borrow from federal funds. Regarding deposits, bank money is not the bank's own money but other people's money. Deposits provide banks with a large pool of capital, and banks don't pay much interest on deposits while charging higher rates for loans and making money from other banking services. In addition, the bank has immediate access to federal funds through the inter-banking system when the bank is temporarily in need of cash at the end of the business day while other banks have a surplus to lend overnight. The overnight rate in most countries is set by the central bank, and is typically the lowest available interest rate.

---

[51] Ibid.; Nguyen, "Lending Innovation," *supra*, note 1.

Overall, banks have a lower cost of funds while nonbanks obtain their funds from investors. Banks can charge lower interest rates on loans, while nonbanks charge higher for the same amount. But banks are heavily regulated and, due to those banking regulations, are reluctant to make loans and often impose stringent borrowing requirements.

A company with traditional assets like inventory, equipment, and accounts receivable can seek loans from banks through asset-based lending (ABL). The loans are revolving credit lines or term loans that are secured by the borrower's assets. Depending on the quality and value of the assets for collateral, the bank determines the availability of the credit to the borrower. That means ABL from banks is typically available to midsized and large corporations with traditional assets.

Businesses use trademarks in connection with marketing, distributing, and selling their products and services. Through such use, the trademark gains recognition in the mind of the consumer and the marketplace accumulates goodwill associated with the trademark. A trademark itself does not have value; the trademark's goodwill does. The trademark's goodwill is the intangible asset that appears on a company's balance sheet, and goodwill is the premium value paid to acquire the company. In other words, the economic value of a trademark represents the goodwill of the trademark. Leveraging goodwill, many trademark owners license their trademark to others, expanding trademark use in different markets and sectors. The licensees do not own the goodwill but generate the goodwill for the benefit of the licensors. The licensees are willing to pay the licensing fees instead of adopting their own trademarks which are unknown to the market. Riding on the existing goodwill of the licensed trademarks, the licensees anticipate that they will be able to distribute and sell products under the licensed trademarks.

The future revenue the licensees plan to earn is essentially the byproduct of the trademark goodwill. Lenders can rely on the future revenue the licensees will earn to provide the needed loan to the licensees. This type of asset-based lending does not involve the trademark itself but the future revenue or the byproduct of the trademark's goodwill. The same type of lending can occur against account receivables generated from patents, trade secrets, and copyrights.

Here is an illustration. The University of Alabama owns the "Crimson Tide" trademark. Crimson Tide, of course, enjoys enormous goodwill, as the football team has captured numerous national championship titles. The University licenses Crimson Tide to a three-person company to make merchandise. As the football team was heading to the national football championship game, the small company desperately needed cash to make 60,000 t-shirts. No banks would lend to the company because it had neither a credit rating nor traditional assets. The company turned to an alternative nonbank lender for the loan by pledging as collateral its future revenue. Taking the future revenue as collateral does not trigger any need for filing with the USPTO.[52]

---

[52] Nguyen and Hille, "The Puzzle," *supra*, note 18.

Obviously, trademark or other IP owners can use future revenue from their own transactions with others as collateral instead of the above licensee's scenario. In both cases, if the future revenue is recurrent and predictable, the lending is the typical ABL with traditional accounts receivable as assets. For the ABL against accounts receivable or for future revenue to occur, the trademark must have established goodwill.

A clever bank can structure its lending practice to extend a credit line or a small loan to tech companies capable of generating receivables from IP-based products or services. In this type of lending, the customers of the tech companies are an important source for lenders to evaluate in ascertaining the risk. The customers will directly pay to a lockbox at the bank ensuring the money of the receivables comes to the bank directly and not through the tech company, therefore reducing the risk for the bank. The bankers must understand the tech company's product and financing cycles. In many circumstances, the tech company may have one major customer for all its products and the customer is a substantially larger corporation or a publicly traded entity. The bankers can therefore easily obtain information about the financial health of the customer entity.

In sum, the tech company receives the funds it needs and its customer is pleased. The bank provides the money without encountering any potential violation of banking regulations. The bankers, of course, must continue to monitor the tech company's monthly statement to verify that invoices are paid. The receivables generated are from the tech company's innovation evidenced by the intellectual property assets they have secured. With the money from the bank, the tech company will be able to grow and can demand a larger future credit line as the amount of receivables increases.

Warrants as the IP Proxy

Tech companies spend some of their hard-earned resources to develop their intellectual property assets. Ownership of proprietary knowledge, trade secrets, copyrights, and patents can distinguish one tech company from another. The intellectual property assets are so valuable that they are the key drivers of the enterprise. In other words, the value of the enterprise is dependent on the intellectual property, and vice versa. The high valuation the enterprise garners reflects, in part, how important investors view intellectual property assets as the key driver of the enterprise.

If the startup survives, thrives, and scales, it will be likely to receive the next round of capital funding at a tremendously increased valuation of the entire enterprise. Consequently, outlier banks make loans to startups for the upside: to obtain some benefits from the enterprise's high valuation at subsequent rounds of capital funding. The outlier banks want warrants as part of the loan's cost to the startup.

A warrant is what an enterprise furnishes to the outlier banks that confers to the banks the right, but not the obligation, to purchase the startup's shares at a certain price, and with a specific expiration on a future date. The startup usually offers the warrant at a very low price. When the startup survives, scales, and advances to subsequent capital funding with the enterprise's new and high valuation, the price of the stock at this time is substantially higher than the price conferred in the warrant. The outlier bank can cash in on the warrant and reap the difference between the current price of the stock and the warrant price.

As with any loan, the enterprise must pay the loan principal and interest payments. Typically, the outlier bank provides free interest payments for the first year, and around a 5 percent interest rate for the subsequent two years of the three-year term loan in IP Venture Banking. The interest rate is substantially lower than the startup can secure from alternative sources. There are several reasons for the lower interest rate on a loan from an outlier bank. Unlike alternative lenders who have no access to cheap money, outlier banks do. As commercial banks, outlier banks receive money from depositors. These deposits are other people's money, and banks pay depositors low interest and charge borrowers high interest. With access to plenty of low-cost money, outlier banks can lend to startups at a lower cost. Of course, outlier banks must still be careful in selecting only the VC-backed enterprises that are most likely to reach new rounds of venture funding, ensuring that the banks will receive payments on the principal loan, fees, and interest.

Overall, in exchange for the warrant as part of the loan cost, the outlier banks can give "more favorable credit terms" to the startups. In other words, the startups get lower interest rates and favorable terms on the loan to extend their runway to meet milestones and the next round of VC funding.

Illustratively, five young tech companies, in six separate transactions, as discussed next, have borrowed money from different outlier banks. In each transaction, the borrower was required to grant the banks warrants for the rights to purchase stock at a fixed low price as part of the loan cost. The banks later exercised their rights under the warrants when each of the borrowers' stock values increased.

Xoom Corporation is a digital consumer-to-consumer online money transfer and payment services company founded in 2001 in San Francisco. As part of the cost to obtain an IP venture loan from SVB, Xoom issued a warrant for 43,114 initial shares of common stock to the bank at the warrant price of $0.05 per share on October 29, 2004.[53] The warrant also granted SVB the right to purchase additional shares for subsequent loans as provided in the agreement. The warrant allowed SVB to exercise its right any time before the expiration date of October 29, 2011. When Xoom entered into the loan agreement with the bank, the startup had just received Series B capital funding on February 13, 2004, for $5.6 million. Xoom excelled and advanced to subsequent rounds of funding. By March 19, 2010, Xoom obtained

[53] "Warrant to Purchase Stock" 1, *Xoom Corp. & Silicon Valley Bank*, 2004, available at: www.sec.gov/ Archives/edgar/data/1315657/000119312513010596/d364901dex44.htm [https://perma.cc/7TFH-HMWA] (last accessed September 19, 2023).

Series F funding and raised $33.2 million. Consequently, SVB greatly benefitted from the warrant that it had demanded from Xoom back in 2004, now that the value of the shares had spiked. Moreover, on April 30, 2012, Xoom needed a new loan for its continued growth, and the company issued another warrant to SVB.[54] Xoom conferred to the Bank the right to purchase 100,000 shares at $1.71 per share.[55] Ten months later, Xoom held an IPO at a price of $16.00 per share. In sum, the valuation of the enterprise Xoom increased, and SVB reaped a handsome return from having the warrant.

Outlier banks can also obtain warrants for convertible stock as part of the price for the loans to startups. An example of this is Etsy, a peer-to-peer marketplace vis-à-vis a smartphone app that enables the buying and selling of handmade and vintage items. Etsy was founded on June 18, 2005, and it subsequently received Series A funding on November 1, 2006, and Series C on July 1, 2007.[56] While flush with new Series C funding, Etsy signed a loan and security agreement with SVB on November 15, 2007.[57] As part of the price of the loan, Etsy issued a warrant of 16,854 initial shares of Series C convertible stock to SVB. Etsy agreed to provide additional shares if the Bank made a loan to Etsy for an equipment purchase in excess of $500,000 in the

---

[54] In the 10-K filing in 2014, Xoom stated:

> In October 2009, the Company entered into a loan and security agreement (the "Loan Agreement"), with Silicon Valley Bank ("SVB"), which was amended in September 2012 to add a second lender and increase the available borrowing amount. In September 2013, the Company entered into an Amended and Restated Credit Agreement (the "Restated Loan Agreement") with SVB and other lenders. The Restated Loan Agreement added additional lenders, increased the available borrowing amount to $150.0 million through September 2016 and changed certain of the financial provisions. The Company is required to repay the outstanding principal balance under the line of credit in full at least once every eight business days. Under the Restated Loan Agreement, the Company pays a fee of 0.50% per annum for the daily unused portions of the line of credit. The interest rate at December 31, 2014 and December 31, 2013 was 4.25%. The Company paid a one-time commitment fee of $430,000 and a one-time arrangement fee of 0.30% of the amount available under the line of credit in 2013. The Company also paid SVB an annual administration fee of $45,000 in 2013 and 2014. These expenses, except the annual administration fee which is expensed over twelve months, are being amortized over the period of the Restated Loan Agreement . . . SVB issued a standby letter of credit for $15.0 million which satisfied an additional collateral requirement to maintain the Company's India operations and a $3.9 million letter of credit in January 2014 as a security deposit for the Company's new office lease.

"Xoom Corp., Annual Report (Form 10-K)," February 27, 2015, available at: www.sec.gov/Archives/edgar/data/1315657/000155837015000240/xoom-20141231x10k.htm [https://perma.cc/T5PN-BEY2] (last accessed September 19, 2023).

[55] "Warrant to Purchase Stock," *supra*, note 52. The issue had the expiration date of April 30, 2022. Ibid.

[56] "Etsy," *CrunchBase*, available at: www.crunchbase.com/organization/etsy [https://perma.cc/PXT4-7SX2] (last accessed September 19, 2023).

[57] "Sample Business Contracts: Warrant to Purchase Stock: Etsy Inc. and Silicon Valley Bank," *Onecle*, available at: https://contracts.onecle.com/etsy/silicon-valley-bank-warrant-2007-11-15.shtml [https://perma.cc/TB88-RFLH] (last accessed April 17, 2020).

aggregate. The warrant price per share was $2.67 per share, and the duration of the warrant was ten years, with an expiration date of November 14, 2017. In 2008, the company received Series D funding of $27 million, and then Series E funding of $20 million in 2010. That meant the bank loan payments were paid off, and the Bank could continue to keep the warrant for a later payout. Holding on to the warrant was fruitful as Etsy had its IPO in 2015, and on November 14, 2017 – the expiration date of the warrant – the value was $16.25 per share. Consequently, SVB could enjoy its investment by cashing in on the warrant before or on the expiration date. As a point of reference, if the bank had subsequently made additional loans to Etsy and accepted new warrants, the price per share for Etsy was around $40 per share in August 2018 should the bank wish to cash in on the warrants then.

The same startup can also borrow from different outlier banks, paying different costs for the loans in warrant amount and interest rate. Celator Pharmaceuticals, Inc. issued a warrant to ComericA Bank on March 11, 2009, in connection with an IP venture loan.[58] The warrant was for the right to purchase 233,333 shares of the Series C Preferred Stock at $0.60 per share. The warrant expired in March 2016. Celator went public in 2013 and was subsequently acquired by Jazz Pharmaceuticals for $1.5 billion in May 2016. As the valuation of Celator increased at subsequent IPO or acquisition, ComericA enjoyed the benefits by cashing in on the warrant.

Celator also issued a warrant to Square 1 Bank on June 15, 2012, for a loan of $3 million at an interest rate of 5.5 percent, with payments for interest only payable for the first six months. In connection with this loan, Celator provided to Square 1 Bank the right to purchase 17,267 shares of common stock at the price of $5.21 per share with the expiration date of June 15, 2019.[59] That meant Square 1 Bank could reap the warrant benefits when Jazz Pharmaceuticals purchased Celator in May 2016 at $30.25 per share.

Joining SVB, ComericA and Square 1 Bank, BridgeBank is another outlier bank active in providing loans to and receiving warrants from startups. For example, BridgeBank holds a warrant to purchase stock issued by GigOptix, Inc. on April 7, 2010, in connection with a loan agreement entered between the two parties.[60] GigOptix was founded in 2001 for the design and manufacture of "high-speed

[58] "Warrant To Purchase Stock" 1, *Celator Pharm., Inc. & ComericA Bank*, March 11, 2009, available at: www.sec.gov/Archives/edgar/data/1327467/000119312512517529/d411577dex43.htm [https://perma.cc/DFZ9-DPPS] (last accessed September 19, 2023).

[59] See "Celator Pharm., Inc., Annual Report (Form 10-K)," April 1, 2013, available at: www.sec.gov/Archives/edgar/data/1327467/000119312513136909/d513410d10k.htm [https://perma.cc/3FEQ-KCP9] (last accessed September 19, 2023). For the Warrant to Purchase Stock Agreement between Celator and Square 1 Bank, see "Amended and Restated Warrant to Purchase Stock," Celator Pharm., Inc & Square 1 Bank, November 13, 2012, available at: www.lawinsider.com/contracts/456JKcpBP6hlSGBYkzRuou/celator-pharmaceuticals/1327467/2012-11-13 [https://perma.cc/9UM4-7YJ7] (last accessed August 28, 2022).

[60] See "Annual Report (Form 10-K/A)," *Gigoptix, Inc.*, June 10, 2010, available at: www.sec.gov/Archives/edgar/data/1432150/000119312510137248/d10ka.htm [https://perma.cc/6T4U-ZUUN] (last accessed September 19, 2023).

integrated circuits that connect the optical and electronic domains."[61] The company subsequently received several venture rounds of funding. In recent years, the company itself has expanding as has recently acquired Magnum Semiconductor Inc. for $55 million.

In some cases, the outlier bank can simply sit back and watch as its warrant grows in value. For example, Square 1 Bank agreed to extend a credit line of seven million dollars to Otonomy. As part of the loan price, Square 1 Bank received a warrant to purchase stock signed by Otonomy, Inc. for Series B Preferred stock at $0.4032 per share.[62] The number of shares, 520,000, is based on the calculation of 3 percent of the principal amount of the loans divided by the initial warrant price of $0.4032. The warrant was entered on July 31, 2013, and has an expiration date of July 31, 2023. Otonomy is a biopharmaceutical company in the development and commercialization of "treatments for diseases of the inner and middle ear." The company was founded in 2008 and went public on August 14, 2014. At the time of writing, its share price was $6.30 per share. The Bank can either cash in the warrant or keep it as a future investment.

In summary, the warrants are the windfall investment on the intellectual property's enterprise value when outlier banks cash in at the enterprise's subsequent acquisition event or IPO. Illustratively, SVB was known for taking the warrants on loans to startup companies with VC backing. Fitbit, the maker of fitness-tracking wristbands, was one of those startup clients that issued a warrant to the bank. The bank held on to the warrant and cashed it in when Fitbit went public. The money that SVB made on the warrant exceeded losses from loans made to startups "over the last 10 years."[63]

SECURITY INTERESTS IN INTELLECTUAL PROPERTY ASSETS AS THE LAST RESORT

There are risks in IP Venture Banking. Startups suffer from high failure rates in trying to meet their milestones and are often not able to obtain the next round of VC funding. Without the new round of cash infusion through VC funding, there is no money to pay back the loans to the outlier banks. Moreover, if the enterprise is struggling financially, its intellectual property assets are not worth much more than liquidation value. That means outlier banks must plan for the downside: taking a

---

[61] "Gigoptix," *CrunchBase*, available at: www.crunchbase.com/organization/gigoptix#section-over view [https://perma.cc/D7H3-WWFR] (last accessed April 14, 2020).

[62] See "Loan And Security Agreement" 1, *Otonomy, Inc. & Square 1 Bank*, July 31, 2013, available at: www.sec.gov/Archives/edgar/data/1493566/000119312514266440/d724113dex1010.htm [https://perma.cc/D8GZ-465T] (last accessed September 19, 2023).

[63] Scott Reckard, "At Silicon Valley Bank, Risky Tech Start-Ups Are Lucrative Business," *The Los Angeles Times*, August 8, 2015, available at: www.latimes.com/business/la-fi-silicon-valley-bank-20150807-story.html [https://perma.cc/6Z2Z-KG52] (last accessed September 19, 2023) (reporting Silicon Valley Bank's unique role in nurturing its startups clients).

TABLE 3.3 *Patents per deals by top banks and outlier banks*

Group	Average	Patents per deal
Top 14 Banks	in Table 3.2	38.5
Outlier Banks	in Table 3.2	9.4

security interest in the intellectual property assets as collateral in the event the enterprise heads into liquidation.

Indeed, anticipating that not all deals will be successful, the banks will insist on taking security interests in the intellectual property, the only asset of value owned by the startup. The intellectual property assets, if the banks foreclose on them, are the resource of last resort in the event of liquidation. Outlier banks often combine the loan and security interest in intellectual property collateral together in the same document. For example, Bazaarvoice was founded in 2005; the company and ComericA Bank entered a Loan and Security Interest Agreement in 2007 wherein the company granted the bank a security interest in the intellectual property collateral.[64] Likewise, SVB has long insisted on taking a security interest in startups' intellectual property assets as collateral. For instance, one of SVB's startup clients was Accrue Software, Inc., which was founded in 1996. It obtained a loan from SVB in 1997 and granted the bank a security interest in the startup's intellectual property, as seen in the Loan and Security Agreement executed by the parties.[65]

Empirical research reveals that outlier banks have recorded their security interests in patents and patent applications as collateral. The banks typically recorded their security interests with the USPTO's Assignment Branch.

Most tellingly, among all banks that have recorded their security interests in patent collaterals with the USPTO, more than 90 percent of the filings are done by banks with traditional lending models that lend to established companies with large patent portfolios. Consequently, the average number of patents per deal done by these banks is 38.5. On the other hand, outlier banks embrace the IP Venture Banking model by lending to startups that are not established companies and have procured very few patents. The average number of patents per deal for outlier banks is 9.4. Table 3.3 shows the average numbers of patents per deal for outlier banks and other top banks.

In taking a security interest in patents as a last resort, in the event that the startup is in liquidation, outlier banks must anticipate potential buyers of the intellectual

[64] "Loan And Security Agreement" 1, *ComericA Bank and Bazaarvoice, Inc.*, July 18, 2007, available at: www.sec.gov/Archives/edgar/data/1330421/000119312511233414/dex1030.htm [https://perma.cc/7EYK-PGNG] (last accessed September 19, 2023).

[65] "Loan and Security Agreement: Silicon Valley Bank and Accrue Software Inc.," *FindLaw*, September 19, 1997, available at: https://corporate.findlaw.com/contracts/finance/loan-and-security-agreement-silicon-valley-bank-and-accrue.html [https://perma.cc/4EJW-PQBF] (last accessed September 19, 2023).

property assets at the outset, when contemplating whether to make the loan. Otherwise, when the startup is in liquidation, and the banks are trying to understand the market and attempting to identify a buyer for the foreclosed intellectual property, it is often too late to recoup the maximum value for the collateral and too uncertain to recover the loan amount. Therefore, the networks of experts, investors, entrepreneurs, and executives that banks have cultivated through their strong and unique relationships with VCs become highly relevant in shaping the outlier banks' understanding of the startup client's business and identifying who may be the potential buyers of the distressed intellectual property assets. The intellectual property collateral would be of little value if there is no buyer when the outlier banks foreclose on the property. In other words, the outlier banks must have their own exit strategy should the client be in financial trouble, and the intellectual property collateral is in liquidation.

As seen, SVB loaned to Ozro, Inc., a startup, and received a security interest in Ozro's patents for which the bank promptly filed its senior security interest on April 2, 2001.[66] Ozro also granted a security interest in the same patents to Cross Atlantic Capital Partners, Inc. (XACP) on the following day, April 3, 2001. A few months later, the startup did not perform well, and the bank quickly exited the transaction and assigned its security interest in Ozro's patents to the junior secured party, XACP. As anticipated, Ozro then "defaulted on its loan obligations" and XACP, which was now the assignee of the senior security interest and the holder of the junior security interest in the collateral of the patents, foreclosed. XACP then became the purchaser of the foreclosed patents at the foreclosure sale, and immediately assigned its rights in the patents to Sky Technologies.

This example shows several things: first, SVB was closely monitoring its client's business. The bank knew when it needed to exit – before the client's business problems became too dire. Second, because SVB insisted on a seniority position in its security interest of the patents, it had the upper hand. XACP was in the circle of networks that the bank had cultivated. With that relationship, the bank could approach XACP to acquire the bank's senior security interest in the patent collateral. That was exactly what the bank did: it assigned its rights to XACP. Finally, SVB exited first, leaving XACP to conduct the actual foreclosure, sale, and assigning of the patents to the purchaser, Sky Technologies.

Moreover, if the outlier banks do not take a security interest in the startup's intellectual property, the banks would insist on a negative pledge that the borrower agrees "not to encumber" any of its intellectual property without the consent of the banks. For example, in the Loan and Security Agreement between SVB and BigBand Networks, Inc., the negative pledge prohibiting security interests in intellectual property is reaffirmed in Exhibit A. The banks, instead, take a security

---

[66] See *Sky Techs. LLC v. SAP AG*, 576 F.3d 1374, 1376–1377 (Fed. Cir. 2009).

interest in the borrower's accounts receivable, which typically are the income generated from the borrower's intellectual property-based products.

In summary, outlier banks accept security interests in startups' intellectual property assets as collateral as a last resort in the event the enterprise is in liquidation. The value of the intellectual property, therefore, is calculated at forced liquidation. That means, from the perspective of outlier banks, the valuation of intellectual property assets at going concern value is not relevant and downright too risky for the banks to issue the loan, as discussed earlier within this chapter.

4

The Stanford Professor and Two Bankers

The three founders of Silicon Valley Bank (SVB) epitomize Californian determination and pragmatism. Medearis, the Stanford professor, who for ten years listened to his students struggling to obtain loans, decided to float an idea of a community bank for tech companies. The professor sought out a banking consultant who brought in a bank executive who carried his dream of founding his own bank, the trio together established a community bank for tech. Their backgrounds and convictions illuminate the startup spirit synonymous with Silicon Valley. Their journey led them to select what was then an uncommon name, Silicon Valley Bank, in 1983.

The inspiration for the creation of a community bank for tech lending is a very American story of an immigrant's aspiration. The founders of the community bank were inspired by Amadeo Peter Giannini, who in 1904 opened the Bank of Italy in San Francisco and later developed this bank into the Bank of America (BOA). Ironically, BOA initiated some of the earliest tech lending but abandoned the business, leaving a gap that the community bank subsequently filled.

MEDEARIS MEDEARIS: THE IDEA MAN

Professor Medearis recalled that throughout the 1970s his Stanford students routinely brought up the dire situation faced by entrepreneurs with new business ideas that banks refused to make loans to them. Venture capital (VC) firms were not yet around in large numbers, Medearis observed, and the students repeatedly made the same statement that no banks were lending to them. Four, five, and ten years passed; yet the statement about the dire situation persisted. Medearis thought that there might be an opportunity for a bank to serve high-tech entrepreneurs. He remembered years later: "The original idea sort of kept hitting me in the head with my students because they literally wanted to find money to start backing a new idea."[1] So Medearis became interested in banks and their operations.

[1] "SVB Oral History," *supra*, Chapter 2, note 17, at 5.

Medearis himself was also a businessman and a founder of his own startup. Financing filled the back of his mind. His curiosity about banks and lending percolated as he prepared the materials to teach his graduate students, coming from different states and countries, about the management of construction projects. He typically brought in outside speakers to provide the students with knowledge and perspectives from a multitude of stakeholders in complex construction projects. Speakers with financing experience from banks and equipment leasing companies were among those invited.

Teaching the Stanford engineering students in the Construction Management class brought the passion for engineering and financing together for Medearis. He considered himself a maverick from Grand View Avenue, Kansas City.[2]

As a first grader, after several days of a family car trip from Kansas City to San Francisco, young Medearis saw the Golden Gate Bridge while going to the 1939 World's Fair and fell instantly in love with the marvels of construction and innovation. He wondered how bridges were built as he experienced the rhythm of the most magical bridge of all as his parents' car crossed it, taking in the 746-foot tall towers, soaking in the sweeping cables, and admiring the orange color and Art Deco styling. The sensory experience expanded his horizon.

He was smitten by the white buildings erected in 1936–1937 on Treasure Island, the glistering water in the Bay, the surrounding hills, the abundance of flora and fauna in California, and the gorgeous weather. He could not fathom that no Kansas winter existed in California and harbored no desire to leave the magical Bay area at the end of the trip. He dreamed of and plotted his return to California.

His father, Donald N. Medearis, was the first pediatrician in Kansas City.[3] Being a physician ran deep in his DNA; his grandfather, father, and older brother, Don, all practiced medicine. Robert Medearis revered his father, who first gained all As from the University of Kansas and then obtained his medical degree from Harvard Medical School. Donald N. Medearis, Jr., Robert's older brother, also graduated from Harvard Medical School and became the Charles Wilder Distinguished Professor of Pediatrics at Harvard. Growing up among the Harvard men, Robert Medearis nursed another dream, in addition to plotting his return to California, that he must find a way to go to Harvard like his father and older brother.

Medearis played basketball in high school. He was a good athlete, and he actively talked to different colleges, including Stanford, for an opportunity to play on their teams. He attended the summer basketball camp for state players under the famous Kansas Coach Forrest Allen or basketball's first great coach, whose booming foghorn

---

[2] James Kirk Robison and Robert Medearis, *Robert Medearis, A Maverick from Kansas* (2015); Interview with Robert Medearis on March 18, 2022 (on file with author).

[3] R. Alan Ezkowitz, John D. Crawford, Michael S. Jellinek, and Ronald E. Kleinman, The Faculty of Medicine, Harvard University, "Obituary: Donald N. Medearis (1927–1997)," October 6, 1997, available at: https://fa.hms.harvard.edu/files/hmsofa/files/memorialminute_medearis_donald_n.pdf [https://perma.cc/2GKA-M75M] (last accessed September 25, 2023).

voice earned him the endearing nickname "Phog" Allen. Coach Allen knew Medearis was good but not good enough for Kansas, so he contacted the Stanford basketball coach and advised Medearis to go for Stanford.

Medearis reached his dream of returning to California eleven years after the 1939 World's Fair. His family was of modest means and going to Stanford would cause financial constraint on his father. But Medearis was determined to get himself to Stanford; he played basketball, joined the ROC, majored in engineering, and worked part-time as a food server at Stanford President Wallace Sterling's house, ensuring that he could financially afford Stanford.

President Sterling was proud that the food servers were Stanford students who worked their way through school, and he insisted that his guests spend some time with the students. Medearis served the food and met the young Senator John Kennedy, the poet Robert Frost, President Dwight Eisenhower, and many distinguished guests who graced President Sterling's residence. Sterling solidified both Stanford's national and international reputations, built the Stanford Shopping Center, leased University land, launched the Stanford Research Park, and hired Frederick Terman, the father of Silicon Valley, as his provost.[4] From Medearis' perspective, both Sterling and Terman are the true founders of Silicon Valley.

Before Terman was the provost, he served as the Dean of the Engineering School from 1944 to 1958, inclusive of the four years the young Medearis was a civil engineering student at Stanford. Clark Oglesby, the professor who created the new Construction graduate program in Civil Engineering with the endorsement of Terman, took Medearis as a protégé.

After graduating from Stanford in 1955, Medearis fulfilled his ROTC obligations with three years of service in the Navy. He was determined to get into Harvard Business School.

In 1958, Medearis achieved his second dream to enroll in Harvard, where his father and older brother had earned their medical degrees. There, like many students of his generation at the Business School, he took a class in his second year with the legendary Professor George Doriot, who is also known as the "father of venture capital." Professor Doriot, a brigadier general in World War II, cofounded the oldest executive MBAs in the world in 1930, and then in 1957 founded INSEAD, the top business school in France. As the father of venture capital, Doriot set up American Research & Development (ARD) in 1946, a VC firm, and scored the first major venture success story by investing $70,000 in Digital Equipment Corporation in 1957, a company that enjoyed a valuation of $38 million in 1968, equating to a return of over 500 times Doriot's investment. Medearis enrolled in Doriot's class called "Production," with a primary focus on startup entrepreneurship and VC

---

[4]   Frederick Terman moved with his parents to Stanford from Indiana. His father, the noted psychologist Lewis Terman, developed the Stanford-Binet IQ test. See, Ben Maldonado, "Eugenics on the Farm: Lewis Terman," *The Stanford Daily*, November 6, 2019.

financing. Young Medearis loved the class because Doriot taught from the approach of "I have been there" in the venture financing and business worlds. Also, Doriot believed in being different. While others used case studies, Doriot lectured, and if they lectured, he would use a different method.[5] Doriot instilled in young Medearis the idea of being a maverick, including attitudes of refusing to be bound by tradition, and truly loving what you do. He also believed if you don't like what you do, you should get out, even at a cost.

In Doriot's class, Medearis got a taste of developing a business plan and strategy for how to grow the business. The final assignment in the class was a group report for a new business plan and strategy. Medearis focused on developing a homebuilding business plan based on his earlier interest as a Stanford undergraduate in Clark Oglesby's construction course. He had witnessed the pent-up demand for housing from returning veterans from the Korean War and the suburbanization across the country. He believed that quality and affordable housing was needed nationwide. The group project was well received and filed in the Library of Congress, and Medearis was exceedingly proud of his idea. He earned his A+ from Doriot. The group project also helped land Medearis his first job at Lusk Corporation in Arizona upon graduation from Harvard.

Lusk built subdivisions, bridges, and retention dams. Medearis spent seven years in Arizona; he rose from a division manager to be the head of all operations in Arizona and served as a member of the company's Board of Directors. Lusk expanded into Northern California and appointed Medearis to open a new California office. Unfortunately, Lusk overextended itself and got caught in the downside of a seven-year economic cycle. The company held more inventories but could not sell. Lusk filed for bankruptcy. It was time for a new job, and Medearis entertained phone calls from recruiters while planning to build his own company.

Medearis went out on his own and founded a construction development company called Hollistic Construction Company (HCC) in the late 1960s. HCC bought land, built multi-units, and sold them. Medearis was later recruited to serve as the president of a new company called Builder's Resources Corporation (BRC) whose money came from American Standard, National Whirlpool, Stanley Works, Donaldson, Lufkin and Jenrette, and a larger real estate firm from Los Angles. BRC raised money and invested in construction projects across the country. He was with BRC for several years until the company was sold to Maersk.

Interestingly, the most exciting phone call came from his old professor and mentor from Stanford, Clark Oglesby. The old kindred spirit asked him to come and teach Construction Management at Stanford. Medearis became an adjunct professor, teaching what he loved about Construction Management.

Medearis brought his real-world, multi-faceted experience in real estate development and construction to his students in the classroom. It was the teaching at

---

[5] *A Maverick from Kansas, supra,* note 2.

Stanford that brought him joy and connection with many different entrepreneurs. He recalled Hernan Martinez who worked in the banking side of a VC firm, and so Medearis reached out to him to learn about the differences between first- and second-rounds of VC. Medearis understood why VC firms didn't like to provide the second round and believed that there was a space for banks to get involved; however, banks were afraid to be in that space to lend to entrepreneurs. Also, Medearis did not know much about banking. He believed when you don't know something, talk to others. That was exactly what Medearis did. He talked to other people about the idea of creating a bank for entrepreneurs who received funding from VCs. Clark Oglesby, his old professor and then colleague, didn't see the need for a bank for entrepreneurial engineers. Medearis spoke to some of the leaders in Silicon Valley and VC contacts, and they were enthusiastic.

Among the people that Medearis spoke to about the idea of creating a new bank was Bill Biggerstaff.

BILL BIGGERSTAFF: THE CONSULTANT

Medearis lived in Atherton and resided in a clubby world of compatible men. They played poker together. The original group included Burton Blackwell, Dave Elliott, Starr Colby, Bob Procter, Fred Rehmus, Bill Biggerstaff, and Medearis Medearis. Burton Blackwell was a well-known builder in the mid-peninsula, while Dave Elliot was Medearis' Stanford fraternity brother who also earned his MBA from Harvard a couple of years ahead of Medearis. Elliot became the Vice President of Administration for Memorex in 1968 and later joined Heidrick & Struggles, an international executive search firm, and served as Managing Partner of the firm in 1974. Starr Colby worked for Lockheed as the manager of the then remote-piloted vehicle project after serving as assistant director for space technology at the Pentagon.[6] Fred Rehmus was the founding principal of Brownson, Rehmus & Foxworth, a financial advisory firm for multi-generation wealth.[7]

Medearis wanted to know everything about banks. He reached out to Bill Biggerstaff, one of his tennis buddies in Atherton.

Bill Biggerstaff was born on March 17, 1919, in Berkeley, California. He loved basketball and played for three years at the University of California, Berkeley. Like many young men of his generation during World War II, he joined the Navy and

---

[6] "Obituaries: Starr J. Colby," *Almanac News*, February 2, 2000, available at: www.almanacnews.com/morgue/2000/2000_02_02.obit02.html [https://perma.cc/VP7W-E8DX] (last accessed September 25, 2023).

[7] Fred Rehmus, Oregon Shakespeare Festival, available at: www.osfashland.org/en/artist-biographies/board-member/Former-Members/fred-rehmus.aspx [https://perma.cc/27JH-TCEB] (last accessed September 19, 2022); Brownson, Rehmus, & Foxworth, available at: https://brfadvisors.com/ [https://perma.cc/6HXS-AM28] (last accessed September 19, 2022).

fought in the South Pacific. He returned from the war and went to Harvard Business School for his MBA in 1947. He was a natural salesman with charm. He started in auto sales, spent a few years at Mechanics Bank in Richmond, and then worked in sales and marketing in the international division of the Ford Motor Company which took him to New York City, Dearborn, Michigan, and Brussels. With his international experience, he returned to California to join Wells Fargo Bank in San Francisco and served banking clients overseas. He worked at Wells Fargo from 1965 to 1976 as a Vice President and from 1976 to 1978 as a Lease Broker. He then joined California Commerce Bank as a Vice President and Manager, Business Development, from 1978 to 1982 until he resigned from that position to devote full time to the organization of SVB.

Biggerstaff and Medearis played tennis every weekend at Medearis's house. They also swam at Fred Mielke's house, as all three men lived in Atherton.[8] Mielke became a trustee at Stanford University in 1978 and CEO and Chairman of the Board at Pacific Gas & Electric Co. in 1979. Like Biggerstaff and Medearis, Mielke was a graduate of Harvard Business School. He also obtained his Juris Doctor from Stanford Law School.[9] Medearis chatted to Mielke about his idea of a new bank.

Medearis talked to Biggerstaff about his students' years of pestering him about banks' rejections and new entrepreneurs in the high-tech sector desiring to gain access to bank money when they needed it.[10] They discussed how banks grow from taking deposits and that the nascent high-tech sector companies had cash that would be deposited at the banks. Utilizing this cash would allow banks to make loans. Medearis himself made several trips to San Francisco to the Federal Reserve Bank and learned about banking regulations and federal and state chartering processes. Medearis wanted to learn from Biggerstaff about bank operations. Medearis believed that there might be something there for both Biggerstaff and him to tackle. Biggerstaff, possessing vast knowledge about the banking industry, talked to Medearis in exchange for a consultant fee of $1,000 per month. Medearis insisted on knowing everything about banking, and they talked for about six months.

Biggerstaff proved both knowledgeable and charming. He could talk business – the banking business was all about relationships. Biggerstaff also knew people who might be interested in starting a new bank. To submit a charter application, Biggerstaff knew the perfect candidate with an understanding of high-tech lending. When the time came, he would recruit that candidate.

Medearis and Biggerstaff forged ahead with the creation of a new bank, which took some time. Biggerstaff finally introduced his perfect candidate, Roger Smith, to Medearis as a potential president of the new bank for the charter filing. Medearis

---

[8] "Frederick W. Mielke Jr. (1921–2015)," *SFGate*, March 20, 2015, available at: www.legacy.com/us/obituaries/sfgate/name/frederick-mielke-obituary?id=8421820 [https://perma.cc/76EB-A6CX] (last accessed September 25, 2023).

[9] Ibid.

[10] "SVB Oral History," *supra*, Chapter 2, note 17, at 6.

and Biggerstaff then received the Findley Reports about the banking industry in California. The Findley Reports provides rankings of the banking industry based on performance through its annual designations of "Super Premier Performing," "Premier Performing," and "Commendable Performing" classifications. The Findley Reports also publishes a monthly newsletter on banking trends, merger and acquisition transactions in the banking industry, and professional topics for the management of financial institutions. They proceeded ahead and selected the name for the new bank, "Silicon Valley Bank." They shared the name with Smith, who had agreed to serve as the president of the new bank and put his name on the charter application, and they received conditional approval by the California Superintendent of Banks on February 16, 1983.

Medearis and Biggerstaff drove down with Dave Eliot to Pajaro Dunes Resort from Atherton for their annual poker game. The setting was late spring. The weather was perfect for a getaway. The men drove down on Friday to play poker before their wives and children arrived on Saturday. The poker group served as the sounding board for Medearis and Biggerstaff to chat about their new bank idea. The men attending the annual poker game all supported the idea and later invested in the bank. The poker game was not where the idea of the bank originated. According to Medearis, in an endearing and complimentary sense, Biggerstaff acted like the greatest schmoozer who enjoyed crafting the poker-game version of the story much more. So, the legend was born. Moreover, a poker game conjuring alluring images of skills and bluffing among men sounds much more enticing than a boring truth.

Biggerstaff was sixty-four years of age when he joined forces with Medearis and Smith to found the new bank. He insisted that Medearis pay him for his consulting fees. Medearis later arranged for the new bank to pay Biggerstaff for the consulting fees incurred during the charting application process and organization of the new bank.[11]

As a true banker at heart, Biggerstaff always carried his legal pad and pens ready to sign up new clients and open their accounts with the Bank. He used his charm and he knocked on doors.

> Bill didn't retire from the bank until he was 85. He was a shining example to our young people. He was still going out and developing new businesses. We didn't have databases. So Bill had legal pads. He had all the prospects out there and he wasn't shy. [W]ithout appointment he just went knocking on doors and said I'm Bill Biggerstaff from Silicon Valley Bank, I want to tell you more about the bank and how we might work with you. So Bill was a true inspiration for our young people showing that if this old guy can do it, we can do it. [H]e did his own filing [because he didn't have an] administrative assistant or anything else.[12]

The founders also believed that the new bank would need someone with international banking stature and experience like Biggerstaff. After the bank opened its

[11] SVB 1983 Prospectus document (on file with the author).
[12] Harry Kellogg Interview, March 14, 2022 (on file with author).

door in October 1983, Biggerstaff would serve clients who would be successful and expand globally. Such clients would need letters of credit, foreign exchange, and the like. Biggerstaff was the mercurial banker in the young bank, not tied down in any particular practice group.

> Bill, as a founder of the bank, did what he really wanted to do. He would be doing stuff [in the tech lending group] for one day and help with our real estate credits the next day. So, he was kind of a roamer which allowed him to do whatever he wanted.[13]

The name "Silicon Valley Bank" was not universally approved when Medearis and Biggerstaff disclosed their idea; but Roger Smith, the high-tech banking executive, thought it was exactly what he would like to name his new bank! The three men with their respective experiences forged their new path to founding the new bank. Each brought specific strengths to complement the others and, together, the trio cemented the foundational three-legged stool, an image the trio often conjured when they recounted their business model for the new bank.

> Roger, with the startups and VC relationships, Bill, with the international, global experience, and Bob, with startup experience through working with several startups as a consultant and at Stanford University created SVB.

Even so, the new bank could not be a reality without the execution of a CEO with a startup mentality.

ROGER VERNON SMITH: THE STARTUP BANK CEO

Smith nursed the idea of creating a new bank with an emphasis on serving the high-technology sector before Biggerstaff approached him. Smith was exceedingly fond of the burgeoning Silicon Valley and noted that, in the early 1980s many new businesses with "Silicon Valley" in their names appeared. Smith was the regional President of Imperial Bank, but he wanted to be in charge of a new startup bank with a new vision. The entrepreneurial spirit ran deep in Smith's psyche, anchoring his belief in what banking should be.

Smith grew up in Colorado and Kansas. His high school class of 26 students was in the city of Elkhart, Kansas, bordered by Colorado on the west and Oklahoma to the south. Elkhart's population was 1,780 people in 1960 when Smith graduated from high school, and it remained relatively unchanged sixty years later in 2020, with 1,888 people. His father graduated from the University of Kansas, but Smith looked west of Elkhart and went to the University of Colorado for a business major. Smith was a man without the typical connection, as the saying goes: if your father doesn't own the bank in the city, you don't have that many opportunities. In the Midwest,

[13] Ibid.

Smith set his eyes for opportunities further west of Colorado, seeking an interview with Wells Fargo bank for an internship in California.

The year was 1964. Smith decided that his personality was most suitable for the banking business. He liked finance but not all the time. He liked sales but not all the time. Banking would be the perfect combination of finance and sales. During Wells Fargo training for the newbies, Smith picked Mountain View, California, as his preference for a branch location. The name "Silicon Valley" didn't exist at the time on the map, but Mountain View exceedingly satisfied his ambition to firmly root himself on the west coast for new opportunities. At the Mountain View branch, the young Smith opened an account for Bill Biggerstaff in 1964! Their paths crossed almost two decades before the birth of SVB. Smith worked at Wells Fargo branches and deepened his experience serving businesses and individuals.

A year later, in Wells Fargo's Menlo Park branch, the young Smith began his first real job as a banker under the tutelage of the branch manager, Robert L. Altick, Jr., a Stanford graduate and a forward thinker who rose to prominence a few years later, becoming the Senior Vice President of Wells Fargo Bank's East Bay Division in 1970.[14]

Young Smith, forever an entrepreneur, left the Wells Fargo branch office for the Stanford Bank, an independent bank in Palo Alto, because he wanted to gain the experience of a full bank business. Smith was also attracted to the very prestigious profile of people on Stanford Bank's Board of Directors. In 1966, Smith saw the connections between Stanford University and new businesses started by Stanford graduates. Smith heard much about Fred Terman, the famous father of Silicon Valley, who then headed Stanford's School of Engineering and spearheaded a new center where research and industries would collaborate, the Stanford Industrial Park, in 1951. Terman counted Oswald Garrison Villard, Jr., Russell and Sigurd Varian, William Hewlett, and David Packard among his students who heeded his advice when founding their own companies. Working at the Stanford Bank marked a major development in the young Smith's banking career. He observed how an independent bank like Stanford Bank, with only one location but with deep ties with the business community, vibrantly served the Stanford area. He experienced how an independent bank operated without hierarchical management in another city and state. He wanted to be the boss of an independent bank in the future. However, there were more steps to climb before he could reach that peak of a banking career.

With a wife and two children, Smith set his eyes on obtaining his MBA to earn a new leadership position in banking. Working at the Stanford Bank during the day, Smith also attended evening classes at 5:30 p.m., 7:00 p.m., and 8:30 p.m. at Santa Clara University. With his MBA, he returned to Wells Fargo as an assistant manager

---

[14] "Executive Changes," *The New York Times*, October 16, 1970, available at: www.nytimes.com/1970/10/16/archives/executive-changes.html [https://perma.cc/4UB3-BA46] (last accessed September 25, 2023).

in the Burlington office and spent four months in the Investment Department to observe how the smart, senior bankers in the Management Committee made their decisions. The prime rate was 12 percent, the interest rate was about 18 percent, and banks were practically frozen in their lending. Young banker Smith quickly learned that the bankers in the Management Committee didn't have all the answers!

Back in the Mountain View branch of Wells Fargo, Smith concentrated on building the business, and he became the manager of the branch in 1971. His exceedingly capable assistant manager of the branch was Harry Kellogg. During the early 1970s, a branch manager assumed enormous power; he could make lending decisions without waiting for approval from upper management at headquarters.

By 1973, Smith was in charge of the Wells Fargo Special Industries Group (SIG) in Palo Alto to go after high-tech companies. Intel was a client of the bank after breaking away from the legendary Fairchild Semiconductor, also a depositor at the bank. Smith's personal clients included notable visionaries, including Bob Noyce of Intel and Wilf Corrigan of Fairchild. Bob Noyce and his cofounder Gordon Moore originally named the semiconductor company with the combined first letters of their last names, "NM Electronics," changing it to "Intel," an abbreviation of "Integrated Electronics" after they purchased the rights to use the name from Intelco.[15]

Smith understood that high-tech companies in the semiconducting business experience good business rapport with their customers. He leveraged that knowledge by providing loans against their receivables, meaning he could monitor and collect their receivables in the event of default on the loan. He devised ways that the bank could monitor the high-tech companies' activities to reduce risks in lending against their receivables.

Smith wanted a piece of a high-tech company's growth, so he insisted on obtaining warrants as part of loan costs for tech companies to borrow from Wells Fargo in 1973. Warrants are rights to purchase a fixed number of shares in a company at a fixed price. When the company's valuation goes up, banks can cash in on the warrants before the expiration. For instance, Smith's Special Industries Group was able to require 10 percent warrant coverage on a loan. If a loan was $1 million, 10 percent of the loan amount would be in a warrant.[16] The duration of the warrant is somewhere between five to eight years with the hope for a liquidity event of mergers and acquisitions or an initial public offering in that time. Around 90 percent of the liquidity events are mergers and acquisitions (M&A).

---

[15] Jennifer Elias, "10 Facts You (Probably) Didn't Know about Intel's 50-Year History," *Silicon Valley Business Journal* (July 10, 2018).

[16] In later decades, when competition in venture debt deals increased, the gold standard for a $3 million loan was that 5 percent of the loan amount would be in warrant.

The first client who granted the Special Industries Group (SIG) a warrant was Timeshare Company, a high-tech entity with a special focus on time-sharing computer systems. SIG put together a loan against account receivables to Timeshare. The loan was typically up to 80 percent of the account receivables or 50 percent of inventory. Timeshare issued a warrant of 10 percent of the loan coverage to SIG, in addition to interest payments. SIG made $50,000 in the warrant on that first deal of a $500,000 loan.

SIG's clients were not limited to the vicinities of Palo Alto. Some of the tech clients were in Utah, meaning the bankers must fly there to close their deals. The bankers followed where they could bank and lend to high-tech clients. As the ecosystem was small back then, Smith's Special Industries Group knew all the high-tech companies at that time and signed them up as either lending clients or depositors. These companies were concentrated in the semiconductor industry and semiconductor equipment industry. The Special Industries Group also networked and got to know the investors in these companies and formed relationships with them.

One of SIG's clients was Atari, the developer of the seminal arcade game Pong and the Atari2600, the ubiquitous video game console. Atari was backed by the legendary venture capitalist Don Valentine who founded Sequoia Capital in 1972. Atari's cofounder, Nolan Bushnell, named the famous game "Pong" after an attractive female employee with the tiniest waist.[17] Bushnell's pictures in hot tubs with women did not please Wells Fargo management; they questioned Smith about this particular SIG client. The loan to Atari, however, was among the deals that cemented the relationship between the bankers, the VC, and the founders in the early 1970s.

Smith's keen sense of action led the Special Industries Group to be housed in the same building as the law firm Wilson Sonsini. Proximity mattered. The bankers in the SIG formed a relationship with Larry Sonsini as they wanted the tech companies and investors who were the law firm's clients to also be clients of the bank.

Among the bankers who worked for Smith in the Special Industries Group was Harry Kellogg, the assistant manager for the Wells Fargo Mountain View branch. Kellogg possessed an intellect and charm that he used effectively in forging relationships with investors at Sequoia, Kleiner Perkins, NEA, and other VC firms in the early days. Kellogg appreciated the proximity with Wilson Sonsini and VC firms and valued Smith's leadership as head of the Special Industries Group.

Kellogg was part of the big brothers banking group that Dave Titus, a young banker fresh out of college, looked up to from his trainee desk. Titus was too young and new to be part of the Special Industries Group, but he observed and admired the Group. Smith hired Titus because he believed the young man was very smart

[17] Keith Stuart, "Atari Founder Nolan Bushnell Loses Award after Sexism Outcry," *The Guardian*, February 1, 2018.

and hard working. Titus understood high-tech companies at that time. He was hungry, craved responsibility, and exhibited an innovative streak.

Things went well in the Special Industries Group but not with Wells Fargo itself. Smith felt that his Special Industries Group was a fish out of water in the Wells Fargo environment. He was acutely aware of being that fish each time he needed to report his Group's latest activities to the Wells Fargo loan committee who were used to GM, GE, and the like. New names in high-tech scared them. Newness worried them. When the Special Industries Group made one bad loan, the Wells Fargo loan committee was ready to shut the Group down for good.

The loan was $6 million to a digital watch company called Litronics. The VC backing the company walked away because the technology was so new, but there were other startup watch companies at that time, and no M&A candidate emerged to buy Litronics. The company could not be liquidated. No firm was willing to buy the company's intellectual property assets. The bank had to write off the $6 million loan loss. Then the call came from Wells Fargo headquarters in San Francisco to eliminate the Special Industries Group. Wells Fargo did not want any risk, and they believed that high-tech was adjacent to high risks. Their belief was shared by other banks, and all banks stayed away from lending to high-tech. Wells Fargo dealt the death blow to Smith's Special Industries Group.

Wells Fargo, however, could not extinguish the conviction that Smith harbored deep inside himself that banking and serving the burgeoning tech industry was the way banks should participate and grow. Smith stayed on to serve the Wells Fargo branch at Stanford Industrial Park with a focus on retail while keeping his eyes on opportunities for his true calling. The call came from Imperial Bank.

Imperial Bank recruited Smith to be the president of a new regional office to capture high-tech companies as clients. Smith would be his own boss to run the new office with a focus close to his heart: lending and banking high-tech clients. Also, Imperial Bank paid Smith much more money than he received from Wells Fargo; yet Smith was biding his time at Imperial Bank because he wanted more. He yearned for an opportunity to start a new bank and execute his vision of a new startup bank. This opportunity came from Bill Biggerstaff.

A long time ago, when the young trainee Smith worked in Wells Fargo's Menlo Park office, Bill Biggerstaff walked in to open a personal account, and Smith served him. Over time they became friends. This time Biggerstaff came in with a new business proposition to recruit Smith to be the president of a new startup bank. Biggerstaff informed Smith that Medearis had been working on the business plan for the new bank. They selected the name "Silicon Valley Bank." Smith was ready to give up his comfortable position at Imperial Bank and jump all in at a startup bank. This time his dream would materialize. He liked the idea of being at a bank from the beginning and building it up. He was not at Imperial Bank during its inception, but for SVB he could be. The entrepreneur in the banker's psyche rose to the challenge.

Smith carried with him a strong belief that a startup bank to serve the community provides a pivotal strategy to help build the economy. Smith was at the University of

Colorado when President John F. Kennedy was elected. During this time, the economy was in bad condition, and the idea of community banking began to take root in Smith's mind. People in the community would be those who start a bank, and their deposits would then be used to loan out to the local businesses in the community. Regulations should be relaxed to allow startup banks to be formed to serve communities across the United States. The early 1980s proved an exciting period to start a new bank.

Smith invited others along for the journey. He would bring Dave Titus with him. He also plotted to bring some people from the former Special Industries Group, including Harry Kellogg and J. Kirens, if he could recruit them. He would recruit some of the former clients in the high-tech sector. He thought of making everything seem bigger than it really was. Different, everything would be different. Others may possible have thought what he planned for the new startup bank was *odd*, not just different. He signed on to the business plan with Biggerstaff and Medearis. He would continue to work at Imperial Bank until the time came for him to resign and work on the opening of SVB. So he thought.

✱ ✱ ✱ ✱

GIANNINI INFLUENCE

A startup bank in 1983 enticed three men with different backgrounds yet the same desire to create something different from the existing banks. Although Smith credited President Kennedy with the community banking idea and the concept that banks should make loans to businesses in the community, there was a specific giant in the banking industry that Smith and his cofounders admired. That giant was Amadeo Pietro Giannini, the founder of the Bank of America.

Nationwide there were 400 new banks in 1983. California alone had 72 new banks that year. The three founders saw large numbers of new banks receive charters with ease. The timing was right to create a startup bank to make loans to the community. The community they envisioned, however, was different, dominated by the growing high-tech semiconductor and semiconductor equipment industry. This type of community can grow and transcend geographical boundaries. For competition in the niche of banking for the high-tech industry, Bank of America (BOA) ranked the number one bank in this area. However, BOA faced massive problems in real estate in the early 1980s and would soon exit the niche, leaving the upstart SVB to capture the high-tech community. Ironically, the three founders based their banking inspiration on Giannini of BOA.[18]

---

[18] "SVB Oral History," *supra*, Chapter 2, note 17, at 7.

When the banking world only served the wealthy and affluent class, Giannini banked ordinary people and small businesses. Typical banks shun little deposits and tiny loans as unworthy of their time. Immigrants and fruit growers were not welcomed to the intimidating bank lobby space. Giannini signed these hard-working individuals and their families up as his customers. He opened bank doors to them wherever they were. His banks came to the valley to serve the small farmers and growers in the Santa Clara valley. He followed the trails of his potential customers.

Giannini was born on May 6, 1870, in San Jose, the same city where 113 years later SVB was born. San Jose was not a center of the gold rush but fertile soil for fruits and vegetables grown by immigrants, including immigrants from Italy. Giannini's father came from a wealthy family in Genoa that afforded him the ability to open a hotel establishment in San Jose. Giannini was the firstborn of the three children. When Giannini was three years old, his father was killed by a workman over a dispute over a one-dollar debt. His mother would soon remarry and moved the family to the North Beach, San Francisco neighborhood.

Giannini, without a college education, began to distribute produce and fruits in the Italian immigrant enclave of North Beach to assist his stepfather in his agriculture distribution business. As a young produce broker, Giannini exhibited his boldness to connect with the farm producers who brought the produce grown in the Santa Clara Valley to him for distribution. He networked with buyers of the produce. He understood what the buyers and producers needed from banks. He also wanted their deposits, and he believed that the deposits in the aggregate of many small accounts would help a new bank to grow. With the business knowledge from being a produce distributor, he founded the Bank of Italy and served the ordinary people, the small businesses, the produce merchants, the growers, and the immigrants. The people with moderate means were "the little people" who never set foot in a bank except when the Bank of Italy welcomed them with open arms.[19]

Through his experience as a produce broker, Giannini observed the new fabrics of America through his daily encounters with individuals who were Italians, Chinese, French, Spanish, Portuguese, Irish, Jews, Syrians, and the local, old Americans. Banks during this time ignored the immigrant population in Giannini's North Beach neighborhood. Giannini saw that as an opportunity for his new bank. The majority of the Bank of Italy's clients in the early years were immigrants. Giannini encouraged them to open accounts and save their money at his bank instead of stashing the cash under their mattresses. He explained to them that his Bank of Italy was for them. He taught them about interest-bearing accounts. He helped to avoid loan sharks by providing small loans of $25 at bank rates while other banks insisted that the smallest loan must be $100. The Bank of Italy also

[19] Marquis James and Bessie Rowland James, *Biography of a Bank: The Story of Bank of America* (Harper & Brothers, 1954).

publicly announced in 1909 that it "is to pay special attention to the affairs of people who speak English with difficulty and will have employees who speak the French, Italian, Spanish and Portuguese languages."[20] No bank in the United States then and now would issue or embrace such a mission to serve such a diverse customer base in the same way.

When San Francisco burst into flames during the 1906 earthquake, Giannini leveraged his boldness and his knowledge as a produce broker by piling the money from the bank vault on a produce wagon and topping the money with the produce. While other banks waited for the fires to die and the vaults to cool, Giannini ran his banking operations directly from the wagon. He allowed withdrawals and made loans on handshake promises, and all of the loans were later repaid. Giannini was fearless and turned the earthquake disaster into an opportunity. Giannini trusted his customers, and they trusted and rewarded him. His reputation grew and his bank attracted attention beyond his North Beach neighborhood.

The Bank of Italy expanded its reach and serviced the agricultural regions in the Santa Clara Valley and beyond. Giannini made loans to small farmers and charged a lower interest rate of 7 percent instead of the going rate of 8 percent. The Bank provided loans for automobile purchases, equipment, and all personal and business assets that were structured in installments. With the expansion in services, the Bank would soon transform to become the first bank in the nation to provide lending services to individuals and small businesses in different fields, displacing loan shark operations that imposed exorbitant rates and often invited violence.

Giannini went into banking at the age of thirty-four, and he did not embrace banking for personal wealth, the goal of many banking executives. He died in 1949 with an estate of $489,279, which was less than he had, taking into account the deflation of the dollar, when he opened the Bank of Italy. He turned to banking to serve the then-unbanked people and followed their trails and money with his new idea of banking expansion. He encountered lots of opposition. When the Bank's Board of Directors and colleagues were discouraged by the resistance and hardship, Giannini reminded them:

> The Bank of Italy was launched and has had a remarkable record of growth on a policy of conservative yet energetic and enthusiastic optimism. The institution has never known and should never know the word "failure" in any matter, large or small; nor will "cold feet" ever bring it enduring or any sort of success. Our flourishing San Jose and Market Street branches are pertinent illustrations of what "boosting" and constant optimistic demeanor accomplished for us in the face of trying and at times disheartening odds.[21]

[20] Ibid., at 51.
[21] Ibid., at 69.

He fought against the banking establishment. They resisted his encroachment into their cities, particularly, Los Angeles. He saw how Los Angeles's population and wealth multiplied and the region of eternal sunshine lured tourists and snowbirds. Los Angeles annexed smaller cities to extend its metropolis boundaries, including Hollywood. Giannini was enticed by Los Angeles' fast growth and potential opportunities. The Bank of Italy attempted to acquire additional banks, including Park Bank, to supplement its then modest presence in Los Angeles. The banks in Los Angeles and the legislators blocked his efforts. A newspaper carried the headline "Park Bank Taken over by Italians."[22] The appeal to racial prejudice failed to deter Giannini. His newly acquired banks in Los Angeles carried on the Bank of Italy's mission. Giannini took out a half-page advertisement that the Bank of Italy would offer money to small mortgage borrowers who needed $1,000 or less:

> It is our purpose to make a specialty of the interest of the small depositor and borrower. We aim to do all in our power to help in the building up of Los Angeles. We have money to loan at all times to the man who wishes to build on property that he owns. We have no money for speculators. We consider the wage-earners or small businessman who deposits their savings regularly, no matter how small the amount may be, to be the most valuable client our bank can have.[23]

Banking is about relationships cultivated through hard work. When Giannini saw speculators drive his Bank's share price up to $300 in January 1925, he warned against gambling and urged the public not to buy the Bank shares in the open market. He insisted that there was no ground for wild trading in expectancy. He instructed all of his banking offices to refuse loans on Giannini shares.[24] His action was unprecedented then and now.[25]

He fought against and worked with the regulators to expand the Bank of Italy and create a bank holding structure. He spent years wrangling with state and federal regulators. He refused to give up the fight to change banking laws and regulations. He fearlessly acquired local banks and turned them into banks of his own vision. Throughout California, along the coast, the valleys, north and south, east and west, he created the modern banking practices of having branches to duplicate and stretch his vision of banking the little fellows whom typical banks shun. He won the state-wide banking battle in 1927[26] and targeted nationwide banking, a dream that he nurtured back in 1924:

> Under nationwide branch banking, an enterprise located in either the big city or the small village would have equal potential reservoirs of credit – perhaps running into hundreds of millions. Big business could do business anywhere. Moreover, this

---

[22] Ibid., at 61.
[23] Ibid., at 64.
[24] Ibid., at 175.
[25] Ibid.
[26] Ibid., at 268.

borrowing power would be absolutely independent of local conditions. The explanation, of course, is found in the word diversification . . . Why has California been an ideal proving ground for branch banking? Because its productive resources are remarkably diversified. But we do not, of course, represent California as being so fully diversified as the entire United States. Hence, a nationwide system has far more assurance of success from the very outset than had our statewide system. Under a nationwide system a section distressed through crop failures, floods, unemployment, or for any other reason, would experience no diminution in its local financial support for any legitimate purpose. A new factory, for instance, would be financed as well in a distressed section as in a prosperous one. The amount of distress would be lessened and recovery greatly speeded up.

Giannini's Bank of Italy then transformed to become Bank of America, National Association on March 24, 1928, when the Reserve Board approved the application of the new bank with trust powers and forty-five city branches.[27] By October 1945, BOA became the largest bank in the world, with more than $5 billion in assets.[28]

Giannini's legacy is etched in the mind of those who deeply care about banking business and innovation, including the three founders of SVB. Giannini never forgot the Santa Clara Valley from his years as a produce broker; he opened his first branch in San Jose. The Valley was dear to Giannini, as it was to the three founders of SVB. With the spirit of Giannini, SVB would seek out the high-technology clients that banks neglected. The high-tech clients would be SVB's "little fellow" in banking.

To realize their startup bank plan, Smith, Medearis, and Biggerstaff agreed to their equity stake distribution in the new enterprise. In recognition of their respective contributions to the founding of SVB, Medearis would receive 12,500 shares, Roger Smith 7,500 shares, and Biggerstaff 4,000 shares.[29] On stock incentive options, the Prospectus stated that the Board of Directors expected to grant Roger Smith 35,000 shares, Medearis 20,000, and Biggerstaff 10,000. Also, Medearis would be Chairman of the Board & Director, Smith the President & Director, and Biggerstaff the Vice President & Director. The new bank would pay Biggerstaff for his consultant fees of $21,000 in connection with the organization of the Holding Company and the Bank. There was a specific mention in the Prospectus about reimbursement to Medearis.

As to Roger Smith, the president of the Bank, his initial annual salary was set at $90,000 in 1983, $100,000 in 1984, and $115,000 in 1985. Regarding a bonus, Smith would receive as much as 25 percent of his initial annual salary in deferred compensation. The Bank agreed to provide Smith with a full-size, four-door automobile with expenses to be borne by the Bank, membership in the Foothills Tennis Club and up to three other clubs, life insurance of $200,000, and other medical insurance for him and his family. The Prospectus seemed to disclose plenty of information!

---

[27] Ibid., at 278.
[28] Ibid., at 477.
[29] 1983 SVB Prospectus.

5

Be Different from the Beginning

Apple Computer, Inc. released its "Think Different" campaign in 1997 to mark the return of Steve Jobs and to resurrect the struggling computer company. The *Think Different* campaign "got an audience that once thought of Apple as semi-cool, but semi-stupid to suddenly think about the brand in a whole new way."[1] Interestingly, *be different* is what Silicon Valley Bank (SVB) embraced and practiced from its beginning in 1983. The Bank distinguished itself from the crowded banking sector by serving entrepreneurs in the region since the early 1980s. At the time SVB was formed and officially named, "Silicon Valley" was considered unattractive for banking to capture the public attention and adopted the available moniker.

THE 45 DAYS OF FUNDRAISING RECORD

After the founders received the tentative approval for a state bank charter on February 16, 1983, the difficult part – fundraising – began. Silicon Valley Bancshares, the Holding Company of SVB, needed to raise the required money ($5,000,000) so the Bank could begin the state charter filing. The Company offered 500,000 shares, with 143,000 in reserve for sale to officers, directors, and organizers, at the price of $10 per share in the stock offering prospectus. The offering was not underwritten by any firm because the three founders, Robert Medearis, Bill Biggerstaff, and Roger Smith, simply didn't see the need to waste money on an underwriter. Also, no public market existed for the common stock of the Company. No one possessed a crystal ball to predict whether an established public market for the Bank's stock would develop after the Company finished selling all of the 500,000 shares. Technically, one could purchase and sell the common stock in over-the-counter markets through securities dealers, but when

---

[1] Rob Siltanen, "The Real Story Behind Apple's 'Think Different' Campaign," *Forbes*, December 14, 2011.

would trading activities occur for SVB's stock in 1983? Not any time soon, for sure, was the safe-bet answer. Consequently, investors who purchased the Holding Company's stock could transfer the shares immediately to others if they could find such buyers![2]

That meant the three founders must hustle to find buyers for the shares initially issued by the Company. It took them only 45 days to raise the $5,000,000 listed in the prospectus. Smith was exceedingly proud of the Herculean fundraising efforts for a startup, a community bank. To his chagrin, he discovered that, after he quit his comfortable and lucrative job as the regional president at Imperial Bank, the holding company of SVB had not secured the $5 million for the new bank to open for business. He was not thrilled; the other two founders and organizers had informed him that they had the money to entice him to join, but it turned out they were very far from the fundraising goal.[3] Fundraising for a new independent community bank was challenging then and still is today.

Going back to Imperial Bank was not an option, so the fearless Smith rolled up his sleeves and plunged himself into the fundraising efforts. Desperation is sometimes the best incentive. Smith had received an attractive investment commitment from North West Trust Company for $500,000, but before he was able to collect the gentlemen who committed the trust company to invest the $500,000 left the trust company! Smith flew up to Edmonton, Canada, to insist that the North West Trust Company pay the committed $500,000 or 10 percent of the shares for what they had promised to invest in the new bank. Among the prospective investors, the trust company was the largest, and only Smith was willing to chase after them for funding. Unfortunately, the prospectus listed that the North West Trust Company had committed to the amount. In a phone conversation with Smith, the management of the trust company acted incredulously in their efforts to back out of the commitment. Smith considered either shooting himself or flying up to Canada the following day. The next day Smith arrived in Edmonton and held a long discussion with the trust company officials. They negotiated back and forth; both sides knew that a lawsuit was possible but should be avoided. The trust company devised a plan; they would provide $250,000 the following week. For a startup bank with no money, the sum of $250,000 was a lot. The bank accepted $250,000 from North West Trust Company. Smith flew back with the check in his pocket.

Smith hustled. Medearis hustled. Biggerstaff hustled. They needed the money. The Prospectus stated that the Bank could not begin without having that amount and the charter approval was only provisional, so the three men were fretting about the prospect of not meeting the fundraising goal. Through personal contacts, some individuals and firms rose to the occasion to invest in the new bank. The largest personal investment was $100,000, a couple of people put in $60,000, but some folks

[2] "1983 SVB Prospectus," *supra*, Chapter 4, note 29, at 5.
[3] Interview with Roger Smith, February 25, 2022 (on file with author).

could only provide the minimum amount of $1,000. Smith noted other new banks at the time took as long as six months to obtain the necessary money to open. Around the same time, there was a bank that called itself a "Hi-tech bank" which failed after two years, and the FDIC took over the bank. The three founders pitched to potential investors with confidence in the idea that SVB would serve "hi-tech" companies and thrive.

Smith planned to keep his word, stating that he and his two cofounders were going to begin their new bank as planned. They promised the early investors that they would succeed with the fundraising efforts, and they would deliver on the promise. They indeed achieved their goal, with 200 shareholders, inclusive of the 100 special individuals who were listed in the Prospectus under "Founders Group."

THE 100 BANK INVESTORS–FOUNDERS

How could they sell off the shares to enable the bank to open its doors as planned? *Be different*, again, was the only strategy to employ in the fundraising efforts. The three founders came up with the idea of having 100 founders of the bank and each of the founders and their affiliations would then be displayed impressively in the prospectus. To be one of the 100 founders, each person must purchase 1,000 shares at the listed price of $10, and that meant the 100 founders at $10,000 each would yield the bank $1,000,000. Smith did not want just any bank founder. As the startup bank aimed at the hi-tech industry, the 100 bank founders should be influential men from that industry. As for women, very few were in tech in 1982–1983, and only two women were included in the list of the 100 individuals in the Founders Group.

Instant credibility was another key purpose behind the list of 100 bank investors–founders. A new bank possesses no credibility to convey. It rests on no goodwill as it aims to generate and build up that goodwill. The most efficient way to achieve the aura of credibility even before SVB was allowed to open would be to harness the credibility of each of the 100 individuals who embodied the business and the spirit of the burgeoning Silicon Valley. Their separate, and collective, reputations would endow SVB with the instant credibility that the three founders craved during the fundraising period and beyond.

All dollars are not created equal. The amount may be the same, but the value they possess is not the same. For Smith, Medearis, and Biggerstaff, money came from the men in the tech industry who would create a long-lasting positive impression on others. The good money carried unquantifiable value related to marketing, networking, business development strategies, and growth efforts of the startup bank. Smith and his two cofounders understood these points well. The good investment money which they raised, coming from known individuals in tech, would cement the startup bank's relationship with the technology sector from the beginning.

Moreover, having 100 important individuals signing up as its Founders Group signaled that the people in the community came together to create a bank for banking and lending for the individuals and businesses in the community. This was Smith's plan and dream influenced by President Kennedy's idea of community banking. The three founders also decided to separate the 100 individuals into subgroups "High Technology," "Professional and Financial Services," "Commercial Business," and "Real Estate and Construction."

One by one, they persuaded those who were in or possessed deep connections within, the technology industry to be the bank investors–founders. Smith made phone calls and personal visits. Medearis also reached out to some of his contacts, but most of the bank investors–founders in the "High Technology" group originated from Smith's network. The men from the "High Technology" group were mostly presidents or senior officers of top-tier tech companies, notably, Quantum Corporation, Convergent Technologies, Advanced Micro Devices, Kera Corporation, KMEGA Technology, Intel Corporation, MCI, Microvertics Corporation, Advanced Crystal Sciences, Inc., General Circuits, General Technology Corp., Mark Telephone Products, Inc., Plexus Computers, Inc., PH Components, Sorcim Corporation, Xidex Corporation, Naramics Corporation, Data Technology Corporation, Intectra, Inc., ASK Computer Systems, Inc., Ultratech Stepper, Selectone Corporation, California Biotechnology, Inc., Systar Corporation, Flextronics, Inc., Wilman Industries, Inc. Pacific Western Systems, Inc., Forward Technology, Inc., Microvertics Corporation, and Plantronics, Inc. Many of these companies continue to operate today. It is worth taking a look at a few of these founders listed in order to see the extensive network of power that was built by the Bank in their Founders Group, which would later be utilized to the advantage of the Bank's clients.

In reaching out to the high-tech industry in Silicon Valley in 1982–1983, Smith admired the individuals who had established themselves as leaders and earned enormous respect from their peers. For example, Dan Worsham typified the innovative entrepreneurial spirit.[4] He established his company, Pacific Western Systems, Inc., to build and manufacture semiconductor equipment that solved many problems that he and his clients witnessed first-hand. Worsham first joined Fairchild Semiconductor in 1959 as an engineer when the integrated circuit was announced by the famed company. Worsham worked with many Fairchild notables like Gordon Moore, Bob Noyce, and Jay Last. Worsham's life story before working at Fairchild is itself an inspiration. He spent several years in the Navy Reserve during high school and fought in the Korean War after he graduated from High School. He was severely wounded and lost his leg in Korea. Discharged after hospital operations and rehabilitation, Worsham went through the junior college system for three years and then transferred to Stanford. Unfortunately, he ran out of money

---

[4] "Oral History Interview: Dan Worsham," *Semi*, available at: www.semi.org/en/Oral-History-Interview-Dan-Worsham [https://perma.cc/P6F4-QF9K] (last accessed September 20, 2022).

just before graduation. In desperation, he appealed to a professor at Stanford for help. The professor sent him to meet Dean Knapic, the founder of Knapic Electro-Physics, known for manufacturing silicon crystals in South Palo Alto. Because Worsham knew how to grow crystals, Knapic recommended him to meet Bob Hall, the foreman of preproduction at Fairchild Research and Development. After an interview with Hall, Worsham received his job working for Dr. Bob Brown, a physicist at Fairchild, and Dr. Harry Sello, a pioneer in the semiconductor industry.[5] Later Worsham left Fairchild for Siliconix to support his family. Having witnessed many unsolved problems at Fairchild and Siliconix, Worsham was determined to found his own company. Pacific Western Systems had annual sales of $20 million in semiconductor equipment during its heyday.

Robert Campbell is another example of an entrepreneurial founder that SVB desired to include in its "High Technology" Founders Group. Campbell, a former Apple employee, founded Forethought in 1983, a few months before SVB opened its doors for business. Together with another Apple employee, Taylor Pohlman, Campbell planned to build a multi-purpose application that would integrate word processing graphics and spreadsheets using object-oriented technology. Their product was Presenter or PowerPoint, the enormously successful presentation software that allows users to tell their narratives powerfully and visually and capture the audience's attention. In 1987, Microsoft acquired Forethought for $14 million. PowerPoint continues to dominate the market today.

Another founder who was an inventor and problem solver was Courtney Phillip Graham. He designed the headsets for pilots and astronauts in 1961 in a tiny garage in Santa Cruz with Keith Larkin. The two men cofounded Plantronics. The company's notable moment arrived when Neil Armstrong declared "That's one small step for man, one giant leap for mankind" transmitted through a Plantronics headset on July 20, 1969. Graham became one of the Bank's 100 investors–founders after his friend, Dan Worsham signed up.

Likewise, C. Woodrow Rea, Jr., the President of Ultratech Stepper, Inc., was a member of the SVB Founders Group. The company was known for its product line of 1x microlithography steppers, using a unique catadioptric lens design. General Signal later acquired the company. Rea himself went on to become a partner at the venerable VC firm New Enterprise Associates (NEA). As Smith was signing up one founder, he made sure to leverage that founder's name to get other founders to sign up.

In embracing the tech entrepreneurs for SVB, Smith and Medearis understood that venture capitalists and venture capital firms were the key forces working with

[5] David Laws, "Harry Sello: Silicon Pioneer and Industry Personality (1921–2017)," *Computer History Museum*, April 14, 2017, available at: https://computerhistory.org/blog/harry-sello-silicon-pioneer-and-industry-personality-1921-2017/ [https://perma.cc/74DP-YAEZ] (last accessed September 25, 2023).

the entrepreneurs. They knew that, in the tech ecosystem, VC investors play the dominant role in selecting, growing, and scaling tech companies. Without VC funds, many tech companies simply could not exist. That meant the startup Silicon Valley Bank, just like their tech entrepreneur clients, needed the VCs to be on the 100 founders list. The startup bank received strong endorsement from general partners of VC firms, including Jamieson & Company, Mayfield Fund, Matrix Partners, L.P., and General Signal Ventures through Smith's relationships with VCs at his prior positions in the Special Industries Group at Wells Fargo.

The VCs whom Smith coveted include the legendary J. Burgess Jamieson, Thomas J. Davis, Jr., Donald Lucas, and Glen McLaughlin.

By 1983, Jamieson was already an established name among the VC community. With his MIT training in electrical engineering, Jamieson worked for Grumman Aircraft Corporation, although he found the job rather boring. Active duty called him out of boredom, and he served as a First Lieutenant in the US Army between 1952–1955. He returned to his passion for engineering by working in the next two decades at various companies, from established enterprises to startup firms, including Honeywell, Adage, Computer Control Company, and Electronic Memories Corporation. With an engineering mind for new technology and a keen business interest, Jamieson got his first taste of venture investment by turning around Sycror, Inc., a financially troubled tech company that received investment from Electronic Memories Corporation. His success with Sycror led to accepting an opportunity to team up with Bank of America and Jamieson cofounded WestVen Management, a venture capital partnership of which Bank of America was General Partner in 1971. Two years later, in 1973, Jamieson took the next leap and cofounded the Institutional Venture Associates and was a general partner at that firm for more than two decades. When SVB approached him, Jamieson had just become the owner of his Jamieson & Co., a private investment firm.[6] A year after Jamieson signed up his name as one of the bank founders, he cofounded Sigma Partners and created one of the highly successful records of venture capital investing for the next several decades.

Thomas J. Davis, Jr., is the Davis of "Davis & Rock," one of the first venture capital firms that he cofounded with Arthur Rock in 1961. Davis exemplified the quintessential east coast establishment product; he graduated from both Harvard College and Harvard Law School, and he was the captain of the polo team at Harvard. He and Rock received funding from several founders of Fairchild Semiconductor and William F. Miller, the then provost at Stanford University.

[6] J. Burgess Jamieson, "Bay Area Venture Capitalists: Shaping the Business and Economic Landscape," conducted by Sally Smith Hughes in 2009, Regional Oral History Office, The Bancroft Library, University of California, Berkeley, 2010; Burgess Jamieson: An Old-Fashioned VC, *Venture Capital Journal* (July 1, 2001), available at: www.venturecapitaljournal.com/burgess-jamieson-an-old-fashioned-vc/ (last accessed September 25, 2023).

They made their first investment in Teledyne Inc. for $200,000 and enjoyed watching their investment balloon to almost $3 million in six years.[7] Davis and Rock raised $5 million and invested $3 million into only fifteen companies in seven years, and the $3 million returned $100 million to investors. In 1969, Davis founded Mayfield Fund and had helped start more than 125 high-tech companies by the time of his death in 1990.[8]

Likewise, Donald Lucas was a known venture capitalist when Smith secured his name as an SVB founder.[9] To all VCs in the community, Lucas was among the earliest venture capitalists. He was bold and tenacious in fundraising; he raised half of the initial equity financing for National Semiconductor Corporation in 1957. He was credited with being instrumental in growing Oracle, Cadence Design Systems, Dexcom, Macromedia, and fifteen other successful companies. He was with Draper, Gaither & Anderson (DG&A), the first venture capital firm, and later with Sand Hill Financial Company. Years later, Santa Clara University named the business school after Donald Lucas. Santa Clara was where Smith earned his MBA before he joined Wells Fargo.

Glen McLaughlin, General Partner at Matrix Partners, grew up in a small town in Oklahoma. He earned his business degree from Price College of Business, University of Oklahoma, in 1956. After college, he served as a troop carrier pilot in the Air Force and then went on to Harvard for his MBA. He spent ten years as the CFO for Four-Phase Systems, Inc., 1972–1982, a VC-backed company. He switched sides, joining Matrix Partners, LLP, to nurture the seed and early-stage companies. He showed he believed in the startup SVB by investing $10,000 and was listed in the "High Technology" group of Bank Founders in 1983. After four years at Matrix Partners, McLaughlin founded his own company, Venture Leasing Associates, and he was the CEO there for seventeen years. Overall, McLaughlin founded fifteen companies and served on thirty-two corporate boards before he retired in 2003.[10] Smith knew that investors like McLaughlin would be tremendously valuable to SVB later when the bank grew and expanded to serve all aspects of the VC ecosystem.

7 "Thomas, Davis: High Tech Investor," *The Los Angeles Times*, September 17, 1990.
8 "Thomas J. Davis, 77, Investment Executive," *The New York Times*, September 13, 1990, available at: www.nytimes.com/1990/09/13/obituaries/thomas-j-davis-77-investment-executive.html [https://perma.cc/HF4C-ZAYZ] (last accessed September 25, 2023).
9 John Shoven, "In Tribute: Donald Leo Lucas, March 18, 1930–Dec. 27, 2019," *Stanford Institute for Economic Policy Research (SIEPR)*, available at: https://siepr.stanford.edu/news/tribute-donald-leo-lucas-march-18-1930-dec-27-2019 [https://perma.cc/GDY7-XZ7F] (last accessed September 25, 2023); "Donald L. Lucas: Special Limited Partner," *RWI Group*, available at: https://geechungdesign.com/rwigroup/team/don_l_lucas.html [https://perma.cc/9X56-KTSU] (last accessed September 20, 2022).
10 "PRESS KIT: Bio of Glen McLaughlin," *Wolfe News Wire*, August 19, 2002, available at: www.wolfenews.com/releases/PRESS-KIT-Bio-of-Glen-McLaughlin/00655/ [https://perma.cc/V2FJ-S4NR] (last accessed August 29, 2022).

As it turned out, thoughts about, and the cultivation of, relationships with VC investors were prescient for SVB's future.

Smith also secured support from individual investors such as H. Myrl Stearns and Charles Ying. They were all listed as the Bank Founders under the "High Technology" group. H. Myrl Stearns cofounded Varian Associates, the famed enterprise that researched and built the linear accelerator.[11] Smith, along with everyone in the area, knew that two tech companies that anchored the tech industry around Stanford University were Hewlett Packard and Varian. The founders of the two companies had all been students of Fred Terman at Stanford University's Engineering Department. Smith aimed for one of the two heavy-weight tech companies and was elated to get Stearns to be a founder of SVB. Stearns' Varian Associates invented and sold the Klystron, high-power microwave vacuum tubes used in radar systems as amplifiers or oscillators. Stearns himself grew up with five siblings on Idaho ranches and in lumber camps, receiving his early education in a one-room schoolhouse. He studied electrical engineering at the University of Idaho. Upon graduation in 1937, he went to Stanford for further education. He spent his first seven years after Stanford at Sperry Gyroscope Co. of New York, a leading defense contractor, to develop radar during World War II. He became a cofounder of Varian Associates in 1948 and served as its first Executive VP & General Manager. Subsequently, he became Varian's president in 1957. Varian Associates was the first business to find a home at the Stanford Industrial Park and Stearns served on the Varian Board until 1991.[12]

Smith was keenly aware that the Asian-American community was important in the tech industry in the Valley. He secured both Charles Ying and David Tsang as investors–founders in the Bank. Ying was born in Chongqing, China and grew up in Hong Kong.[13] At the early age of 16, Ying was accepted to MIT, along with his brother. He earned his engineering degree from MIT in two years and stayed in Cambridge to obtain both his MS in electrical engineering from MIT and his MBA from Harvard. He cofounded Atex Inc. in 1973 while pursuing his MBA. The company built automated-digital-printing press computers to replace the antiquated Gutenberg-type printing presses. Atex machines transformed how newspapers across the country printed their issues. Eastman Kodak acquired Atex in 1983. Ying then

[11] "Varian Associates: An Early History," *Varian Associates*, available at: www.cpii.com/docs/files/ Varian%20Associates%20-%20An%20Early%20History.pdf [https://perma.cc/YR24-HTYZ] (last accessed September 20, 2022); "Varian Associates: 1948 to Present," *Collection of Historical Scientific Instruments: Harvard University*, available at: http://waywiser.fas.harvard.edu/people/ 1020/varian-associates [https://perma.cc/44SP-V4DJ] (last accessed September 20, 2022).

[12] Sabin Russell, "H. Myrl Stearns: President, Co-founder of Varian Associates." *SFGate*, October 19, 2006, available at: www.sfgate.com/bayarea/article/H-Myrl-Stearns-president-co-founder-of- 2467937.php [https://perma.cc/54YF-BYSL] (last accessed September 25, 2023).

[13] "Charles Ying, Part-Time Vail Resident, 1946–2010," *Vail Daily*, September 29, 2010, available at: www.vaildaily.com/news/obituaries/charles-ying-part-time-vail-resident-1946-2010/ [https:// perma.cc/5PA2-C3R4] (last accessed September 25, 2023).

founded an investment group to invest in various startup companies. Silicon Valley Bank was one of the startups where Ying invested his money. Later, Ying founded his pet project, MyFonts, a digital fonts distributor in 1999. He also served as president and CEO of Information International Inc., a corporation in the automated document production and publishing sector.

David Tsang, a notable figure and founder of Data Technology Corporation, demonstrated success as one of the best semiconductor pioneers when Smith approached him. Tsang, a first-generation Taiwanese-American, worked at a Jewish club in New York City upon arrival from Asia to save money for college tuition at Brigham Young University in Utah. He majored in electrical engineering and later worked for Hewlett-Packard, but left the company in 1974 to cofound Xebec, a manufacturer of disk controllers. Xebec had an IPO for $70 million in 1982. The restless Tsang also founded Data Technology Corporation in 1979 to manufacture disk controllers and high-density disk drives. Again, this company had its IPO, for $140 million, in 1987. Tsang worked relentlessly and founded Oak Technology. He took this to its IPO for $200 million in 1995.[14]

Smith also signed up Francis Alan Moore, President of Shop Tools, Inc., to join the list of investors–founders. Moore is the brother of Gordon Moore, one of the founders of Intel. Smith was very pleased that he could get notable brothers because fame and credibility through association or blood were sufficient for Silicon Valley Bank's fundraising efforts. Another notable brother was Mark Wozniak, cofounder and general manager of Computer Plus, Inc. His brother is Steve Wozniak, cofounder of Apple Computer. The Computer Plus store was known as the original Apple store where individuals and businesses could see the latest Apple products, and Apple enthusiasts and developers could meet. Wozniak built his company to be one of the most respected computer resellers in the United States with exclusive Apple Education Reseller product rights for five states in the Western region. The store became the model and inspiration for Apple Store.

Another important individual in the VC ecosystem was S. Allan Johnson, Vice President, Western Technology Investments. His company carved out a niche to provide loans to tech companies to acquire their equipment. Western was ahead of its time in understanding what tech companies need and how debt financing would be crucial to the tech companies in their growth cycle. Smith welcomed Western into his referral network. Who could imagine that Smith would later join Western after he left the Bank in 1993?[15] Johnson signed his investment in Silicon Valley Bank.

---

[14] Qidong Zhang, David Tsang: Building a Better Future, *China Daily*, April 4, 2014, available at: www.chinadaily.com.cn/a/201404/26/WS5a30c814a3108bc8c672eb8c.html [https://perma.cc/GGK 8-WHBZ] (last accessed September 25, 2023).

[15] See Chapter 8.

Smith persuaded Mary Pacifico Curtis to become an investor. She was one of the two women included in the list with the ninety-eight men. She was an entrepreneur and maintained connections in the high-technology ecosystem. In 1977, Curtis founded her own advertising and public relations firm called Pacifico & Associates when she was only twenty-four years of age, two years after she moved from New York to California and changed jobs twice in the two years. She saw that, in Silicon Valley, young people founded companies, and she could too.[16] She built the firm into an award-winning advertisement and public relations agency for global tech companies and selected startups.[17] As a serial entrepreneur, she became an angel investor and advised Silicon Valley startups.[18] As the CEO of Curtis Electronic Music Chips, she worked to revive the Curtis Electromusic business as a unit of OnChip Systems with a new branding campaign, created new demand for old chips producing the "Curtis analog sound," and resumed manufacturing the authentic CEM3340 and CEM3320 chips in response to the new demand.[19] She served on the boards of many performing arts non-profits, and she herself later became an accomplished poet, literary critic, and author. Her firm is still in operation under the name "Pacifico Inc." and leads integrated advertising and public relations campaigns. The firm counts international tech companies like Samsung, THX, and TSMC as clients.[20]

The Founders group of 100 influential individuals were beyond doubt more impressive and valuable to the Bank than the names listed on the Board of Directors, according to Smith. The Bank would later rely on the Founders Group for referrals and to expand its services to meet the needs of tech companies. Most, if not all, of the Board members were not connected to the high-tech sector. The individuals who were in the real estate sector were brought in by Medearis to serve on the Board. One individual who stood out on the Board was Barbara Fairhurst. She was the only woman. Such was a rarity then and a testament to the three founders to invite a talented businesswoman to join the Board. Fairhurst was Executive Vice President and part owner of Sequential Circuits, Inc., in San Jose,

[16] Erik Chalhoub, "Los Gatos Author Mary Pacifico Curtis Releases Memoir," *Los Gatan*, January 19, 2022, available at: https://losgatan.com/los-gatos-author-mary-pacifico-curtis-releases-memoir/ [https://perma.cc/M66B-XGS6] (last accessed September 25, 2023).

[17] "Pacifico," *Pacifico.com*, available at: https://pacifico.com/ [https://perma.cc/A3ZG-MAN4] (last accessed September 20, 2022).

[18] "Mary Pacifico Curtis on Gitta Ryle," *Look What She Did*, available at: https://lookwhatshedid.com/story/mary-pacifico-curtis-on-gitta-ryle/ (last accessed September 20, 2022); Pacifico is a partner at Mighty Capital in San Jose. "Mary Pacifico Curtis," *Signal*, available at: https://signal.nfx.com/investors/mary-pacifico-curtis [https://perma.cc/QCT2-PYJP] (last accessed September 20, 2022); "Mary Curtis," *CrunchBase*, available at: www.crunchbase.com/person/mary-curtis (last accessed September 20, 2022).

[19] "Board of Directors: Mary Pacifico Curtis," *EMEAPP*, available at: https://emeapp.org/board-of-directors/ [https://perma.cc/JK4A-CSX4] (last accessed September 20, 2022).

[20] "Case Histories," *Pacifico*, available at: https://pacifico.com/case-histories/ (last accessed September 20, 2022).

a manufacturer of electronic keyboards, synthesizers, and other musical instruments. She joined Sequential Circuits in 1977 and worked her way to the executive vice president position at a time very few women held such a position in the music industry.[21] Fairchild made significant improvements in how products were manufactured at Sequential Circuits and stayed there until it was acquired by Yamaha in 1987. She was also an active leader in many civic organizations, including the San Jose YWCA and the Resource Center for Women in Palo Alto.

Most of the 100 individuals in the Founders Group were initially Smith's contacts. He invited them to invest their money in a new startup bank. He was committed to starting a bank with their money. He would hate to return the money to the 100 individuals if he and his two cofounders failed to reach their goal to open the Bank. He leveraged their names, credibility, and connections to raise the rest of the money.

LAWYERS AS CONNECTORS IN HIGH TECHNOLOGY

Medearis always believed that a good business plan includes a good lawyer. Smith understood the value of having lawyers as connectors in the high-tech industry. He learned that from his experience when his Special Industries Group at Wells Fargo shared the same building as the Wilson Sonsini law firm in Palo Alto. He felt he needed to get Larry Sonsini to be one of the 100 bank founders.

Think about it, Smith thought, a new tech company needs lawyers to assist in forming the new business entity or drafting documents for a deal. If the bank knows the lawyers, the lawyers would recommend the bank to serve their clients. Banking is about relationships. Smith wanted SVB to be part of the ecosystem where the lawyers play a key role on the legal side and the Bank would occupy a role on the financial and banking service side. If SVB were in that ecosystem, the tech company would stop by the Bank to deposit the check they had just received from investors based on the recommendation of the lawyers. Knowing the VC investors remains a pivotal part of the ecosystem. Knowing the lawyers who serve exclusively tech companies is another piece of the puzzle in the ecosystem. Larry Sonsini is definitely the lawyer that the Bank must know on a personal basis. Moreover, Sonsini solved potential legal problems for the Bank from the very beginning and, for that, Smith was so grateful.

Sonsini was born in Rome, New York. In 1949, he traveled across the country with his parents to Los Angeles where his father sought new employment. His entrepreneurial and dynamic father rose to the top of Hughes Tool Company. Sonsini went to the University of California, Berkeley, and played on both the football and rugby teams. He came down to the San Francisco Peninsula sometimes to play against

---

[21] "1983 SVB Prospectus," Chapter 4, note 29, at 18; "Barb Fairhurst," NAMM, July 26, 2010, available at: www.namm.org/library/oral-history/barb-fairhurst [https://perma.cc/6KHW-SLH9] (last accessed September 25, 2023).

Stanford. Law school was next for Sonsini. He graduated in 1966 from Berkeley Law School with an interest in securities law even though the corporate securities jobs were typically on the east coast. Instead of seeking a job with a traditional law firm, he listened to his law professor's advice about new excitement in the Peninsula and sought a position at a small firm there.

The firm was named after the four men comprising it: McCloskey, Wilson, Mosher & Martin. These four lawyers represented startup entrepreneurs and venture capitalists who invested in and built companies in the high-tech industry. No firm was doing this type of work exclusively. Newly minted lawyer Sonsini was excited to have the opportunity to be at the front line. Immediately, literally! He started to meet the young entrepreneurs of that time. He met Bob Noyce, the inventor of the transistor and brainchild at Fairchild and later Intel. He met Gene Kleiner, who, along with Bob Noyce, was among the famous "traitor eight" who jumped from Shockley Electronics to Fairchild Semiconductors in 1957. Bob Noyce, Gene Kleiner, and the other six men of the "traitor eight" each owned 10 percent of Fairchild. The venture capitalist behind the Fairchild deal was none other than Arthur Rock, who later joined forces with Thomas Davis, Jr. to create Davis and Rock. Kleiner subsequently formed Kleiner Perkins, one of the top-tier VC firms in Silicon Valley. The young lawyer also met other very early venture capitalists through his work for the law firm. They included Tommy Davis, Arthur Rock, and Don Lucas, among others. Many of these names were listed in Silicon Valley Bank's "High Technology" group! The circle was small back then.

By 1968, Pete McCloskey, one of the four partners of McCloskey, Wilson, Mosher & Martin, left to run for Congress. Sonsini and John Wilson, one of the partners of the firm, decided to build the firm to become a national, full-service firm to serve their tech clients and to grow with them. As the tech industry quickly transformed, the law firm must quickly adapt by having both expertise and deep relationships with clients. Wilson Sonsini added intellectual property, and antitrust, among their core expertise to serve the growing client base.

Wilson Sonsini was known by 1983 as the firm with a strong relationship-driven business model in the VC ecosystem. They were also novel by making investments in their startup clients. They accepted a warrant for the right to purchase shares in startups in exchange for the legal services the startups could not afford. Smith watched Wilson Sonsini and he liked what he saw. Smith also liked the law firm's client relationship practices by the lawyers, and he decided that, at Silicon Valley Bank, the Bank would not have customers because law firms, the Wilson Sonsini law firm, and the like, have clients, and so would his bank! After all, Smith would like all the lawyers who serve tech clients to send them along with their checks for deposit at his bank!

In addition to Wilson Sonsini, Smith and Medearis recruited the following lawyers and law firms to be on the 100 Bank Founders list. Smith wanted to list each lawyer and their affiliates separately to create a bigger perception:

Edward M. Alvarez, *Ferrari, Alvarez, Olsen & Ottoboni*
Chester H. Brandon, *Thelen, Marrin, Johson & Bridges*
Scot N. Carter
Matthew Hurley, *Hurley & Hurley*
Christopher Ream, *Ream, Train, Horning, Ellison & Roskoph*
Jane Relyea, *Howell & Hallgrimson*
Paul H. Roskoph, *Ream, Train, Horning, Ellison & Roskoph*
Warren R. Thoits, *Thoits, Lehman & Love*

The list seemed to include all the known lawyers and their associated law firms on the Peninsula! Moreover, Smith and Medearis circled in on the VC ecosystem by identifying the accounting firms, insurance agents, and executive search firms. They reached out to them and got $10,000 from each, along with their valuable networks.

THE THREE-LEGGED STOOL BUSINESS CONCENTRATION

Smith, Medearis, and Biggerstaff articulated to investors that the new bank was going to be different from other banks. The Silicon Valley Bank would concentrate on three areas: high technology, professional/business/commercial, and real estate. They loved the image of the three-legged stool.

That meant they reached out to individuals in areas outside of high technology. Medearis was in real estate and construction businesses through his work at Lusk and HCC, Inc. He brought in several individuals for the real estate subgroup listed in the 1983 Prospectus. Among those individuals was a real estate lawyer who was also one of the two women listed in the Founders Group. Jane Relya was an attorney with Howell & Hallgrimson when she agreed to invest in the new Silicon Valley Bank and be listed in the Founders Group. Relya graduated from The Ohio State University Moritz College of Law and then moved to California for a position at Howell & Hallgrimson in 1979. She became a partner and left the firm in 1990 for Terra Law for two years. Subsequently, she joined McPharlin Sprinkles & Thomas and practiced with that firm for 18 years until her retirement in 2019. Relya was known for her expertise in real estate transactions, including purchases and sales, financing, leasing and development, and loan workouts.

The fundraising efforts in the real estate and commercial areas rounded out what SVB's founders would need for the total sum. In addition, Medearis provided his HCC, Inc. corporate space to the Holding Company as its administrative office at 735 Live Oak, Menlo Park. He charged the Holding Company of the Bank $7,000 in rent for the office space that they used from March 1, 1982 until finding their own space. The management of the Holding Company during the fundraising period believed that the monthly rent of $500 was "as favorable as would have been available from an unaffiliated party."[22]

---

[22] "1983 SVB Prospectus," Chapter 4, note 29, at 24.

With the three-legged stool story as their sales pitch, Smith, Medearis, and Biggerstaff worked very hard and reached deep into their relationships in different circles of their networks within the Silicon Valley community to build a new bank. The 100 influential individuals in the high technology, business/commercial, and real estate sectors believed in the three men's pitches. They all came together for a new startup, invested some of their money, and trusted the three founders' belief that the new enterprise would be successful. The 100 individuals in the subgroups of the Founders Groups reflected the three-legged stool in fundraising efforts and business concentrations that Smith would execute as the first President and CEO of the Bank. Smith would later continue to emphasize the three-legged stool in his subsequent letters to shareholders along with the annual reports.

Finally, at the conclusion of the fundraising time, Smith could exhale after the money came in so the Bank could open for business. But not so fast, there were many new problems to solve before the big opening day.

AN ODD LOCATION AND THE ELECTRICITY PROBLEMS BEFORE THE OPENING DAY

The three founders selected an office space located in an industrial area surrounded by fields in the middle of nowhere. To the average person, the location seemed strange but to Smith, the location was perfectly different. He and his two co-founders wanted the new bank to be very different from all banks out there. Forget downtown offices. All banks occupied downtown areas. The industrial area seemed to be as different as it could be for a bank location. Indeed, there were no bustling commercial buildings nor foot traffic in action where typical bank offices were situated. Forget Menlo Park. Forget Palo Alto. Those locations would cost too much for a startup bank. The industrial area in San Jose would be wonderfully different because the Bank would be in the center of an area where its new high-technology clients were located and where all the action was taking place. The location would signal to everyone that the new bank would emphasize high-technology services as one of its three legs. Smith thought the location was ideal. It would attract attention, which meant free advertisement!

Look at it this way: instead of calling the building and location odd, Smith referred to it as "modern," with 5,300 square feet of interior space. The leasehold improvements included the installation of the bank vault, carpeting, and interior finishing work at the cost of $60,000. The Bank budgeted an additional amount of $90,000 for computers, printers, copying machines, telephones, furniture, fixtures, and other furnishings.[23] The monthly rent was $5,500 for the first couple of months and climbed to $7,206 when the fiscal year began on July 1, 1984. Nothing came cheap, even in a modern building at an odd location.

[23] "1983 SVB Prospectus," Chapter 4, note 29, at 8.

Dave Titus was incredulous when he saw the odd location; yet, he was happy he had decided to come for the ride when one day his boss at Imperial Bank, Roger Smith, asked him to take a walk. Odd, Titus thought. Smith never asked him to take a walk before.[24] Why walking? In California, you drive. On the walk, Smith offered the young smart banker an irresistible position to be different: a young banker to be in charge of the "Technology Lending" group at the startup bank. His new title would be "Vice President," which sounded impressive. He could not say no to the opportunity of exhilarating responsibility and more money. Titus was still young, still in his learning mode within the banking business. He did not have a family yet, so he stood to lose less by taking on this new adventure. He accepted the offer without knowing how odd the location would be. The new bank had four desks. The new bank used computers, the most precious and hi-tech equipment the young banker coveted. He was ready to lead the "Technology Lending" group of one as he was among the original first five employees of the Bank. Years later, the old building is still standing at 2262 North First Street in San Jose near the intersection of Charcot and North First Street, though the Bank moved out years ago. It would still be strange for any new bank to hang its sign for business there today.

Getting ready for the opening of the Bank was an exciting time. The organizers of the Bank had many necessary steps to complete before the Bank could commence its operation. They anticipated that the Bank would be ready by September 1983, but they could not pull it off. The application and organization activities took time. The organizers advanced funds for the organization's costs and operating expenses during the organization period. The Holding Company planned to repay these advances from the proceeds of the line of credit of $400,000 from a commercial bank. The organizers needed to secure the office space, hire contractors to remodel the space for banking purposes, furnish the new offices, and hire a couple of people, in addition to planning the festivities for the grand opening.

The opening would be on Thursday, October 20, 1983. All investors, shareholders, and friends were invited to celebrate the special occasion. The day before the opening, the Wednesday that Smith years later could not forget, he received a phone call from the building contractor. "You cannot open tomorrow," said the contractor. "Say what, again?" asked Smith. "You cannot get electricity to the building. We cannot get the electricity," the contractor convincingly declared to Smith. Immediately, Smith thought of the several hundred people who would walk through the door tomorrow for the open house. Too late to call each of them to cancel. It would be a crushing blow to not have the opening because there was no electricity in the "modern" building in an odd location!

Smith remembered Bill Biggerstaff's tennis buddy, Mr. Don Elliot, the President & CEO of Pacific Gas & Energy Company, and he suggested that Biggerstaff contact Elliot. Medearis was also a fraternity brother of Elliot at Stanford. Elliot

---

[24] Interview with Dave Titus on May 4, 2022 (on file with author).

was among the men in the poker group whom both Medearis and Biggerstaff had shared their business idea of a new bank with, and they had received encouragement and support from the group. Silicon Valley Bank, less than 24 hours from its scheduled opening, desperately needed Elliot and his connection at Pacific Gas & Energy Company more than ever! Everyone was from the same community. So Biggerstaff made the call to Elliot.

Biggerstaff dialed and reached Elliot's secretary and described the dilemma to her. Smith and Biggerstaff waited for hours as the problems were solved by Elliot's people. They got the electricity connected and the bank hosted its open house as planned. Again, the close-knit community came together, as it had for the fundraising in 45 days!

ANOTHER ODDITY: NO ADVERTISING SPENDING

Roger Smith believed that the Bank would never obtain enough money for advertising. That led to the conclusion that the Bank should not spend even a dime on advertisements. So, how did they get people to know about the Bank without spending any money on advertising? Smith and his group came up with an idea for getting free advertising for the opening of the Bank: "Clean suits."

Smith and Dave Titus concocted a plan to get some "clean suits" and wear them at the opening festivities on Thursday, October 20, 1983! Not suits that are professionally cleaned by one of those dry cleaning establishments in Palo Alto! One of the three legs the startup bank focused on was the high-tech industry so the "clean suits" were the white suits, the overall garment, static-free, with the ability to eliminate all dust and particles from contaminating the cleanroom that technicians needed to wear while making computer chips. These clean suits belonged to the semiconductor sector. These clean suits turned the wearers into Easter bunnies but without ears and tails. They certainly looked peculiar to the semiconductor sector as they are used to protect precious and delicate computer chips. Wearing the clean suits would definitely cause a stir and make an impression on everyone, Smith's instinct whispered loudly to him. One of the best candidates to wear one of the clean suits would be Paul N. McCloskey, Jr., also known as Pete McCloskey, a Director on the Silicon Valley Bank's Board.

McCloskey was all game. He was a Republican Congressman, representing San Mateo County from 1967 to 1983. They all knew him! He won the election after defeating Shirley Temple, the child star of the *Glad Rags to Riches* movie who turned politician and ambassador in her later years. McCloskey co-authored the 1973 Endangered Species Act while he was in Congress. He challenged Richard Nixon in the 1972 Republican primary without success but became the first Congress member to issue a public call for Nixon's resignation after the famous event called the Saturday Night Massacre. McCloskey then unsuccessfully sought the Republican nomination when one of the two US Senate positions representing

California became available. McCloskey was a graduate of Stanford Law School, and the first name listed in the four-man law firm joined by Larry Sonsini.

At the opening of the Bank, McCloskey took his place there. Dave Titus assisted him in getting in the clean suit. The photographer snapped the shutter and the picture landed in a nice big spread in the San Jose and San Francisco newspapers.[25] Everyone talked about it. Everyone saw it. Silicon Valley Bank indeed displayed its festive opening! Years later, people still remember the picture. That was exactly what Smith had hoped for – a free and notoriously effective advertisement, capturing Smith's idea of running a startup on its shoestring budget. The image also distilled a moment of ingenuity and displayed the spirit of a community getting together for the birth of a new business.

BIGGER PERCEPTION

From the very beginning, Smith aimed for a "bigger perception"; that is, whatever the bank was going to do, it must appear bigger to others. This audacious "bigger perception" became part of the bank's DNA. For instance, the list of 100 Bank Founders included all 100 names along with their affiliations in the 1983 Prospectus. Their names and affiliations certainly attracted attention because these were men of instant recognition who served in the three sectors the bank intended: high technology, real estate, and commercial. A few names for inclusion would not be sufficient to impress friends and competitors. One hundred calls to mind not only a large number but also pride, perfection, or fulfillment as seen in 100 percent. To be able to refer to the list and say to others that the bank had 100 founders conveyed the influence and intention that Smith, Medearis, and Biggerstaff possessed what it took to achieve success for the new bank and its investors. After all, the new bank began as a startup business that received money from investors, and investors expected returns from the enterprise. In subsequent years, the bank removed the affiliations but kept the names of the 100 founders in its annual reports. Some founders dropped off the list, but others were added, enabling the bank to tout the "100 founders list."

Smith wanted the "bigger perception" on the Bank's opening day. Smith wanted everyone to know that a new bank opened its door for business, and it would not be just any bank, it is the Silicon Valley Bank. He got the "bigger perception" for the Bank from former Congressman Pete McCloskey in the famous photograph of Dave Titus assisting the Congressman into his "clean suit." The photograph furnishes instant recognition, association, and influence. Smith and his men embedded

---

[25] See "Pete McCloskey, a Director of the Silicon Valley Bank's Board and a (Rep.) Congressman running for Senate, being helped into a clean suit by Dave Titus, SVB's Vice President of the Technology Lending division, during the ceremony opening Silicon Valley Bank held on October 20, 1983." Photo by Bill Andrews, available at: https://historysanjose.catalogaccess .com/photos/62311 (last accessed October 3, 2023).

"bigger perception" deep in the bank's DNA and years later people still recall the photograph.

Smith understood that people cared about "Who is in the deal?," so he selected names of influencers to amplify the Bank's image. Bill Walsh, the President of the '49ers, signed on at the beginning among the 100 founders. Each name illustrated the Bank's exposure to different niches of potential business. The power of referrals was the backbone of a successful community bank. Also, Smith kept his eyes open for new ways to constantly keep his startup Bank engaged in conversations in different circles. In many ways, Smith embodied the hustle we see today on social media, with influencers touting products and encouraging consumers to buy, but Smith did it all without the reach of social media.

Smith practiced "bigger perception" by appearing and speaking at many civic and industry events. When the Stanford Center for Entrepreneurship hosted its Third Annual Conference on Saturday, May 12, 1984, Smith was there to speak on "Alternatives to Venture Capital." He explained how his Bank could provide debt financing to startups, so they could maintain an equity base. He spoke immediately after Brooks Byers, cofounder of Kleiner Perkins, talked about capital formation for startups. When the White House hosted a conference on small businesses, Smith served proudly as a delegate, wearing his credentials imprinted with Silicon Valley Bank, Palo Alto, CA. He participated in many local clubs and his participation and attendance impressed others on the presence of SVB.

The bigger perception in accordance with Smith's vision, however, did not mean excessive spending. The opposite occurred. It was all about engaging in activities that magnified the Bank's presence. That meant he and his bankers must not be sitting at their desks but be out in the wider community to sign up accounts, knock on doors, follow up on leads, and cultivate relationships.

In projecting the bigger perception, Smith instilled frugality into the startup bank's DNA.

FRUGALITY

The young banker, Dave Titus, wanted a steak lunch or dinner to celebrate a loan or a big deposit, but Smith would not allow such frivolous expenses. IHOP or Wendy's was the only choice. Years later, Titus recalled fondly that he wished Smith would have given him a steak. A few years later, Smith relented by having dinner at Sizzlers with Kellogg. Still, frugality was running deep inside the Bank's DNA.

Smith worried from the very beginning about the bank's bottom line. As the President and CEO of the startup bank, he identified ways to minimize costs. To do that he was creative! His clients and employees knew that Smith's ideal business lunch was a sandwich eaten at his desk. Smith avoided all the expensive restaurants in town. The bank needed a blackboard for conducting meetings. Smith purchased one at a garage sale and was very proud of the acquisition. Personalized stationery?

Just forget about it at Silicon Valley Bank! The fancy personalized stationery would become scrap paper the moment the person received a promotion or quit. Smith refused to waste money on personalized stationery. It was not considered a good idea for an employee to talk too long on a local phone call. Smith implored his employees to cut the local phone call short, so they could take incoming long-distance calls in order to avoid situations of telephone tag.[26]

Smith tried to think of the bank's money as his own. He set examples for his employees. If he needed to make two short trips to the same city and airlines required Saturday night stays for cheaper fares, he would book both trips at the same time so he would make his trips look longer to qualify for the cheap fares. He outfoxed the airlines and their Saturday night stay requirement; he saved two-thirds of the regular weekday fare. Phone calls to the East Coast were cheaper if you made them before 8:00 a.m. Smith urged his employees to come in early to make the phone calls, so they could achieve two objectives of saving the bank some money with the cheaper rate and devoting the rest of the day to their work on West Coast time; but, if an employee had to spend a long time on a long-distance conference call, it was fine by Smith if it meant saving the employee from traveling or sitting in a waiting room later.

As the boss, Smith knew all too well the truism of "When the money is gone, the doors close," and he treated the responsibilities seriously. The startup bank must succeed. Smith never deviated from that focus. His nickel-and-dime mentality might draw sniggers from others. So be it: Startups must control costs and meet what they have promised to deliver. Smith's bank was a startup. Also, many of the bank's clients were startups or possessed a startup's frugal mentality. Smith proudly joined the tightwad executives and clients in the area.

One of the known tightwad executives then was Scott McNealy, CEO of Sun Microsystems. McNealy hung a sign in his office that CEO meant Cheap Executive Officer. To McNealy, cost-cutting was a competitive weapon and a corporate trade secret. He declined to reveal how his company eliminated waste and functioned efficiently.

Randy Hawks, Executive Vice President of Identix, noted that his employees were frequently on the road but must make phone calls to check in with their offices, and the company reduced the cost by installing a toll-free line that the employees could use whenever they needed to call the office. Hawks reduced the use of the cellular phone in his car when he was traveling by making a call to a client of interest ahead of time. He wanted to make sure that the person would indeed be available when he called, he would then pull over and use the less-expensive pay phone.

T. J. Rodgers, CEO at Cypress Semiconductor, drove a Honda Accord and used generic shampoo. Any managers who overshot the quarterly budget by 2 percent had

---

[26] Mark Schwanhausser, "Tips for Tightwads, Execs Tell How to Save Bucks," *The Mercury News*, October 14, 1991.

to face Rodgers in his office and explain why their spending was out of control. If his company projected a 10 percent increase in revenues, hiring could not rise more than 9 percent, manifesting his rule that productivity must increase faster than payroll. Each employee at Cypress Semiconductor was posted at a position guaranteeing the most productivity. To control the monthly bill from PG&E, Rodgers instituted a conservation policy that every non-essential light would run on an automatic timer and the roofs of AC housing units were coated with a white sealant to reduce the temperature around AC units by three degrees.

Eric Benhamou, CEO at 3Com, clarified that cost-cutting does not mean cutting down on quality. The competition requires companies to cut costs but enhance quality. Benhamou saved his company money through recycling. His employees salvaged pounds of materials that were typically discarded by peers. The salvaged materials were gold and silver used to make printed circuit boards! The company implemented a new method of cleaning its printed circuit boards to eliminate the use of ozone-depleting chlorofluorocarbons. The implementation earned his company favorable free publicity in addition to qualifying for tax benefits and earning extra savings.

Smith, the CEO of a startup bank, joined McNealy, Hawks, Rodgers, and Benhamous of the then high-tech sector in being tightwad executives strategically counting beans to ensure the survival of their enterprises.

THE HOLDING COMPANY, THE BANK, AND THE RISKS FROM THE BEGINNING

Medearis worked hard on getting Silicon Valley Bank's charter approved. On February 16, 1983, the Bank received approval to organize as a California banking corporation. On February 22, 1983, Medearis filed the Articles of Incorporation for the Bank with the Secretary of State's office, but approval did not mean the Bank could open for business immediately. There were a number of necessary steps which the organizers of the Bank had to comply with to enable the Bank to commence banking operations. They selected the initial office, acquired the lease for the premises, obtained Federal Deposit Insurance, purchased equipment and furniture, hired the first group of employees, promoted and prepared for the opening festivities, among others.

Following the prevailing banking structure, Medearis and other organizers created Silicon Valley Bancshares, the holding company of the Silicon Valley Bank. The Company was incorporated under the laws of California on April 23, 1982. Upon creation, the Company submitted an application to the Board of Governors of the Federal Reserve System also known as the "Federal Reserve Board" for permission to serve as a bank holding company pursuant to the Bank Holding Company Act of 1956 and to purchase 100 percent of the shares of the Bank. The Company planned to offer to sell common stock and raise $4,750,000 of the net proceeds from the offering to provide the capital required to operate the Bank. If all things went as planned, the Holding Company would function as a holding company of the Bank and invest any funds of the Company. They anticipated expanding by forming or acquiring new subsidiaries in both banking and non-banking areas.

The 1983 Prospectus stated that the Company would issue 500,000 shares to obtain gross proceeds of $5,000,000. The money would then be used by the Company to purchase all the shares of the Bank, to pay application and organization expenses, stock offering expenses and general corporation expenses. The Bank would receive $4,750,000 in proceeds for working capital, leasehold improvements, furnishing, application, organization, and preopening expenses of the Bank. Neither the Company nor the Bank could commend the operations of the Bank until the organizers completed the offering of the shares and received the requisite approvals of both the California State Banking Department and the Board of Governors of the Federal Reserve System. Actually, the California Superintendent of Banks would not authorize the Bank to commence until the Bank received $4,750,000 for its stock and satisfied all conditions.

Medearis and Smith knew that creating a new startup bank faced numerous competitions and risk factors in 1982–1983. The Bank aimed to engage in providing banking services to entrepreneurs and businesses in northeast San Jose in Santa Clara County. Not only did the Bank face competition from well-established banks with offices in desirable service areas, savings and loan associations, but other financial institutions also enjoyed superior financial resources compared to what were available to the new startup bank, which all made the banking sector extremely competitive. Additionally, there were many independent banks with money market funds that were not required to maintain interest-free reserves against the money market fund equivalent of deposits. Competitors surrounded the startup bank. In the Bank's primary service area, which covered portions of San Jose, Santa Clara, and Milpitas, the Bank faced one banking office with total deposits of $4,482,000. Meanwhile, the secondary service area encompassed a larger geographic area including San Jose, Santa Clara, Milpitas, and Sunnyvale. The Bank countered twenty-two competitive banking offices with a combined $411,835,000 deposits or $18,720,000 per office! The big banks with large geographic coverage possessed a larger war chest to finance wide-ranging advertising campaigns and enjoyed the ability to move their investment assets to regions of higher yield and demand. These banks were capable of instituting substantially higher lending limits than the new startup bank. In addition to these banks, saving and loan associations and credit unions circled the new bank. In fact, there were four of these offices with a total of $22,640,000 in deposits![27]

Bring them on, Smith was undaunted by the competition. His bank would leverage its independent bank status to flex its ability to aggressively court clients,

[27] "1983 SVB Prospectus," Chapter 4, note 29, at 11–12.

bank them, and lend to them in primary and secondary areas. With the specialized services in three targeted sectors, Smith believed local promotional activities and personal contacts by the Bank's officers, directors, and employees to all the 100 founders and their contacts would enable the Bank to compete. He figured as long as his bank could be profitable for a couple of years, some acquirers would buy out the bank. That would not be a bad idea. Just like many startups in tech, acquisitions become excellent prospects.

But there were things beyond Smith's control in the banking sector. The general economic and political conditions, whether domestic or international, governmental monetary and fiscal policies, directly affect banks. Economic conditions, from inflation, recession, unemployment, high-interest rates, and fluctuations in the money supply – you name it – may impose risks on banks. With his deep banking experience, Smith believed that he was ready to run his bank his way to weather economic conditions and uncertainties.

Smith knew the certainties of banking and that both the Holding Company and the Bank would be subject to extensive banking regulations. The nature of banking ensured such outcomes. Current and future legislation and government policy could drastically impact the entire banking industry in general and his new startup bank in particular. Around this time, proposals existed to permit banks to have interstate branches. Smith noted that recent federal legislation facilitated non-bank financial institutions (like savings and loan associations and credit unions) to provide checking accounts and to compete for deposits. This type of legislation might cause his bank to have to pay more on the interest expense. Like any bank CEO, Smith needed to stay on top of government regulations.[28]

Smith and Medearis targeted the tech sector as clients for the new bank. Under the "Proposed Services" described in the 1983 Prospectus, they clarified that the Bank would direct its attention to the high technology companies. This was a risk the Bank took because regulators did not like the term "high tech" which to regulators was synonymous with "high risk" at the time. They identified their three primary areas of service: high-tech, commercial, and real estate in the Prospectus. Under these proposed service areas, the Bank intended to provide "a high level of personalized banking services" to its clients. For lending to clients, the Bank promised that the clients would deal directly with experienced professionals who possessed the authority to make loan decisions. For deposits, the Bank anticipated being competitive with money market funds in order to attract clients for depositing their checks. All of these intentions meant that Smith must follow through with clients to consistently deliver on all the promises.[29]

---

[28] "1983 SVB Prospectus," Chapter 4, note 29, at 4–5; SVB's Annual Reports 1984, 1985, 1986, 1988.
[29] "1983 SVB Prospectus," Chapter 4, note 29, at 10.

As the holding company of the Bank, the Company's initial primary source of income, other than interest income earned on the Company's capital, would be the dividends distributed by and management fees paid by the Bank. The banking regulations even controlled the Bank's ability to make these payments. Paying dividends by the Bank would be subject to California banking law, which imposed certain restrictions on the amount. As a new startup bank, paying dividends was not on its immediate horizon. Survival was the focus! Thriving and growing revealed the next steps!

Smith was convinced that the Bank, with its three-legged stool and a strong emphasis on banking and lending to the high-technology sector, would work.[30] Confidently, he wanted on his tombstone:

I TOLD YOU IT WILL HAPPEN.

---

[30] All references to Smith are based on interviews with Smith conducted in March 2022 (on file with author).

6

Against All Odds

SVB AS THE STARTUP, CHEERLEADER, AND CONNECTOR

The unconventional approaches Silicon Valley Bank adopted in the early years challenged banking culture. SVB transformed into one of the largest fifteen banks in the United States by serving exclusively tech companies in innovation centers across the nation.[1] SVB was the startup, cheerleader, and connector to and for its clients in the tech sector.

MAKING PROFITS THE FIRST YEAR

Roger Smith could take a nice deep breath and exhale. The startup bank made profits in its first year of existence! This was nothing short of an astounding success story.

Smith was elated when he signed "R. V. Smith" above his name along with the title "President" on the very first Management's Report to the shareholders of Silicon Valley Bancshares or Holding Company that detailed Silicon Valley Bank's first full year of operations. The Company earned $222,000 or $.44 per share for the year. The number sounded and looked almost perfect, triple "2" for the total earned amount. After all, how many startups made profits in the first year of operation?

Glancing at the Bank's statistics of growth, Silicon Valley Bank saw deposits grow from $31,576,000 at the beginning of 1984 to $45,087,000 at the year's end, representing a 2.34 percent growth rate. All deposits arriving at the Bank were from local clients. On the loan side, the Bank noted an increase from $7,619,000 to $30,013,000 in 1984! The loan growth stemmed from referrals from existing clients, the Bank's 100 Founders Group and other shareholders, Venture Capitalists (VCs), lawyers,

---

[1] This chapter is partially based on interviews with: Roger Smith on February 25, April 18–19, 2022; Harry Kellogg on March 4, 30; and April 18, 2022; Dave Titus on May 4, 2022; and Aaron Gershenberg on April 18–19, 2022 (all on file with author).

and accountants in the local community. The Bank generated interest income in 1984 of $4,459,000, resulting from both interest and fees on loans of $3,425,000. That meant the average yield on loans and investments was 13.5 percent. Comparatively, the interest expense that the Bank incurred for the same period totaled $2,496,000, representing an average cost of funds at 7.9 percent Indeed, the numbers easily demonstrated how the Bank earned its profits in the first year!

With these numbers, the Bank demonstrated that the community needed the Bank, and the community helped build the Bank. Smith was right on target with his business model to be different in every aspect and to build a network of referrals in the community. Banking is truly about relationships. His bank grew and prospered in the first year because of the special relationships formed before the opening and subsequently nurtured and expanded every day by SVB's team of believers. No question about it, hard work coupled with smart work propelled the Bank to its first finish line at the end of 1984 with outstanding results. Like all startups, the Bank needed to continue to innovate and grow, and that is what Smith intended to do in 1985.

During the first full year of operations, Smith solidified the three major business areas for the Bank: High Technology, Commercial, and Real Estate.[2] He strongly believed that "by focusing specific resources on these three separate markets we have been able to establish a fine reputation as a place to receive quality banking service."[3] The three areas anchored the Bank's business; the three-legged stool encapsulating Smith's strategy from the beginning and cementing the Bank's services. In fact, Smith was particularly fond of the three-legged stool image, a known wonder of physics, a more stable stool than its cousin with the extra leg – a four-legged stool, a daring sitting device that allows a person to sit on an uneven surface because the ends of the three legs are always situated on the same plane. Each market area of the Bank's services was one leg of the three-legged stool. The three areas, at least in the early years of the Bank's operation, would provide stability and flexibility because the Bank's business in one market contributed to the other two and, in return, all three markets established the whole, so they could lean on each other and grow. For instance, the deposits from the High Technology clients would be used to make loans to the Real Estate clients. High Technology clients received their infusion of money from investors and these clients actually didn't need many loans. Real estate clients needed more loans. The Bank would achieve earnings by paying low interest on deposits and lending at high-interest rates. The commercial sector didn't need as many loans as the Real Estate and Construction clients, and they didn't generate as much in deposits as the High Technology clients; but the Commercial clients were an important segment of the community and provided

[2] Roger V. Smith, "Management Report to Shareholders," *Silicon Valley Bank*, 1984 (on file with author).
[3] Ibid.

excellent referrals. Smith kept the image of the three-legged stool in his mind, even years later.

The Bank's 1984 growth in earnings, deposits, and loans in the three areas confirmed to Smith that the Bank operated in "one of the most exciting market-places in the world,"[4] and he was serious about creating enthusiasm. In the High Technology market or "one of the three legs" of the stool, Smith strived to "establish and maintain a well-balanced client portfolio of quality companies and individuals" in this market. He saw that, in the first full year of operation, the client base expanded tremendously to cover a "solid cross-section of companies" and he noted that high technology meant much more at the time because it consisted of telecommunications, defense electronics, semiconductor manufacturing, computer peripherals, application software, and medical electronics. The base continued to expand as entrepreneurs and their enterprises innovated at a fast speed. Smith also observed that the client base in these broad sections included not just the companies but many private and institutional venture capital firms.[5] The key ingredients for the expansion of the high-technology client base were "the strength" of the Bank's "network of contacts in the Silicon Valley."[6] In the 1984 Management Report to shareholders, Smith promised that the Bank would work "to enhance our reputation as one of the major forces in the financing of emerging technology-based companies."[7] That could only be done with the assistance of the Bank's "excellent group of Founders and Stockholders from the technology community."[8] In many ways, Smith predicted the network effects with amazing prescience stemming from the 100 founders and the VC community as crucial to the Bank's identity as the bank for the innovation economy in years to come.

The exciting community, for the Silicon Valley Bank officers and employees, was where they would recruit potential clients, build relationships, and provide quality banking services. The bankers at Silicon Valley Bank didn't wait for the clients to come to them. They searched for new clients. They called on every high-tech startup in their first or second year in operation.[9] They tried to sign all of these companies up for their deposits at the Bank. Smith reminded his bankers, "We're mainly knocking on doors for deposits, not loans."[10] The startups often possessed lots of cash from the VC funding rounds. The Bank wanted the startups as clients from their early years.

[4] Ibid.
[5] Ibid.
[6] Ibid.
[7] Ibid.
[8] Ibid.
[9] Ralph King Jr., "Electronic Banking, Making Loans to Young High-Tech Companies Only Sounds Risky. That's Why Silicon Valley Bancshares is So Profitable" *Forbes*, August. 20, 1990.
[10] Ibid.

The Bank refused to use the word "customers" but warmly embraced the word "clients."[11] Clients are not merely customers. Just like law firms, especially the Wilson Sonsini firm for tech companies, SVB had clients. SVB opted for the idea of having bank clients, with relationships cultivated and enhanced, so the Bank would become the indispensable partner of the clients in their growth. The Bank would grow with the clients. Smith shared with Joel Kotkin, who wrote in an *Inc. Magazine* article recognizing Silicon Valley Bank as one of a rare breed of new banks in 1984:

> In a way, we are trying to be like a small-town bank. We look at the explosion of small companies around here and spend our time helping them develop. We want to be there at every level, helping them plan their growth and giving them the advantage of our networking.[12]

What Smith described was exactly what entrepreneurs like Ron Murphy and John Dillon needed in 1984. Murphy and Dillon sought assistance from the Bank when the men founded their own company with a couple of engineers from ESL Inc., a subsidiary of TRW Inc. in Sunnyvale. The men didn't know much about building and financing their startups. After an encounter with the tireless SVB CEO, Roger Smith, at the Junior League of Palo Alto's annual "Silicon Valley Follies," the men received the services that they craved. Smith allowed the young startup company to use a conference room for meetings in the evenings and on weekends when the Bank was not in operation. Smith introduced Murphy to an attorney and financial advisers to form their legal and corporate team. Bob Gunderson, the attorney whom Smith recommended, then connected Murphy and his engineering team to receive venture capital from Hambrecht & Quist and Seidler Amdec Securities. Murphy and Dillon's startup company, Delfin Systems Inc., flushed with VC investment, subsequently deposited its new money with Silicon Valley Bank. As the company expected to reach its milestones, new deposits received from VCs would make their way to the Bank.

Another fledgling company, Legacy Computer Systems, founded by entrepreneur Rick Ramras, needed a loan to meet the demand of a big order of $750,000 from AT&T for 210 customized Kaypro portable computers. Ramras' company would add printed circuit boards that allowed these devices to run on the then three major operating systems CP/M, MS-DOS, and Bell Telephone Laboratories Inc.'s Unix. Ramras was required to deliver the computers before AT&T finished its corporate restructuring scheduled at year's end. The company was desperate to borrow $300,000 for payments to suppliers and subcontractors. Ramras himself sought help

[11] Smith, "Management Report," *supra.* note 2.
[12] Bradford W. Ketchum Jr., "The Inc. 100," *Inc. Magazine*, May 1, 1984, available at: www.inc.com/magazine/19840501/5649.html [https://perma.cc/UUG8-HGR2] (last accessed September 26, 2023); Joel Kotkin, "The New Small Business Bankers," *Inc. Magazine*, May 1, 1984.

from a local branch of a well-known giant bank but was told that he must wait 60 to 90 days for a decision on the loan. He then went to a small, locally-owned independent bank, but the bank also declined because it was unfamiliar with the computer market sector. However, this independent bank suggested Ramras reach out to Smith at Silicon Valley Bank for high-technology lending. Ramras met up with Smith and the young Dave Titus at the Bank located in the odd location in the middle of the industrial part of northern San Jose. Smith and Titus welcomed Ramras, quickly obtained all the details of Ramras' deal with AT&T and assessed how Ramras would be able to fill the order for the customized computers. The company's revenue for 1983 reached $2.3 million from the add-on circuit boards to computer devices. Smith and Titus made their calculations. No loan committee existed to decide on the loan applications. Smith and Titus constituted the de facto committee, they looked at the loan as a money-making deal for the Bank, and they offered a resoundingly positive answer to Ramras. Within 48 hours Ramras picked up a cashier's check for $300,000. The swift action from Smith and Titus enabled Ramras to fulfill the order on the clock and facilitated the company's reception of subsequent orders from AT&T. Consequently, the company's sales were expected to reach $5 million at the end of 1984. The company picked the right bankers, and the bankers met the company's demand. To Smith, the way SVB served clients "happens to be a hell of a good way to build a bank."[13]

Both Smith and Titus worked together to craft the Service Statement that the Bank issued before the opening day in 1983. They envisioned how they wanted to be treated as a client and articulated the Bank's promise to all clients with the following bullet points, which sound like the Bank's manifesto:

- Each Client will have a Banker and an alternate Banker.
- Each Employee will have Clients assigned to them.
- Each Client will be treated in the same manner as we would treat a good friend.
- Our treatment of Clients and potential Clients will be consistent, whether in person, on the phone, or in written communication.
- We will strive to accommodate our Clients' needs by handling the transaction, referring it to our friends if appropriate, or counseling the Client to reexamine their needs.
- Training of our staff will be continually available to allow each of us to do our jobs in the most professional manner.

Smith was very proud of his decision adopting the approach of calling the tech entrepreneurs and enterprises "clients" instead of "customers" in 1984. He made sure that his *Management Report* to shareholders included the Bank's preference for "clients," setting the Bank apart from its peers at the time and forming the Bank's

[13] King, "Electronic Banking," *supra*, note 9.

long-term version of the banking relationship as a partnership for years into the future of Silicon Valley and tech communities nationwide. But of course, at that time in 1984, Smith and his officers at the Bank could not predict the future. They needed to see how 1985 would unfold.

THE STARTUP BANK BEYOND THE FIRST YEAR

Silicon Valley Bank changed its legal counsel in 1985. The leading and innovative tech law firm Wilson Sonsini Goodrich & Rosati accepted the position of General Counsel to the Bank, signaling a new and exciting chapter at the Bank. Indeed, the Bank declared for the first time that it would distribute dividends of $279,000 to its Holding Company on December 31, 1985. The return on shareholders' equity jumped from 4.9 percent in 1984 to 9.5 percent in 1985. The total number of shareholders hovered around 350 shareholders of record.

The Bank's growth in earnings, loans, and deposits in 1985 attracted the banking sector's attention. *The Findley Reports*, a California banking newsletter, rated the Bank as a "Premier Performing Bank" because it met stringent growth and profitability goals and belonged among the 24 percent of independent banks achieving this top rating recognition. The Bank experienced strong growth in deposits which increased by 50 percent from 1984 to reach $67.5 million in 1985. The loan portfolio, likewise, leapt to a 52 percent increase over 1984 to $45.5 million. The astounding growth in 1985 yielded earnings of $451,000 or $.90 per share or a 103 percent increase over 1984's numbers. Both Smith and Medearis jointly signed their *Letter to Shareholders*, attributing the tremendous growth to the efforts of cementing the Bank's reputation as the bank that serves "clients" not mere customers. The bank was where clients received timely superior service and extensive networking relationships.

After just a little more than two years in operation, the Bank had transformed into "a front-runner" in the technology market. The Bank was daring; on the second anniversary of October 17, 1985, the Bank opened its first Regional Office in Palo Alto to be near the heart of the tech community in Silicon Valley. The Technology Division of the Bank had now developed specialized products and services as the client base became so diverse. One interesting development occurring in 1985 was the Bank's change of phrase from "High Technology Division" to just "Technology Division." Omitting that word was not an accident but an evolution in the Bank's understanding of its business and an attempt to educate the regulators that "high technology" did not mean "high risks."

Technology companies, as the Bank explained to the regulators, covered a wide spectrum, including "electronics, computers, semiconductors and equipment, medical technology and others." These enterprises were mostly in the business-to-business segment, meaning they invented, manufactured, or made devices for other businesses. These enterprises generated accounts receivable because they had a strong and established customer base. That meant loans to these companies were against the receivables. Given their revenue, sales, customer orders, and deliverability, the Bank's loans to these companies were not "high risk," as regulators had mistakenly believed. Dave Titus could not bear the sight of the federal and state bank regulators whenever they arrived at the Bank and spent days inspecting it. He had to gather and pile his stack of loans to tech companies in front of the regulators. Titus showed them that each loan to tech companies was paid. Not a single loan was a bad loan. No nonperforming loan resulted. Loans to the Bank's tech company clients were the safest and soundest. One by one, Titus made sure that the regulators saw the loans that his group made were repaid. He felt vindicated that lending to tech companies was not "high risk" as the regulators often assumed. Eventually, it was time to retire the word "high" from the "High Technology Division" for good.

Smith noted that some of these technology enterprises were growing fast, and the Bank must adaptively respond to clients' demands in the Technology Division. In 1985, the Bank met the then-new challenges by providing the following specialized products and services to tech companies at that time in Silicon Valley when no bank came close to serving the tech entrepreneurs and their enterprises:

- Cash management services – advising, designing, and implementing investment programs for liquid companies.
- Multiple pricing options – offering clients the choice to include warrants or other equity participation incentives in the credit pricing model.
- Leasing – arranging traditional and tax-oriented capital equipment leases for the needs of companies in all stages of development.
- International banking – providing and negotiating import, export, and standby letters of credit.
- Investor-assisted bridge financing – helping smooth out the timing of equity offerings.

That list was a startling transformation of tech lending. No bank had ever devoted significant expertise and resources to serve the tech community as Silicon Valley Bank did. Smith's two decades of technology lending and banking at Wells Fargo and Imperial Bank paid off handsomely; the list exhibited Smith's vision of serving the technology sector within the VC financing ecosystem.

Dave Titus, two years older and a wiser banker from when he joined the Bank in October 1983, rose quickly and became the Senior Vice President and Manager of the Technology Division of SVB; but Titus decided to leave in 1986. The fast-growth Technology Division also included Robert C. Pedersen, Vice President of the Palo Alto Regional Office; David Harvey, Assistant Vice President; Leslie Leonetti, Client Service Officer; and Emelysa Delpasen, the Administrative Assistant in the group. Restless, Titus sensed that he had learned as much as he could from the banking side, and he wanted more. He left the Bank but continued working in the technology sector. In 1986, Titus joined a firm that put together the second-largest fund in the VC financing ecosystem.

Thereafter came Harry W. Kellogg III as the new Senior Vice President in charge of the Technology Division in 1986. Kellogg reunited with Smith in churning the tech banking and lending process with fast speed and elevated the meaning of relationships to new heights. Another milestone in the Bank's early history in 1986 was the merger with National InterCity Bancorp which allowed the Bank to gain additional capital. This was no small accomplishment for a bank that had been open just three years! The Bank opened a new office in Santa Clara to serve its expanding client base.

Kellogg, with his understated charm and keen intuition for networking, greatly enhanced the tech lending division in the years to come.

HARRY W. KELLOGG III, SVB'S HEAD OF TECHNOLOGY DIVISION IN 1986

Kellogg considered himself lucky to be born in California. Grass Valley, California, not the glamorous Hollywood or shiny San Francisco, was his birthplace. Grass Valley was an area where farmers loved talking of goats of all colors (solid blacks, solid reds, solid tans, red paints, black paints, tan paints, black spotted, red spotted, tan spotted, correct spotted, and all quality percentage, full blood and purebred Boer goats). Kellogg's father was in service and was sent to a camp in Grass Valley in 1943 just before the war. Both of Kellogg's parents and grandparents came from Cleveland, Ohio. The baby Kellogg departed Grass Valley with his parents soon after birth and spent his first three years in Cleveland, Ohio.

When the war was over, in 1946, Kellogg's father spoke to some of his buddies, all of whom yearned for a permanent move to California. Fortunately for baby Kellogg, his father secured a job at Ames Research Lab in Mountain View, so the family moved to Palo Alto. At that time Palo Alto was a small town with a small Main Street and Stanford University. Kellogg loved growing up in Palo Alto. He went to elementary school, junior high school, and high school in Palo Alto. He was tall and strong, and he loved playing football. Years later, with modesty, Kellogg said that he hated to admit that he was an ex-football player. He played football at both Menlo Park, an all-men college in Atherton, and San Jose State University. He was good at football, so he was recruited while at Menlo Park and then transferred to play at San Jose on a football scholarship! He majored in finance at San Jose State.

In the early 1960s, employers conducted campus interviews to select trainees. Kellogg scored interviews with several firms, including Wells Fargo Bank. He liked the story of Henry Wells and William G. Fargo who founded the bank in 1852 when trains, canals, and stagecoaches forged an elaborately interconnected means of transportation, communications, and commerce that transformed economies and communities throughout the United States, from California to New York. Wells

Fargo bank and its branches served both established and new communities, industries, and individual customers across time. Kellogg was inspired by the stagecoaches
that brought Wells Fargo customers to what they valued most and drove them
forward. He desired to be a branch manager at Wells Fargo and settle down with
a wife along his career path. He accepted his position in retail banking at Wells
Fargo in the Mountain View branch. The boss and branch manager was none other
than Roger Smith! Kellogg was the assistant manager.

In those olden days, Kellogg liked to say, the branch manager was powerful
because the corporate accounts were controlled by the branch. That meant
Smith's Mountain View branch possessed a powerful portfolio of many high-
technology companies: Intel; Fairchild; Rambus. All the who's who of the high-
tech industry were the customers of Wells Fargo's Mountain View branch. Smith
and Kellogg cultivated connections and relationships with the founders, the officers,
the established and the new entrepreneurs, and practically all who were in the
semiconductor industry and semiconductor equipment industry. Bob Noyce, the
CEO and one of the founders of Intel, was a customer. Gordon Moore was one of
the founders of Intel and was also a customer of Wells Fargo's Mountain View
branch. Smith, Kellogg, and other bank officers got to know the investors in these
tech companies. The VC relationships with the bankers blossomed in the late 1960s
at Wells Fargo.

Kellogg remembered how the visionary Smith later decided to start a new
corporate bank service called the Special Industries Group in the Palo Alto office
of Wells Fargo. Smith's business acumen astounded Kellogg because the Special
Industries Group was located in the same building where the famous law firm
Wilson Sonsini was situated. Picture this: an entrepreneur came to the building to
see the Wilson Sonsini lawyers for counsel, signed various documents and received
a brand new check from investors, then the entrepreneur took the elevator down to
the first floor of the building, and the entrepreneur would drop by the bank at the
end of the elevator ride and deposit the check on his way out! Literally, the Special
Industries Group followed their clients and operated within the circles of connectors. Kellogg loved working as one of the lenders in the Special Industries Group,
where he spent three years. The bankers cultivated and deepened their ties with the
investors and the VCs. They formed long-term and invaluable relationships with
Sequoia, Kleiner, Perkins, NEA, and many other marquee VC firms in the
early days.

In the Special Industries Group, the bankers displayed great innovation. They
observed how some companies with VC backing grew very fast and of course were
flooded with money at later rounds of financing or at an exit event of being bought
out by bigger companies. The bankers wanted to serve these companies in their
early stages and meet their needs in getting equipment leases, in addition to banking
and lending needs. Most importantly, the bankers also wanted part of the growth
experienced by the companies. How could they get in at the early stages though

when companies lacked traditional prerequisites for loans? The bankers asked for warrants! A warrant is the right to purchase a certain number of shares, typically at a low price and a specific date. The company must issue the warrant as part of the cost of obtaining a loan. The bank would hold on to the warrant and cash out at a later time when the company, for instance, is acquired by a bigger company at a very high valuation. This practice was quite novel at the time when Smith implemented it at the Special Industries Group.[14]

Young Dave Titus, who had just started at Wells Fargo as a trainee at that time, learned about the Special Industries Group and how they served the high technology industry, and he was in awe. He wanted to be in that type of practice. He looked up to Smith, Kellogg, and other experienced bankers in the Special Industries Group, and recalled them with fondness and reverence years later.

The Special Industries Group, however, faced its demise in the Wells Fargo environment. Smith felt that the management at Wells Fargo headquarters in San Francisco didn't understand or appreciate high technology customers. The management was dismissive of Smith's presentations on high-technology companies and loans to such clients. He felt like a fish out of water each time he attended meetings with management and informed them about loans made by the Special Industries Group to companies with unfamiliar names. Unfamiliarity, unfortunately, meant fear and uneasiness regarding lending to high-tech companies because "high technology" meant "high risk" to the powers that be.

Their fears were realized when one big bad loan was made by the Special Industries Group. A call from senior management in San Francisco to Smith conveyed what management had believed all along – that high technology indeed meant high risk, and the group was to be shut down. All the bankers in the Special Industries Group either left or moved to different groups in Wells Fargo.

Kellogg was crushed. He stayed briefly in the middle market group at Wells Fargo but escaped to Bank of the West to meet his calling on high-technology lending. Kellogg believed that the technology sector was the future, and he wanted to be part of the action. At Bank of the West, he started a high-technology lending group for that bank. The bank was a wholly owned subsidiary of the French international banking group BNP Paribas, with its executive office in San Francisco. Kellogg received a very comfortable salary and incentives to build the high-technology lending group at the bank. He hired a banker who had worked for him in the Special Industries Group at Wells Fargo. Kellogg leveraged his expertise and connections in the tech ecosystem and started a fund to invest in companies. Among his famous accounts at the Bank of the West were Sun Microsystems and entrepreneurs "who have gone on to do important things." Scott McNealy and Andreas Bechtolsheim were among those entrepreneurs that Kellogg nostalgically recalled years later.

---

[14] Interview with Roger Smith, *supra*, Chapter 5, note 3.

Kellogg learned about Smith's new startup Silicon Valley Bank in 1983 when Smith called him to entice him to join, but he didn't want to give up his high-level executive job at the Bank of the West along with the support that his group received from the BNP, especially the international banking service portion. However, the honeymoon period with the Bank of the West did not last long. Kellogg felt that BNP, the owner of the Bank of the West, was "a little onerous and overbearing." Kellogg was fed up. Years later, Kellogg recalled a fancy dinner that he had organized for the President of BNP San Francisco office to meet with Scott McNealy, Vinod Khosla, and Andreas Bechtolsheim of Sun Microsystems. With the dinner, Kellogg sought to make future referrals to BNP given the French bank maintained an extensive international network. Sadly, the French man at the dinner was snobbish and didn't care for the referrals. After the dinner, Kellogg concluded that BNP didn't understand the business of lending to new tech companies and never would, leaving him feeling uncertain about his future at the Bank of the West.

Smith called Kellogg again in 1986 when Kellogg was feeling "a little vulnerable" about his career. In October 1986 Kellogg reunited with Smith at the Silicon Valley Bank upon hearing about the three-legged stool business strategy and that Kellogg would be the banker in charge of one of the three legs: The Technology Division of Silicon Valley Bank. He would remain for the next thirty-one years.

GROW WITH THE CLIENTS: EXTENDING A CREDIT LINE AGAINST RECEIVABLES

Smith and his bankers understood that their clients, the startups and the entrepreneurs, worked really hard, and the Bank must work equally hard. The bankers put in long hours. They held meetings at seven in the morning. Smith worked seven days a week. Like their startup clients, the bankers consciously watched all their spending. No three-martini lunches existed. No cocktails and dinner. Like their clients, they were ready to seize new opportunities, sign up for new accounts whenever they met somebody new, and to identify unique ways to help tech companies. Smith and Kellogg instilled the working-hard-like-startup-clients ethics deep in the Bank's DNA. New hires quickly learned that SVB was not a traditional bank.

Smith spent significant time promoting the bank. He understood public relations well, but he aimed for effective PR without a high price tag. Instead, he sought speaking engagements in town and with out-of-state banks and industry meetings to talk about his unique bank. Through this networking, Smith met bankers at different banks for potential partnerships whenever SVB needed corresponding banks, and a hunting ground for luring the top bankers to work at SVB.

One of the unique ways the Bank assisted its startup clients was by lending against receivables to tech companies and requiring warrants as part of the loan cost. This strategy allowed the Bank to grow with the clients and benefit from the client's fast growth. Here is how that strategy worked.

In the early years, the Bank made loans to tech companies that already had customers and generated accounts receivables, and the customers of these tech companies were typically large entities with lots of cash that had no problem paying for the orders. Hewlett-Packard and AT&T were among the examples of large customers of the tech companies. Understanding the business-to-business model under which the tech companies then operated, the bankers at Silicon Valley Bank did not turn these potential borrowing clients away when the entrepreneurs called or walked to the Bank's offices for a loan or a line of credit.

As the sales order sizes increased for the tech companies, the Bank enjoyed the larger-size loans and accompanying interest and fee payments. Practically all other banks in the Silicon Valley area didn't understand the business model of tech companies at the time and stayed away from tech companies as potential clients. Also, those banks believed that without "hard assets" backing the receivables, there was nothing for the banks to rely on for collateral in case the borrowers failed to pay; the banks were afraid of the perceived risks stemming from making loans to tech companies. Consequently, the field was left wide open for Silicon Valley Bank to be the one and only go-to bank for tech companies.

With the hiring of Harry Kellogg, who was the Head of Tech Lending at Bank of the West, Smith eliminated any potential competition in the area. Wells Fargo had already shut down its Special Industries Group several years ago. Tech companies faced slim prospects for finding bankers at a bank that truly understood and welcomed their business and quirks. The only bank with enormous resources to compete in Tech Lending then was Bank of America (BOA), but they decided not to compete after seeing what Wells Fargo did with the Special Industries Group. BOA's management was similar to Wells Fargo's in its lack of understanding and appreciation for tech entrepreneurs. Further, BOA was deep in real estate loans and enjoyed its dominant role in that sector. Smith seized the opportunity left by BOA and accelerated his Bank to be number one in serving the technology sector. Without BOA, Wells Fargo, and Bank of the West in the competition, SVB was indeed the number one bank in this sector.

Kellogg grew the Technology Division at SVB and expanded his group of bankers from two groups: those who were either the lone banker doing tech lending at a bank that didn't care deeply about tech lending (as Kellogg had experienced at the Bank of West) or bankers from the former Special Industries Group at Wells Fargo. The like-mind group of bankers at the Technology Division carried their mission of serving and growing with their clients. The bankers poured over every financial statement of the company, analyzing everything about them. Loan decisions were made in committees, and the bankers informed the clients of the loan decisions as promised. Committees met early and frequently to render loan decisions. The company could expect to learn the decision within a week of requesting a loan.

For these tech loans based on receivables, Silicon Valley Bank worked hard to track the borrower's monthly progress on the sales and payments. Some of the

borrowers were tech companies backed by VC firms. The Bank was always conservative in making the loan against accounts receivable. The Bank also took a security
interest in all the assets owned by the borrowing company. Illustratively, Plexus
Computers grew spectacularly and then crashed. VCs and creditors lost more than
$40 million in total when the company filed for bankruptcy in 1989. Silicon Valley
Bank was Plexus' primary lender and recouped its $344,000 loan by collecting on
the company's receivables because those were among the assets that served as
collateral to secure the loan. The Bank's loan got paid, but the VCs and other
creditors got nothing.[15]

As the Bank perfected its lending against receivables in the early years, the bankers
anticipated their rewards as the Bank began trading stock on NASDAQ under the
symbol SIVB in 1987. Unfortunately, the Black Monday market crash occurred in
October 1987, as Kellogg recalled:

> All I remember is that we were supposed to get listed on what was called, I don't
> even remember all the particulars behind it, it was called Black Monday because
> the stock market just went cratered in one day and they had a shutdown, the stock
> market. That's the same day the Silicon Valley Bank was going to get listed on the
> stock exchange. Because I don't know if that was the savings and loan debacle that
> happened more exactly what it was, but the whole market went down. And we got
> lost in the shuffle obviously because of everything that was going on in the market
> itself. ... it wasn't good. We had all our investment bankers lined up. We were
> going to have a party and all that kind of stuff. And yeah, we had to wait a few weeks
> or months, as I recall to get listed, essentially.[16]

The Bank completed the IPO in 1988 and raised $6 million in equity. The Bank,
as a practice in the early days, issued stock option plans to key employees while
attracting and retaining talents unique to the Bank's philosophy. Smith opened
additional offices in Palo Alto and San Jose. Specifically, the new office to serve the
tech community was in Two Palo Alto where the law firm Wilson Sonsini was also
located. Kellogg believed that being in the same building with Wilson Sonsini
exhibited Smith's ingenuity as a CEO of a startup bank. It reminded him of the
Special Industries Group under Smith's leadership which had done something very
similar. Nothing was sweeter than being the Bank where entrepreneurs could
deposit their checks after they signed documents at Wilson Sonsini. All they needed
to do was take the elevator down and drop off the checks before exiting the building.

GROW WITH THE CLIENTS: WARRANTS FOR GROWTH

Smith and Kellogg, however, wanted more; they wanted part of the tech company's
growth. As a client grows with more sale orders, the client's stock became more

---

[15] King, "Electronic Banking," *supra*, note 9.
[16] Interview with Harry Kellogg, March 14, 2022 (on file with author).

valuable, and the client might be acquired by others. The Bank, under Smith and Kellogg's leadership and their experience from tech lending in the Special Industries Group, asked tech clients to provide warrants as part of the loan cost. No other bank did such a thing back then because banks did not help grow their clients the way Silicon Valley Bank did.

By 1987, Silicon Valley Bank took warrants from 15 companies in connection with credit lines backed by accounts receivable. For example, Chips & Technologies Inc., a startup from Milpitas, California, was founded by Gordon A. Campbell, a former Intel Corporation executive in 1985.[17] The company specialized in standard application-specific integrated circuits. The company raised $1.35 million from William Marocco and other investors at the time. All banks, however, declined to extend a line of credit to the young company. Silicon Valley Bank was the exception! The Bank provided the startup with a $250,000 line of credit against its receivables and inventory as collateral. The Bank received warrants in connection with the credit line. A year later, the startup grew handsomely. With careful monthly reviews of the startup's financial reports, the Bank increased the startup's line of credit to $1 million and asked for a bigger warrant as part of the new loan cost. The startup was able to quickly go public and raised $9 million in just two years of existence. The startup didn't need the larger line of credit from the Bank but remained as the Bank's client. Gary Martin, Chips & Technologies Inc.'s Vice President of Finance appreciated that the Bank provided the company with a small line of credit at first to allow the company to grow, "and give you more if you deserve it."[18]

SVB bankers then understood why entrepreneurs were willing to issue warrants to the Bank as part of the loan cost. Smith explained the origin of warrants:

> The warrant idea came from the old Wells Fargo Special Industries Group. We took warrants. Depending on each situation, the amount of capital, we got warrants . . . We even got warrants on these receivable lines, too, because we were doing it early, no one else was doing it . . . And now put yourselves in the chair of the entrepreneur, so the way it works is that you have this idea, and you bootstrap it at first. Then you go out and get capital. But you need more money and you could go out to get capital. If you could wait, say six months, then you would get a higher price for your stock. So, that's where the Bank would come in. We would loan money, and you could, if you will, survive for another six months and prove your concept. And so, that's where as an entrepreneur, you would give us the Bank a very small number of warrants. That was a lot cheaper than selling your stock at that time. So, it was a win-win for both of us and the company.[19]

[17] "A Decade of Semiconductor Companies, 1988 Edition" (Table 1c) 4, *Dataquest*, June 1988, available at: http://archive.computerhistory.org/resources/access/text/2013/04/102723194-05-01-acc.pdf [https://perma.cc/Q3K7-QM3C] (last accessed September 26, 2023).

[18] Marie-Jeanne Juilland, "Lending without Fears," *Venture*, January 1987.

[19] Smith Interview, February 25, 2022 (on file with the author).

Let's unpack Smith's explanation with some numbers to illustrate why a VC-backed startup takes on a loan from the Bank and that startup willingly issues a warrant to the Bank. What are the costs and benefits to the startup?

To answer these questions, consider a hypothetical offered by the Bank: Assume that the startup has just received a Series A round of $10 million from a VC. Typically, VC investors will take "20 percent ownership (on a fully diluted basis)" in the enterprise, rendering the total valuation of the enterprise at $50 million (20 percent of $50 million is $10 million of the VC fund). As startups generally burn lots of cash to meet their milestones, for our purposes, we assume that the enterprise's monthly cash burn rate is $1 million. The $10 million Series A will allow the enterprise to survive for 10 months. What if the enterprise is unable to meet some of its milestones and needs two or three additional months before it can reach the Series B round? To ameliorate the problem, the enterprise could have approached an outlier bank immediately after it obtained the Series A funding. When the enterprise is awash in cash and confidence is the ideal time to request a venture loan of $3 million to be drawn later. That means the enterprise would have three extra months of cash burn to lengthen its runway by 30 percent in order to meet its milestones and reach the Series B round.

In exchange for a 30 percent additional runway, the enterprise is required to issue a warrant to purchase stock from the outlier bank. The warrant has a "dilution equivalent to 25–50 basis points" fully diluted (meaning 0.25 percent to 0.5 percent of ownership of the enterprise). If the warrant has 50 basis points, the bank has the right to purchase $250,000 worth of shares of the company with a $50 million valuation. Further, the warrant here constitutes only 1/40th of the dilution for 30 percent additional runway compared to the $10 million Series A capital fund with 20 percent ownership! In other words, the enterprise would be able to meet its milestones, survive, and excel to Series B, without diluting its equity as it would have if it sought the loan from a non-bank lender.

As with any loan, the borrower must pay the loan principal and interest payments. Typically, the bank provides free interest payments for the first year, and around a 5 percent interest rate for the subsequent two years of the three-year term loan. The interest rate is substantially lower than what the startup can secure from alternative sources. There are several reasons for the lower interest rate on a loan from SVB. Unlike alternative lenders who have no access to cheap money, banks do. As a commercial bank, SVB receives money from depositors. These deposits are other people's money, and banks like SVB pay depositors low interest and charge borrowers high interest. With access to plenty of low-cost money, SVB could lend to startups at a lower cost. Of course, they still had to be careful in selecting only the VC-backed enterprises that were most likely to reach new rounds of venture funding, ensuring that the Bank would receive payment on the principal, fees, and interest.

Overall, in exchange for the warrant as part of the loan cost, the Bank could give "more favorable credit terms" to the startups. In other words, the startups got lower interest rates and favorable terms on the loan to extend their runway to meet milestones and the next round of VC funding.

The Bank, in helping the entrepreneurs, asked for warrants from tech companies when they sought loans based on receivables lines and loans between rounds of VC funding. Holding on to these warrants became part of the Bank's investment.[20]

NO BRIDGE LENDING BUT AN EXTENSION OF THE RUNWAY

To Smith and Kellogg, the Bank had to serve some of the startup companies, including startups without products and no accounts receivable. These startups needed a line of credit from the Bank. If the Bank provided a little line of credit to a startup, this allowed the startup to tinker with the concept, improve their product, and finally make their product ready for market and generate receivables. The bankers believed that the line of credit would allow startups to grow and, as the startups advanced into later stages, the startups would continue to turn to the Bank for banking and lending services. If the Bank could not keep up with the massive and fast growth of a particular client, the Bank could rely on the Boston-based Bank of New England, SVB's correspondent bank.[21]

In providing a line of credit to a startup between its VC rounds of funding or making a loan on 80 percent of accounts receivable, Kellogg explained that the Bank was extending the runway for that startup company. With VC-backed startups, growth is important. Without growth, the companies will die. Growth does not necessarily mean making profits. The VCs fund the startups to grow them to the next round. Meanwhile, the startup needs a loan from the Bank before it can reach the next round. That means the money from the Bank is helpful to both the startup and the VCs because the Bank helps extend the runway a little bit longer. The Bank helps the VC's portfolio companies to grow.

With the connections the Bank cultivated with the VCs for many years, Kellogg and his bankers gained access to the visibility of whether VCs would continue to fund certain startups in the next round. VCs may walk away because the management team failed to deliver growth, spent too much cash without meeting specific milestones, or deviated to something else. The close working relationship with the marquee VC firms like Sequoia, Kleiner Perkins, NEA, and Benchmark translated into unique knowledge of which VC firm and which partners at a VC firm the Bank should extend a line of credit to or provide a loan to the VC-backed startup. For the VCs, in their long-term relationship with the Bank, they would not walk away early

[20] See Xuan-Thao Nguyen, "Lending Innovations," *Brooklyn Law Review* 86 (2020): 135; "Banking the Unbanked Innovators," *Journal of Corporation Law* 45 (2020): 715.
[21] Cris Oppenheimer, "Bank Thrives on High-Tech Loans," *The San Jose Mercury News*, December 7, 1987.

because there was no other bank in the area at the time that would help finance the growth of VC-backed companies.[22]

Extending the runway, Kellogg explained, did not mean the Bank was making bridge loans or engaging in bridge lending. Think about it for a few minutes: Kellogg suggested to anyone, including the SVB Board of Directors and the federal and state regulators, who uttered the "bridge loan" phrase, the Bank took a security interest in all the startup's assets, including its most valuable assets – the technology, the intellectual property assets, in addition to the fixed assets like equipment and inventory. The security interest in all of the assets served as the backstop to reduce the Bank's exposure. Kellogg made sure that the Bank did not use the incorrect phrase "bridge loans" in this unique VC ecosystem and tech accounts receivable line of credit. He knew regulators generally do not like the words "bridge loans" and educated the regulators about the uniqueness of the lending practices in his Technology Division.[23]

SVB AS THE CHEERLEADER

When Kellogg joined SVB as the Head of the Technology Division there were only eight people in the group. He held a daily meeting with the group. No one person was endowed with the authority to approve the loan by himself, including Kellogg. Eight years before Kellogg joined SVB, while he was in the Special Industries Group, Kellogg had a $3 million lending limit, but everything was different at SVB, and he possessed no lending authority. He liked the SVB approach because it was all about building a new bank for startups in the tech sector. Loans in the Technology Division were made by the loan committee on Tuesday and Thursday, and the bankers would immediately inform the client. In fact, the Bank built its reputation on promptly providing clients with quick answers because the loan committee met both on Tuesday and Thursday to render decisions on new loan applications of the week. Moreover, the lenders in the Technology Division held their informal meetings daily and shared their input about certain software, medical tech, or semiconductor companies of interest. The members brought their different skill sets to the group. The information flowed, and everyone was involved while learning about new and potential clients and their businesses.

With intimate knowledge about clients and their sale orders, milestones, acquisitions, and other achievements, SVB cheered their successes in many different ways.

The Bank celebrated the clients with a "Did You Know?" newsletter and sent copies to 3,000 Silicon Valley "kingpins."[24] For instance, the newsletter included "Red Pepper Software Company of San Mateo, CA recently raised $2.6 million

---

[22] Interview with Kellogg, *supra*, note 16
[23] See Chapter 7.
[24] Juilland, "Lending without Fears," *supra*, note 18.

through a Series B preferred offering. Merrill Pickard, Anderson & Eyre and Matrix Partners led the offering. Red Pepper, a Bank client, develops intelligent decision-making support tools for scheduling and streamlining operations for the industrial and government markets." Red Pepper was among the Bank's fourteen clients with major news in the newsletter of the month. The Bank seemed to relish in the clients' successes and didn't hesitate to brag about their news. Yet the Bank bragged in its own way without incurring the advertisement costs in local media outlets. This newsletter was Smith's brainchild for marketing to all entrepreneurs, professionals, and VCs in the Valley.

Smith was the ultimate cheerleader CEO in his intense, calm, and conservative manner. When the news spread with headlines about layoffs in tech companies and the declining growth rate around Silicon Valley, Smith refused to accept the ill-fated conclusions. He took a stand and cheered on the entrepreneurs and new tech companies for their contributions to diversifying the local economy and their innovation. Here is a letter Smith wrote in "Other Voices" in the local newspaper on December 16, 1985:

Silicon Valley remains one of the most rewarding and exciting places in the world in which to do business today. What keeps business people's faith in the valley alive? With all the persistent sour-grapes economic news, there is still a corps of investors and lenders bullish on the valley's immediate future. The reasons they are still eager to invest in local companies can be summarized in a few basic observations.

Diversity. People often overlook that the Silicon Valley economy is not built upon a single industry but consists of a diversity of technologies and services. The technology-based economy is more than semiconductor manufacturers or personal computer companies, two segments that get a lot of the press. Segments such as defense electronics, medical electronics, factory automation and telecommunications are healthy and growing, the varied business segments that we refer to as the high-technology industry reduce the economic risks associated with dependence on one industry. Silicon Valley's business environment is more resilient by virtue of its diversity.

Innovation. If science is the mother of invention, her children have found their happiness in Silicon Valley ... [W]hen we read of layoffs, unpaid vacations, and declining growth rates, many small and medium-sized companies have continued to thrive and hire new employees at geometric rates. Fremont-based Sysgen Inc., a maker of tape drives and other personal computer peripherals, had only 15 employees in October 1984 and now employs 80 people. Sysgen has also demonstrated a steady growth in sales and profits. Maxim Systems, a defense electronics company, has experienced a five-fold increase in personnel, sales and profits in the past two years.[25]

[25] Roger V. Smith, "Other Voices," *Peninsula-ime Tribune*, December 16, 1985.

Smith was prescient in his understanding of innovation and how innovation creates new markets and wealth for reinvestment in the community. He even mentioned artificial intelligence as one of the new technologies being developed in 1985! He indeed learned about and from entrepreneurs and innovators through his clients. He cheered on the entrepreneurs and innovators in the public forum. In other words, he did not run his Bank to solely make money but leveraged his position as the President and CEO of the Bank to openly support the tech sector with nuanced explanations and to elevate the role of business leaders in a community at large with civic engagement. Here is another paragraph in the same letter from Smith:

> Innovation in developing new products often creates whole new markets and opportunities. As a new product market grows, it attracts more companies, thereby increasing competition and the need for developing methods to improve efficiency. The new types of technologies being developed here today, such as artificial intelligence and genetic engineering, may bring about the next economic revolution, thereby providing more wealth that is reinvested in our community.[26]

In addition, Smith cheered the entrepreneurs and investors for their integrity and knowledge. Smith wrote in the same public letter to express his observation that "[d]oing business in a community where people are honest about their endeavors and stand by their commitments has proven to help stimulate support for new companies and economic growth." Smith proudly added his signature to the letter because he stood by what he believed in – serving as the unbashful cheerleader for his clients.

When clients had their initial public offerings, the Bank took out a small section in a local publication to congratulate them for having "just taken flight." For instance, in 1996, the Bank included 38 clients who had achieved their IPO. These clients were tech companies from different innovation centers in the country. They came from Mountain View, Hayward, Los Altos, Berkeley, Sunnyvale, Palo AltoPleasanton, Oakland, Redwood City, San Jose, Tustin, Menlo Park, and Sacramento in California, from Burlington and Cambridge in Massachusetts, from Boulder and Denver in Colorado, from Beaverton, Oregon, from Wenatchee, Washington, from Oklahoma City, Oklahoma, from Austin, Texas, and from New York City. The Bank counted itself on "helping emerging companies spread their wings" and "enabling technology."

Another crucial way the Bank cheered the clients was believing in them by connecting them with other professionals and firms, so they could receive the assistance they craved, the funding they sought, and the advice on which they depended to move forward.

---

[26] Ibid.

SVB AS THE CONNECTOR

The Bank kept attorneys, accountants, insurance agents, and equipment leasing companies as contacts at the bankers' fingertips to dispense to the Bank's clients when the occasion arose. With the Bank's name as a stamp of approval, a client might encounter an easier time acquiring what it sought from others. For instance, after the Bank extended a small line of credit based on receivables, the Bank might refer the client to see an equipment leasing company. The lessor was more willing to work with the client knowing that the Bank had already extended the credit line.

When the Bank signed a new entrepreneur for a bank account, the Bank might have connected the new client to one of the law firms, accountants, insurance, or VC firms in the Bank's 100 founders and extensive business circles. The Bank may have introduced the client to one of the investors. These firms and investors may then have introduced the new client to others. The network effects widened for the client and, in turn, the Bank benefited from the network effects. The clients, the various professional firms, and the investors in these circles introduced their clients and prospects to the Bank for banking and lending services. Smith noted these support circles:

> The professional and service companies supporting our high-technology economy provide an excellent climate for doing business. The professional firms of attorneys, accountants, and bankers have worked with many young and growing companies and are sensitive to their needs. Many service firms are quick to support a new company with an eye toward a profitable long-term relationship. These relationships or networks are invaluable in conducting business in our area.[27]

Additionally, when an entrepreneur possessed a concept that the bankers might not understand, the Bank could tap into its network and ask others with relevant expertise to help the bankers to acquire a better understanding of the entrepreneur's technology. In so doing, the Bank would connect the entrepreneur to the experts and advisors. Smith and his bankers knew best that in the Silicon Valley community where the Bank anchored its offices, the entrepreneurs, experts, and advisors were all willing to learn from past mistakes because these mistakes "provide a continuous graduate school of business!"[28]

In the *Did You Know?* newsletter, the Bank both marketed itself and connected clients or their partners to one another with their latest milestones. In other words, the Bank constantly sought and promoted connections through its own marketing strategy in the form of a newsletter. In fact, Arthur Rock, one of the most famous venture capitalists in VC history, remarked with enthusiasm to Smith about how much he loved the *Did You Know?* newsletter. Smith and his bankers were pleased! In the 1980s era, decades before Crunchbase and Pitchbook, Silicon Valley Bank already understood the value of information as an enabler to bring those in the technology sector closer together.

[27] Ibid.
[28] Ibid.

The *Did You Know?* newsletter continued for a couple of years after Smith left in 1993. Here are a couple of entries from the July 1994 *Did You Know?* newsletter:

#3. San Jose client, Western Technology Investment, completed its $50 million Venture Lending and Leasing Fund. The Fund will provide venture-backed companies with leases and loans for equipment acquisitions and other asset-based financing.

#7. Celtrix Pharmaceuticals, Inc., a Santa Clara, CA client, and Green Cross Corporation, have signed a license agreement covering the development and commercialization in Japan of SomatoKine, a novel IGF complex, for the treatment of osteoporosis. Green Cross is a Japanese pharmaceutical company based in Osaka that has been working with Celtrix in conducting preclinical studies.

#13. Our client, Theratx, Inc. completed its IPO selling 4.0 million shares at $12.00 per share for a total of $48 million The offering was underwritten by Robertson, Stephens & Company, Alex, Brown & Sons, and Donaldson, Lukin, & Jenrette.

Likewise, here are some entries in the *Did You Knows?* No. 3, 1995 newsletter:

#2. Our San Francisco, CA client, Preview Media, Inc., has recently raised $5 million of preferred equity from Kleiner Perkins Caufield & Byers, America Online, and Landmark Communications. Preview produces travel-related programming for broadcast and cable television stations.

#8. Over the last three months, our San Jose, CA client, Meris Laboratories, has made four acquisitions: Sierra Medical Lab, Norcal Laboratory, West Cost Pathology Laboratory and Physician Biomedical Laboratory. Meris offers medical testing services throughout California.

#9. Genus, Inc. our Sunnyvale, CA client, completed a private placement with a group of institutional investors led by Bachow & Associates Inc. for $17.5 million. The equity was raised to meet backlog requirements and to capitalize on additional market opportunities. Genus manufactures chemical vapor deposition machines and ion implantation machines for semiconductor manufacturers.

As cheerleaders and connectors, SVB counted many entrepreneurs as repeat clients. Take Gordon Campbell: in 1981 he founded Seeq Technology Inc. which was an SVB client. Seeq had its initial public offering in 1987 and was among the Bank's first clients that went public.[29] Campbell later founded Chip & Technologies, Inc. in 1985, and the startup was also a client of the Bank.

[29] Silicon Valley Bank Oral History panel on Robert Medearis and Roger Smith conducted by Stephen Smith, November 11, 2014 (hereinafter "Oral History").

ENDING THE FIRST DECADE AND BEGINNING 99 PERCENT OF
SERVING THE TECH SECTOR

From loans against receivables to tech lending to VC-backed companies, SVB cemented itself in the venture capital community by opening a new office in Menlo Park at 3000 Sand Hill Road in 1989. SVB's reputation as the key partner in the VC ecosystem grew with its presence on the famed street in Silicon Valley.

In 1989, the Bank noted that competing financial institutions had retreated in their efforts of serving the tech sector in the last six years. Taking advantage of the new opportunities, the Bank had increased its commitments and penetration into the tech sector to gain additional market share over the same six years. The Bank revealed new layers of its understanding of the tech sector and how it would serve this growing sector, ensuring the bankers meet the fast-evolving demands. In many ways, the Bank and its bankers were growing and changing along with the transformation of Silicon Valley each year. The 1989 Annual Report indicated:

> Technology companies possess unique financing needs. Rapid growth, specialized capitalization structures, product evaluation, and substantial foreign sales and offshore manufacturing, all contribute to their characteristic makeup.

Interestingly, the tech companies that were able to secure external funding from VCs presented a new type of private company. They consisted of the typical private entities, from the Bank's observations, but "have all the ingredients of their public brethren": Namely, these companies "[a]long with their external funding … have an "outside" Board of Directors, their financials are audited by major accounting firms, and they retain major law firms that specialize in emerging tech companies."

Consequently, the Bank must respond to the market changes by "establishing a service philosophy which promotes product customization." Where would the bankers extract information to understand market trends and shape their service philosophy to serve the private tech companies with characteristics of public companies? The officers of the Bank's Technology Division regularly attended industry meetings, for instance, the seminars and conferences hosted by the American Electronics Association. The Bank hosted informal lunches with clients, turning these lunches into forums for discussion and the exchange of ideas. The bankers kept their eyes and ears open and brought the information learned back to the Technology Division. Together, the bankers would adjust their portfolio "as the industry and economy dictates and therefore maintains its strong position within the industry sector." The breakdowns of the Technology Division's portfolio are included in Figure 6.1.

The bankers utilized the new location at 3000 Sand Hill Road in Menlo Park to further embed themselves into the venture capital community. Smith appointed one of his top bankers, Donald Cvietusa, to be in charge of the new location. Cvietusa was a top high-tech loan officer at Bank of America until May 1988 when

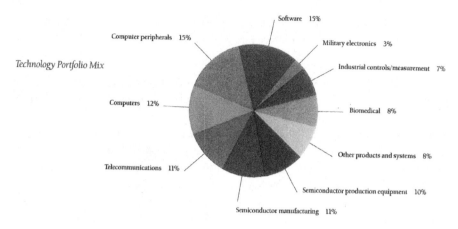

Software 15%

Computer peripherals 15%

Military electronics 3%

Technology Portfolio Mix

Industrial controls/measurement 7%

Computers 12%

Biomedical 8%

Other products and systems 8%

Telecommunications 11%

Semiconductor production equipment 10%

Semiconductor manufacturing 11%

FIGURE 6.1 1989 Annual Report.

he joined SVB. Cvietusa was known as a "disciple of the Giannini approach," just like his boss Roger Smith. The Giannini approach prized highly personalized lending policies.[30] The loan officers, through loan committees, made their loan decisions based on their assessment of their tech clients, and they delivered their decisions promptly after they held their loan committee meetings at 7:00 a.m. on Tuesday and Thursday weekly! After spending thirty years at BOA, Cvietusa loved the energy of the Technology Division at SVB and thought that his time at SVB was an exciting finale to a rewardingly successful banking career.[31]

The VCs were the conduit of referrals to the Bank. Tirelessly cultivating the relationships with partners and investors in the VC ecosystem, the bankers, under Kellogg's leadership, saw $48 million in deposits generated in the Sand Hill Road office in only six months from March 1989 to December 1989. Instead of having one breakfast meeting, Kellogg became known for having three breakfast meetings, so he could reach out to as many clients and potential clients as possible. Building a startup bank SVB for the exciting tech startups and growing companies never proved easy. Kellogg loved the hard and smart work, and three breakfasts were significantly cheaper than the industry's three-martini lunch!

The Bank aimed to keep the clients happy and to grow with the dynamic technology sector. By 1989, the Bank prioritized its strategy to meet some clients' need for bigger loan amounts. The Bank reached out to other banks and US financial institutions and international affiliations to serve new client's expansive and complex needs. Also, some clients demanded both vertical and horizontal

[30] Joel Kotkin, "Still Flying High in the Valley," *Inc. Magazine*, October 1, 1988, available at: www.inc.com/magazine/19881001/5977.html (last accessed September 26, 2023).
[31] "Donald Steven Cvietusa, 1933–2015," *East Bay Times*, October 31, 2015, available at: www .legacy.com/us/obituaries/eastbaytimes/name/donald-cvietusa-obituary?id=16556905 [https:// perma.cc/N5TK-X9K5] (last accessed September 26, 2023).

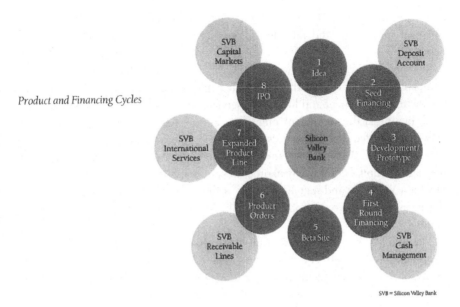

SVB = Silicon Valley Bank

FIGURE 6.2 Product and financing cycles, 1989 Annual Report, page 9.

services. The Bank met both by implementing an approach that Smith called "financial engineering" in offering "solution-oriented services and customized product applications" to growing tech companies in a dynamic marketplace. Figure 6.2 shows product and financing cycles, indicating where and how the Bank rose to the challenges in the latter part of the first decade of the Bank's existence.

The inner circles demonstrated phases one to eight of a successful Bank's tech client advancing from having an idea to an IPO. The five outer circles denote the Bank's financing services to phases two, four, six, seven, and eight of the tech company's product cycles. A tech company begins with an idea or concept. The idea or concept may be novel or innovative to attract some seed funding. Here, in the company's phase two, the Bank's service is useful to the tech company. The Bank signs up the tech company as a client for the deposit of the seed funding. The company utilizes the seed money to develop a prototype. Success in developing the prototype may attract the first round of financing. Now, in the company's phase four, the Bank's service to the company expands to include cash management. With the infusion of capital, the company will perfect its product development to a beta site. Soon, after beta testing, the company can begin to fill orders for its new product. To assist the company in filling the sale orders, at the company's phase six, the Bank will extend a line of credit based on the company's receivables. With further success, the company expands its product line and may attract international orders. In the company's phase seven, the Bank responds with international services to handle the client's international sales orders, payments, foreign exchanges, etc. The company grows and heads to IPO at phase eight. The Bank teams up with other banks and financial institutions and provides its services in the capital markets to help the client.

In other words, the Bank was banking on loyalty from the young startup tech company, planning to serve them from the beginning phase to the exiting phase and intertwining its vertical and horizontal services for the life of a tech company. The Bank identified the significant milestones and phases of a growing company and actively expanded and inserted its services to be the long and continuous partner. In so doing, the Bank must secure the best leads from the investors and lawyers in the venture capital community in order to know which startups received the backing of which VC firms and specific partners at the relevant VC firms and to know that the investors who would not abandon the startups in the middle of a particular phase.

The Bank not only worked with the tech company executives but also the customers of the tech client in connection with the Bank's credit line against receivables, cash management, and international services phases. To maintain a proactive role in the cycles, the Bank offered and conducted "industry informational seminars and other value-added events" to keep all clients informed and broadened "network affiliations and continued industry expertise." That meant the SVB bankers worked very long hours, atypical for bankers in a commercial bank, but not atypical for a startup entrepreneur. Smith knew that he was relentless in pushing himself and his bankers. To Smith, working hard was the only option for the Bank to thrive, achieve the status as the number one Bank for startups and entrepreneurs, and to remain the number one. The key to the Bank's future success was a "high-level commitment of providing financial services to the technology marketplace." This could only be achieved by having "an expanding base of referral sources and a loyal following of venture capitalists and technology company executives." These statements squarely articulated what the Bank would later transform into – a financial institution with 100 percent devotion to the tech industry, eliminating the much riskier leg – the real estate concentration – of the three-legged stool. Smith correctly forecasted the Bank's future business model before the Bank got into trouble with the real estate concentration two years later.

Smith's version of a community bank for technology refused to confine "community" in the geographical sense. As long as there is a vibrant VC ecosystem to support tech companies, Smith wanted the Bank to craft a presence there. When some of the investors expanded their investments to Taiwan and Hong Kong, Smith allowed Peter Mok, one of his bankers, to create an office there to serve the entrepreneurs and the investors within the VC community in Asia. Peter Mok grew up in Hong Kong, understood the language and culture, and possessed strong relationships with clients. Mok was the perfect person to begin the Bank's Asia practice. The Bank launched international services with the Pacific Rim & Trade Finance groups under Peter Mok's leadership. In many ways, the Bank followed the clients in their expansion.[32] Or, more precisely, the Bank followed the money from the VC trail. In Smith's explanation, the Bank behaved like a lawyer in serving the clients, not a typical commercial bank.

On the VC trail, the Bank seized the opportunity to open a new office near Boston, Massachusetts, establishing a nationwide, bicoastal footprint for a community bank that was not even nine years old! By 1990, many banks in Boston faced serious problems. Both Bank of Boston and the Bank of New England went out of business. SVB had already developed a corresponding banking relationship with Allan Woodward from the Bank of New England for loans that were larger than SVB's bank limit when the Bank was smaller. Woodward understood tech lending as his group served the tech industry on Route 128. Smith sought out the bankers from the Bank of New England and welcomed them to join the SVB's new office near Boston.[33]

For the Beaverton, Oregon, office, the Bank received a call from Dan Case of Hambrecht and Quist, a well-regarded investment firm behind the IPOs of Apple Computer, Genetech, and Adobe Systems in the 1980s, recommending Art Hiemstra, a banker at First Interstate in Oregon, to Smith as a potential hire. Hiemstra wanted to continue his work in Oregon through SVB but preferred to be in Seattle. Nevertheless, Smith seized the opportunity and hired Hiemstra, along with all the VC and tech connections that Hiemstra brought with him, to serve both Portland and Seattle. Being a cost-conscious bank, Smith saw the opportunity presented a win–win situation because Hiemstra could start the new SVB office in the basement of his house! At least for three months the rent was really cheap before Hiemstra's wife requested the SVB office be located outside their home![34] SVB's new office under Hiemstra went immediately into loan production action to the tech industry in the Pacific Northwest. Hiemstra stayed with SVB from 1991 to 2003 and his "Northwest Division" of SVB generated more than $1 billion in deposits from tech companies and several hundred million in loan commitments.[35]

With the expansions to Boston, Newport Beach, Beaverton, and Hong Kong in 1990 and 1991, Smith steadied his Bank where focus and consistency would be maintained throughout the offices. With focus and consistency, Smith knew that his bank would continue to distinguish itself from the mainstream, traditional banks. Smith pushed the offices to always keep their eyes on being cost conscious. At all times, the bankers at SVB breathed and behaved like their entrepreneurial, startup clients in the technology industry.

Aggressive in his approach to the expansion of the Bank in serving the technology industry, Smith also aggressively took the cash from tech deposits to make loans in

---

[32] Oral History, at 26–27.

[33] Ibid., at 24.

[34] Ibid., at 25.

[35] "Art Hiemstra," *Walker's Research*, available at: www.walkersresearch.com/Profilepages/Show_Executive_Title/Executiveprofile/A/Art__Hiemstra_400181302.html [https://perma.cc/FX4H-VH2E] (last accessed September 22, 2022).

real estate. The Bank made lots of money in real estate loans. Soon the real estate industry-wide problem caught up with the Bank and, because real estate was one of the legs of Smith's three-legged stool, the Board acted swiftly to replace Smith with John C. Dean in 1993. The Bank immediately recovered and returned to the black after the first loss ever recorded in the Bank's history.

Dean, a bank restructuring specialist, implemented a systematic process and technology infrastructure for the Bank. Kellogg left the Bank for less than a year and returned to reclaim his place in the Tech Lending division. The Bank doubled its business focus on serving the tech sector. Dean proudly claimed that he grew the Bank from a market capitalization of $65 million in 1993 to over $3 billion in 2000. The Board then named Ken P. Wilcox as president of Silicon Valley Bank in 1999 and by 2001 elevated Wilcox to be president and CEO of the Holding Company, Silicon Valley Bancshares, and John Dean was named the chairman of the Board.[36] Under Wilcox's leadership, the Bank moved the one-third tech sector concentration to 99 percent of the Bank's business, cementing the Bank's presence as the only bank focusing on helping to grow entrepreneurs and investors in the innovation economy.[37]

Under both Dean and Wilcox's leadership, the Bank approved the creation of the first two venture capital funds in 2000, Strategic Investors Fund and BancVentures Fund, which included a $150 million fund of funds, and a $65 million direct equity fund, respectively. Interestingly, the creation of the two funds traced their origin to Harry Kellogg, the ultimate representative of banking is all about relationships.

According to Kellogg, the Bank had already formed deep relationships with VC firms and other investors for many years. These relationships should be put to good use in new ways to bring value to shareholders! The Bank's proximity to the VCs meant the bankers gained information not available to those outside the tight circle. Many investors who wanted to invest in funds simply didn't possess access to the kind of information that SVB bankers possessed. Kellogg went to the Board to formally ask for $5 million "walking money" so he could grow two funds. Beaming with excitement, Kellogg designated his "dream team" of Greg Becker and Aaron Gershenberg. By the end of December 31, 2000, SVB invested in 208 venture capital funds and had direct equity investments in 60 companies.[38]

[36] "Silicon Valley Bank Celebrates 20 Years of Dedication to Entrepreneurs," *Silicon Valley Bank*, October 17, 2003, available at: www.svb.com/news/company-news/silicon-valley-bank-celebrates-20-years-of-dedication-to-entrepreneurs [https://perma.cc/L8E8-XZED] (last accessed September 26, 2023).

[37] "C-Suite: Dr. Ken Wilcox – Former CEO of Silicon Valley Bank," *Oregon State University College of Arts and Sciences*, September 18, 2018, available at: https://artsandsciences.osu.edu/news-events/events/c-suite-dr-ken-wilcox-former-ceo-silicon-valley-bank [https://perma.cc/NWF4-58PX] (last accessed September 26, 2023).

[38] "SVB 2001 10K Filing for the Fiscal Year Ended December 31, 2000," *SVB Financial Group*, March 16, 2001, available at: www.annualreports.com/HostedData/AnnualReportArchive/s/NASDAQ_SIVB_2000.pdf [https://perma.cc/M2YJ-YL2T] (last accessed September 26, 2023).

FROM HARRY KELLOGG TO AARON GERSHENBERG FOR SVB CAPITAL
ON RELATIONSHIPS

Kellogg's dream team got to work. In 2000, the bank holding company formed SVB Strategic Investors, LLC, the general partner of SVB Strategic Investors Fund, L.P. In just twelve months, the SVB Strategic Investors Fund, L.P. raised approximately $135.3 million in committed capital, to invest as a limited partner in top-tier venture funds, leading regional venture funds, and venture funds with a unique niche. The top tier referred to Sequoia, Kleiner Perkin, Benchmark, NEA, and so forth, all among the who's who in the VC community.

Also, in 2000, the bank holding company formed Silicon Valley BancVentures, Inc., the general partner of Silicon Valley BancVentures, L.P. The amount raised by Silicon Valley BancVentures, L.P. was $56.1 million in committed capital, to make direct equity investments in emerging growth companies in high technology and life sciences throughout the United States. SVB proudly reported that the two funds yielded a return of about 11 percent.

Like Smith and Kellogg of the generation before, Gershenberg was a leader who understood that SVB investment is a relationship business. He cared deeply about cultivating and maintaining relationships. In the subsequent decades, Gershenberg flew around the world to meet with investors. He remembered the early days when Kellogg told him about going to meet and talk to VCs and get his free meals! He deepened the Bank's long-term relationship with VCs to bring proposition value to investors in the fund of funds he created. That meant he also possessed the knowledge and experience of evaluating what would be important for investments and the impact of such investments.

Though Smith had long left the Bank and Kellogg retired, the SVB DNA and philosophy of focus, consistency, and cost consciousness in serving clients in the VC ecosystem echoed in Gershenberg and his group at SVB Capital. They leveraged their relationships with general partners and founders to bring value to the limited partners of funds created by SVB Capital. They drew circles within circles and overlapped circles to reach all aspects of different clients' phases in their own product and life cycles. They worked hard and smartly to render the work to appear to be effortless. Along the way, Gershenberg consumed more than Kellogg's three breakfasts a day, metaphorically speaking.

Gershenberg later became the Managing Partner and Co-Founder of SVB Capital. He was credited with using his tireless and creative energy to found ten funds.[39] The $5 million expanded to $7 billion, furnishing unique proposition value to global institutional investors who, as Kellogg knew, did not possess, but

---

[39] *See* Chapter 9. See also "Annual Reports & Proxies – 1996 to 2022," *Silicon Valley Bank,* available at: https://ir.svb.com/financials/annual-reports-and-proxies/default.aspx (last accessed September 23, 2022).

wanted to gain, access to investment opportunities in the innovation economy.[40] Kellogg retired to Danville, California. Gershenberg planned to hand his baton to the next leadership at SVB Capital but would remain focused on building impactful funds.

> It's not about making more money. It's how can I take the money that I've made and deploy that in a way that creates a positive impact.

> I am interested in education. I think about the way people learn and how technology can be leveraged to help people. I want people to have the opportunity that I had without going to fancy schools . . . I think fintech is super important. I think taking friction out of the movement of capital, savings, and all of that, everybody should have the opportunity, not just because you're a billionaire, to create wealth, savings, and investments.

> I've recently been learning about mental health. If we help people with depression, addiction, and PTSD, just think about the impact of homelessness. We don't have a system that helps people with mental health, to understand the problems, and we don't talk about it.[41]

The SVB values fell on the shoulder of Greg Becker for the last ten years before SVB's sudden death. Becker had been the fearless leader of 8,000 employees and succeeded in shaping SVB values and corporate culture.[42]

---

[40] Interviews with Aaron Gershenberg on April 18–19, 2022 (on file with author); "Aaron Gershenberg," *Silicon Valley Bank*, available at: www.svb.com/profile/aaron-gershenberg [https://perma.cc/YUA5-HBZ7] (last accessed September 23, 2022).
[41] Interview with Gershenberg, *supra*, note 39.
[42] See Chapter 10.

7

Convincing the Banking Regulators

The unique success enjoyed by Silicon Valley Bank was the result of a long process that began at the vision of the bank by the original three founders, Medearis, Biggerstaff, and Smith. The key to success involved convincing the regulators to establish a bank for the tech sector. Educating the regulators required ongoing efforts in the first decade and thereafter. SVB lenders, including Harry Kellogg, convinced the regulators about the efficacy of tech lending.[1]

A CHARTER FOR A NEW BANK FOR HIGH-TECH

Medearis nursed the idea of a new bank for quite some time, seeking to learn everything he could about banking operations before he discussed the bank idea with, and then hired with his own money, Bill Biggerstaff. They drove around and talked. They discussed the idea in Medearis' office in Menlo Park. Biggerstaff, with his vast banking knowledge and outgoing personality, served as a consultant to Medearis for six months regarding bank operations. As of March 31, 1983, Biggerstaff had received $21,000 for his consultant fees. Medearis also spoke to many others in the banking industry.

Medearis and Biggerstaff spent many months contemplating their ideas for the new bank before finally submitting the bank charter application. They received conditional approval from the California Superintendent of Banks on February 16, 1983. Medearis also relied on Gary Steven Finley & Associates for the Findley Reports of financial information and performance of banks in California's banking industry. Medearis, Biggerstaff, and Roger Smith agreed that the Bank's proposed services would be a "high level of personalized banking services to its customers,"

---

[1] This chapter is based in part on interviews with Harry Kellogg on March 4 and 30, 2022, Roger Smith on February 25, 2022, Smith and Kellogg on April 18–19, 2022, and Dave Titus on May 4, 2022 (all on file with author).

and that the Bank would emphasize "short-term business loans" directed toward "professionals and small- to medium-sized commercial businesses." They also noted that the Bank would pay "particular attention" to "high technology, professional services, and real estate development companies." With the diversification of services instead of sole concentration in the high technology sector, the organizers secured the approval of the bank charter.

They submitted the Articles of Incorporation of the Bank to the California Secretary of State on February 22, 1983. The Superintendent would not allow the Bank to begin its operations until the Holding Company raised the necessary amount and furnished the Bank with $4,750,000. Medearis always believed that obtaining a good lawyer was essential to a business plan. He sought out legal assistance from Lillick McHose & Charles to represent the Holding Company and the Bank in connection with the offering of the Holding Company's stock to investors.

Overall, organizing the new bank proved to be a complex task. The organizers had to explain their business plan, risk-management framework, and internal controls to illustrate how the new bank would generate revenue through banking and lending products and services, make profits and furnish a return to shareholders.[2] Once its operations started, the young bank faced the pressure of growing quickly. The pressure might have led to riskier lending practices, causing problems with the regulators, that potentially might then have led to elevated capital and supervisory expectations imposed by the regulators. Here, SVB organizers articulated their business plan, identified risks, and mapped out their strategies in the Prospectus filings.

Organizing a bank costs money. SVB organizers advanced a total of $105,000 in 1982 and 1983 to pay for the Holding Company's and the Bank's application and organizational expenses. Some of the organizers obtained a line of credit of $400,000 from First Interstate Bank of California for the organization application, organizational and preopening expenses, leasehold improvements, furnishings, and other expenses. The Bank would later pay off these advances. According to the Prospectus, the Board of Directors would determine whether the Bank would pay any of the Bank organizers' fees, but Biggerstaff's fees would definitely get paid.

Looking back, the 1980s appears to have been an exciting period to organize new banks. There were seventy-two new banks chartered in California in 1983 alone. Today, the situation greatly differs due to mergers and bank failures; the total number of banks chartered in California as of December 31, 2021, was only 102.[3]

---

[2]   Governor Michelle W. Bowman "Speech: The Lack of New Bank Formations Is a Significant Issue for the Banking Industry," *Board of Governors of the Federal Reserve System*, October 22, 2021, available at: www.federalreserve.gov/newsevents/speech/bowman20211022a.htm [https://perma.cc/2BTV-CXFR] (last accessed September 26, 2023).

[3]   "Profile of State-Chartered Banks, 2018–2021," *California Department of Financial Protection and Innovation*, March 2022, available at: https://dfpi.ca.gov/wp-content/uploads/sites/337/2022/03/bpro4q21.pdf [https://perma.cc/UU7T-4CLC] (last accessed September 26, 2023).

Twenty years earlier, in 2001, the total number of California-chartered banks reached 196.[4] Nationwide only 5,000 banks were state-chartered. The state with the most state-chartered banks was Iowa, with 249 banks, based on the data available for 2017. In the entire country, only nine new FDIC-insured commercial banks were chartered in 2021 compared to 391 new banks chartered in 1984.[5] The FDIC also maintains a list of bank failures every year.

With the money raised from the 100 investors–founders, Silicon Valley Bank commenced its operations as planned in October 1983. True to the founders wishes, the Bank used its personal touches and referrals from 100 investors–founders to sign up clients. Biggerstaff was hired as Vice President for Business Development by the Holding Company, and his initial compensation was $42,000 annually. Roger Smith understood through his years in serving the tech community at Wells Fargo, Imperial, and Stanford banks that many tech companies started with lots of cash when they had just received capital infusion from VCs and investors. Dave Titus shared Smith's understanding. Smith knew that, as a new bank, SVB should make loans to tech companies against their accounts receivable. Of course, the question was: how did they convince the regulators to support this type of tech lending?

The Holding Company and the Bank faced federal and state examiners from different regulatory bodies every year. Primary bank regulators include the:

- Board of Governors of the Federal Reserve System (Federal Reserve);
- Federal Deposit Insurance Corporation (FDIC);
- State banking regulators; and
- Consumer Financial Protection Bureau (CFPB).

Typically, bank examiners conduct "safety and soundness," "target and horizontal," and Consumer Financial Protection Bureau (CFPB) examinations. The examiners may issue formal examination reports of "factual findings" and "opinions and recommendations". The examiners' reports are confidential and privileged to serve two underlying policy concerns: (1) Bank management must be open and forthcoming in response to the inquiries of bank examiners, and the examiners must, in turn, be frank in expressing their concerns about the bank; and (2) Disclosure of confidential portions of a bank report might breed public misunderstanding and unduly undermine confidence in the bank.[6]

---

[4] Profile of State-Chartered Banks, 2001–2004," *California Department of Financial Protection and Innovation*, February 2019, available at: https://dfpi.ca.gov/wp-content/uploads/sites/337/2019/02/bankprof4q04.pdf [https://perma.cc/ZJU2-WXF6] (last accessed September 26, 2023).

[5] "BankFind Suite: Find Annual Historical Bank Data," *Federal Deposit Insurance Corporation*, available at: https://banks.data.fdic.gov/explore/historical?displayFields=STNAME%2CTOTAL%2CBRANCHES%2CNew_Char&selectedEndDate=2021&selectedReport=CBS&selectedStartDate=1934&selectedStates=0&sortField=YEAR&sortOrder=desc [https://perma.cc/4ACU-8B35] (last accessed September 23, 2022).

[6] *In re Subpoena Served upon Comptroller of the Currency*, 967 F.2d 630 (D.C.Cir. 1992); *Delozier v. First Nat'l Bank of Gatlinburg*, 113 F.R.D. 522 (E.D.Tenn. 1986).

As the descriptor "safety and soundness" suggests, examiners conduct inspections to evaluate the soundness of the institution's assets and the effectiveness of its internal operations, policies, and management. Mnemonically speaking, bank examiners use a CAMELS rating to describe a bank's soundness in Capital adequacy, Asset quality, Management, Earnings, Liquidity, and Sensitivity. The examiners then rank the bank from one to five, where one is the highest and five is the lowest rating.

In the early days, at Silicon Valley Bank, the young banker Dave Titus recalled that he monitored all monthly activities of every loan to tech companies against account receivables. He kept track of all the invoices paid. He showed the examiners that every single loan to tech companies was paid back. He demonstrated that tech lending the SVB way alleviates any concerns relating to whether the Bank's loans are likely to be paid back and whether the bank's investments are profitable. Titus' data, including piles of loan documents and payments in tech lending at SVB, confirmed that the Bank's management made sound decisions. Titus was annoyed that the examiners spent days at the Bank wasting his time. He would rather use his time on his tech clients. He enjoyed helping clients get the financing they needed so they could expand, grow, and deliver their most promising ideas to the market.

After Dave Titus left in 1986, Harry Kellogg arrived and took charge of the Tech Lending division at SVB. The accounts receivable-based lending was the Bank's bread-and-butter product as Kellogg remembers. The loans were structured at 80 percent of eligible receivables. Though SVB took a lien on all the assets, including the intellectual property, the loan was only based on the account receivables. Kellogg asked auditors to conduct audits of the tech company's books on the receivables. With the security interest and loan structure, SVB minimized the risks in tech lending. Ultimately, the regulators agreed that the tech lending as performed by SVB was safe lending practice. Still, convincing the regulators took years, as Kellogg recounted the educating of the regulators by SVB lenders:

> We had to educate the regulators that this is relatively safe lending. We would get
> collateral on all the company's assets, the accounts receivable, the inventory, the
> fixed assets, equipment, and the IP. And I don't think there was any other bank
> around that really understood what's the value of the IP. But we had to educate the
> regulators, and it was year after year. We had to show them [the technology lending]
> write-offs are less than our middle market lending. It was an educational process
> [letting] them [see] our results year after year. The big fear for us: once the
> regulators understood, a new crew from the regulators would come in that didn't
> understand the lending model. In fact, we didn't lose a lot of money, if any, in
> lending to high-tech companies. But then, they sent in a new batch of regulators,
> and we'd have to re-educate them all over again.

Each year, when the regulators showed up at SVB for the annual examination, Kellogg and his lenders knew that they must spend weeks educating the examiners. The examiners arrived and occupied the board room. They requested individual files on VC investors, the portfolio companies or borrowers, the financial statements, the forecast, product information, and market research. "Literally, they made their second home" in the SVB board room with all the files. Each year Kellogg and other SVB bankers hoped that the next year the same group of examiners would come, so they "didn't have to start from scratch."

With respect to educating the regulators on giving tech loans at up to 80 percent of the receivables, SVB lenders needed to watch what they said to the regulators in their efforts to assuage any concern about the perceived risks associated with lending to high-tech companies in the 1980s:

> We said we had an uncovered amount in addition to our receivables. We pointed out to the regulators that we had all the assets. We will only lend against accounts receivable. But we still have some value, like the equipment of the company and its intellectual property assets. So it's not like we were going to lose everything just because we had eighty percent of receivable lending. We had a backstop because we had [an] all assets lien to include the fixed assets with the equipment, the inventory as well.

In connection with these tech lending transactions against account receivables, SVB took warrants as part of the loan cost that borrowers must pay. Borrowers did not have to pay for SVB's audit of their receivables. Kellogg recalled that SVB worked with the law firm Wilson Sonsini in the 1980s to get the first warrant agreement in place.

SVB's tech lending was later morphed to be called venture lending or venture debt. This meant SVB lenders must educate the regulators about venture lending. The regulators here were the federal regulators. Silicon Valley Bank was subject to examination as detailed in the Federal Reserve's Commercial Bank Examination Manual.[7] Interestingly, among the long list of nineteen different types of lending presently described in the Manual, there is no mention of "venture lending."

Types of Lending

2080 Commercial and Industrial Loans
2090 Real Estate Loans
2100 Real Estate Construction Loans
2102 Real Estate Appraisals and Evaluations
2103 Concentrations in Commercial Real Estate Lending, Sound

Risk-Management Practices

2110 Floor-Plan Loans
2115 Leveraged Lending

---

7 *Commercial Bank Examination Manual* (Federal Reserve May 2022), at 2, available at: www
  .federalreserve.gov/publications/files/cbem.pdf [https://perma.cc/KWR5–7PEK] (last accessed
  September 26, 2023).

2120 Direct Financing Leases
2130 Consumer Credit
2133 Subprime Lending
2135 Subprime Mortgage Lending
2136 Nontraditional Mortgages – Associated Risks
2138 Mortgage Banking
2140 Agricultural Loans
2142 Agriculture Credit-Risk Management
2150 Energy Lending – Reserve-Based Loans
2160 Asset-Based Lending
2170 Securities Broker and Dealer Loans
2180 Factoring

All of these types of lending failed to cover the venture lending practices employed by Silicon Valley Bank.[8] The list does include "leveraged lending," but that type of lending does not mean venture lending for startups and growing tech companies.

Leveraged lending is a type of corporate finance used for mergers and acquisitions, business recapitalization and refinancing, equity buyouts, and business or product line build-outs and expansions. Banks and other financial institutions participate in leveraged lending by providing senior financing, mezzanine financing, and short-term or bridge financing.[9] In addition to fees, the institutions may take equity positions in leveraged companies with direct investments through venture capital firms, securities firms, and small business investment companies. The institutions may also accept warrants. The Manual explains under "Risks Associated with Leveraged Lending" that there are nine categories of risk for bank supervision purposes when examiners assess banking risks. These risks are credit, interest rate, liquidity, price, foreign exchange, transaction, compliance, strategy, and reputation. The primary risks associated with leveraged lending, however, are credit, price, liquidity, reputation, compliance, and strategy.[10]

Venture lending is not leveraged lending. Venture lending is for startups while leveraged lending is for established firms. Immediately after receiving an infusion of capital in Series A, a startup seeks a venture loan in the form of a credit line for the purposes of facilitating the company to grow into the Series B round of funding, not for merger and acquisition, business recapitalization, refinancing, and the likes which are typical under leveraged lending. The loan that the startup needs is not

---

[8]   Ibid.

[9]   Richard E. Farley, "The Volcker Rule's Impact on Bridge Loans," *Stay Current by Paul Hastings*, November 2011, available at: https://webstorage.paulhastings.com/Documents/PDFs/2043.pdf (last accessed September 26, 2023).

[10] *Commercial Bank Examination Manual, supra*, note 7, at Section 2115, available at: www.federalreserve.gov/publications/files/cbem.pdf [https://perma.cc/KWR5–7PEK] (last accessed September 26, 2023).

bridge financing. In leveraged financing, banks provide temporary bridge financing during the syndication period. When the time commencing on the closing date and ending on the date the Loan and Commitments have been completed, they are to be repaid through subsequent debt or equity offerings. There are risks associated with bridge financing because the repayments may not occur due to investor appetite, liquidity, and market demand change during the syndication period.

Venture lending in the form of a short-term loan and a line of credit received after Series A is to be repaid by the next round of capital funding, Series B. At first glance, it reassembles a bridge financing. However, in substance, venture lending is on the growth of a startup that is on its way to meeting its milestone to get to Series B. Further, the VC firms who have already invested in the startup by providing Series A capital are working in their best interest to see the startup advance to Series B. The VC firms will benefit significantly when the portfolio company grows to subsequent rounds as the valuation of the enterprise increases and, in turn, the VC investments multiply. In addition, other VC firms would want to participate in the subsequent rounds as the startup meets its milestone and is ready to scale. Multiple VCs typically participate to spread out the risks in Series A, B, and subsequent rounds.

Kellogg recalled that the bank examiners were concerned about venture lending when SVB increased its focus on providing short-term loans and extending lines of credit to startups backed by VC firms. According to Kellogg, SVB lenders stayed away from mentioning the word "bridge loan" in their tech lending to avoid invoking fear in the bank examiners. To qualify for a bridge loan, a company must demonstrate strong credit and stable finances. These criteria were not applicable to tech startups with Series A funding because they had neither credit history nor stable finances. A conventional bank could take from thirty to forty-five days to approve a bridge loan and charge higher interest rates and fees. The lengthy approval process does not work for tech startups that must grow and continue to grow aggressively. Bridge loans are often used to finance the purchase and/or renovations of real estate properties. For businesses, a bridge loan provides short-term financing until the borrower obtains permanent financing. Bridge loans are risky because the business may not be able to obtain permanent financing. SVB lenders also did not like the "bridge loan" image because the bridge loan could turn into a pier inviting danger even though SVB lenders structured the deals like bridge loans:

> We had a saying that a bridge loan could turn into a pier, essentially, so yeah. And you fall off the pier at the end of the day. So, that's why we don't want the regulators to think we were making bridge loans. But in reality, we knew that's what we were doing. So, we loan money on accounts receivable. Let's say it's a million dollars, the company would raise $5 million. They rest their line of credit with us or accounts receivable allowance for thirty days, ninety days, or whatever. And as they ramped up to grow and generate revenue, then they would start borrowing on the accounts receivable. So, those were the annually renewable accounts receivable loans. So, we renew the line every year, get a new note, documentation, and all that.

Kellogg and SVB lenders had to convince the federal regulators that venture lending was safe. The lenders spent their time explaining to the bank examiners the VC ecosystem and VC-backed financing. They showed SVB received repayments on loans made to VC-backed companies who held no credit history nor products in the marketplace. They explained how these portfolio companies grew and that growth was the key factor. They explained how a loan or a line of credit to VC-backed companies lengthened the runway enabling the companies to get the next round of funding, enabling the companies, therefore, to pay back the loan from SVB. The Bank received lots of cash from deposits, and the Bank only loaned out one-third of the deposits. Venture lending suffered a significantly small number of default loans.

SVB decided to convince the skeptical examiners by arranging for the VCs to meet with the federal regulators. Kellogg recalled this strategy with pride because the meetings with elite VCs abated the examiners' concerns about venture lending.

> Meeting with the federal regulators was important. The investors had to meet with them, to give the regulators some idea because the VC industry was still kind of nascent at the time. So, they give them a better understanding of what the venture capital business was all about and how they selected the companies to invest in and they conducted due diligence.

Not all VC firms become the winners. Not all VC firms select winners only, and many VCs are simply not good investors. SVB's long-term relationships with the best VC firms and the best general partners in the industry enabled Kellogg to reach out to them in the Bank's efforts to win over the regulators in their examination of venture lending. After all, who knew more about the VC ecosystem than the reputable top VC firms in Silicon Valley? Of course, Silicon Valley Bank was the only bank that worked with the best VCs.

> We knew [who] the better VCs were. And we wouldn't lend money to certain companies backed by VCs because we knew what their record was or they'd walk away early. I mean, the valley was really small. So, you knew that some, certain VC firms would walk away at the first sign of a problem. That's not a Kleiner Perkins, that's not a Sequoia, that's not an NEA, that's not a Benchmark. So, we got to know the VCs that were going to have success. These VCs were not going to leave Silicon Valley Bank holding the bag because we were the only bank working with their companies. So, if Silicon Valley Bank went away, there had been no bank to help finance the growth of these companies. So, it's all about the investors, knowing their pattern of investing, and partners and theirs funds. Who were the successful general partners of these funds?

SVB was able to get Don Valentine, who founded the famed Sequoia Capital in 1972, to speak to the regulators. Valentine was among the first generation of venture capitalists who shaped and elevated Silicon Valley to its global status. As the marquee VC firm, Sequoia Capital has invested in over 500 technology companies.

Valentine helped in the creation of key industries like semiconductors, personal computers, personal computer software, digital entertainment, and networking. In 1987, Sequoia financed Cisco Systems and Valentine served as the Chairman of Cisco until 1996. Valentine had also invested in Atari in 1974, Apple Computer in 1977, and Electronic Arts in 1982, among many other important tech companies, by the time SVB approached him to meet with the regulators. SVB's relationships with Valentine, in fact, went way back to the early days when Smith and Kellogg were at Wells Fargo. Smith signed up Cisco's founders, the husband and wife team, Leonard Bosack and Sandy Lerner, as clients of SVB, in their kitchen when Cisco had just received its funding from Sequoia.

Dick Kramlich, the Founder & General Partner of the famous New Enterprise Associates (NEA), also came in to meet and talk to the regulators. Kramlich first worked with Arthur Rock in their VC investments in 1969. In 1977, he personally became an early investor in Apple Computer with his own account. A year later, in 1978, he founded NEA. Kramlich's investments in many tech companies turned into billion-dollar results, including Ascend Communications, ImmuneX, Juniper Networks, and Macromedia. His other notable winners included Xoom Corp, Financial Engines, Force10 Networks, Wayport, and CITIC Pharmaceuticals; they either went public or were acquired for substantial sums.

Franklin Pitch Johnson also pitched in to meet with the regulators at SVB's request. Johnson was also among the elite leaders of the first generation of VCs. In 1962, he became the cofounder of Draper and Johnson Investment Company, and three years later in 1965 became an independent venture capitalist as the founder of Asset Management Company. Under his leadership, the firm has made over 250 venture investments in the past five decades, including Amgen, Applied Bio Systems, Applied Micro Circuits, Conductus, Hybritech, IDEC Pharmaceuticals, Octel, Qume, Red Brick Systems, Remedy, Sierra Semiconductor, Tandem Computer, Teradyne, and Verity.

SVB also got John Doerr of Kleiner Perkins to meet with the regulators. In 1974 Doerr joined Intel in sales and then came to Kleiner Perkins in 1980. He was known for backing entrepreneurs and making investments in many successful tech companies, including Compaq, Netscape, Symantec, Sun Microsystems, drugstore.com, Amazon.com, Intuit, Macromedia, and Google. In 2015, Americans heard more of his name through Ellen Pao's sex discrimination case when she served as Doerr's chief of staff. She recounted instances where he declared that he'd specifically requested an Asian woman because he liked the idea of a "Tiger Mom-raised" woman and gave the male chief of staff investing work but the female chief of staff the grunt work. She must travel with him because he was more comfortable asking a woman to do such tasks.[11]

---

[11] Ellen Pao, "This Is How Sexism Works in Silicon Valley: My Lawsuit Failed. Others Won't," *The Cut*, available at: www.thecut.com/2017/08/ellen-pao-silicon-valley-sexism-reset-excerpt .html [https://perma.cc/U8FY-AZB6] (last accessed September 26, 2023).

In addition to Don Valentine, Dick Kramlich, Franklin Pitch Johnson, and John Doerr, SVB also persuaded elite venture capitalists from Mayfield Fund and Menlo Ventures to speak to the regulators. SVB wanted the regulators to see that the VCs are sophisticated, smart, and highly educated investors in tech companies. SVB relied on the VCs to convey the assurance that the loans will be repaid by the capital the VCs invested in the companies.

> These were investors in the companies. These were John Doerr from Kleiner Perkins, and Don Valentine from Sequoia. These were the actual investors in the companies. So they would see that these investors were pretty sophisticated ... They could see that these guys were smart, educated, and articulate. So they got a better assurance that we weren't just then lending money to some flaky investors in a company out there.

For five years the regulators were relentless. They demanded to see the evidence and hear the explanations from the important men of the venture capital community year after year about the VC ecosystem, VC financing, early-stage financing, late-stage financing, how SVB loans are made to tech companies, how the loans fit in the VC financing, how the loans are paid, whether the VCs abandon the deals, and so forth.

However, not all portfolio companies backed by VC firms succeed. What due diligence did the Bank conduct on the portfolio companies in making loan decisions? The Bank brought in the VCs to explain their due diligence, which the Bank relied on for underwriting venture loans.

> [The VCs] do due diligence. That was important. We didn't do our own technical due diligence on [portfolio companies] because we didn't have the ability and skill set to do that. So, we leverage off the due diligence [of the VCs]. Sometimes, they'd share it either orally or potentially in writing about what that IP was all about. So, we'd leverage the due diligence the venture firms get. And they were willing to share it with us because we will loan money. We were the only bank around that will lend money to these early-stage companies. So then we wanted to know the value of all the assets, including the IP. So, that's what the VC shared with regulators, the extent of the due diligence that they did before making it an equity investor.

The regulators learned that, because the VCs put more money into their portfolio companies through their investments, it was in the VCs' interest to conduct the due diligence. Due diligence is costly. The Bank could not incur such a cost and pass it to the borrower. The VCs spent their time explaining their risk, their due diligence, and selection of companies to the regulators.

> We knew the VCs who know a lot more in-depth about these industries than we ever would. So, they were the ones that were vetting the IP essentially for us, the underwriter of loans. We didn't, we didn't go deep and understood it [technology].

The VCs put in their hundreds of millions of dollars into these companies and they vetted the IP. So, we brought the investors in to meet with the regulators. That was unheard of in those days and maybe still is.

Kellogg and his team knew that many of these portfolio companies created intellectual property assets. But, as bankers, they simply did not possess the technical expertise to understand the intangible yet important assets. Also, if the deals went bad, who would purchase the intellectual property assets when the Bank wanted to foreclose or get out before the company further imploded? The VCs, as the investors with much capital sunk into the portfolio companies, always knew much more than the Bank about those potential outcomes.

In summary, the Bank relied on the VCs for their understanding of the intellectual property value and selling the intellectual property assets if needed to recover the loans.

The Bank, nevertheless, demonstrated to the regulators that they appreciated the value of the intellectual property assets owned by the portfolio companies and vetted by the VCs. The Bank insisted on taking a lien on all the assets. If a bad time occurred, the Bank could recover the loan by selling the most valuable assets of all, the intellectual property. Again, the Bank would turn to the VCs for potential purchasers of the intellectual property assets.

> We took a blanket lien on all the assets. IP was important for us, not that we necessarily understood that, but we knew the investors did, and the investors don't want to lose all their money ... We didn't understand deeply the semiconductor technology, the processes, and all the rest of it. But we know working with the investors, we could sell the IP potentially to a potential buyer or sell the company as well. That we just knew and relied on the VCs who knew and vetted it, or if there was a problem with a credit, who the potential buyers may be out there.

If a company must shut down, the VCs would work with the Bank to identify potential purchasers. It is in the VCs' interest to find a purchaser for the IP assets because that money recouped would help pay the outstanding loan. The more money they could recoup, the better. It is in the VCs' interest to keep their good relationship with the Bank because a VC firm generally caters to many portfolio companies, and the Bank worked with all of them. The VC firm wouldn't want one bad case to poison all the remaining transactions and existing relationships. It is also in the Bank's interest to recover what it loaned out and to work closely with the VCs. Most importantly, the VCs know more about the IP assets, the players, and the market – much better than the Bank.

> [The VCs] would know who the potential buyers might be out there of the IP or the company itself. If we had to wind down a company or shut down a company, we'd work with the investors who figured out who out there would buy the IP or the company. And there, as in everything else in Silicon Valley, there are specialized

firms out there I've worked with when companies are going out of business, Sherwood Partners, liquidate companies. That's what they do. So they worked with VCs to wind these companies down, and they get enormous fees if they're successful. So, there are specialty companies that do wind down bankruptcies, all the rest of it.

The VCs agreed to meet and speak to the regulators because VCs knew that their investments come in stages. Startups burn lots of cash. VC Series funds are not sufficient for the startups to grow as planned. Also, growing a company and executing a business strategy are not a straightforward process. There are many unanticipated problems along the journey of going from Series A to Series B and so forth. The efficient way of obtaining the needed cash to bridge between the two rounds of funding is not going for a half-round or a bridge equity round but a venture debt. A half-round or bridge equity round would cause further dilution of the VC investments. A venture debt will not cause dilution.

In providing venture lending to the portfolio companies, the Bank did not demand guarantees from the VCs. Because the Bank understood that the VCs had already put in their own risk money, the VCs appreciated the no-guarantee demand. In other words, VCs knew that they needed Silicon Valley Bank in the VC ecosystem to grow new tech companies and disrupt existing niches and subsectors.

> Well, they understood the value of what Silicon Valley Bank was, knowing what their bank was doing. So, they understood the value that Silicon Valley Bank was to their portfolios. And we would not share where non-public knowledge is concerned.

Finally, the regulators relented. The successes were in plain sight; the Bank's deposits grew so fast from VC money invested in portfolio companies who opened accounts at the Bank, to tech companies actually borrowing very little, for every $3 of deposit there was a $1 tech loan, and the write-offs were so small compared to other loans. The regulators could see that the deposits in the accounts at the Bank came from the VCs' portfolio companies. The Bank made venture loans to the portfolio companies from the money sitting in those accounts. The loans enabled the portfolio companies to grow and reach the next round of funding. The VCs infused new money into the portfolio companies that allowed the companies to pay back the loans. The Bank relied on the VCs and the VCs relied on the Bank. Both VCs and the Bank played necessary roles to nurture and grow new companies for the innovation economy. The regulators could see and hear all of it in those meetings over the five years. The regulators were educated in the end and never asked again about venture lending.

Considering that by 2022 Silicon Valley Bank was the thirteenth largest bank in the nation, and it had been dominating the venture lending market, why didn't the regulators include venture lending among the nineteen different types of lending subject to examination? The federal regulators saw the evidence of success every year during examinations at Silicon Valley Bank, noting that venture lending is safe.

They accepted that the technology-focused bank is the model of success and that no bank in the entire country was in this market. Perhaps they didn't need to identify and include venture lending as the twentieth type of lending in the Federal Reserve's *Commercial Bank Examination Manual*. SVB, with the help from VCs in those meetings, cemented that venture lending at a commercial bank is the federal regulators' best-kept secret.

Uniquely, the best-kept secret is perhaps the most notoriously open and has appeared on display in practice and in plain sight for the last forty years. Perhaps the best-kept secret opened the door for later comers like Square Bank and Bridge Bank to enter the venture lending practice without facing the five years of relentless examination by the federal regulators and without asking their VCs to meet and explain to the examiners the fundamentals of the VC ecosystem and financing.

The relationships between the Bank and the VCs were a type of partnership uniquely formed without formal contractual agreements between them. No statute or regulations was dictating the terms of the partnership. There was no contract signed between them. The understanding that the two sides had morphed into customary standards governed their dealings over time and carried into subsequent decades. The regulators, inadvertently, played a role in the morphosis of the partnership between the Bank and the VCs.

The partnership must constantly be nurtured with care, but often the care came from the Bank itself. Kellogg took the care to heart. One of Kellogg's many proud achievements in fortifying the relationships with the VCs is his creation of the VCs Advisory Board. Kellogg "layered" the Board with "early-stage investors, mid-stage, and late-stage investors" and added "prominent lawyers from Wilson Sonsini and someone from one of the CPA firms." SVB lenders wished to know trends in the different niches and subsectors in the tech industry and wanted advice on SVB's potential products, area of practice, and geographic expansion. It turned out the VC Advisory Board became more valuable to SVB than its regular board!

> I started a VC advisory board ... So, we didn't share nonpublic information with them. But we thought here are the area and the places we're thinking of expanding into. These are some of the products we're thinking about, and we got feedback from the VCs on the advisory board. In my opinion, our advisory board was more valuable than our regular board.

What would be the best way to receive experts' attention and advice? Of course, attending the VCs Advisory Board's quarterly meeting would be the answer. How could they entice the busy and important men in the VC community to attend the meeting?

Kellogg got Don Valentine and other prominent VCs on the Board. He would fete them with dinner. However, the dinner alone would not work. SVB gave stock options to the VC Advisory Board for their efforts. Their input was very important to SVB. At these dinner events, SVB bankers got to know the VCs and "bond with them." A few years later, the Holding Company's Board decided that giving away stock options to the VC Advisory Board was not a good idea. So, they put an end to that stock option incentive.

Kellogg got creative. Crisp $100 Franklin bills might do the trick. SVB gave out the $100 bill only if the Board members showed up on time for the meeting. It did it for Don Valentine. Regardless of being one of the most prominent and successful venture capitalists in history and the founder of the storied Sequoia Capital, Valentine would make sure to get to the Board's quarterly meeting so he could fetch the $100 bill. He wanted to show it to his wife each time he got that crisp $100 bill. Years later, Kellogg nostalgically recalled Don Valentine running for the $100 bill.

> And we give them a $100 bill for showing up on time for VC dinner. Don Valentine, one of the most famous VCs who passed away a year ago ... [O]ne night, we were having our advisory board dinner. And Don is running down the street because he wanted to get that $100 bill. I mean, the guy was a billionaire at the time, but so it was important for his wife ... I always remember that here's a guy, one of the most prominent venture capitalists ever running down the street to get a hundred-dollar bill. I can still visualize Don running down the street for his hundred-dollar bill.

Seeking valuable advice and comments from those on the VCs Advisory Board, again, was part of SVB's efforts to build long-lasting relationships with its clients. The bond distinguished the Bank's relationships with VCs from other banks. Fortunately for SVB, banks such as ComericA, Square, and Bridge Banks tried numerous times to compete in the tech lending space but could not. They didn't have Kellogg's VC Advisory Board with $100 bills and Don Valentine.

The partnership between SVB and the VCs was tested when Roger Smith was fired by the Holding Company's Board in 1993 in light of the Bank's overextending in the real estate market and suffering its resultant losses. The regulators inspected the Bank's operations and were very unhappy with the situation at the Bank. They conducted the examinations and issued their letter. Kellogg was present at the Holding Company Board's meeting when the examiners' letter was read out. The meeting took place before Christmas 1992. Years later, recalling the meeting, Kellogg remembered it as though it happened just yesterday.

The federal regulators issued the cease and desist order on April 16, 1993. The Board of Governors of the Federal Reserve System later issued its final order against the Holding Company and its primary subsidiary, the Silicon Valley Bank, pursuant to 12 U.S.C. §1818(b). This statutory section carried the title "Termination of status as insured depository institution." The federal regulators found the Bank was engaged in unsafe and unsound practices in conducting the business of a depository institution. Specifically, the Bank was growing too fast with deposits placed in accounts from investors and tech companies who received funding from VCs.

The Bank took the deposits and turned them into loans in the real estate sector. The real estate crisis left the Bank with nonperforming real estate loans and exposed the Bank's weaknesses, along with its unsafe and unsound practices. The Bank violated the banking law regarding the deposits. The consent order required the Bank to cease and desist from engaging in real estate practice and to take "affirmative action to correct the conditions resulting from any such violation and practice."

The Board fired Roger and the rest of the management team at the Bank. Kellogg was not fired but he and his team needed to dig deep in their relationships with the VCs and urge them not to abandon the Bank.

The bankers at the Sand Hill Road office raced into action. They spent day after day in meetings with VC after VC. They assured the VCs that the Bank would not fail, the Bank would get out of real estate lending, and the Bank would take corrective actions to address the violations. They told the VCs that the Board would soon find a new CEO to replace Smith. They lived in fear that the VCs would call up the portfolio companies to withdraw their deposits at the Bank and move the money to other banks. That would be the end of Silicon Valley Bank. Kellogg recalled:

> I and a colleague spent all of our time at Sand Hill Road assuring the VCs that the bank would not fail. Because if we would've had, if the VCs called all their companies to get your money out of Silicon Valley Bank, and move it to a safe bank like Bank of America and Wells Fargo, we would not have survived. So, we were hand-holding the VCs to assure them that the bank wasn't going to fail, or we were gonna find a new CEO to replace Roger. We would not do any more real estate. We just gave them assurances. But yeah, I remember those days, you know, like they were yesterday, meeting with the VCs to let them know Silicon Valley Bank is not going to fail.

The relationships that took years to build smoothed the rough time. The VCs listened to the SVB bankers and did not tell the CEOs of the portfolio companies to remove their deposits from the Bank. Kellogg deeply appreciated the VCs' strong support, and he always reserved the highest respect for the VCs who stood by the Bank in 1993.

> But the good news for us yet, those relationships worked out. I mean, we had built those relationships [in a] solid way that, you know, that they believed in us, and they didn't leave the bank, or they didn't tell their portfolio to leave the bank.

> So, that's why I still have high respect from somebody from those venture firms because they could very easily just phone the CEO of the company, and get your money out of Silicon Valley Bank.

Kellogg understood that the federal regulators examined both the tech lending practice and the deposits. Kellogg and the SVB bankers succeeded in their persuasion of the clients to keep the money in the accounts so the Bank could quickly shed the troublesome real estate lending division and concentrate its efforts on safe and sound lending – the tech lending practice.

> The regulators looked not only at your loans but at your deposits as well. Are these deposits going to stick around or at the first sign of a problem, are they going to leave? I mean, that was when the bank had its issues in 1993. We got a cease and desist from the regulators.

SVB swiftly addressed the problems. The Board brought in John Dean, a bank turnaround specialist, to be the CEO. Dean implemented new measures, put systems in place, and shed the real estate lending division, in compliance with the federal regulators' order.

That meant during 1993 the Holding Company and the Bank consented to formal supervisory orders by the Federal Reserve Bank of San Francisco and the Bank itself consented to a formal supervisory order by the California State Banking Department. Specifically, the orders required the violators to comply with the following actions:

- suspension of cash dividends; restrictions on transactions between the Company and the Bank without prior regulatory approval;
- development of a capital plan to ensure the Bank maintains adequate capital levels subject to regulatory approval;
- development of plans to improve the quality of the Bank's loan portfolio through collection or improvement of the credits within specified time frames;
- changes to the Banks' loan policy requiring the Directors' Loan Committee to approve all loans to any one borrower exceeding $3 million and requiring the directors to become more actively involved in loan portfolio management and monitoring activities;
- review of, and changes in, the Bank's loan policy to implement (i) policies for controlling and monitoring credit concentrations, (ii) underwriting standards for all loan products, and (iii) standards for credit analysis and credit file documentation; development of an independent loan review function and related loan review policy and procedures;
- development of Board oversight programs to establish and maintain effective control and supervision of Management and major Bank operations and activities; development of a plan, including a written methodology, to maintain an adequate allowance for loan losses, defined as a minimum of 2.0 percent of total loans;
- development of business plans to establish guidelines for growth and ensure maintenance of adequate capital levels; review and evaluation of existing compensation practices and development of officer compensation policies and procedures by the Board of Directors of the Company and Bank;

- changes in fees paid to directors and bonuses paid to executive officers receive regulatory approval; and,
- development of a detailed internal audit plan for approval by the Board of Directors of the Bank.

The State Banking Department order further required the Bank to maintain a tangible equity-to-assets ratio of 6.5 percent.[12]

The Holding Company and the Bank were in substantial compliance with such orders on March 31, 1995. The Bank was back on track and turned profits again with a net income of $1.7 million or $0.21 per share for the first quarter of 1994, and a net income of $3.3 million or $0.37 per share for the first quarter of 1995.

One thing that the regulators learned was that real estate lending, not tech lending, was the riskiest. But the Bank must make profits from its lending practices. Dean devised new specialty practices that were non-tech. The third CEO, Ken Wilcox, then eliminated all those specialties and concentrated SVB 100 percent on serving the tech ecosystem. SVB thrived spectacularly by focusing both its identity and business as the only bank with 100 percent in tech lending and banking.

In the subsequent decade after the Great Recession, in 2010, the Dodd-Frank Wall Street Reform and Consumer Protection Act created the Consumer Financial Protection Bureau (CFPB). To protect the consumers, the CFPB examiners conduct their own bank inspections in accordance with the CFPB policy. Typically, the CFPB examiners perform the following in the course of an examination at Silicon Valley Bank, or any depository institution:

- collect and review available information (from within the CFPB, from other Federal and state agencies, and from public sources), consistent with statutory requirements;
- request and review supplementary documents and information from the entity to be examined;
- develop and obtain internal approval for a preliminary risk focus and scope for the onsite portion of the examination;
- go onsite to observe, conduct interviews, and review additional documents and information;
- consult internally if the examination indicates potential unfair, deceptive, or abusive acts or practices; discrimination; or other violations of law;
- draw preliminary conclusions about the regulated entity's compliance management and its statutory and regulatory compliance;
- consult internally about follow-up corrective actions that the institution should take, whether through informal agreement or a formal enforcement action, if warranted by findings;

[12] "SVB 10Q Filing," *Silicon Valley Bank*, March 31, 1995.

- draft the examination report;
- obtain appropriate internal review and approval for the examination work and draft examination report;
- share the draft report with the prudential regulator and obtain and consider any comments they may offer, consistent with statutory requirements; and
- after final internal clearance, finalize and transmit the report to the supervised entity.[13]

It is no surprise that, since 1993, SVB was never again found in violation of unsafe and unsound practice requirements associated with its lending practices. Even so, Kellogg could never forget the dark day at the Board meeting before Christmas 1992.

Kellogg was in shock that Smith was gone and everyone in management at the Bank was gone. Dean brought in a banker from Boston to head the technology lending division. Kellogg was ordered to report to this new immediate supervisor instead of reporting directly to the CEO as Kellogg used to do under Smith. The new boss was a banker cut from the same cloth as traditional bankers. He and his lending group spent all their time in the bank office. They were all suited up. They didn't go to where the tech clients were meeting and working. They avoided the tech entrepreneurs. They didn't reach out to the VCs. They ignored the lawyers. Kellogg could not recognize SVB's DNA in this new technology lending group. Feeling very vulnerable, Kellogg received a call to head a new tech lending group at a local bank. He accepted the offer and left SVB.

With the new job that came with a new car, Kellogg spent eleven months at the new bank. Still, his heart ached for SVB. He finally received a phone call from Dean informing him that the banker from Boston was fired and that Dean wanted him to return to head the technology banking division. There was no banker in Silicon Valley with VC relationships as deep as Kellogg's. Both Dean and Kellogg made wise decisions. Kellogg rejoined SVB to cultivate and maximize his relationships with VCs, ensuring the partnership foundation between SVB and the VC community for years.

---

[13] *CFPB Supervision and Examination Manual* (Consumer Financial Protection Bureau (CFPB) March 2022), Overview 5–6, available at: https://files.consumerfinance.gov/f/documents/cfpb_supervision-and-examination-manual.pdf [https://perma.cc/Q4YQ-B7PM] (last accessed September 26, 2023).

8

SVB Tech Lending and the Birth of Venture Debts

Roger Smith and his bankers from Wells Fargo's Special Industries Group brought their experience in tech lending to Silicon Valley Bank (SVB). According to Smith, Bank of America (BOA) was the first bank to take warrants for the right to purchase shares as part of the loan cost that they charged tech companies who were backed by Venture Capitalists (VCs) in Silicon Valley's early days. After both Bank of America and Wells Fargo exited tech lending, SVB became the sought-after bank for lending to tech companies. SVB perfected its tech lending practice to startups that were VC-funded entities. This practice would later be called venture lending, venture loans, or venture debts in the United States and overseas.[1]

Smith observed from his experience of running Wells Fargo's Special Industries Group that two characteristics existed relating to tech companies. One, there is a lot of cash when tech companies receive their capital infusion from VCs' rounds of funding. Tech companies focus first on growth but may not generate profits until later. If a tech company can wait for a few more months before obtaining its next round of capital funding, the company will receive a better valuation, assuming that it continues to grow and meet its milestones. What can a creative banker like Smith do to serve these VC-backed tech companies? Banks always insist on the creditworthiness of a potential borrower. Could Smith and his lenders ignore the traditional approach to lending practice implemented by banks? What if the VCs walked away from funding the tech company for the next round? How did SVB minimize the bank's risks? What type of due diligence did SVB conduct before the approval of loans to VC-backed companies?

Two years after Smith opened SVB, the VC community garnered $3.8 billion in total commitments from limited partners in 1985. By 1987, when Harry Kellogg

---

[1] Nico Lehnertz, Caroline Plagmann, and Eva Lutz, "Why Deep Pockets Make Great Borrowers: An Empirical Analysis of Venture Loans," *Journal of Business Economics* 92.9 (2022): 1–23.

joined forces with Smith to strengthen tech lending practice at SVB, the total commitments to VC funds climbed to $4.9 billion.[2] To Smith and his lenders, that large amount of cash and capital infusion to increase new growth of new tech companies just exploded. Some of the money should be in accounts at SVB! Silicon Valley epitomized the best place to do business, especially for Smith's new bank. To put the VC community in the economics of that time, one could feel the excitement about the 1980s. New firms were incorporated at a rate not seen before. There were 1.3 million new startups in all areas spruced up annually.

During the 1980s, for the first time in the United States, small firms were more innovative than large firms; more innovations were created by small firms comparatively speaking.[3] Before 1980, large firms created the majority of new jobs in the United States, but in the 1980s job creation shifted to small firms. Fortune 500 companies lost 4 million jobs while small firms created 16 million new jobs.[4] The astounding increase in new firms meant lots of capital infusion being poured into funding startups.

One of the major sources for capital infusion into the VC community came from the change in the 1979 Employee Retirement Income Security Act's (ERISA) "prudent man" rule. This change urged the fiduciary to manage a pension fund in a manner that a man "acting in a like capacity and familiar with such manners would use in the conduct of an enterprise of like character with like aims."[5] The unlocking of the ERISA pension funds allowed a vast amount of money to be invested in high-risk assets, VCs included! Pension fund managers could invest up to 10 percent of their capital in VC funds, propelling the annual contributions to VCs from the meager $100–200 in the 1970s to more than $4 billion at the end of the 1980s. VC money, however, first exploded in 1958 due to the change in the Small Business Investment Act (SBIA) which authorized tax breaks for investors. Also, in 1978, Congress reduced capital gains tax from 49 percent to 28 percent, and then further reduced it to 20 percent by 1981. The combination of the flow of money from pension funds and the low tax rate on capital gains encouraged the explosion of the VC community in the 1980s.

A VC firm consists of a limited partnership with general partners and limited partners. High-net-worth individuals, family offices, endowments, foundations, pension funds, insurance companies, and other investors are the limited partners providing the money. The investment professionals who make investments in

---

[2]   Paul A. Gompers, "The Rise and Fall of Venture Capitals," *Business and Economic History* 23.2 (1994): 1–26.

[3]   F. Scherer, "Changing Perspectives on the Firm Size Problem," in *Innovation and Technological Change: In International Comparison* (Z. Acs and D. Audretsch, eds., University of Michigan Press 1991), 24–28; Lehnertz et al., *supra*, note 1.

[4]   D. Birch, "Sources of Job Growth and Some Implications," in *Jobs, Earnings, and Employment Growth Policies in the United States* (in J. Kasarda, ed., Kluwer Academic, 1990), 71–76.

[5]   ERISA, §404 (a)(1), 29 U.S.C. §1104(a)(1) (Supp. V 1975).

startups and manage the funds are the general partners (GPs). Limited partners (LPs) understand the high risk–high reward in VC investments and contribute 99 percent of the money and keep 80 percent of the net gains. That means the GPs who invest the LPs' money by selecting startup companies or portfolio investments, assisting those companies to grow, and then liquidating them through a private sale or a public offering, will spend a period of up to ten years to grow a particular fund or investment. GPs seek a return of at least five times their investment. GPs will keep 20 percent of the net gains and charge a 1–3 percent annual management fee. LPs may impose various restrictions on GPs in the limited partnership agreements to ensure the GPs' main responsibilities involve maximizing the investors' return. For instance, GPs cannot invest all the money in a single startup or personal funds. LPs don't want to see all their money evaporate in a highly concentrated failed investment made by the GPs.

The idea of selecting the startups with potential for fast growth and assisting those startups to grow through providing counsel and support to entrepreneurs and management teams originated from Harvard Business School Professor George Doriot. VC firms often adhere to Doriot's philosophy. They conduct due diligence before making their investments and extend their technical expertise in helping entrepreneurs in the management and growth of startups. Robert Medearis, one of the three founders of Silicon Valley Bank, always spoke fondly of his old Professor Doriot. Medearis happily recalled his class and project assignments in Doriot's course during Medearis' MBA pursuit.

Both Medearis and Roger Smith knew that VC investments in Boston and Route 128 during the 1970s had made their way to Silicon Valley because they saw the creation and growth of Fairchild Semiconductor, reportedly the first tech company to receive VC funding with the money from wealthy industrialist Sherman Fairchild. Arthur Rock helped arrange the VC funding of Fairchild. Later, Rock's VC firm funded Intel and Apple. Smith met the legendary Arthur Rock when the venture capitalist opened an account at Wells Fargo. Meanwhile, the founders of Silicon Valley Bank were keenly aware of the release of cash from pension funds, foundations, endowments, family offices, and wealthy investors and that cash was being unleashed by the low tax rate on capital gains of 20 percent in 1981 into tech companies in the West Coast via VC funds.

Smith and his lenders strongly believed that banking is about relationships and the only way to get some of the VC investments into Silicon Valley Bank meant building meaningful, reciprocal relationships with the VCs, the investors, the entrepreneurs, the lawyers who do the deals, the equipment leasing companies, and the accountants. All the players were part of an entrepreneurs' ecosystem. Bank of America, Wells Fargo, and Bank of the West were no longer contenders in the tech lending space. Smith and his bankers focused on signing up accounts from new tech companies while Harry Kellogg and his lenders concentrated on making loans to tech companies; yet Smith and Kellogg knew that they didn't want to repeat the mistake made by the Special Industries Group at Wells Fargo in venture lending.

In venture lending, as the name suggests, the tech company must be a VC-funded entity. Unlike conventional loans where metrics such as historical cash flow and creditworthiness are scrutinized, venture loans focus on the startup's ability to raise the next round of capital from VCs to fund its efforts to meet the next milestone, to grow the company a little longer, and to repay the outstanding loans. That means SVB could only make loans to VC-funded tech companies in order to reduce its risk of nonperforming loans and the irks of the banking regulators. Also, to minimize risks, venture loans should be short-term to enable the startups to focus on the pivotal activities to reach their milestone for advancement to the next round of VC capital. The entrepreneurs could use the money from the venture loan to bolster the sales team, lease critical equipment, enhance marketing efforts, invest in needed development, and begin scaling the enterprise. The ratio of venture loan to valuation should be between 6 and 8 percent of the startup's last post-money valuation.

For SVB lenders, in the venture lending niche, tech startups need an alternative source of financing. Debt is better than equity from the tech startup's perspective. First, let's understand VC-funded tech startups versus the millions of new businesses annually created since the 1980s.

The universe of VC-funded tech companies is small compared to the total number of startups each year. Globally, the number of newly created businesses approximates 100 million annually. In the United States, there were 804,398 new businesses founded in 2020. This number is smaller than the 1980s boom when Silicon Valley Bank began its journey and witnessed 1.3 million new businesses start every year.[6] Generally, startups suffer large failure rates. For example, of all businesses started in 2014, 80 percent made it to the second year, 70 percent to the third year, 62 percent to the fourth year, and 56 percent to the fifth year. In other words, half of new businesses fail in five years.

Without financing, startups wither. One in four new startups are not able to receive the necessary funding and quickly face the reality of limiting the growth of their business.[7] When an entrepreneur forms a startup, the first source of funding typically comes from the entrepreneur's personal savings and credit, family, and friends. One in three startups commences their business with less than $5,000. Personal funds of startup costs contribute 77 percent of all financing methods for startups.

Some research universities and affiliated foundations create pre-incubation centers or accelerator programs to assist student entrepreneurs in all areas. Indiana University's Shoemaker Innovation Center provides office space for student entrepreneurs and collaborates with the Hoosier Hatchery pre-incubator at the Kelley School of Business and Bloomington's Dimension Mill startup accelerator to assist

---

[6]   Gompers, *supra*, note 2.
[7]   "106 Must-Know Startup Statistics for 2023," available at: www.embroker.com/blog/startup-statistics/ (last accessed September 28, 2023).

students to build and launch their business idea. IU Philanthropic Venture Fund cultivates an entrepreneurial culture for students at Indiana University by providing pre-seed funding to viable early-stage IU student-led companies. The University of Washington created UWComotion to support startup creations and launch their ideas. Similar tech startup incubation hubs are at the University of Michigan, University of Wisconsin, University of Utah, Georgia Tech, and UC San Diego. Obviously, with its proximity to Silicon Valley, Stanford is a leader among universities in entrepreneurship and the incubation of new startups.

If the tech startup can survive and advance, it must next obtain outside funds in the form of seed capital or money from incubation funds or angel funding. In financing parlance the term "angel" traces its origin to affluent patrons of Broadway theaters who advanced the funds for a theatrical production and received the capital and interest payments afterward, assuming the productions were successful in generating revenue. In tech financing, the term "angel investor" has been credited to William E. Wetzel, who coined the term to describe supporters of new tech ideas in 1978.[8] In 1983, Wetzel interviewed 133 angel investors in the New England area to identify their roles and recommend steps to improve the efficiency of this type of informal risk capital. Angels have now spread their wings to more than 300,000 startups and there are more than 400 angel groups.[9] Angel round financing often means a very small check that occurs when a startup is about to launch or is launching. The check, however, is too small for the entrepreneur to meet the daily operation.

Seed funding represents the first official money that a tech startup secures. The entrepreneur typically must start with a prototype or proof of concept and establish demand for the product. Just like planting a tree, the entrepreneur needs seed money at the infancy stage. An investor invests capital at the seed stages in exchange for an equity ownership or convertible note stake in the startup. Founders learn very soon that they must give away 20 percent of their company as they engage in the seed round if they wish their companies to have a chance to survive and quickly grow to the next round of funding. Founders discover that the money from personal savings, friends, family, and university pre-seed innovation centers depletes very fast. Top seed investors today are Andreessen Horowitz, Accel, Founders Fund, Balderton Capital, Y Combinators, Techstars, and 500 Startups, among others. The amount of a seed fund round depends on the technology and the market, and on how well the entrepreneurs can get the startup to the next fundable milestone. Yatrikart, a tech-enabled transit retail chain, raised $450,000 in a seed funding round from Shuru-Up's Digital platform and Artha Venture Fund. Jit, a Tel

---

[8] William E. Wetzel, Jr., "Angels and Informal Risk Capital" (1983). University of Illinois at Urbana-Champaign's Academy for Entrepreneurial Leadership Historical Research Reference in Entrepreneurship, available at: https://ssrn.com/abstract=1505193 (last accessed September 28, 2023).

[9] John May and Manhong Mannie Liu, *Angels without Borders* (World Scientific, 2015).

Aviv, Israel-based provider of a platform simplifying product security for developers, raised $38.5 million in seed funding from Tiger Global Management and strategic angel investors. Jit, founded in 2021, was nurtured by FXP, a new Boston–Israel startup venture studio. Typically, the newly raised seed funds would be utilized to expand the platform's infrastructure, improve technology, and hire talent.

Seed money is not free unless it is from America's Seed Fund. The National Science Foundation through America's Seed Fund awards more than $200 million in research and development funding to 400 startups across the United States. Most of the startups receiving the funding employ fewer than five employees. Unlike private sources, America's Seed Fund does not demand equity from the startups. The entrepreneurs retain full ownership of their startups and intellectual property.[10]

For many startups, 12–18 months encompass the usual time to go from seed funding to a Series A financing round. The rare and fortunate few among startups can then attract funding from VC firms.

Startups' funding statistics provide a sobering reminder of the competitive nature of obtaining funding. Of all the startups in 2013, only 0.05 percent received VC funding and 1 percent received angel funding. Angel investors invested in 61,900 companies, with an average amount of $74,955. Nevertheless, for the very fortunate few of all startups that received VC funds – a total of 3,700 companies in 2012 – the average investment by VCs was $5.94 million. In other words, angel investors write sixteen checks for every check VCs write, but the average amount from angel investors is extremely small compared to VC's funding rounds. Breaking down the VC-funded companies further, early-stage companies receive an average of $2.6 million from VCs. Only 1 percent of tech startups evolve into unicorn companies like Uber, Airbnb, Slack, Stripe, and Docker.

In 2021, less than 10 percent of companies that received seed capital advanced to Series A. In the Series A round, the venture capitalists receive the first series of preferred stock after the common stock is issued during the seed financing round. The amount of funding through Series A reached $22.2 million in 2021, representing a 30 percent increase from $15.6 million in 2020. In the entire United States, only 880 companies with seed money advanced to Series A funding in 2021.[11] The 880 Series A deals mean 7,920 other unfortunate companies with seed money failed to reach the next round of funding. The sobering statistics confirm why banks don't dare to make loans to young startups in the seed round of funding. The shocking failure rate among startups prevents banks from engaging in courting and signing startups as clients for banking and lending services.

---

[10] "About America's Seed Fund Powered by NSF," available at: https://seedfund.nsf.gov/about/ (last accessed September 28, 2023).

[11] "Series A, B, C, Funding: Averages, Investors & Valuations," available at: www.fundz.net/what-is-series-a-funding-series-b-funding-and-more (last accessed September 28, 2023).

A company that obtains a Series A round demonstrates that it supports a minimum viable product. The Series A capital furnishes the company with a couple of years of runway enabling the company to develop its product, hire a management team, and create a market strategy. Major VC firms that provide Series A funding include Accel, 500 Startups, Bessemer Venture Partners, Andreessen Horowitz, Greycroft Partners, IDG Capital, NEA, and Sequoia Capital, among hundreds of other venture firms.

VCs are active investors. When they invest in startups, they obtain seats on the boards of directors. They shape all major decisions at the startups. They distribute money based on milestone attainment. They monitor the startup progress. They possess the right to hire and fire the management and entrepreneurial team. They introduce entrepreneurs to experts, consultants, lawyers, and bankers. To SVB, the "bankers" should be Silicon Valley Bank, and SVB must work very hard to secure its role as the "Bank for the Innovation Economy" so VCs encourage their portfolio companies to open new accounts and become long-term clients with SVB.

Smith and his bankers all saw that VC firms hold power. Some of the late-stage, high-growth VC-backed companies went public. The bankers witnessed that in the two decades from 1972 to 1992, 962 VC-backed companies reached the initial public offering (IPO) stage. The impact of VC-backed companies on the economy was well documented as seen in the 1993 statistics, 30 VC-backed companies employed more than 420,000 people in the United States and their market value then already reached $88 billion. Also, VCs invested in high-tech startups like Apple Computer, Microsoft, Lotus, and Genentech and low-tech startups like Staples, TCBY, and Federal Express. Most importantly, all companies desired high growth.

Silicon Valley Bank fostered and promoted its venture debt practice by coveting some of the billions of outstanding VC money in addition to the Bank's existing business of using accounts receivable or assets-based lending to tech companies in the early years after its opening for business in 1983. Like all pioneers, creating and doing something new does not come easy. SVB must disregard old concepts of creditworthiness and traditional factors in lending and embrace the startup's growth instead of the startup's lack of profit.

Silicon Valley Bank organically learned and leveraged its relationships with VCs to find the answers to the original question concerning how to minimize the Bank's risks in tech lending.

Given only 0.05 percent of all startups or 10 percent of seeded companies are selected to receive Series A from VCs, Silicon Valley Bank rode the VC's coattail in its strategy of banking and lending tech startups. In selecting the 10 percent of all seeded companies for its Series A funds, VCs are careful in their analysis and due diligence of worthy startups. These efforts cost time and money. VCs can afford to engage in these efforts, but banks comprise neither the expertise nor the resources to conduct analysis and due diligence of seeded startups. Banks cannot and do not know which seeded startups are more worthy startups that would advance to the next stage of funding to pay back bank loans. A solution to this conundrum happens to be for the Bank to follow the VCs.

Indeed, SVB knew that while top-tier VCs tolerate higher levels of risk, the Bank must still be very careful in their lending decisions. Only startups that represent potentially the most disruptive and best technology can secure pitch meetings with top-tier VCs. Out of 100 pitches, VCs select only ten startups for further scrutiny. Through intensive due diligence, VCs then narrow the ten investment opportunities even further, ultimately funding only one.[12] VCs conduct a "thorough due diligence process on the entrepreneur or scientist, the technology, and the potential market."[13] The due diligence focuses on minimizing risks by aiming to address questions such as, "Does the technology work? Is there a market for it? Is the market accessible? Who are the competitors? Does the entrepreneur possess the skills to bring the concept to the market?" Moreover, for startups with technology in regulated indus-tries, VCs focus on additional risks: "Can clinical trials be conducted? Will they be successful? Can regulatory approval be obtained?"[14]

The level of due diligence conducted by VCs can be extensive and costly. SVB simply could neither afford to conduct the same nor absorb the cost. Nor could the Bank then pass the cost on to the startups or high-growth companies. That would make the total cost of the loan prohibitive for potential tech clients whose resources are concentrated on growth, not high loan costs and fees. To minimize the total cost of the loan, the Bank leveraged its extensive and unique relationships with VCs and depended on the VCs for their due diligence in selecting potential clients from among the startups that have already received VC funding. Consequently, SVB targeted VC-backed companies that recently obtained Series A funding *and* who would most likely receive Series B funding. Without receiving the Series B funding, the company will not have the money to pay back SVB's loan!

SVB faced the same concern as any commercial bank when SVB bankers executed loans: the risk that their loans may be in default. Even so, a tech startup's business model is about trying to perfect its technology and succeed at specific milestones for high growth. This means the startup constantly needs a cash infusion and is not in the position to be paying back a loan even if it could obtain such a loan. The only way for SVB to lend to a VC-backed startup would be if there is a strong likelihood that the startup will pay back the loan. That can only happen if there is a strong likelihood that the startup will receive new funding. This is when the next round of VC Series B funding comes in to provide the startup with the needed cash infusion and to pay back the loans to SVB.

[12] Brief of Amici Curiae Venture Capital Firms Aberdare Ventures et al. in Support of Respondents, Microsoft Corp. v. i4i Ltd., 564 U.S. 91 (2011) (No. 10-290), 2011 WL 1042210.
[13] Ibid.
[14] Ibid.

Consequently, relying on the same VCs for their due diligence alone is not sufficient to ascertain whether the startup, which has already received funding from the VCs, will pay back the loan, because the VCs may abandon the startup, or other VCs may not be interested in joining the original VCs to provide the startup with the next round of funding. In other words, to ensure the likelihood that SVB must get paid on loans to startups, the Bank must feel comfortably certain that the startup that has just received Series A funding from VCs will be likely to receive Series B funding from the same VCs and, perhaps, additional VCs.

Startups that have received VC funding for Series A face only a 50 percent chance to survive to the next round of Series B funding. That meant SVB could not lend to just any startups that have received Series A funding, as it is still too risky for default. There is information asymmetry that SVB confronted because the startups and the VCs simply knew more about the startup's situation than the bankers at SVB. To overcome the information asymmetry problem, SVB cultivated and built a uniquely strong relationship with the VCs, as well as a nurturing relationship with the Series A startups. There are quality signals that SVB and others can rely on to independently verify the likelihood that the VC-backed companies will secure the next round of VC funding.[15] Because SVB accumulated four decades of relationships with thousands of VCs, including the marquee VCs in the industry, SVB overcame the information asymmetry faced by its competitors. Accordingly to Harry Kellogg, SVB knew all the VCs and gathered knowledge of whether the VCs would continue to invest in the next round of funding or abandon a particular portfolio company even before the company's management team learned the bad news!

Aligning the information symmetry in its favor, SVB imposed a cost to its loan to the Series A companies. On the one hand, the VCs wanted SVB, the experienced bank in tech lending, to work with their portfolio companies; so, the VCs sent the companies to the Bank or nudged the founders to work with the Bank. It was in the VCs' interest that the Bank furnished a loan to lengthen the startup's runway for a couple of months, so the startup can reach Series B without VCs furnishing their money or helping to secure capital for the startup between Series A and Series B. Also, some VCs may abandon the company and not want to waste additional money. The Bank's money is relatively cheap and money that VCs don't have. On the other hand, the startup does want and need the loan because it must grow to reach specific milestones, so it can enjoy a higher valuation. The startup does not want to dilute itself too soon with more equity capital. The startup also does not want to expire prematurely or to belong to the 50 percent failure group of Series A companies that could not get to Series B. All founders and entrepreneurs know that reaching Series B is the most challenging time in early-stage companies. It is in

---

[15] See Xuan-Thao Nguyen and Erik Hille, "Disruptive Lending for Innovation: Signaling Model and Banks Selection of Startups," *University of Pennsylvania Journal of Business Law* 21.1 (2018): 200.

this scary death valley where entrepreneurs learn if they can make it, Series C would be easier. To SVB and all stakeholders in the VC ecosystem, startups looked to SVB for loans and paid for the cost of securing the loans.

Startups at Seed and Series A rounds backed by accelerators and VCs, respectively, park their new infusion of capital in accounts at the Bank. SVB sat on lots of cash, and it must make prudent loans and investments. Kellogg explained that generally, the Bank loaned $1 for every $3 in deposits. SVB acquired so many deposits from tech money that it sometimes had to turn away deposits. Meanwhile, making tech loans required SVB to avoid the 50 percent failure of Series A companies that failed to advance to Series B. SVB, by utilizing its relationship strengths with VCs, suffered incredibly little default in tech lending. SVB became richer from tech lending!

SVB dominated tech lending by working with companies that had just obtained Series A funding from VCs. The Bank grew its venture lending based on several factors. First, it demanded warrant coverage in addition to the typical interest rate payment and fees. Second, the Bank enjoyed a long-term relationship with the startup and, when the startup moves forward with subsequent funding rounds, the Bank would make additional loans and receive additional warrants. Third, the Bank could monitor the startup's financial health because the startup maintained its account at the Bank. Fourth, the Bank developed a special relationship with the VCs and learned insider information from the VCs about the startups to help the Bank make its decision regarding the loans.

SVB was known for taking warrants on loans to startup companies with VC backing. Fitbit, the maker of fitness-tracking wristbands, was one of those startup clients that issued a warrant to the bank. The bank held on to the warrant and cashed it in when Fitbit went public. The money that SVB captured on the Fitbit warrant was more than the losses from loans made to startups over the preceding last 10 years.[16]

SVB exported venture debt practice to the United Kingdom and Europe as the Bank worked with new startups and investors in innovation centers in the region. SVB bankers convinced startups who were unfamiliar with venture debts to consider the importance of this type of necessary loan for their growth in the innovation economy. The Bank explained to the founders there that SVB's venture debt was free of covenants and the interest costs were lower than some founders otherwise believed. Further, in comparison to the cost of dilution associated with equity fundraising, SVB educated the founders in these new geographical markets that venture debt allows founders to retain more equity for themselves and their key employees. SVB also quickly pointed out to potential borrowers that, unlike other venture debt lenders, the Bank did not insist on taking a board observer seat or

---

[16] See E. Scott Reckard, "At Silicon Valley Bank, Risky Tech Start-Ups are Lucrative Business," *L. A. Times* (August 8, 2015), available at: www.latimes.com/business/la-fi-silicon-valley-bank-20150807-story.html [https://perma.cc/6Z2Z-KG52] (last accessed September 28, 2023).

having voting rights. Overall, by securing a venture loan from SVB immediately after a startup received its Series A funding, the startup gained financial flexibility to address any unanticipated events, lengthened the runway to the next round of capital funding, and lowered the average cost of capital.

For instance, GoCardless, a startup in the UK with a focus on fintech offering solutions to simplify direct debit payments, obtained a venture debt through SVB during the COVID-19 pandemic for the needed cash to lengthen its runway to reach its next capital fundraising round. Likewise, TrustPilot, a startup in Denmark and a popular online consumer review site, turned to SVB for venture debt to launch more products and invest more in R&D and sales and marketing. Most importantly, according to Peter Holten Muhlmann, the company's cofounder and CEO, the venture debt from SVB provided a helpful non-dilutive supplement to equity in fueling growth at his company and proved beneficial in bridging a gap between larger equity financing events. Similarly, Signal AI, a startup founded by three people in a garage in 2013 to use artificial intelligence to enable companies to track critical information in real-time, turned to SVB for venture loans twice in 2020. Signal AI's fast growth demanded non-dilution and an efficient way to fund the business outside or alongside equity which rendered SVB venture loans highly attractive to Signal AI. Signal AI employed 150 people in New York, London, and Hong Kong to serve global customers, including Global Fortune 1,000 businesses.[17]

SVB's venture debt charged an arrangement of 1 percent and in some cases a back-end maturity fee of 1 percent and a warrant of the right to purchase the startup's stock at an agreed price. SVB explained:

> Take a simple example of a company valued at $100 million looking to raise $10 million in equity, a move that would require the founder to give up 10% of the business. By opting instead to take a portion as venture debt – say $3 million which might typically come with a 0.5% warrant – the founder would instead be getting $10 million of capital whilst giving away just 7.5% of the business. It is easy to see how, when following this approach over several capital rounds, equity dilution can be significantly reduced.

During the pandemic some tech startups faced challenges. SVB's debt deferral scheme allowed all borrowers to defer their capital repayments for six months. SVB worked hard to establish itself overseas since its early decade in operations. Its efforts yielded favorable results. In the United Kingdom, an SVB branch gained independent bank status in August 2022 to exclusively serve the innovation economy in the United Kingdom and Europe. Venture debt practiced by SVB in the United States was imported into the United Kingdom and Europe to grow a new generation of tech startups and talents.

---

[17] "Busting the Myths of Venture Debt," available at: www.svb.com/startup-insights/startup-growth/busting-the-myths-of-venture-debt (last accessed September 28, 2023).

Competitors didn't sit still while they were watching SVB perfecting and dominating the lucrative venture debt market. Smith left SVB in 1993 and later worked with a private venture debt lender. Dave Titus also worked for a private venture debt lender. Venture debts in the United States were subsequently embraced by both private and publicly traded lenders.

SVB's practice of taking warrants was not limited to venture-backed companies. In some cases where the tech companies were in post-IPO and receiving rounds of post-IPO equity, SVB furnished credit facilities and took warrants as part of the credit cost to the borrowers. In some instances, where the deals were too large, the Bank teamed up with a finance company to deliver the credit facilities to the clients. Alphatec Spine, a medical technology company with a focus on revolutionizing the approach to spine surgery and developing new standards for spine surgery to achieve the goals of decompression, stabilization, and alignment, went public on June 1, 2006. The company needed new capital. On December 5, 2008, Alphatec entered into a Loan and Security Agreement with SVB and Oxford Finance Corporation that permitted Alphatec to borrow up to $30 million, comprising of a $15 million term note and a $15 million working capital line of credit. The term note carried the initial interest rate of a three-month LIBOR rate[18] plus 8 percent and the interest rate for the working capital line of credit was SVB's prime rate plus 2 percent. In addition to the interest rate payments to the two lenders, Alphatec issued to SVB a warrant to purchase 190,4976 shares of its stock at $1.89 per share, exercisable for a term of 10 years, and to Oxford Finance a warrant of 285,714 shares for the same price and term.[19]

89bio, Inc., a spin-off of Teva Pharmaceutical Industries Ltd., is known for its lead product, BIO89–100 for the treatment of nonalcoholic steatohepatitis, a severe form of nonalcoholic fatty liver disease. 89bio is headquartered in San Francisco, with its development center in Herzliya, Israel. In 2018, 89bio received $60 million in Series A funding. By 2020, Teva faced cash flow difficulties following its acquisition of Actavis in 2015, and it decided to spin off 89bio into a separate company. On July 14, 2020, 89bio went public and raised $84 million in Nasdaq secondary offering. The company then needed loans and entered into an amended Loan and Security Agreement with various lenders and SVB for an aggregate principal amount equal to $25 million. On June 4, 2021, the company also issued to the Lenders and SVB a warrant to purchase 33,923 shares of the company's stock at $19.12 per share with a term of 10 years.[20]

Commercial banks generally do not engage in venture debt. Banking regulations and regulators generally don't allow banks to make loans to companies between VC

---

[18] LIBOR rates are benchmark interest rates which serve as a globally accepted key benchmark interest rate that indicates borrowing costs between banks.
[19] Alphatec Holdings, Inc. Form 8K (December 5, 2008).
[20] 89bio, Inc. Form 8-K (May 28, 2021).

rounds of funding because half of these companies will not meet their milestones and cannot advance to the next round of funding. Estimates indicate about 75 percent of VC-backed companies do not survive. That is too much of a risk for banks.

However, SVB's experience in serving the tech industry reveals that much capital infusion is poured into startups. If commercial banks cannot participate in venture debts, nonbank lenders play an active role. Lenders can charge a higher interest rate than banks would because lenders don't have cheap money from depositors. These lenders get their money from investors and the investors want high returns, whereas depositors at banks don't expect much from having their checking and saving accounts at the banks. According to Smith, as he is on the Board at a venture lender, the investors are institutions, including university foundations like Stanford and Notre Dame.[21] This leads to the next discussion about non-bank tech lenders in venture debt.

VENTURE DEBT MARKET AND PUBLIC VENTURE LENDERS

There are now many venture lenders. These lenders are not banks; they are not subject to banking laws and regulations. The venture debt market has grown fast in the last few years. In 2020, in the United States, VC-backed companies received a total of $25 billion in venture debt, marking the third consecutive year the venture debt market reached past $20 billion. This huge growth is startling when compared to $5 billion in venture debt in 2010 and 2011. The venture debt market grew faster than VC and PE markets. One key explanation for the fast growth is that startups have learned that debt is cheaper than equity financing. Debt financing provides a good alternative to capital for growing startups to lengthen their runway, so they can reach a better valuation. Most importantly, venture debt does not dilute the startup's equity. As the name implies, venture debt activities depend on VC activities. An increase in VC and capital funding deals leads to an increase in venture debt activities.[22]

Publicly traded companies in venture debt include Triplepoint, Horizon Technology Finance, and Hercules Capital. Triplepoint devotes its business to venture debt to VC-backed high-growth companies in the tech, cleantech, and life science sectors. Triplepoint positions itself as the only debt provider equipped to meet the needs of VC-backed companies at every stage of their development. Likewise, Horizon Technology Finance is a venture lender that focuses solely on making loans to startups in emerging technology, life science, healthcare information and services, and cleantech. Horizon claims that it has provided over $1.3 billion in loan commitments. Hercules Capital asserts that it is the largest non-bank lender to VC-backed companies at all stages of development.

---

[21] Interview with Smith, April 19, 2022 (48 minutes into the tape).
[22] PitchBook Analyst Note: Venture Debt a Maturing Market in VC (March 19, 2021).

Interestingly, these public companies are organized as business development companies or BDC under the Investment Company Act of 1940. As BDC entities, they are permitted to finance their investments through borrowings subject to a 150 percent asset coverage that means for every $100 of net assets a BDC holds, it may raise up to $200 from borrowing and issuing senior securities. A BDC entity is also required to invest at least 70 percent of its total assets in "qualifying assets," including securities of private US companies, cash, cash equivalents, US government securities, and high-quality debt investments that mature in one year or less. Furthermore, as a Regulated Investment Company (RIC), the public entity is subject to Subchapter M of the Internal Revenue Code of 1986. That means the entity does not pay corporate-level income taxes on its investment income. The entity instead distributes its net capital gain as dividends to its stockholders.

Moreover, one of the striking features that separate public venture lenders, who are BDC entities, from commercial banks is the requirement that BDCs must make managerial assistance available to the borrower portfolio companies. This feature makes BDCs more similar to VC firms and is known to provide a nurturing role to VC's portfolio companies.

Hercules Capital, Inc., with $1.2 billion in aggregate market value, as stated in its 2021 10K Annual Report and $2.6 billion in total assets, is the largest public entity in venture debt. Its shares are listed on the New York Stock Exchange. The company began its investment operations in September 2004 when it identified that VC-backed tech companies are underserved by commercial banks in the venture lending area. Commercial banks are typically more comfortable with assessing the credit worthiness of a potential borrower through traditional means and therefore cannot underwrite the risk associated with VC-backed tech companies. Hercules meets the demand for structured debt financing for VC-backed companies in broadly defined tech industries in all stages of development.

Hercules stakes itself as a specialty finance company focused on providing senior secured loans to high-growth, innovative VC-backed companies in a variety of technology, life sciences, and sustainable and renewable technology industries. As of December 31, 2020, approximately 87.2 percent of the fair value of Hercules' portfolio are investments through venture loans in three tech industries: 33.1 percent in the "Software" industry, 32.2 percent in the "Drug Discovery & Development" industry, and 21.9 percent in the "Internet Consumer & Business Services" industry.[23]

The loans are typically secured by either some or all of the assets of borrowers. Hercules makes venture loans with warrants to purchase shares from private companies and some public companies. In some situations, Hercules even takes an equity position in the portfolio companies. Unlike commercial banks, Hercules can take equity ownership in the portfolio companies and may exceed 25 percent of the

---

[23] Hercules 2021 10K Filing, page 42.

voting securities of such companies.[24] This amounts to a controlling interest under the Investment Company Act of 1940. Hercules receives the equity ownership stake in the portfolio companies in connection with future equity financing rounds while the VC-backed companies use the venture loans provided by Hercules for growth, working capital, and, in some instances, acquisitions or recapitalizations.

Hercules's venture loans float in the range from $15 million to $40 million. There are three portfolio companies that Hercules made loans for with a fair value above $80 million each, constituting greater than 5 percent of Hercules's net assets. BridgeBio Pharma LLC, a clinical-stage biopharmaceutical company of drugs for patients with genetic diseases, borrowed $93 million; EverFi, Inc., a web-based media platform to teach and certify students in the core concepts of financial literacy, fetched $85 million; and Tricida, Inc., a biopharmaceutical company on the discovery and clinical development of novel therapeutics to address renal, metabolic, and cardiovascular diseases incurred $80 million in loan amount from Hercules.

The loans are secured by the portfolio company's tangible and intangible assets but intellectual property assets are often not included in the collateral. That means Hercules cannot claim first priority on assets in which it does not hold security interest. Hercules instead prohibits the borrowers from pledging their intellectual property as collateral in subsequent deals with others. The venture loans carry interest rates ranging from 7 to 11.5 percent. Hercules imposes exit fees, balloon payment fees, commitment fees, success fees, and prepayment fees. With respect to equity enhancement features in the form of warrants or other equity-related securities that Hercules charges borrowers in connection with venture loans, the warrants typically contain terms of five to ten years or three to five years after IPO. Hercules targets a total return inclusive of interest, fees, and value of warrants at 12–25 percent for its venture loans.

Hercules also provides equipment loans to VC-backed companies. The loans are typically for three to four years and secured by underlying equipment. The borrowers must issue warrants to purchase stock from Hercules.

Systematically, Hercules devises its venture debt process to potential tech borrowers in the VC-backed financing ecosystem, as shown in Figure 8.1.

Figure 8.1 reveals that Hercules must engage in formal due diligence and approval of the proposed venture loans to prospective portfolio companies. Hercules claims that it performs standardized due diligence methodologies, which entails due diligence on financial performance and credit risk and analysis of the operations, legal, and applicable regulatory framework of a portfolio company. Consequently, Hercules' underwriting team members work together to conduct both due diligence and ascertain the prospective borrower's business plan, operations, and financial performance. Hercules has also implemented an investment

[24] Hercules 2021 10K Filing.

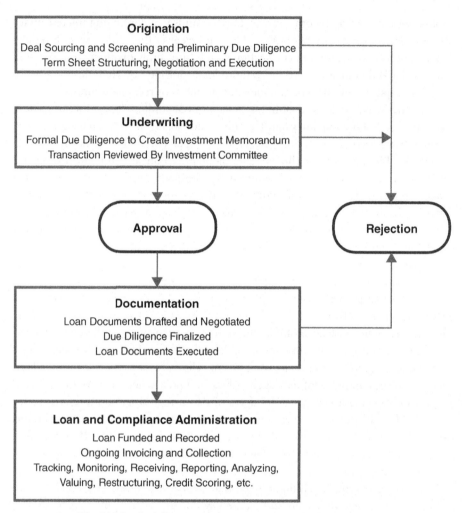

FIGURE 8.1 The VC-backed financing ecosystem

grading system from Grade 1, being the least risk, to Grade 5, when the borrower is in a workout, to all venture loans made to its clients. Under its grading system, all Hercules' venture loans experienced a weighted average investment grading of 2.16, as of December 31, 2020.

To generate new deals, Hercules boasts that it has developed a proprietary and comprehensive structured query language-based database system to track its investment process steps from sourcing, originations, tractions monitoring, and post-investment. With 54,000 tech companies and 13,000 venture capital firms, investors, and industry contacts, Hercules asserts that its database enables the company to maintain, cultivate, and grow necessary relationships for deal sourcing.

An interesting aspect of these public venture lenders involves the assistance from the Small Business Administration (SBA) to the lender's wholly-owned SBIC subsidiaries. Hercules subsidiaries HT III and HC IV are Small Business Investment Company (SBIC) subsidiaries subject to SBA regulations. Both HT III and HC IV may make long-term loans to small businesses, invest in the equity securities of those businesses, and provide them with consulting and advisory services. Through the subsidiaries, Hercules gained access to up to $175 million of capital through the SBA debenture program on October 27, 2020.

Horizon Technology Finance, with its stock listed on NASDAQ, made 45 debt investments with an aggregate fair value of $437.3 million in 2021. Among the venture debt deals, 87.6 percent, or $383 million, consisted of Senior Term Loans where Horizon held first priority in the security interest of the collateral secured in the loans. Horizon took a security interest in borrowers' tangible and intangible collateral assets except for intellectual property. The applicable portfolio tech companies did not want to pledge their intellectual property as collateral. Horizon instead imposed a negative covenant wherein the tech companies cannot pledge intellectual property as collateral in subsequent transactions with others. Horizon's venture loans covered principal amounts between $3 million and $28 million, repayment terms of between 15 and 60 months, and annual interest rates of between 8 and 13 percent. Horizon's shareholders enjoyed a total return of 29.7 percent based on market value as of December 31, 2021, which is calculated as (x) the sum of (i) the closing sales price of Horizon's common stock on the last day of the period plus (ii) the aggregate amount of distributions paid per share during the period, less (iii) the closing sales price of Horizon's common stock on the first day of the period, divided by (y) the closing sales price of Horizon's common stock on the first day of the period.[25]

With respect to the warrants to purchase stock in the portfolio companies, Horizon typically acquired preferred stock. Preferred stock typically does not grant voting rights in the company but does maintain priority over common stock in dividends. In 2021, Horizon received warrants in seventy-three portfolio companies. In addition, Horizon obtained equity positions in three portfolio companies and success fee arrangements in six portfolio companies.

In making venture loans, public entity lenders employ certain core strategies. In addition to interest rates, fees, and warrants, these lenders rely on "enterprise value" to structure and underwrite loans. What this means is that the lenders take the valuation based on the portfolio company's most recent equity capital round of funding. In some cases, the lenders also include the intrinsic value of the portfolio company's technology, service, or customer base. With the enterprise value, the lenders take a security interest on the company's assets in the event the company fails to pay, and the lenders must foreclose on the assets in order to recover the

---

[25] Horizon 2022 10K Filing.

outstanding loan and fee. Like Hercules, Horizon conducts due diligence on prospective borrower loans by obtaining and evaluating the information on the tech company's technology, market opportunity, management team, fundraising history, investor support, valuation considerations, financial condition, and projection. In addition, Horizon requires private portfolio companies to furnish monthly financial information to the lender for monitoring purposes. The companies also regularly provide updates on performance and future plans.

PRIVATE VENTURE LENDERS

The majority of venture lenders, however, constitute private companies. Western Tech Investment (WTI) touts that it accumulated forty years of experience in venture debt and counts high-growth public and private companies like 3PAR, Ablation Frontiers, BeVocal, Brocade, Cerent, Facebook, Google, IDEC Pharmaceuticals, InvenSense, Juniper Networks, Neutral Tandem, Palantir, Postini, and Youku.com as clients. Over forty years of investing in tech companies through providing venture loans to them, WTI has committed more than $7 billion to 1,421 portfolio companies. The company claims that it pioneered the concept of venture debt by serving tech companies from the advent of the semiconductor industry to the present time. WTI can make venture loans to tech companies from its institutional fund which receives investments from institutional Limited Partners (LPs) including endowments, non-profits, academic institutions, and select family offices.

As a pioneer, non-bank lender in venture debt, WTI sets itself apart from other lenders by publicizing its transparency pledge in encouraging every entrepreneur to make demands from venture debt lenders. WTI's transparency pledge sets a baseline for entrepreneurs to compare and hopefully return to WTI for venture loans:

> *For the avoidance of doubt and notwithstanding anything to the contrary contained in this Agreement or the other Loan Documents:*
>   (a) *the occurrence of a Material Adverse Change or Material Adverse Effect shall not constitute an Event of Default or otherwise allow Lender to declare the outstanding Loans due and payable;*
>   (b) *Lender shall not be entitled to (i) require Borrower's investors or members of Borrower's Board of Directors to make written or verbal commitments of ongoing financial support, or (ii) require Borrower to conduct its banking or hold its deposits at any specific bank or financial institution;*
>   (c) *Borrower shall not be required to maintain any minimum tangible net worth, working capital, current ratio, quick asset ratio, liquidity ratio, or debt-to-equity ratio or comply with any similar financial covenant; and*
>   (d) *if Borrower becomes insolvent then Lender shall not be entitled to declare an Event of Default or otherwise demand that the outstanding Loans shall be due and payable provided Borrower continues to be able to pay its debts as they become due.*

What that transparency pledge means is WTI offers money to VC-backed startups enabling them to spend on what they need in order to grow, extending their runway, and taking opportunities to maneuver when their business conditions experience unexpected changes. The transparency pledge states key terms governing the loans but does not include "material adverse changes" and "insolvency default" clauses, does not require investors to serve as guarantors, and does not contain any subjective requirements to allow lenders to accelerate the loan payments at the worst moment. In other words, WTI's venture loans show favorable to the borrowers.

WTI's credit facilities including term loans, equipment loans, and credit lines are available to tech companies from the Seed stage through IPO. WTI is exceedingly proud of its total portfolio of 1,421 companies; it lists clients every year from 1994 to the present time on its website. Through its list, clients come from a wide range of subsectors in the tech industry. Browsing through the list of 1,421 companies and descriptions of each company brings to mind the *"Do You Know?"* newsletter that Roger Smith championed at SVB. It is no surprise that Smith resides among the directors on the Board of Directors of Venture Lending and Leasing of WTI! He has been serving as a director there since he parted ways with SVB in 1994. Also, on a proxy statement filed with the SEC for a shareholders meeting in 2000, Smith was listed among eight directors as nominees to the Board of Directors of Fund I. Smith continues to actively serve in his directorship role at WTI. He pioneered venture debt at Wells Fargo and SVB banks, then brought his knowledge and expertise to WTI in 1994. He has never left venture lending to tech companies.[26]

Among many notable venture loans, WTI made to various tech companies involved the loan to Facebook. In 2004, Peter Thiel invested $500,000 in Facebook with a valuation of $5 million. At that time Facebook comprised one employee in California. WTI extended its venture debt deal with Facebook.[27] Likewise, WTI provided its venture debt to Google in 1999. Given WTI's leading position in venture debt, Harvard Business Publishing includes WTI's venture debt deal with Juvo, a fintech company with mobile identity scoring software designed to establish financial identities of creditworthy, among its case studies for study to purchase and analyze for their startup financing courses.[28]

[26] 2014 Smith and Medearis Interview; Notice of Joint Annual Meeting of Shareholders November 15, 2000, Venture Lending & Leasing, Inc., available at: www.sec.gov/Archives/edgar/data/1039802/000091205700046292/0000912057-00-046292.txt (last accessed September 28, 2023).

[27] "Tracking Facebook's Valuation," *New York Times* (February 1, 2012), available at: https://archive.nytimes.com/dealbook.nytimes.com/2012/02/01/tracking-facebooks-valuation/ (last accessed October 3, 2023); "About Us," *fvd*, available at: www.findventuredebt.com/about-us (last accessed October 3, 2023).

[28] See Syllabus for Financing Startups, Coller School of Management, The Leon Recanati Graduate School of Business Administration, Rel Aviv University (Summer Semester 2021), available at: www.ims.tau.ac.il/Tal/Scans/Syllabus_Download.aspx?kurs=12313950&syllabus=kr_syllabus_s20203_koo_voo.pdf&dt=12082021004032 (last accessed September 28, 2023).

WTI expands its venture debt practice to clients outside the United States. For instance, Eguana Technologies, Inc., entered into a loan for working capital of $10 million on April 1, 2022, with WTI. Eguana is a company based in Calgary with a focus on the designs and manufacturing of high-performance residential and commercial energy storage systems. WTI has been serving as a lender and key partner to Eguana for many years. Under the latest loan, Eguana gave WTI first priority of security interest in all Eguana's assets. The loan carries an interest rate of 12 percent per annum, with interest-only payments in the first six months, and both interest and principal payments in the subsequent thirty months. Eguana issued a warrant that entitles WTI to purchase 4,934,309 common shares of Eguana at $0.355 per share. The warrant agreement contains various vested and unvested timing of the warrants. Further, if WTI holds on to the warrants, the vested unexercised warrants will be exchangeable after the earlier of a liquidity event for Eguana and September 30, 2025, for "an amount equal to the sum of: (i) US$1,500,000; and (ii) the product obtained by multiplying US$1,500,000 by the percentage of the principal amount of the Loan actually advanced by the Lender relative to US$10,000,000."[29] In other words, Eguana pays a large warrant coverage for the $10 million loan.

On the other spectrum of WTI in the venture debt sector is Arc, a full-service finance platform for the software-as-service (SaaS) subsector, founded in 2021. Arc targets software startups with customized financial products. In terms of capital, Arc holds $150 million available in loans to customers. Arc claims to be on a mission to help startups grow because the founders know firsthand and through meetings with hundreds of software founders that startup funding is both costly and distracting. Arc distinguishes itself by providing from a meager $50 thousand to $50 million to startups. Hundreds of startups have leveraged Arc to accelerate their growth, extend their runway, and make strategic bets.

Besides WTI and Arc, Crunchbase includes 481 organizations under its venture debt investors category. Mercury Technologies, Inc. is a young upstart that wants to take on SVB in venture debt.

Mercury, a startup banking service fintech platform founded in 2017, decided to stake out a position in the venture debt sector in 2022. In total, Mercury has raised a total of $152 million from Coatue, CRV, Andreessen Horowitz, and other VC firms. Mercury at first offered banking services to startups but added a new offering of venture debt to its platform. The company's banking platform offers FDIC-insured products through Evolve Bank & Trust, an Arkansas-based bank, to serve 60,000 startups. The banking platform also provides services like checking and savings accounts, debit cards, ACH payments, check payments, and domestic and international wire transfers. Mercury makes its money primarily through its debit card

---

[29] "Eguana Enters into a US$10 Million Loan Agreement with Western Technology Investment," available at: www.nasdaq.com/press-release/eguana-enters-into-a-us%2410-million-loan-agreement-with-western-technology-investment (last accessed September 28, 2023).

interchange fees and on float deposit transactions from client checks into their accounts and fund availability for withdrawals.

The venture debt business looks attractive to Mercury. With the advantages of its platform, Mercury believes that it positions to make the process of obtaining venture loans with great ease, enhanced efficiency, and a less cumbersome process. Mercury's head of capital and relationship management is Jason Garcia, a former SVB senior vice president. In extending venture loans to startups, Mercury will take a small warrant and charges origination fees. The company plans to make a total loan amount of $200 million this year and up to $1 billion next year. Potential clients are startups that have already raised $2 million in funding from at least one institutional investor. In other words, Mercury is aiming at very early-stage startups. Moreover, understanding that venture loans immediately follow the capital funding round, Mercury plans to offer a loan amount of 25 to 50 percent of the startup's equity round.

Mercury's founders targeted taking a piece of SVB's market with its easy-to-use platform, larger venture debt amount, and smaller warrant cost. One of Mercury's founders and CEO Immad Akhund voiced his frustration and disdain for the old-fashioned ways that SVB and commercial banks continue to operate and that banks fail to understand the new entrepreneurs who develop products today. Akhund then argued that Mercury's advantage over SVB was because "it is a product-first startup."[30] Mercury was able to score several clients including AirGarage and PreAct Technologies for venture debts. Both AirGarage and PreAct Technologies received their Series A funding.

Whether Mercury will succeed in dominating the venture debt market in the aftermath of SVB's demise remains to be seen.

OTHER COMMERCIAL BANKS IN VENTURE DEBT

There are only a handful of banks who dared to enter the venture debt space. Interestingly, none of these banks devote 100 percent of their business practice to serving the innovation economy of tech and life sciences. These commercial banks dedicate only a division or a group practice to serve the tech and life sciences. After several years of planning, Avidbank debuted venture lending in December 2018 by making some key hires. The lead professional of the new venture lending group was someone who began his career at none other than Silicon Valley Bank.[31] Bank of Commerce retained a tech lending group and hired Ted Bojorquez to lead its

---

[30] Connie Loizos, "Startup Banking Service Mercury Jumps into Debt Lending to Take on Silicon Valley Bank," *TechCrunch* (March 15, 2022).

[31] "Sam Bhaumik Joins Avidbank to Lead New Venture Lending Group" (December 19, 2018), available at: https://ir.avidbank.com/news/news-details/2018/Sam-Bhaumik-Joins-Avidbank-to-Lead-New-Venture-Lending-Group/default.aspx (last accessed September 28, 2023).

Silicon Valley region to focus on venture debt deals. The more significant banks in venture debt include ComericA, PactWest, and Bridge Bank.[32]

ComericA Bank acquired Imperial Bank in 2001 to solidify its emerging growth and venture banking division. Imperial Bank was the bank where Roger Smith served as the President of the regional office before he left to found Silicon Valley Bank with Robert Medearis and Bill Biggerstaff in 1983. Imperial Bank developed a tech lending practice, but it was significantly smaller compared to Silicon Valley Bank. In one study of 529 tech firms that went public from 1996 to 2000, half of the firms identified their bank lenders in the IPO filings. The leading bank that made loans to these tech companies was Silicon Valley Bank, which occupied 65 percent, and Imperial Bank took 20 percent.[33] Before the acquisition of Imperial Bank, ComericA bought Plaza Bank in San Jose, University Bank in Palo Alto, and Metrobank in Los Angeles as part of ComericA's expansion into California. As of 1995, about 10 percent of ComericA's business in the California offices was with small, high-tech companies.[34] With the acquisition of Imperial Bank, ComericA eliminated additional competition. Because ComericA identifies as a large commercial bank, it could take on loan deals with tech companies in the late-growth stages, including IPO deals.

ComericA's Technology and Life Science Division (TLS) operates in Seattle, Boston, New York, California's Palo Alto, San Francisco, San Jose, and Los Angeles, Central/Mid-Atlantic region, Canada, and Israel. Illustratively, TLS furnished $10 million in venture loan to Delix Therapeutics, a neuroscience company developing novel disease-modifying therapeutics for psychiatric and neurological conditions. Delix Therapeutics raised $70 million in their Series A financing round in late 2021. Similarly, TLS extended a $10 million venture debt facility to Alida, the creator of the world's first Customer Experience Management and Insights platform, in 2021.[35] Solegear Bioplastics, a leading developer of high-performance plant-based plastics for packaging and durable product applications, closed a venture debt facility with ComericA Bank in 2014. Similarly, ComericA agreed to provide a revolving credit line of $80 million to Montauk Renewables, an energy company specializing in the

[32] https://kruzeconsulting.com/venture-debt/#:~:text=Venture%20Debt%20Market%20Size%20%
      2D%20%24%20in%20Billions&text=We%20estimate%20that%20the%20US,the%20market%20
      was%20in%202016 (last accessed September 28, 2023).
[33] Laura Gonzalez and Christopher James, "Banks and Bubbles: How Good are Bankers at
      Spotting Winners?" Department of Finance, Insurance, and Real Estate, Warrington
      College of Business Administration, University of Florida (May 19, 2006), available at: www
      .newyorkfed.org/medialibrary/media/research/conference/2006/fin_intermed/Gonzalez-James_
      UofFlorida_June21.pdf (last accessed September 28, 2023).
[34] Peter Sinton, "High-Tech Bank Loves Startups," SF Chronicle (May 22, 1995), available at:
      www.sfgate.com/business/article/High-Tech-Bank-Loves-Startups-Silicon-Valley-3033000.php
      (last accessed September 28, 2023).
[35] "Alida Secures US$10 Million Debt Facility from Comerica Bank," Business Wire (June 28,
      2021).

TABLE 8.1 *Venture lending landscape*

Company	HQ	Assets	Market cap
ComericA	Dallas, TX	$65.3 bln	$8.3 bln
Silicon Valley Bank	Santa Clara, CA	$33.3 bln	$5.1 bln
City National	Los Angeles, CA	$30.8 bln	$3.9 bln
Square 1	Durham, NC	$2.6 bln	$533.1 mln
Bridge Bank	San Jose, CA	$1.6 bln	$360.3 mln
Hercules	Palo Alto, CA	$1.2 bln	$855.2 mln

recovery and processing of biogas from landfills and other non-fossil fuel sources for beneficial use.[36]

As expected, bankers who have worked at a tech lending division of a bank like ComericA Bank may experience frustration that the bank has no appreciation for the tech ecosystem. For instance, John Benetti, one of the two Managing Directors at ComericA's California offices left for SVB after 18 years at ComericA. Though Benetti left ComericA for more than four months, the Bank had not updated its TLS pages. Moreover, a visitor to ComericA's website would encounter difficulties to search for TLS pages. Overall, ComericA's once dominant position in tech lending has declined. Back in 2014, ComericA held the assets and led venture lending space ahead of SVB as seen in a report from CNBC (Table 8.1).[37]

Interestingly, five years after ComericA's acquisition of Imperial Bank, a group of ComericA bankers, formerly with Imperial Bank, left to found Square 1 Bank to exclusively focus on startup tech lending, because they felt that ComericA did not adequately serve the tech startups. Square 1 Bank itself, after 10 years of operations, was acquired by PacWest.

In October 2015, PacWest acquired Square 1 Bank, a startup full-service commercial bank serving the tech industry and providing venture loans to tech companies. Square 1 distributed their offices to Austin, the Bay Area, Boston, Chicago, Denver, Durham, Los Angeles, Minneapolis, New York, San Diego, Seattle, and Washington, DC. Square 1 was active in venture debt deals to VC-backed companies. Before the acquisition by PacWest, Square 1 teamed up with TriplePoint Venture Growth BDC Corporation to deliver large debt financing commitments to clients. For instance, Square 1 and TriplePoint jointly provided $40 million in venture debt to Optoro after the startup closed a $50 million Series C funding round led by Kleiner Perkins Caufield & Byers, a Silicon Valley venture capital firm, as well as Generation Investment Management, a VC company founded by Al Gore. Optoro is a tech company specializing in reverse logistics that assists

---

[36] www.sec.gov/Archives/edgar/data/1826600/000119312520316007/d939445dex1015.htm (last accessed September 28, 2023).
[37] Ari Levy, "Out of the Way VCs: Banks Muscle in on Tech Boom," *CNBC* (October 14, 2014).

retailers and manufacturers to manage and then resell their returned and excess merchandise. Optoro helps place the products on Amazon, eBay, Buy.com, and BestBuy. The company uses its subsidiary BULQ.com to liquidate goods in bulk.

Square 1 Bank was founded in 2005 by a husband and wife team, Richard and Susan Casey. The bank obtained its charter in North Carolina with an initial capitalization of $105 million from 200 shareholders. Richard Casey was a former executive with Imperial Bank in the venture division which was created to compete against Silicon Valley Bank for tech startups venture lending business. Susan Casey was President of the Technology & Life Science Division of ComericA Bank and CCO of the Emerging Growth Division at Imperial Bank before that bank was acquired by ComericA. In addition, she was with Silicon Valley Bank for five years before joining Imperial Bank. Richard Casey served as the CEO at Square 1 Bank while his wife was COO and Chief Credit Officer.[38] In addition to the Caseys, other executives from ComericA joined them at the new Square 1 Bank in 2005.[39]

Square1/PacWest counts CallRail, Inovoca, MeUndies, The RealDeal, Credit Karma, PhenomPeople, PinDrop, All Traffic Solutions, Cardlytics, ShopRunner, MapAnything, and Renovo as clients on its website for Technology, Life Sciences, and Startup Services. In the deal with ShopRunner in 2016, for instance, the Bank provided a multi-year credit facility to the company – a membership-based online shopping service for high-value consumers. For the transaction with Appboy in 2015, Square 1 Bank received the warrant to purchase 12,000 common stock at the price of $2.09 per share, with an expiration date of June 8, 2025. Appboy was founded in 2011 with the plan to use "technology to help brands humanize their customer relationship by communicating in responsive, highly personalized ways" and subse-quently its cofounder and CEO Bill Magnuson changed its name to Braze in 2017.[40] Braze went public and was traded at $37.17 on June 23, 2022. Square 1 Bank certainly gained on its warrant issued from Appboy.

Square 1/PacWest, like the other commercial banks in the venture debt space, serves late-stage tech companies. For example, in 2014 Square 1 Bank made a $3 million term loan to Obalon Therapeutics and obtained a second warrant to purchase Series D preferred stock in addition to customary interest and fees. Obalon Therapeutics issued a total of shares that were equal to 3 percent of the principal amount of the loan of $3 million, or 90,000 shares under the Loan and Security Agreement dated June 14, 2013. The price per share was fixed at $2.5983.

[38] "Square 1 Bank Founder and CEO Richard Casey Dies," available at: https://wraltechwire .com/2010/11/11/square-1-bank-founder-and-ceo-richard-casey-dies/ (last accessed September 28, 2023).

[39] Brad Meikle, "VC Bank's Cashes Huge Check," *Buyouts* (August 15, 2005), available at: www .buyoutsinsider.com/vc-bank-cashes-huge-check/ (last accessed September 28, 2023).

[40] Marissa Aydlett, "'Change Everything': What It Takes to Rebrand a Company in Six Months, Warts and All" (June 15, 2018), available at: www.braze.com/resources/articles/braze-appboy- rename-rebrand (last accessed October 3, 2023).

In 2019 PacWest retired the name Square 1 bank and turned the tech lending practice to the Venture Banking group, offering a comprehensive suite of financial services focused on entrepreneurial businesses and their venture capital and private equity investors.

Interestingly, the veteran bankers in the Venture Banking group honed their skills at Silicon Valley Bank before they joined Square 1 and then subsequently became employees at PacWest. Pete McDonald, SVP of Venture Relations and Startup Services at PacWest Bank, was a Relationship Manager at Silicon Valley Bank for 23 years from 1994 to 2017 before he joined PacWest. Likewise, Jay McNeil, Managing Director, Life Science, Venture Banking at PacWest, was with Silicon Valley Bank for 16 years. Bejermin Colombo, Managing Director, Life Sciences at PacWest Bank was Senior Relationship Manager, Life Science, at Silicon Valley Bank for eight years. To compete with Silicon Valley Bank, PacWest's Venture Banking Group offered a low cost of capital and low warrant coverage. The PacWest bankers include material adverse change and investor abandonment clauses in their venture loan agreements to mitigate their risk in the event the startups face a downsizing situation.[41]

PacWest promises to entrepreneurs that they "will experience our unrivaled high-touch service, delivering quick turnarounds, transparent credit terms and thoughtfully structured banking solutions to preserve and manage your resources and capital." A team of client service will be assigned to a client, making PacWest "nimble and highly responsive." The team promises to provide "the best-tailored service, delivered with the speed and consistency that today's innovators deserve."[42]

Ken Fugate, a cofounder of Square 1 Bank and Managing Director of Square 1's Mountain Northwest Venture Banking Region, left his position to lead Signature Bank's Venture Banking group in 2019.[43] Fugate helped build Square 1's reputation and IPO before PacWest acquired Square 1 in late 2015. Fugate brought with him a group of bankers from Square 1 Bank to form a new 24-person Signature Bank's Venture Banking Group to focus on serving venture capital firms and venture lending to VC-backed companies. Unsurprisingly, Ryan Incorvaia, who spent 10 years at Silicon Valley Bank before joining Square 1 Bank became involved in the newly formed group at Signature Bank.[44]

---

[41] Scott Orn, *Venture Debt Scouting Report: Square One Bank* (February 9, 2018).

[42] www.pacwest.com/lending-solutions/venture-lending (last accessed October 12, 2022).

[43] In addition to shutting down SVB, the regulators also closed Signature Bank to prevent further bank crises in March 2023. See Hannah Lang and Nupur Anand, "Signature Bank becomes Next Casualty of Banking Turmoil after SVB," REUTERS (March 13, 2023), available at: www.reuters .com/business/finance/new-york-state-regulators-close-signature-bank-2023-03-12/#:~:text=March% 2012%20(Reuters)%20%2D%20State,that%20stranded%20billions%20in%20deposits (last accessed October 3, 2023).

[44] "Ken Fugate to Lead Signature Bank's Venture Banking Group" (April 15, 2019), available at: https://newyork.citybizlist.com/article/543169/ken-fugate-to-lead-signature-banks-venture-banking-group (last accessed September 28, 2023).

A few months before PacWest acquired Square 1 Bank, Western Alliance Bank acquired Bridge Bank on August 11, 2015, for $425 million, to expand its presence in Northern California and foray into the venture debt banking business. Bridge Bank was founded as a full-service professional business bank in Silicon Valley in 2001, serving tech companies that were both VC and non-VC-backed entities. Bridge Bank's products included growth capital, equipment and working capital credit facilities, and treasury management solutions. Bridge Bank, at the time of the acquisition, held $1.8 billion in assets with its main office in San Jose and six lending offices across the United States. Western Alliance Bank kept Bridge Bank as a division and did not retire the name "Bridge Bank" in subsequent years.

At Bridge Bank, venture debt is a unit under the "Commercial & Corporate Solutions." Bridge Bank explains on its website that "Investor-backed companies seeking growth without ownership dilution look to venture debt as a strategic financial tool. Venture debt can provide a level of flexibility not found with investors while supplementing an existing equity round. You can trust our expertise as a venture debt lender to assess funding options that can fuel your momentum." Bridge Bank further details to potential clients that venture debt financing is a "loan designed to extend the runway for fast-growing companies," and that venture debt allows investors, founders, and employees to preserve control because the loans are the least dilutive early-stage financing option, that ventures loan offers a "bridge" between equity rounds so the startup may be able to raise equity at a higher valuation after it was able to grow and meet critical milestones with the infusion of the cash from the venture loan, and that venture loan supplements the startup's existing equity allowing founders to "leverage venture capital investments and preserve investors' dry powder for your company's future needs."

Mike Lederman leads as the current Senior Managing Director, Technology & Innovation at Bridge Bank. Like many professionals who operate in the venture debt business, Lederman began his career at Silicon Valley Bank and held positions with Horizon Technology Finance, one of the publicly-traded and non-bank lenders in venture debt. Ryan Dammeyer, another Senior Managing Director, Technology & Innovation, possesses a similar background, as he spent nearly a decade at Silicon Valley Bank. Essentially, two out of the three senior leaders in tech lending at Bridge Bank sharpened their skills first at SVB.

In addition to venture debt, Bridge Bank offers to explore other funding options with potential clients, such as asset-based lending, which is accounts receivable and inventory-based lending.

Like SVB, Bridge Bank demands warrants as part of the loan costs charged to borrowers. For instance, in the venture loan with Precision Therapeutics, an early-stage, VC-backed company that provides cancer management services to doctors, Bridge Bank received a warrant at the price of $0.10 in connection with a short-term convertible promissory note. The warrant presented an expiration date of ten years or August 22, 2023. Bridge Bank made its loan days before Precision Therapeutics received its $15 million capital funding from local venture funds, Adams Capital, Birchmere Ventures, and Draper Triangle Ventures in Pittsburg, and three out-of-town VC firms.[45]

In a deal with Vapotherm, an early-stage startup with a Series A round of funding, Bridge Bank received a warrant to purchase 60,000 shares at the price of $1 per share for the Series A Preferred Stock in connection with the loan the Bank extended to the company. Vapotherm, specializing in respiratory care medical devices, issued the warrant to Bridge Bank on September 27, 2013, and the warrant carried an expiration date of September 27, 2020. A few months later in 2014, Vapotherm advanced to a Series B financing round of $24 million led by Glide Healthcare Partners. The company proceeded to subsequent rounds until it went public in 2018.[46] In other words, Bridge Bank did the right thing to bet on its venture loan to Vapotherm. The company paid back the short-term loan, and the Bank kept the warrant until it wished to exercise it before the expiration date. As the company received subsequent funding rounds and an IPO event, the Bank enjoyed a high return on the warrant.

In a different deal with Inuvo, a publicly traded company engaging in artificial intelligence-driven commerce solutions, Bridge Bank provided debt financing on March 1, 2012, for a $10 million accounts receivable revolving credit line and $5 million term loan. Inuvo agreed to pay interest on the credit line monthly at prime plus 0.5 percent plus a monthly maintenance fee of 0.125 percentage points on the average daily account balance and interest on the term loan at prime plus 1 percent. In connection with establishing the credit facility, Inuvo also incurred origination fees payable to Bridge Bank of approximately $100,000.[47] With respect to the warrant, Inuvo granted Bridge Bank the right to purchase 51,724 shares. Interestingly, in this deal, the Bank received a security interest in Inuvo's intellectual property.[48] In the Intellectual Property Security Agreement, the Company granted to the bank a security interest in all patents, copyrights, trademarks, licenses thereof, and proceeds and products deriving from the intellectual property, to secure the loan.

As mentioned before, in deals with banks and non-bank lenders, many tech companies generally do not want to pledge their intellectual property assets as collateral to secure loans. The intellectual property assets are too valuable to the

---

[45] "Betting on Biotech," *Smart Business News* (September 22, 2003), available at: https://sbnonline .com/article/betting-on-biotech-there-are-plenty-of-reasons-to-believe-that-biotechnology-is-the-next-big-thing-but-will-it-blossom-in-pittsburgh/ (last accessed September 28, 2023).

[46] "Vapotherm raises $56M via an IPO at NYSE," available at: https://glidehealthcare.com/news/ venture-and-growth/vapotherm-raises-usd56m-via-an-ipo-at-nyse/ (last accessed September 28, 2023).

[47] Inuvo 8K Filing (March 6, 2012).

[48] Intellectual Property Security Agreement dated March 1, 2012, between Bridge Bank and Inuvo, available at: https://investor.inuvo.com/sec-filings/all-sec-filings?form_type=8-K&year=2012&page=2##document-3517-0001354488-12-001000-1 (last accessed October 12, 2023).

company's operations. Borrowers instead agreed to a negative covenant wherein they are prohibited from using the intellectual property assets as security for subsequent transactions with others. Illustratively, in the deal between iSpecimen and Bridge Bank dated August 13, 2021, for a term loan facility of $5,000,000, the Bank charged an interest rate equal to the prime rate plus 0.75 percent and customary fees and expenses. The company agreed to pay interest payments only until February 2023 and then payments of principal and interest for the remainder of 30 months. In connection with the loan, the company issued Bridge Bank a warrant to purchase 12,500 shares of the company's common stock at $8.00 per share. The warrant will expire 10 years from issuance in 2021. Concerning assets as collateral for the loan, the company pledged all assets except for its intellectual property.[49]

Providing banking and lending services to VC-backed companies was a lucrative business. Some banks wanted to add a variation of that business to their platform by acquiring former bankers from Silicon Valley Bank. However, none of these banks were able to compete against SVB. Simply, those banks didn't have a culture of devoting 100 percent of their practice to serving the tech and license industries. The venture banking groups at those banks must operate within the larger culture of traditional banks that do not understand the VC and tech ecosystem. The traditional culture did not appreciate growth because the bankers in typical banks still insisted on seeing profits and demanding guarantees when they evaluated new customers with only intangible assets. Consequently, the venture banking groups would not be able to expand their practice.

Moreover, the venture banking groups at the traditional banks did not acquire the contacts and relationships that SVB had perfected for more than forty years. These groups are still young even though some have the experience of a couple of SVB's bankers. SVB did not fear competitors in venture debt because its relationships in the tech and VC ecosystem ran deep and wide. As a bank, SVB succeeded in both banking and lending services to meet the short-term and long-term needs of each of its clients. Competitors didn't have SVB's network and the benefits of the network effects.

Wells Fargo, after shutting down Roger Smith's Special Industries Group, never appeared as a contender in venture debt to VC-backed companies. Instead, Wells Fargo today lists "Technology" under its "Industry Expertise" and states that it offers simply a Startup Accelerator program. But the Startup Accelerator program will only furnish up to a $1 million deal in exchange for Wells Fargo to take a minority equity stake.[50] Wells Fargo also claims that it provided seed funding for VC funds to back tech and healthcare startups founded by women.[51] Besides those activities, Wells

---

[49] iSpecimen Inc. 8K filing 2021.
[50] https://accelerator.wf.com/ (last accessed October 12, 2023).
[51] "Wells Fargo Provides Seed Funding to Fuel More Venture Capital for Women-owned Businesses," available at: www.bizjournals.com/bizwomen/news/latest-news/2022/03/wells-fargo-provides-seed-funding-to-fuel.html?page=all (last accessed September 28, 2023).

Fargo is not known as a major player in the venture debt space; it never recovered from its own elimination of Smith's Special Industries Group.

With the handsome results from the warrants, SVB declared in its 10K filing for 2002 year-end that "[o]ver the long term, Silicon Valley Bank seeks to generate strong operating results by leveraging its lending practice to obtain warrant agreements to purchase equity in the technology and life sciences companies of the future."[52] Because the Bank coveted more than 9,500 clients, primarily in the tech and life science sectors, across the country through twenty-seven regional offices, the Bank asserted that it would "focus on specialized markets and extensive knowledge of the people and business issues driving them, that [the Bank] provides a level of service and partnership that contributes to [its] clients' success." What the Bank was saying was that its bankers and lenders had carved out a successful niche in venture lending.

As of 2022, SVB remained the leader in the venture lending market while other banks and other non-bank lenders subsided.

---

[52] SVB 2003 10K Filing, page 3.

9

Leveraging the VC Relationships for Expansion

Roger Smith and Harry Kellogg frequently remarked that Silicon Valley Bank (SVB) was all about relationships. The statement sounds like a cliché but until one truly absorbs its meaning it does not resonate and may soon be forgotten as relationships are challenging to understand, cultivate, and nurture strategically. Relationships with marquee VC firms and tech startups in the VC ecosystem were what set SVB apart from public venture lenders, private venture lenders, and other banks that dared to compete in venture debt lending. SVB bankers worked hard at building relationships and expanding the products and services to capture 100 percent of the VC ecosystem. The path was not always smooth, but the bankers tried; they finessed the edges and founded SVB Capital, SVB Premium Wine, and SVB Securities. Peculiarly, no bank rivalled to SVB on its path of expansion.

SVB CAPITAL

Through the arrays of banking products and venture lending, SVB bankers knew the investors, the entrepreneurs, the attorneys, the accounting firm, the equipment leasing companies, the insurance agents, and everyone else in the VC ecosystem in different innovation centers across the United States. SVB lenders monitored the investors' successes, their acquisitions, their exits, their IPOs, and their record on investment returns. The question was of course how to utilize the value from the proximity to the VCs, in addition to SVB's dominant position in the innovation sector.

On some occasions, SVB lenders made loans to VC firms. Periodically, some investors asked SVB to invest in their funds. This proposition of investing in VC funds intrigued Kellogg. He decided to take a month or so to research the idea of investing in VC funds and wrote a paper to prepare for a presentation to the Holding Company Board of Directors. Kellogg had neither the luxury of time nor the resources to conduct in-depth research. He already knew who the best VCs and funds were. He met and spoke to the VCs regularly. Perhaps some of them would let the Bank invest as a Limited Partner in their funds. Kellogg recounted the genesis of making investments in VC funds and how such investments strategically helped the Bank's expansion:

> We wanted to be able to invest in some of the brand-name venture capital firms on Sand Hill Road, just because we had relationships with them. And we banked a number of their portfolio companies. So it was kind of an informal thing.

> Part of the deal right from the onset is we banked their funds as well. We have a huge practice in banking ventures, venture capital, and private equity firms around the world. That's a multi-billion-dollar business at this point.

> So, if we were able to invest as an LP in some of these funds, we wanted them to be a client of the bank on the fund side.

As Figures 9.1 and 9.2 reveal, a venture capital fund is a limited partnership consisting of Limited Partners (LPs) and a General Partnership (GP). LPs include public pension funds, family offices, endowments, foundations, fund-of-funds, and sovereign wealth funds. The LPs are accredited investors with certain net worth and income qualifications. The LPs write most of the checks for the venture capital fund, own most of the fund, and take no operational responsibilities.

The General Partnership (GP) consists of Partners, who are the investment professionals like the notable Don Valentine, Pitch Johnson, and John Doerr, among others, who manage the venture funds. The GP in each venture capital fund, in an effort to reduce their liability, is typically comprised of two Partners from a VC firm, and they form an LLC legal structure. The GP stakes some ownership in the venture capital fund and receives operation management fees paid by the fund. The venture fund makes investments in a portfolio of companies over a period, from five to ten years.

A VC firm – Sequoia, Kleiner Perkins, NEA, or Benchmark – for instance, forms separate funds. Each fund is its own limited partnership. Consequently, liability is reduced by forming separate funds. To consider potential investments, conduct due diligence, manage portfolios, and engage in exit strategies, the VC firm hires its own analysts, associates, principals, and vice presidents to work with the partners. The VC firm may also rely on outside experts and consultants for advice and evaluations.

Each capital venture fund is governed by the Limited Partnership Agreement (LPA) which details the fund, the operation of the fund, the rights of the LPs, the responsibilities of the GP, the management fees of the GP. The LPs put in the money, and the GP serves as the agent of the LP. The GP holds a fiduciary duty to operate and manage the fund in the best interest of the LPs.

With respect to the compensation for the GP, the standard "2 and 20" is often reported in the media for private equity investments. The "2" refers to a 2 percent management fee. For instance, if each LP invests $1 million into Fund I, the

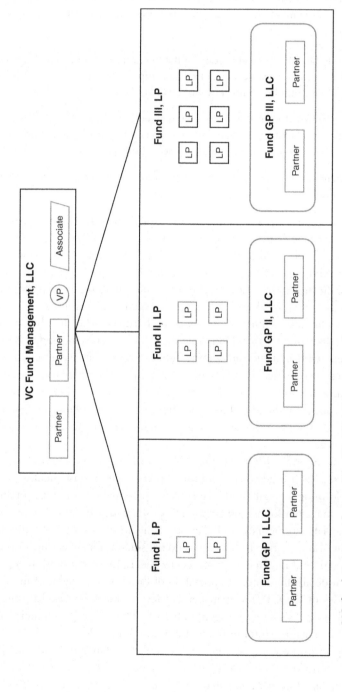

FIGURE 9.1 VC fund structure (designed by Khai-Huy Nguyen)

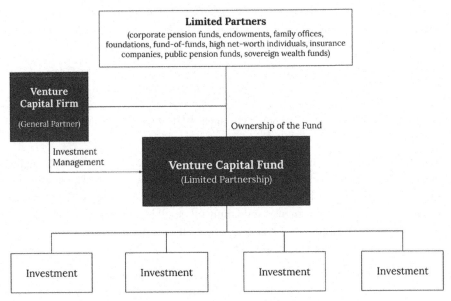

FIGURE 9.2 VC partnership structure (designed by Khai-Huy Nguyen)

investor is expected to pay 2 percent of the $1 million or $20,000 each year. The "20" refers to 20 percent of the profit of the fund and is called "carried interest." For example, if the capital commitment in Fund I was $100 million, for ten years, with a return of five times. After ten years the fund grows to $500 million, the fund must give the $100 million capital commitments back to the investors and payout management fees in ten years of $20M (2 percent of $100M times ten), leaving the remainder of $380 million for distribution. The LPs will take 80 percent or $304 million, and the GP will get 20 percent or $76 million. The GP involves two Partners so each Partner will take $38 million.

Axios reported in 2021 that Sequoia Capital would require its sub-funds to impose a 30 percent carried interest, the Sequoia Fund with a less than 1 percent management fee, and a long-term performance fee.[1] For the size of funds, in 2016, Kleiner Perkins raised a total of $1.3 billion for two funds: $800 million to the growth fund of mature startups and the remainder to early-stage startups. The funds are Kleiner's seventeenth core early-stage fund and third growth fund.[2] Andreesen Horowitz raised $4.5 billion for its fourth crypto fund.[3]

[1] Dan Primack, "Scoop: Sequoia Capital just Blew up the VC Fund Model," *Axios*, October 26, 2021.
[2] Ari Levy, "Kleiner Perkins Raising Close to $1.3 Billion for Two Funds," *CNBC*, May 23, 2016.
[3] Kate Rooney, "Andreessen Horowitz Raises $4.5 Billion Crypto Fund to Take Advantage of Bargains in Down Market," *CNBC*, May 25, 2022.

Kellogg thought that the Bank should be an LP. He wanted the Board to approve a small amount of money to invest as LPs in the funds of various elite VC firms with which he and his colleagues had built relationships over the years.

> I went to the Board, and they gave me $5 million to invest as an LP and in the funds. And they said, "This will give you some walking stick money." It just happened because we knew who the best VCs were. Some of them would let us come as an LP for various reasons. We made a lot of successful investments as a limited partner in funds.[4]

The Bank enjoyed its fruitful relationships, proximity, and rare access to make investments in the world's top VC funds as LPs. The access to make such investments is typically not available to others, including commercial banks, institutional investors, university endowments, and family offices. The access yielded handsome successes for the investments. Of course, many other investors in the United States and overseas would like to gain such access.

> It seems like yesterday, but it was a long time ago ... Everyone on the board at the time knew what better VC funds were. And we had access which the whole world would want access. So, we made a quarter million dollars here and there.

Originally, Kellogg managed the investments. The investments as LPs in VC funds were not limited to the funds in Silicon Valley. SVB lenders knew many VCs on the East Coast and that meant investments as LPs in VC funds in other innovation centers there as well.

The Board was pleased with the successes and increased the amount of investments. Soon, Kellogg and his dream team decided to expand by going out and raising money and bringing them in as LPs. Aaron Gershenberg, cofounder of SVB Capital, recalled the presentation to the SVB Board of Directors explaining to them how SVB Capital would bring value to new investors as LPs within the existing ecosystem:

> And Harry will probably remember this presentation to the Board where we created a PowerPoint slide that had a triangle. And on that triangle, we had the general partners; we had the entrepreneurs and the founders of the companies, and we had limited partners. And what we argued to the Board was that the bank had built an unbelievable brand with the general partners and the founders of companies, but had no brand with the limited partners. We didn't know who they were. We didn't know what they thought. We didn't know how they behaved or acted, but they were the fuel for the venture capital industry. And our vision with SVB Capital was to build that same value proposition for those limited partners as we had for the GPs. And SVB is in the middle of this triangle and shows the money flowing from the limited partners to the general partners, to the entrepreneurs, and then back to the limited partners. We wanted the money to never leave Silicon Valley Bank. They

---

[4] Interviews with Harry Kellogg on March 4 and 30, 2022 (on file with author).

literally would go from one corner to the other. And in the end, we stayed in the middle.[5]

After Kellogg started the investments in the VC funds, Gregg Becker and Aaron Gershenberg became the cofounders of SVB Capital, managing some of the world's top-rated venture fund-of-funds and direct investment funds. Becker led the efforts to formalize the LP investment system, as Kellogg recalled:

Greg Becker, who's now the CEO, we brought him in to run SVB Capital about three or five years after I started that initial fund. So, Greg and the other people at Sand Hill Road went out and recruited the limited partners. And most of that [time] in the early years, it was investors in the US, limited partners in the US.

He and Aaron Gershenberg really got on planes around the US and then subsequently went around the world, in Europe, in Asia, in the Middle East as well, to recruit LPs.

Becker and Gershenberg built the team in-house by recruiting some of the SVB bankers who were already at the Bank's Sand Hill Road office to get involved in the funds management business. They flew to different parts of the country to recruit new LPs in the SVB funds. They flew to cities in Europe, Asia, and the Middle East to meet with potential LPs. They prepared the documents to pitch their funds to investors.

Why would investors in the United States and abroad participate in the funds formed by SVB Capital? Why didn't the investors reach out to the top VC firms for investing in the VC funds? Only a few investors gained such direct access to VC firms. There were many investors without such access, and they really wished to make their investments in the VC funds. Everyone wants to make money! They turned to SVB Capital because they could indirectly gain access by participating in funds formed by SVB Capital. SVB Capital then invested the funds in the VC funds. Kellogg recalled:

What really enamored the LPs is the access we had with some of the better brand funds, and venture capital funds initially in the US. So the fact that we were able to get into Sequoia and Kleiner, Perkins, NEA, and Melo Ventures and some of the ones on the East Coast as well.

The responses SVB Capital received from investors were extremely positive. The combination of the brand reputation of both SVB and the top VCs was irresistible to university endowments, foundations, family offices, and sovereign wealth funds. To these investors, they finally came nearer to the marquee VC funds that were closed shut on them for years. Kellogg explained:

We've got LPs from all over the world, companies, and university endowments. We've got money from the Abu Dhabi Investment Authority. The list goes on and

---

[5] Interview with Aaron Gershenberg, April 19, 2022 (on file with author).

on who the LPs are. There are a lot of big university endowments. Stanford and Harvard, MIT and some others are LPs in our funds. And then we have some Family Offices as well that invest because they don't have the access directly, but through being an LP in our funds, they're able to get into some of the better venture capital and private equity firms around the world.

Kellogg was listed as the Chairman of SVB Capital, and he modestly insisted that it was merely for formality reasons. He believed that he was just the idea guy. The credit for founding and managing SVB Capital should go to Greg Becker and Aaron Gershenberg, Kellogg insisted:

> That was just a formal title because we had to organize it that way. But we didn't have any, we don't have any annual meetings or anything else. It was sort of a title because I think we have to have someone have a title like that as far as we're concerned.

Kellogg recalled that the investments in VC funds and direct investment funds became formalized over five years from the time he commenced. When the group created SVB Capital, there were approximately $25 million in funds. SVB Capital's 100 team members managed more than $7 billion in 2022. Gershenberg summed up that he and his team "identified what were the crown jewels of Silicon Valley Bank and monetized it."[6]

Legally, the birth of SVB Capital can be traced to November 2000.

In late November 2000, Silicon Valley Bancshares, the holding company of Silicon Valley Bank, seized new opportunities presented by the change in the law by acquiring a new legal status as a financial holding company. This new legal entity status allowed Bancshares to no longer require the prior approval of the Federal Reserve Board to conduct or to acquire ownership or control of entities engaged in financial activities. In addition, Bancshares may invest in companies "that engage in activities that are not otherwise permissible, subject to certain limitations, including that Bancshares make the investment with the intention of limiting the investment in duration and does not manage the company on a day-to-day basis."[7] In the same year, Bancshares formed SVB Strategic Investors, LLC. The LLC entity is the general partner of the SVB Strategic Investors Fund, L.P. This Fund raised $135.3 million in committed capital to invest as a limited partner in the top-tier venture funds. The holding company committed $15 million to the SVB Strategic Investors Fund, L.P., and that meant the holding company held 11 percent of ownership interest in the Fund, of which $3 million had been funded as of December 31, 2001.

In addition to investments in VC funds as LP, SVB also made equity investments directly in companies in "emerging growth technology and life sciences companies" throughout the United States. SVB was careful to not invest in companies that

---

[6]   Ibid.
[7]   SVB, "2004 10K Filing," page 6; SVB, "2001 10K Filing."

would render the Bank in competition with their VC clients. Instead, the SVB team made the investments when certain VCs asked them to invest directly in particular startup companies. Again, SVB relied on the VCs for their due diligence in making the investments directly in the startup companies because, as a commercial bank, SVB does not possess the technical expertise to understand the startup technology and science. The investments directly in the startups could not have happened without assistance from some of the VC clients. This strategy ran parallel to the venture lending practice employed by the Bank as a direct result of the Bank's reliance on the VC's due diligence and investments in the startups.

> We started making direct investments in companies, but we never wanted the VCs to think that we were encroaching on what they would do. We would not want them to see Silicon Valley Bank as a competitor in investing in startup companies. But we selectively – when we are asked by some VCs – invested in those companies. And again, our due diligence [is minimal] in comparison to the VCs; we didn't have any technical knowledge or engineers or staff. So, [decisions were] just based on the VCs and all the due diligence conducted by the VCs who made major investments. We came in for $100 thousand or $50 thousand.[8]

Along with the creation of SVB Strategic Investors Fund founded in 2000, the holding company also formed Silicon Valley BancVentures, Inc., the general partner of Silicon Valley BancVentures, L.P. This was a smaller fund compared to SVB Strategic Investors Fund; the Silicon Valley BancVentures, L.P. raised $56.1 million in committed capital. The managers of this fund made private equity investments in emerging growth technology and life sciences companies throughout the United States. At the end of December 31, 2001, the holding company committed capital of $6.0 million to Silicon Valley BancVentures, L.P., representing an ownership interest of 10.7 percent, of which $1.5 million had been funded.

As of December 31, 2000, SVB had made investments in 208 venture capital funds and direct equity investments in sixty companies.[9] Two years later in 2002, SVB reported in its 10K filing that "we had private equity investments in 24 companies through our venture capital fund, Silicon Valley BancVentures, L.P., and made investments in 20 venture capital funds through our fund of funds, SVB Strategic Investors Fund, L.P." Bancshares categorized the two funds and various investments under a "Merchant Banking" group.

In 2003 SVB celebrated its first twenty years of serving entrepreneurs.[10] The year 2003 was also special in venture debt practice. Bancshares created the Gold Hill

---

[8] Interviews with Harry Kellogg, March 4 and 30, 2022 (all on file with author).
[9] SVB, "2001 10K Filing," page 6. The Bank also held 1,324 warrants in 1,038 companies as of December 31, 2000. SVB, "2002 10K Filing," page 28. The Bank also held 1,673 warrants in 1,278 companies.
[10] "Silicon Valley Bank Celebrates 20 Years of Dedication to Entrepreneurs," *Silicon Valley Bank Company News*, October 17, 2003, available at: www.svb.com/news/company-news/silicon-

Venture Lending 03, L.P. and affiliated funds (the "Gold Hill Funds") and held a majority interest in the general partner of the Gold Hill Funds, in addition to serving as a limited partner of the Gold Hill Funds. The creation of the Gold Hill Funds demonstrated that the venture debt sector had grown significantly in serving startups in the VC ecosystem. The money that SVB loaned to the startups could not meet the demand. "The total size of the Gold Hill Funds is approximately $214 million . . . Our combined commitment total in the general partner and the Gold Hill Funds is $20.0 million."[11]

In addition to creating and controlling the Gold Hill Funds for venture debt, Bancshares also invested in Partners for Growth II, LP., "a special situation debt fund" created in 2005 with a total size of $43.7 million. Some of Bancshares' directors were limited partners in the special debt fund.[12]

With the celebration and fortification of its place in the venture ecosystem of fueling the innovation economy, SVB decided in 2004 to replace its "Merchant Banking" group with SVB Capital. By now, SVB Capital covered two funds of funds that invested in venture funds and one fund that invested in privately held startups in the tech and life sciences.

> SVB Capital focuses on the business needs of our venture capital and private equity clients, establishing and maintaining relationships with those firms domestically and internationally. Through this segment, we provide banking services and financial solutions, including traditional deposit and checking accounts, loans, letters of credit, and cash management services.
>
> SVB Capital also makes investments in venture capital and other private equity firms and in companies in the niches we serve. The segment also manages three venture funds that are consolidated into our financial statements: SVB Strategic Investors Fund, LP and SVB Strategic Investors Fund II, LP, which are funds of funds that invest in other venture funds, and Silicon Valley BancVentures, LP, a direct equity venture fund that invests in privately held technology and life-science companies.[13]

Cleverly, SVB Capital also focused on investments in venture debt funds. Specifically, in 2004 SVB Capital covered investments in Gold Hill Venture Lending Partners 03, LP and its parallel funds (collectively known as Gold Hill Venture Lending Partners 03, LP), which provided secured debt to emerging growth startups, and Partners for Growth, LP, a fund that provided secured debt to higher risk, emerging growth clients in their later stages. SVB's 10K report for the year-end 2004 defined "emerging-growth" startups as "companies in the start-up or early stages

valley-bank-celebrates-20-years-of-dedication-to-entrepreneurs   [https://perma.cc/8V9K-N2SS] (last accessed September 29, 2023).
[11] SVB, "2005 10K Filing," page 140.
[12] Ibid.
[13] Ibid.

SVB Capital   203

TABLE 9.1 *SVB funds*

Ownership in limited partner	Capital commitment	Unfunded commitment	SVB ownership percent
	(Dollars in thousands)		
Silicon Valley BancVentures, LP	$6,000	$1,440	10.7%
SVB Strategic Investors Fund, LP	$15,300	$4,590	12.6%
SVB Strategic Investors Fund II, LP	$15,000	$12,375	8.6%
SVB Strategic Investors Fund III, LP	$15,000	$14,488	100%
Partners for Growth, LP	$25,000	$10,750	50%
Partners for Growth II, LP	$10,000	$10,000	22.9%
Gold Hill Venture Lending 03, LP	$20,000	$8,551	9.3%
Other Venture Capital Funds (1)	$72,661	$23,643	

of their lifecycle. These companies tend to be privately held and backed by venture capital; they generally have few employees, have brought relatively few products or services to market, and have no or little revenue." The report also defined "middle market companies" to include the "more mature" entities which may be "publicly traded and more established in the markets in which they participate, although not necessarily the leading players in the largest industries."

SVB Capital's 2004 scope of coverage included Private Equities Services (a division of SVB Securities) to assist private equity firms, and the partners of those firms, with liquidating securities following initial public offerings and mergers and acquisitions.

By the end of 2005, Silicon Valley Bancshares retired its name and rebranded itself as SVB Financial Group. In its 10K filing for the year-end of 2005, SVB Financial Group, a bank holding and financial holding company, announced that its net interest income was $299.3 million and non-interest income from its fees and investments was $117.5 million.

SVB Financial Group provided a summary of its own venture capital funds, debt funds, and funds of funds, and SVB Capital's investments in those funds (see Table 9.1). As is typical with venture funds, commitments to invest are ten years from the inception of the fund and the timing of future cash requirements for the commitments is dependent upon the venture capital investment cycle, the overall market conditions, and the tech and life science subsector conditions.

SVB Capital expanded and became the venture capital and credit investment arm of SVB Financial Group but narrowed its scope to focus primarily on funds management. SVB Capital occupied an important space in the core four segments of SVB Financial Group. The team that managed the SVB Capital family of funds principally operated out of the SVB Menlo Park offices. SVB Capital manages over $7.3 billion of funds mostly on behalf of third-party limited partner investors. From funds of funds that made investments in other venture capital funds, direct venture funds that invested in companies, to venture debt funds, SVB Capital claimed a position in the VC ecosystem in the United States and worldwide. Who would ever anticipate that the $5 million "walking stick" money asked for by Harry Kellogg would mature into SVB Capital? In 2000, there was the first SVB Strategic Investors LLC. Twenty-two years later, the tenth fund SVB Strategic Investors X, LLC came into existence. To Kellogg and his "Dream Team," as reflected in the 2022 leadership at SVB Capital, the essential part of the work was about building, cultivating, and leveraging relationships with VCs, entrepreneurs, and investors in different cities in the United States and the world. That meant lots of hard work and ingenuity were involved while competitors were eager to find ways to chip away at SVB's foundational relationships.

SVB Financial Group depended on SVB Capital for the noninterest income generated through investment returns including carried interest and management fees. In 2021 alone, SVB Capital brought in $487 million in noninterest income compared to $226 million in 2020. The $487 million income comprised of net gains on investment securities of $398 million, fund management fees of $77 million, and gains on equity warrant assets of $6 million derived from SVB's joint venture bank in China.

Interestingly, the Office of the Comptroller of the Currency, for example, reminds all *national* banks that they are prohibited from making most equity investments in venture capital funds.[14] The OCC Bulletin highlights the following about the prohibition:

- Banks generally may not make passive equity investments in venture capital funds.
- Equity investments in venture capital funds may be permissible if they are public welfare investments or investments in small business investment companies.
- Qualifying for the Volcker rule's venture capital fund exclusion does not make a fund a permissible investment for a bank.
- As with any investment, before a bank invests in a venture capital fund, the bank must determine whether the investment is permissible and appropriate for the bank. Impermissible and inappropriate investments expose the bank and its institution-affiliated parties to enforcement actions and civil money penalties. National bank directors may be personally liable for impermissible investment losses.

---

[14] "Investments: Venture Capital Funds, Bulletin 2021–54," *Office of the Comptroller of the Currency*, November 23, 202, available at: www.occ.gov/news-issuances/bulletins/2021/bulletin-2021-54.html [https://perma.cc/HXT9-YCZC] (last accessed September 29, 2023).

Nevertheless, Silicon Valley Bank was *not* a national bank, it was a California-chartered bank and a member of the Federal Reserve System. The Bank is subject to primary supervision and examination by the Federal Reserve Board through the Federal Reserve Bank of San Francisco and the Commissioner of the California Department of Financial Institutions. Also, Silicon Valley Bancshares (later changed to Silicon Valley Financial Group), the holding company and financial holding company was subject to the Federal Reserve Board's supervision and examination under the Bank Holding Company Act, as revised by the Gramm-Leach-Bliley Act. Consequently, the OCC's prohibition did not apply to Silicon Valley Bank. Moreover, the equity investments at SVB were conducted by SVB Capital, a different legal entity from the Silicon Valley Bank.

SVB Capital was an example of the expansion of a bank originally executed by Roger Smith that embodied the 3Cs of Courage, Creativity, and Consistency. The Bank embraced the courage to serve the tech sector and embark on what commercial banks generally don't dare to venture into creatively and consistently. The SVB Capital story, unsurprisingly, is complementary to the SVB's Premium Wine story.

PREMIUM WINE AND SVB BANKING RELATIONSHIP

One of the most perplexing industries among technology, life science/healthcare, and private equity/venture capital sectors served by SVB was premium wine. Certainly, to the casual observer, premium wineries seem completely unrelated to the technology and life sciences niche. However, to the SVB bankers, premium wine brought tremendous value to the other sectors of the Bank. How did premium wine become a part of SVB's DNA?

In 1993 when John Dean, a bank turnaround specialist, took over the reins of SVB, he devised a new plan to replace the real estate niche. The Bank sat on so much cash from its technology and life sciences niche, and the Bank needed to make money the way that all banks do best – based on the interest rates differentiation. The Bank must make loans and generate income from lending out the money. Dean identified industries whose financial services needs were underserved at that time. He called them "Special Industry Niches" and directed SVB lenders to court potential businesses and extend loans in these niches. SVB lenders knocked on the doors of churches, temples, schools, and other religious organizations nationwide offering them term loans for refinancing existing debt, acquiring new property, and renovating, remodeling, or constructing buildings in this special niche. Dean also directed SVB lenders to open its entertainment niche in Beverly Hills, California, focusing on production loans for film, television, and new media, and commercial loans to entertainment-related entities who were producers, distributors, and sale agents. Dean looked at the manufacturing companies in

Northern California as another niche called the "Diversified Industries" practice. The list of "Special Industries Niche" looked fine when Dean was in charge but conveyed both a desperation and a startup pivot. For sure, the list was indeed a product of a bank turnaround specialist who was not afraid of trying to reshape a young bank in its efforts of making money with new lending practices because the young bank with a strong focus on tech and life sciences was sitting on so much cash infused from tech companies' deposits.

The Bank praised its foresight on religious lending practice, equating its own entrepreneurship spirit with American growth in independent churches!

> Growth in independent and non-denominational churches in America provides us with exceptional revenue opportunities. Entrepreneurs can come in all forms. Having the foresight to grow a church or move into a new area requires the same visionary instincts prevalent in our technology clients. Our religious lending practice focuses on providing the entrepreneurs in this segment with the expertise and financial solutions necessary to expand their facilities.[15]

In 1994, the Bank began to focus on lending to premium wineries among the special industry niches. A casual observer may jokingly comment about mixing premium wine with technology and life science niches under the same independent bank. But similarly, wine is about relationships, and banking is about relationships. The program demonstrated great success, and the Bank opened an office in St. Helena, California, in 1996 to establish a stronger presence in this niche.[16] The premium wineries practice made loans to wineries that produce select or exclusive vintages of up to 150,000 cases annually. SVB lenders extended both short-term inventory loans and term loans related to vineyard acquisition and development, equipment financing, and cooperage.

Soon, SVB became one of the leading providers of financial services to premium wine producers in Napa Valley, Sonoma County, and Central Coast regions of California. SVB reached out to premium wine producers in Oregon and Washington. Most of the loans to the premium wine producers were secured by real estate collateral such as vineyards and wineries.

Rob McMillan is credited with founding the SVB Wine Division. When Ken Wilcox, who succeeded John Dean as CEO, considered eliminating all special industry niches, including the wine division, McMillan made a passionate speech to save the division.[17] After many discussions, the wine division was saved. Everyone later appreciated McMillan's wisdom.

---

[15] SVB "1994 10K Filing."
[16] SVB, "1996 10K Filing," page 4.
[17] Interview with Harry Kellogg, April 19, 2022 (on file with author).

McMillan concentrated on ultra-premium wine.[18] It turned out that lots of VCs desire the exclusive, ultra-premium wine. Who would imagine the connection between premium wine and VCs? Premium wine plays an important role in relationship management and building, inclusive of VCs and investor relationships. Harry Kellogg relocated to SVB's Napa offices for five years, working with colleagues on client relationships. Kellogg held the title of President of SVB Private Client Services and Wine Division.

SVB formed a concierge service for prominent people worldwide who would like to visit the wine country, enjoy wine tasting at exclusive wine estates, and stay at posh hotels. These special visitors want access to Harlan Estate, the leader of the low production, top quality wine, and high prices model. Harlan vintages are often described as one of the ten best wines in the country. The waiting list for a bottle is long, despite the released price of $850 per bottle. The speculative market price generally fetches from $1,000 and up per bottle. The people desire a trip to Scarecrow and to listen to its fabled history. They seek an opportunity to see Screaming Eagle Winery and be a part of the cult wine culture. In many ways, these individuals are the people who would like to enjoy what Katie Kelly Bell described in *Forbes*:

> An exclusive wine tasting near Billionaire's Beach: The Malibu Beach Inn, Los Angeles, has an exclusive partnership with the Dierberg Estate in Santa Barbara County to give guests access to its vineyard. The estate is not open to the public, only guests booking the Dierberg Suite can experience the winery and estate with a private tour and tasting followed by a catered gourmet lunch overlooking Happy Canyon.[19]

Premium wine and the attraction of Napa Valley hold an allure for venture capitalists. Richard Kramlich, the cofounder of New Enterprise Associates and Greenbay Ventures, serves on the Board of Festival Napa Valley.[20] VCs and other investors descend to Napa for retreats[21] or to invest in or purchase a prized property.[22]

---

[18] Rachel Louise Ensign, "This Banker Gets to Drink Wine All Day, Rob McMillan Was a Pioneer in the Business of Financing Wineries, but Almost Missed the Grape Opportunity: He First Proposed his Bank Specialize in Mortuaries," *The Wall Street Journal*, July 19, 2019 9:00 am ET, available at: www.wsj.com/articles/this-banker-gets-to-drink-wine-all-day-11563541201?mod=hp_lead_pos11 [https://perma.cc/K45U-7RZF] (last accessed September 29, 2023).

[19] Katie Kelly Bell, "Seven of the Best Wine Tastings and Culinary Experiences to Book Now," *Forbes*, June 13, 2022.

[20] "Richard Kramlich, Board of Directors," Festival Napa Valley, available at: https://festivalnapavalley.org/about-us/board/richard-kramlich/ [https://perma.cc/DRX3-XF3P] (last accessed September 29, 2023).

[21] Brooke Southall, "Upper-Crusty Napa Valley Retreat Brings Together Top Family Office Execs, New Age VCs and Top VCs: At Least Locationally," *RIABiz*, October 23, 2013.

[22] Craig Karmin, "Four Seasons Hotel in Napa Selling for Near Record Valuation: Sunstone Hotel Investors Agrees to Pay about $175 Million for the 85-Room Luxury Hotel," *The Wall Street Journal*, November 2, 2021 8:30 am ET, available at: www.wsj.com/articles/four-seasons-hotel-in-

Some bring their investment strategies and VC experience to investing in wine brands.[23] From politicians like Nancy Pelosi[24] and Donald Trump to celebrities like Brad Pitt, Drew Barrymore, and Sting; they all own vineyards in California.[25] Wine, wealth, and power collide at the vineyards.

SVB bankers learned that premium wine would add value to the rest of the Bank. The concierge service complimented the private banking to serve SVB clients in its growing private banking services. SVB understood the psychology of gaining access to special vineyards producing ultra-premium wine and leveraged that for its banking expansion. Harlan Estate, Scarecrow, Screaming Eagle, and over 400 premium wineries in Napa, Sonoma, Santa Barbara, Oregon, and Washington are SVB clients. The bankers could leverage the wine relationships to entertain and enchant new businesses. The bankers knew that Harlan wine bottles were not available anywhere, but they could help clients to get on the waiting list. Just like in the SVB Capital business, investors worldwide wanted access to invest in VC funds, and that is why the investors participated in funds formed by SVB Capital. An ultra-premium wine division attracted prominent people and investors who covet access to the exclusive vineyards and the most expensive and impossible-to-fetch bottles. Bragging rights are alluring, after all.

> . . . a lot of people from around the US, if not around the world, want to go to wine country. So we did, we had a concierge service. We still have it. If people, prominent people, want to go up to wine country, we get them a hotel. We've set up a wine tasting. And so the whole thing kind of melded together that we have the wine group and then our private banking efforts.[26]

Some VCs would like to invest in certain vineyards, and they sought to obtain loans through SVB's private banking business. Top wine producers looked to the Bank for their loans and financial services.

napa-selling-for-near-record-valuation-11635856200 [https://perma.cc/A9PN-ZWKB] (last accessed September 29, 2023).

[23] The disgraced Charles Banks raised the price from $250 per bottle to $750 bottle to elevate Screaming Eagle's vineyard stature. Adam Teeter, "Meet the VC Who Actually Makes Money Investing in Wine Brands," *VinePair.com*, February 2, 2016, available at: https://vinepair.com/wine-blog/charles-banks-wine-vc-profile/ [https://perma.cc/94N4-NS9K] (last accessed September 29, 2023); W. Blake Gray, "Charles Banks: From Screaming Eagle to Jailbird," Wine-Searcher, February 15, 2017, available at: www.wine-searcher.com/m/2017/09/charles-banks-from-screaming-eagle-to-jailbird [https://perma.cc/RK9L-YPWX] (last accessed September 29, 2023).

[24] Javier Panzar, "Nancy Pelosi's Vineyard Makes Her Fourth-Richest Californian in Congress," *The Los Angeles Times*, November 6, 2015.

[25] Natalie Stayse Owala, "Brad Pitt and Other Celebrities Who Own Vineyards and Wineries," *TheThings*, August 26, 2021.

[26] Interviews with Harry Kellogg, March 4 and 30, 2022 (all on file with author).

By 2002 SVB reevaluated its "Special Industry Niches" and eliminated the religious, media, and real estate niches. But SVB kept the premium wine division because that division enhanced SVB's growing private banking division.

> For many years, Silicon Valley Bancshares pursued a strategy of niche expansion that translated into reaching beyond the boundaries of technology and life sciences sectors, to penetrate what we thought to be under-served markets. In late 2002, we decided to focus our resources on the most profitable industry sectors served by us, which are technology, life sciences, and premium wineries. As a result of narrowing our focus, we deliberately exited three niches: real estate, media, and religious lending. We will continue to service our existing real estate, media, and religious niche loans until they are paid off. However, we will not seek any new lending opportunities in these niches. We expect the termination of these niches to enable us to focus on more profitable aspects of our business and improve overall profitability.[27]

The Bank counted more than $4 billion in loans extended to premium wine clients since 1994. Kellogg shared that the Bank's loan losses in the premium wine industry had been zero. Most importantly, SVB continually provided industry insights and strategic advice to vintners. Every year the Bank issued the *State of the Wine Industry Report* showcasing its industry expertise and long-term relationship with clients.

In its 10K filing for year-end 2010, the Bank curiously listed "SVB Specialty Lending" and stated that, under this lending practice, the Bank provided "banking products and services to our premium wine industry clients, including vineyard development loans, as well as community development loans made as part of our responsibilities under the Community Reinvestment Act." Simply put, one could hardly keep a straight face trying to speak in the same breath as premium wine clients and underserved minority communities given that the minority communities faced serious discriminatory redlining practices nationwide.

PRIVATE BANKING FOR VC/PE AND SENIOR MANAGEMENT TEAMS

SVB bankers soon observed that not only tech companies were flushed with cash when they obtained capital rounds of funding, but the VCs and entrepreneurs were also enriched with new cash. The Bank received deposits from clients within the technology, life sciences, and premium wine sectors, and some deposits from individuals served by its private banking division. The Bank did not seek deposits from conventional retail sources. But what else to do with all the cash?

High-net-worth individuals may need one-off loans and wish their assets would be managed. The Banks provided an array of loans, personal asset management, mortgage services, and trust and estate planning tailored to such individuals.

27 SVB 2002 10K Filing.

In fact, the SVB 10K filing for year-end 1998 stated that the "Executive Banking Division focuses on serving the personal banking needs of senior executives and owners of the Bank's client companies, partners and senior executives of venture capital firms, attorneys, accountants, and other professionals whose businesses are affiliated with the Bank's niches."

On October 1, 2002, SVB acquired Woodside Asset Management, Inc., to be its new subsidiary. Woodside operated $200 million under management for seventy clients. The SVB incorporated Woodside's services as part of the Bank's then-existing private banking services. But Woodside Asset Management experienced an impairment in 2004, and SVB sold off the subsidiary in early 2006.

As the relationships between SVB and VCs, investors, and entrepreneurs flourished, the Bank expanded its services to private clients. In January 2004 the Bank changed "Private Banking" to "Private Client Services" to capture a wide range of credit services, including long-term secured and short-term unsecured lines of credit to venture capitalists and entrepreneurs within the VC ecosystem that the Bank had cultivated. SVB Private Client Services also helped private clients meet their cash management needs through checking accounts, money market accounts, certificates of deposit, and other personalized banking services.

By 2005 SVB included home equity lines of credit, secured lines of credit, restricted stock purchase loans, airplane loans, and capital call lines of credit to individual clients. Owning a private jet was becoming a part of the bragging rights among the individual clients in the VC ecosystem. The Bank did not want to lose out to competitors on that front given that the Bank had known many venture capitalists personally for many years. Harry Kellogg remembered:

> We would just make one-off loans. if Don Valentine from Sequoia wanted to upgrade his aircraft, we would make an aircraft loan. So we did it on a one-off basis essentially. But we didn't have a private bank, a separate private bank. We just did those on a one-off basis essentially.

Like the Premium Wine division, SVB saw its Private Clients division as "Relationship Management" where the Bank nurtured, built, and leveraged the relationships with selected individuals for its lending services. Both divisions brought value to the rest of the Bank's business. The Bank thrived as a one-stop shopping center for its VC clients, observing and anticipating what VC clients need and expanding the services to meet the newly identified need. Also, SVB observed that VC professionals and senior management teams of portfolio companies were going to the First Republic and Bank of America for mortgages. SVB then set into motion discovering how to best serve the individuals through private banking.

Making personal loans to VC individuals and senior management teams of portfolio companies meant the Bank was in the consumer lending sector. It also meant the Bank was subject to a different set of regulations and must comply with these regulations. To adequately serve the clients and stop running afoul of the regulations, SVB decided to set up a separate private bank and hired new bankers to operate the personal lending and mortgage lending lines for private clients.

> But as the bank grew and that was more demand for personal lending by the VCs, we decided that we need a more formalized private bank. There were a few reasons we wanted to do that because we want to be organized, but we didn't know what the heck we were doing as far as the regulations and lending money to individuals. So we were probably breaking a lot of regulatory rules because we didn't know all the compliance and everything else that went into the personal loans. I think we got slapped on the wrist by the regulators because we were making all these personal loans, but we weren't in compliance with all the regulations around those loans. We decided that if we wanted to do this, we should do it effectively, making sure we complied with all rules at the time. So, we set up a private banking group. We hired a person to run that group.[28]

The Bank retired "Private Client Services" and adopted a new name "SVB Private Bank" for its private banking division. This new change in 2010 reflected the recognition that the division primarily provided a range of personal financial solutions primarily to venture capital/private equity professionals, executive leaders of the companies in the tech and life science sectors, and other influencers in the innovation economy. These individuals are the new economy's high-net-worth people. These are the individuals that the Bank aimed to make sure don't go to other banks for their personal loans in connection with purchasing their houses and recreational crafts and satisfying their personal financial requests. Essentially, to serve these clients, the Bank offered a "customized suite of private banking services, including mortgages, home equity lines of credit, restricted stock purchase loans, capital call lines of credit, and other secured and unsecured lending."

SVB returned to personal wealth management in private banking again in 2013 by launching a new subsidiary called SVB Wealth Advisory for individual clients. This time SVB attained both substantial experience and an excellent client base that enabled the Bank to form the SVB Wealth Advisory subsidiary in-house, unlike in 2002 when the Bank acquired Woodside Asset Management, Inc., which was later sold off due to losses. SVB Private Bank then began to include SVB Wealth Advisory, the new investment advisory subsidiary of the Bank, to provide private wealth management services to individual clients. The Bank strategically housed both SVB Capital and SVB Private Bank in the Menlo Park offices near all the top-tier VCs. Believing relationships require a short distance for enhancement, the Bank always knew to be near the clients was a key to its longevity.

The Bank lending to Private Bank clients represented 11 percent of the total gross loans the Bank made beginning in 2015. Home mortgages constituted 86 percent of the Private Bank's portfolio.

---

[28] Harry Kellogg Interview, *supra*, Chapter 6, note 16.

Several years later, with a new opportunity to expand SVB Private Bank, SVB decided in 2021 to make a bold move by acquiring Boston Private, the premier institution for private banking and wealth management.

When SVB announced in January 2021 to acquire Boston Private, the United States and the world were suffering from the raging COVID-19 pandemic. The January 2021 statistics reported the unemployment rate fell to 6.3 percent, more than ten million Americans were unemployed, fourteen million renters were behind on payments, and twenty-nine million adults were struggling with food insecurity. In the peak of the COVID-19 pandemic when many businesses suffered a precipitous downfall, and Congress passed aggressive rescue plans to stall the death spiral, SVB accumulated plenty of cash in deposits from clients. SVB paid $900 million for Boston Private to accelerate the growth and capabilities of its private bank and wealth management strategy. SVB didn't want to stand on the sideline and watch VC/PE investors and entrepreneurs with so much wealth go elsewhere. SVB Private Bank lacked the capability to serve such clients, but Boston Private offered the expertise and experience.

Boston Private, a Massachusetts state-chartered trust company and the sole banking subsidiary of Boston Private Financial Holdings, Inc., operated twenty branches including nine branches in Massachusetts and eleven in California. When the proposed merger was announced, Boston Private enjoyed total assets of $10.5 billion compared to SVB's $140.3 billion.

By acquiring Boston Private, SVB aimed to both extend and diversify its business and geographical influence while maintaining its position as the bank for all leaders and participants of the VC/PE-backed innovation economy. SVB Financial positioned itself to be the arch financial partner for the innovation economy with its four core businesses: commercial banking, investment banking, private banking and wealth management, and fund management to accommodate its existing and growing clients.

Specifically, the acquisition of Boston Private allowed SVB's private bank clients to gain access to the larger and more experienced financial advisor group from Boston Private, in addition to an expanded portfolio of commercial and specialty lending operations, and an improved digital platform. SVB's private bank clients received services related to complex strategies to manage their concentrated stock positions, tax planning, trust services, philanthropy, and estate planning. Most importantly, SVB stood to deliver "the understanding, guidance and solutions" to fuel its clients to build wealth.

Overall, the growth in the last four decades and the massive growth in the Bank's deposits in 2021 translated into ways that SVB identified to capture 100 percent of all facets of VC/PE business and personal wealth investments, finance, banking, lending, and management needs.

SVB INVESTMENT BANKING

SVB noted in its 10K filing for year-end 1995 that the then proposed regulations would allow bank holding companies to control both a bank and a securities affiliate, which could engage in the full range of investment banking activities, including corporate underwriting. The proposed legislations would revise the Glass-Steagall Act and the Bank Holding Company Act of 1956 by expanding permissible activities for banks, principally to facilitate the convergence of commercial and investment banking. The Glass-Steagall Act was enacted in 1933 to separate commercial banks from investment banks. On November 12, 1999, President Bill Clinton signed the Gramm-Leach-Bliley (GLB) Act allowing the consolidation of commercial banks, investment banks, securities firms, and insurance companies.

The GLB Act revised the Bank Holding Act to permit a bank holding company to be a financial holding company and engage in banking, securities, insurance, and merchant bank activities. The bank holding company can acquire and own different types of financial firms without the Federal Reserve Board's approval. For instance, Citicorp, a bank holding company, merged with Travelers Group, an insurance company, to form the new Citigroup, a corporation combining banking, securities, and insurance services under the familiar names Citibank, SmithBarney, Primerica, and Travelers. The GLB Act also removed the blanket exemption for banks from being considered brokers or dealers under the Securities Exchange Act of 1934 and imposed only limited exemptions. In addition, the GLB Act eliminated the exemption that prevented bank holding companies and banks that advised mutual funds from being considered investment advisers under the Investment Advisers Act of 1940.

As a bank holding company, if SVB wanted to be qualified as a financial holding company under the GLB Act, it must demonstrate that its depository subsidiary, the Silicon Valley Bank, is well-capitalized and receives at least "satisfactory" ratings in general, managerial, and Community Reinvestment Act examinations. SVB planned to elect the new "financial holding company" status when it could qualify in the future.[29]

By 1998, SVB undertook its first baby step in investment banking, noting that the Corporate Finance Division would pursue "opportunities in leasing, mezzanine lending and debt placements, targeting bank-eligible investment banking transactions." But SVB was too small and could not grow at the same rate as some tech clients as they grew rapidly in the late stages. Consequently, SVB lost the investment banking business to bigger investment banks.[30] SVB decided to change all of that:

> For clients in the more advanced stages of growth, we pursue opportunities in mezzanine lending and will provide private equity and debt placement services, high-yield debt services, and mergers and acquisitions advice. We also assist our clients through investment bank referrals for public offerings, equity research, sales and trading services, asset securitizations, and fixed-income services.[31]

[29] SVB, "10K Filing Yearend," 1999.
[30] Ibid.
[31] Ibid.

Embarking on a new strategy of investment banking, on September 28, 2001, SVB Securities, a subsidiary of Silicon Valley Bank, completed the acquisition of SVB Alliant, an investment banking firm providing merger and acquisition and corporate partnering services. At first Silicon Valley Bank operated the investment banking under the name "Alliant Partners" and then "SVB Alliant." On October 1, 2002, SVB Alliant was sold by the Silicon Valley Bank subsidiary to the Silicon Valley Bancshares parent company because the transfer allowed SVB Alliant to "operate under less restrictive bank holding company regulations and increased capital ratios at Silicon Valley Bank."

SVB Alliant investment banking subsidiary provided merger and acquisition advisory services (M&A), strategic alliance services, and specialized financial studies such as valuations and fairness opinions. In October 2003, SVB enhanced its investment banking product set by launching a Private Capital Group that provides advisory services for the private placement of securities. SVB Alliant was a broker–dealer registered with the National Association of Securities Dealers, Inc. (NASD). By the end of 2003, however, SVB Alliant did not achieve its originally forecasted results of operations and incurred aggregate impairment of goodwill charges of $63.0 million.[32] In subsequent years, SVB Alliant continued to perform poorly. Additionally, according to Harry Kellogg, the investment bankers and commercial bankers at SVB did not work out well, and SVB closed out investment banking.

> We thought it would be a great fit to be in the investment banking business. So, we did some due diligence on the local investment banks. We acquired an investment bank. And unfortunately, that didn't work out. I mean that one of the biggest differences between it, commercial banking and investment banking, are the people essentially. So, the investment bankers were a little arrogant and thought the people on the commercial side were so-so bankers. It was all about investment banking, doing deals, doing IPOs, and making big fees and all that. So, that was under Ken Wilcox actually who was the CEO at the time when we got into the investment banking business. And then subsequently, we wrote that investment off and shut that business down.

In July 2007, SVB announced its decision to cease operations at SVB Alliant. The completion of wind-down activities meant that SVB Alliant ceased operations by March 31, 2008.

Still, SVB could not sit out for too long. Investment banking generated large fees and handsome commissions, and SVB salivated for the opportunities as it watched deals when late-stage companies went to other banks with big investment bank operations. SVB then identified Leerink, a leading investment bank, specializing in healthcare and life sciences that would complement SVB's commercial banking and lending products with a full range of investment banking services focused on

---

[32] SVB, "10K Yearend," 2004, pages 112–113.

healthcare and life science companies. Under Greg Becker's leadership, SVB returned to investment banking by acquiring Leerink on January 4, 2019. SVB acquired Leerink for $280 million in cash up front and agreed to provide a retention pool for employees of $60 million to be paid over five years.

Leerink Holdings LLC was the Boston-based parent company of healthcare and life science investment bank Leerink Partners LLC. With the acquisition, SVB's investment banking now called SVB Leerink, specialized in equity and convertible capital markets, M&A, equity research, and sales and trading for growth- and innovation-minded healthcare and life science companies. SVB Leerink operated as a wholly-owned subsidiary of SVB Financial and emphasizes two primary lines of business: (i) investment banking focused on providing companies with capital-raising services, financial advice on mergers and acquisitions, sales and trading services and equity research, and (ii) sponsorship of private investment funds. Furthermore, in December 2021, to complement the SVB Leerink investment banking unit, SVB agreed to acquire a boutique technology, media, and telecom equity research firm, MoffettNathanson, to expand the Bank's research coverage. In February 2022, SVB finessed its brand identity by replacing the "Leerink" with "Securities," and the investment banking unit was now named SVB Securities.

In four decades, through different attempts at different types of banking services, acquisitions, exits, and acquisitions again, SVB transformed from being a small, independent bank with the conviction to serve the tech community to becoming SVB Financial Group. Who would have anticipated that its businesses, including Silicon Valley Bank, would offer commercial, investment and securities, asset management, private wealth management, brokerage, and investment services, and funds management services to companies in the technology, life science, and healthcare, private equity, and venture capital, and premium wine industries?

As SVB expanded and became one of the big banks in the United States, Harry Kellogg expressed his concerns about the future of SVB's DNA in banking and nurturing startups. The large, handsome fees generated from investment banking and M&A advisory services were too enticing to the bankers in that they preferred to move away from banking and lending to early-stage startups.

> I hope we never lose focus on banking startups. Because it's easier to grow with a company than if, as they've grown, they will have a bank relationship with Deutsche Bank or JP Morgan, to get them away from somewhere else. It's easier to start with them and grow with them, as opposed to dragging them out from another relation-ship with another powerhouse. But I told Greg Becker, who is the current CEO of SVB, I worry today because we're having to hire people from JP Morgan, Wells Fargo, and Bank of America. Are these people going to have the same mentality for going after startups? Because there's a lot of work involved in lending money to startups as much expertise and time underwriting a loan for an early-stage company as is for a late-stage company. And someone says I don't want to spend all the time working with startups where I'm not making a whole lot of money or get warrants to

a late, late stage. So, I told Greg, I hope we always have the hunger, the fire in the belly to work with startup companies. And there is a special group at the Bank that's all they do is working with startups.

As the Bank shifted its stature as one of the fifteen largest banks in the United States, SVB was leaving behind many early-stage startups. The percentage of early-stage startups the Bank served was small. That opened potential opportunities for new upstart banks to serve the many startups in the innovation ecosystem across the United States and overseas. Take the lessons learned from SVB, coupled with the right timing for a new Bank, and the next Silicon Valley Bank could be formed. Perhaps such thinking may amount to nothing less than wishful in light of the drastic economic contraction in 2022, after companies including banks drenched in cash during 2021, when the economy went into override.

10

Into the Premature Future and Banks' Almost Embrace of ESG

The Black Lives Matter movement and the pandemic propelled many financial institutions, including banks, to adopt Environment, Social, and Governance (ESG) principles. Banks disclosed their metrics in various reports showing that they were somewhat implementing efforts to address ESG in their business, operations, and management.

In 2020, SVB released its report on the gender gap in startup leadership, noting that only 40 percent of US startups have at least one woman in the C-suite or on the board of directors. The elephant in the valley is the gender parity gap permeating the tech sector, yet without meaningful redress at the top by those who hold the power. Releasing the report without itself leading to the change renders the report partially empty. SVB rectified that by cultivating and installing Kay Matthews as chair of SVB Financial Group's board of directors in May 2022. Matthews became the first woman to hold that role at the parent company of Silicon Valley Bank. Matthews herself joined SVB's board in 2019 after spending 36 years at Ernst & Young advising VC-backed startups and Fortune 500 companies. Matthews' leadership on the Board affirmed SVB's visible step in demonstrating that ESG is indeed in its DNA. Diversity and inclusion begin at the Board level.

SVB released its sixty-six page 2022 *Environmental, Social, and Governance Report* on August 18, 2022, revealing the details of its commitments and strategies to "help create a more just, equitable and sustainable world." Bank of America issued its ESG reports, encompassing an *ESG Performance Data Summary* of thirty pages, *Bank of America's Task Force on Climate-Related Financial Disclosures* of twenty-five pages, and ESG highlights in the 2021 *Annual Report* of 221 pages. Wells Fargo produced its ESG reports, including the 2021 *Report*, with ninety-eight pages. Citi Bank bragged that it reported each year on ESG activities and performance and published 183 pages for its 2021 *ESG Report*. Commerce Bank insisted that it leveraged ESG best practices to publish ESG reports about its initiatives and published thirty-eight pages for its latest *ESG Report*. TD Bank asserted that its

ESG reports have evolved over the years and issued 118 pages for 2021 for its *Environmental, Social, and Governance Report.*

It seems that all banks in which people have expressed their hate or strong dislike all cloak themselves under the blanket of ESG reports. SVB was not among the banks interfacing daily with the average American and thus escaped their wrath.

ESG METRICS AND BANKS

In June 2004 a group of 20 financial institutions with combined assets under management of over $6 trillion publicly endorsed the United Nations Global Compact's report entitled *Who Cares Wins: Connecting Financial Markets to a Changing World.* The report included recommendations to integrate ESG value drivers into financial market research, analysis, and investment. Subsequently, as a follow-up, on August 25, 2005, the stakeholders expanded their list and invited additional participants to the *Who Cares Wins* conference in Zurich hosted by the UN Global Compact, the Federal Department of Foreign Affairs Switzerland, and the World Bank Group/International Finance Corporation. The conference brought together for the first-time institutional investors, asset managers, buy-side and sell-side research analysts, global consultants, and government regulators to review the program made in implementing recommendations of *Who Cares Wins* by financial market actors. In addition, the conference fostered a dialogue among stakeholders, identified key obstacles for a better integration of ESG factors in investments and solutions, improved the consistency of the ESG-related message, and explored new emerging issues in the ESG field.[1]

In 2006, a key development occurred. The United Nation's Principles for Responsible Investment (PRI) report, which consisted of the *Freshfield Report* and *Who Cares Wins*, set forth the criteria on environmental, social and governance to be incorporated into the financial evaluations of companies. Incorporating ESG in investments began to gain serious traction.

By 2022, the momentum for incorporating ESG in investments led to a total of 5,020 signatories, representing over $121 trillion in assets under management.[2] The number clearly indicated that institutional investors were holding their asset

[1] "Conference Report, Investing for Long-Term Value," *Federal Department of Foreign Affairs: Switzerland, International Finance Corporation: World Bank Group, United Nations Global Compact,* October 26, 2005, available at: www.ifc.org/wps/wcm/connect/9d9bb80d-625d-49d5-baad-8e46a0445b12/WhoCaresWins_2005ConferenceReport.pdf?MOD=AJPERES&CVID=jkD172p [https://perma.cc/8LQ3-NMT8] (last accessed September 29, 2023).

[2] David Atkin, "2022 April–June Quarterly Signatory Update," *Principles for Responsible Investment,* June 2022, available at: www.unpri.org/signatories/signatory-resources/quarterly-signatory-update [https://perma.cc/SM5B-DV9K] (last accessed September 29, 2023); "Become a Signatory," *Principles for Responsible Investment,* 2022, available at: www.unpri.org/signatory-resources/become-a-signatory/5946.article [https://perma.cc/N3QA-LBPB] (last accessed September 29, 2023).

management firms to ESG commitments. For instance, State Street Global Advisors voted against the re-election of directors at 400 companies that failed to appoint women to their all-male boards.[3] Also, in May 2017, 62 percent of ExxonMobile shareholders voted against management's recommendation, instead demanding the company report on the climate change impact to its business.[4] In 2021, ESG-themed proposals advanced by shareholders during the proxy season trended significantly higher than in prior years.[5] Encouragingly, State Street Global Advisors conducted a global survey of 475 asset management institutions, including pension funds, endowments, foundations, and official institutions, which revealed that 80 percent of the respondents incorporate an ESG component in their investment strategies and the integration of ESG driven investment strategies "has a future in institutional portfolios."[6]

One of the exciting developments in the ESG movement occurred in 2020. Deloitte, PwC, KPMG, and Ernst & Young, along with the World Economic Forum and the International Business Council of 120 corporate members, translated ESG principles to standardized measurements. They established a set of measurements of twenty-one core and thirty-four expanded metrics and disclosures for companies to report their results. This allowed the acceleration of ESG integration because the metrics measure "stakeholder capitalism" and the metrics are designed "to improve the ways that companies measure and demonstrate their contribution to a more prosperous and fulfilled society and a more sustainable relationship with our planet."[7]

Interestingly, the metrics are named "Stakeholder Capitalism Metrics" or SCM. Brian Moynihan, President and CEO of Bank of America and chair of the International Business Council, seemed very proud of the standardizing of ESG measurements under the Stakeholder Capitalism Metrics approach. In fact, Moynihan gushed that SCMs represent "the world's first standardized ESG measurements." Additionally, the SCM approach will help "reward companies making progress, hold companies accountable that need to make better progress, and act on the major issues facing the world."[8]

3   Betsy Atkins, "Demystifying ESG: Its History & Current Status," *Forbes*, June 8, 2020.
4   Diane Cardwell, "Exxon Mobil Shareholders Demand Accounting of Climate Change Policy Risks," *The New York Times*, May 31, 2017.
5   Emily Chasan, "A Record-Breaking, Angst-Filled Proxy Year," *GreenBiz*, July 1, 2021.
6   "Asset Owners Say Integration of ESG has Significantly Improved Returns, State Street Global Advisors Study Shows," *Businesswire*, April 19, 2017, available at: www.businesswire.com/news/home/20170419006214/en/Asset-Owners-Integration-ESG-Significantly-Improved-Returns [https://perma.cc/Z3QK-CB5V] (last accessed September 29, 2023).
7   "Measuring Stakeholder Capitalism: Towards Common Metrics and Consistent Reporting of Sustainable Value Creation." *World Economic Forum*, www.weforum.org/stakeholdercapitalism [https://perma.cc/6A2G-TSHL] (last accessed September 29, 2023).
8   "A New Standard for Measuring Global Sustainability," *Bank of America*, 2020, https://about.bankofamerica.com/en/making-an-impact/stakeholder-capitalism-metrics#:~:text=The%20Stakeholder%20Capitalism%20Metrics%20represent,nonprofits%20and%20the%20European%20Commission [https://perma.cc/W5EX-CKLK] (last accessed September 29, 2023).

STAKEHOLDER CAPITALISM METRICS

SCMs perhaps look familiar with some best practices in existing measurement frameworks covering a wide range of subjects from corporate anti-corruption practices to greenhouse gas emissions and the health and safety of workers.[9] SCM metrics are divided into four pillars: People, Planet, Prosperity, and Principles of Governance.

People Pillar

The metrics for the People Pillar comprise of (a) *Dignity and Equality*, (b) *Health & Wellbeing*, and (c) *Skills for the Future* categories.

Under the *Dignity and Equality* category, there are four core metrics: (i) *diversity and inclusion*, (ii) *pay equality*, (iii) *wage level*, (iv) *risk for incidents of child, forced or compulsory labor*, and five expanded metrics: (i) *discrimination and harassment*, (ii) *freedom of association and collective bargaining at risk*, (iii) *human rights review, grievance impact and modern slavery*, (iv) *living wage*, and (v) *pay gap*.

Diversity and inclusion, the first of the four core metrics under the *Dignity and Equality* category, requires the signatory company to report the percentage of employees per employee category, per age group, gender, and other indicators of diversity (e.g., ethnicity). The rationale for this metric is that gender, ethnic and cultural diversity, particularly within executive teams, correlates to financial performance. More diverse companies are "better able to innovate, attract top talent, improve their customer orientation, enhance employee satisfaction and secure license to operate."[10] The rationale also states that companies that focus on diversity and inclusion in their workforce through improving the representation of a diverse workforce and utilizing diversity and inclusion to develop their talent, reap tangible and intangible benefits. Cynics can easily assert that this metric and rationale are nothing new; they are adapted from GRI 405-1.[11]

The *pay equality* core metric asks the signatory company to report the ratio of the basic salary and remuneration of women to men and minority to major ethnic groups in each employee category by significant locations of operation. The rationale for this core metric is that diversity and inclusion can only be achieved by promoting equal pay for the same jobs. This will assist in reducing disparity and ensuring opportunities for people regardless of gender, race, class, and religion.

[9] Ibid.

[10] "Explore the Metrics," *World Forum*, 2020, available at: www.weforum.org/stakeholdercapital ism/our-metrics [https://perma.cc/2R6T-RDQV] (last accessed September 29, 2023).

[11] GRI is the Global Reporting Initiative that issues independent standards to help businesses, governments, and other organizations understand and report on ESG. GRI 405-1 is designed specifically to report on diversity of governance bodies and employees. "GRI 405: Diversity and Equal Opportunity 2016," *Global Reporting*, 2016, available at: www.globalreporting.org/standards/media/1020/gri-405-diversity-and-equal-opportunity-2016.pdf [https://perma.cc/4E2R-W55V] (last accessed September 29, 2023).

Without addressing pay equality, companies may face reputation and legal risks. The sources for this core metric come from GRI 202-1, UK Companies (Misc. reporting) regulations 2018, and the Dodd-Frank Act.[12]

The *wage level* core metric measures the signatory company's ratio of entry-level wage by gender compared to local minimum wage and the ratio of CEO's total annual compensation to median total annual compensation of all employees excluding the CEO. This core metric addresses fair compensation and benefits to employees which are important to the eradication of inequality and poverty. Further, the wide gap between the CEO compensation and the median perpetuates inequality and hinders the company's long-term value creation. CEO compensation is an area where investors can make meaningful changes.

The *risk for incidents of child, forced or compulsory labor* core metric requires the signatory company to provide an explanation of the operations and suppliers considered to demonstrate significant risk for violation of fundamental human rights. This type of violation has been identified as a hindrance to development. The link between poverty and child labor is well established and can prolong to subsequent generations. Companies ignoring this risk may face legal and reputational consequences.

In addition to the four core metrics under the *Dignity and Equality* category, there were five expanded metrics SCMs advocate signatory companies to consider and include in their reporting practices. For the *discrimination and harassment*, the signatory company reports the number of incidents, the status of the incidents, actions taken, and the total amount of monetary losses resulting from legal proceedings. Regarding the *freedom of association and collective bargaining at risk* metric, the company reports the percentage of its workforce that is unionized and provides an assessment of whether the workforce union efforts at the company's suppliers are at risk along with measures implemented by the company to reduce the risk. On the *human rights review, grievance impact and modern slavery* metric, the company includes the total number and percentage of its operations that have been subject to human rights reviews or human rights impact assessment. The company also discloses the number and type of grievances reported with associated impacts related to human rights issues in the reporting period along with an explanation. Furthermore, the company reports the number and percentage of operations and suppliers considered to display significant risk for incidents of child, forced, or compulsory labor. For the *pay gap* expanded metric, the company includes "mean pay gap of basic salary and remuneration of full-time relevant employees based on gender" and indicators of diversity at the company. The company reports the ratio of the annual total compensation for the organization's highest-paid individual to the median in each country of significant operations. With respect to the *living wage* expanded metric, the company releases the current wages against the living wage for employees and contractors in all of the company's locations.

---

[12] "Explore the Metrics," *supra*, note 10.

The next category under the People Pillar is *Health & Wellbeing* which includes one core metric of *health and safety* and two expanded metrics of *well-being* and *monetized impacts of work-related incidents on organization*. For the core metric of *health and safety*, the signatory company discloses the number and rate of fatalities as a result of work-related injury, work-related injuries, types of work-related injuries, and the number of hours worked. The company must provide an explanation of the company's non-occupational medical and healthcare services to employees. The rationale for maintaining health and safety standards is that it improves productivity and efficiencies which supports the core metric. Also, employees' mental health and emotional wellbeing are important to the company's innovation drive. Regarding the expanded metric of *monetized impacts of work-related incidents on organization*, the company multiplies the number and type of occupational incidents by the direct costs for employees, and employers per incident (including actions and/or fines from regulators, property damage, healthcare costs, compensation costs to employees). This calculation reveals the impact of work-related incidents on the company and persuades the company to invest in occupational health and safety.

The last category under the People Pillar is *Skills for the Future* which encompasses one core metric of *training provided* and two expanded metrics of several *unfilled skilled positions and monetized impacts of training-increased earning capacity as a result of training intervention*. To comply with the *training provided* core metric, the company reports average hours of training per person during a particular period by gender and employee category. The company also provides the average training and development expenditure per full-time employee. The company's investment in training its employees signifies the company's commitment to its workforce and the transformation of the entity. Under the *expanded metrics*, the company discloses the number of *unfilled "skilled" positions and the percentage of such positions for which the company will hire unskilled candidates and train them*. The company expresses, "the investment in training as a percentage of its payroll and the effectiveness of the training as expressed through increased revenue, productivity gains, employee engagement and/or internal hire rates."[13]

Planet Pillar

The Planet Pillar is comprehensive, encompassing seven categories: *Air Pollution, Climate Change, Freshwater Availability, Nature Loss, Resource Availability, Solid Waste*, and *Water Pollution*. These categories dictate four core metrics pertaining to (i) *greenhouse gas emissions*, (ii) *Task Force on Climate-related Financial Disclosures* (TCFD), (iii) *land use and ecological sensitivity*, and (iv) *water consumption and withdrawal in water-stressed areas*.

---

[13] Ibid.

Regarding the *greenhouse gas emissions,* the company reports in metric tons of carbon dioxide equivalent emissions, along with estimates and reports material upstream and downstream emissions where appropriate. Scientific studies have confirmed that greenhouse gas emissions are the culprit of rising global temperatures. This problem has been the focus of multiple responses to climate change. Consequently, a business that produces significant greenhouse gas emissions will be at risk of transitioning to a lower carbon economy.

Concerning the *TCFD implementation,* the company is required to be fully in compliance with the TCFD recommendations. If the company is not compliant, the company discloses whether it has set, or has committed to set, greenhouse gas emissions targets to limit global warming and to achieve net-zero emissions before 2050. These goals are consistent with the Paris Agreement.[14] Signatory companies are well aware of the TCFD recommendations which establish the framework for the disclosure of information on climate-related risks and opportunities in the company's annual filings.

For the *land use and ecological sensitivity* core metric, the company reports the number and area of sites owned, leased, or managed in or adjacent to protected areas and/or key biodiversity areas.

Under the core metric of *water consumption and withdrawal in water-stressed areas,* the company furnishes reports for operations where material water is withdrawn, water is consumed, and the percentage of each in water-stressed areas. Such water consumption and water withdrawal are indicators of the potential negative societal impacts resulting from competition with other users and business risks of operational disruptions and shutdowns.

In addition to the four core metrics, there are twelve expanded metrics under the Planet Pillar. These require disclosures from signatory companies on the following: *impact of freshwater consumption and withdrawal, air pollution,* the *impact of air pollution, nutrients, impact of water pollution, Paris-aligned GHG emissions targets,* the *impact of Greenhouse gas emissions, single-use plastics,* the *impact of solid waste disposal, land use,* and *ecological sensitivity, resource circularity,* the *impact of land use and conversion.*

Prosperity Pillar

The Prosperity Pillar covers *Community and Social Vitality, Employment and Wealth Generation, Innovation in Better Products and Services,* and *Wealth Creation and Employment* categories. Layers underneath these categories are six core metrics and seven expanded metrics for disclosures.

---

[14] The Paris Agreement is an international treaty on climate change which sets goals for nations to substantially reduce global greenhouse gas emissions. "The Paris Agreement," *United Nations Climate Action,* 2021, available at: www.un.org/en/climatechange/paris-agreement [https://perma.cc/KAU4-MHVA] (last accessed September 29, 2023).

Under the *total tax paid* core metric of the *Community and Social Vitality* category, the company reports the total global tax borne, including corporate income taxes, property taxes, non-creditable value-added taxes and sales taxes, employer-paid payroll taxes and other taxes that are costs to the company by separate categories of taxes. This reporting shows how the company contributes to governmental revenues in support of government operations and public benefits.

The *Employment & Wealth Generation* category contains two core metrics of (i) *absolute number and rate of employment* and (ii) *economic contribution*. On the first core metric, the company must disclose the total number and rate of new employee hires and turnover by gender, age group, and other indicators of diversity and region during the reporting period. These numbers are also related to the *People Pillar*, but they reveal the company's employment capacity within a region. On the second metric of *economic contribution*, the company provides numbers demonstrating direct "economic value generated and distributed" to local economies. The company reports on revenue, operating costs, employee wages, and benefits, payments to providers of capital, payments to government, and community investment. Further, the company discloses the total monetary value of financial assistance the company received from the government during the reporting period. Providing economic contribution numbers demonstrates how the company has created wealth for stakeholders.

For the *Innovation in Better Products and Services* category, the core metric is *total R&D expenses*. The company discloses the total costs related to research and development. Such reporting is important to show the company's efforts to innovate its products and services in response to market and future demands. The numbers illustrate the company's capacity for creating new products and services that may be socially and environmentally beneficial.

Under the *Wealth Creation & Employment* category is the requirement for the company's *financial investment contribution disclosure*. The company indicates the total capital expenditures minus the depreciation, together with an explanation of the company's investment strategy. Also, the company reports on share buyback and dividend payments, along with a narrative describing the company's strategy for returns of capital to shareholders.

The Prosperity Pillar encompasses seven expanded metrics: *infrastructure investments and services supported, significant indirect economic impacts, the social value generated, vitality index, total social investment, additional tax remitted,* and *total and additional tax breakdown by country for significant locations*. Some of these metrics are self-explanatory but others welcome rationale. For instance, the *social value generated* metric shows the percentage of revenue from the company's products and services designed to deliver specific social benefits to address specific sustainability. The *vitality index* measures the effectiveness and productivity of the company's investment in innovation. In the *total social investment*, the company discloses the total resources it used in community investment beyond traditional charitable giving investments. This amount is the company's total "resources used for the 'S' in ESG efforts defined by CECP valuation." CECP stands for Chief Executives for Corporate Purpose.[15]

Governance Pillar

The Governance Pillar covers *Ethical Behavior, Governing Purpose, Quality of Governing Body Oversight, Risk and Opportunity Oversight*, and *Stakeholder Engagement* categories. These categories include six core metrics and six expanded metrics.

Ethical Behavior covers two core metrics: *anti-corruption* and *protected ethics advice and reporting mechanisms*. The *anti-corruption* metric requires the company to disclose the total percentage of governance body members, employees, and business partners who have received training on anti-corruption policies and procedures by the region where the company operates. In addition to training on anti-corruption, the company must report the total number and nature of incidents of corruption in the current year but related to previous years. This reporting seems to cover ongoing corruptions only. Additionally, the company discloses the number and nature of incidents of corruption confirmed in the current year only. Moreover, the company reports on discussions of initiatives and stakeholder engagement to combat corruption. This means the company must take on new initiatives to improve its operating environment and culture in order to yield evidence of anti-corruption for its subsequent reporting. Similarly, under the *protected ethics advice and reporting mechanisms* metric, the company describes its ability to prevent and remedy ethical issues by providing a mechanism for employees in seeking advice and reporting ethical and lawful behavior and organizational integrity.

In addition to the two core metrics under the *Ethical Behavior* category, there are two expanded metrics, *alignment of strategy and policies to lobbying* and *monetary losses from unethical behavior*. The former expanded metric insists that the company's lobbying activities are consistent with its publicly stated purposes and strategy. In the later expanded metric, the company discloses the total amount it incurred as a result of legal proceedings associated with fraud, insider trading, antitrust, anti-competitive behavior, market manipulation, malpractice, or violations of other related industry laws or regulations. This disclosure presumes a formal process though regulators and the judiciary are already in place to enforce against unethical illegal conduct.

For the *Governing Purpose* category, the company articulates its stated purpose, "as the expression of the means by which a business proposes solutions to economic, environmental, and social issues." As typically understood in the business world,

---

[15] "What Does CECP Stand For?" *CECP*, https://cecp.co/about/ [https://perma.cc/6TWW-W7MF] (last accessed September 29, 2023).

corporate purpose creates value for all stakeholders, including shareholders. Paralleling the stated purpose, the company may consider embedding the purpose within its strategies, policies, and goals. The company then reports how it has imbedded the stated purpose in management under the expanded metric of *purpose-led management*.

Quality of Governing Body Oversight category covers one core metric *governance body composition* requiring the signatory company to state the composition of the board and committees "by competencies relating to economic, environmental, and social topics; executive or non-executive; independence; tenure on the governance body; the number of each individual's other significant positions and commitments, and the nature of the commitments; gender; membership of under-represented social groups; stakeholder representation."[16] This is a more extensive requirement going beyond the usual single factor like the gender makeup of a board. With a much wider capability and perspective, the board can make robust decisions that bring value to the company.

In connection with the one core metric on board composition, there are two expanded metrics of *remuneration* and *progress against strategic milestones*. For the first expanded metric, the report ties performance criteria in remuneration policies to the company's economic, environmental, and social objectives. That means the company explains how the performance criteria are related to board members' and senior executives' objectives for economic, environmental, and social topics and are consistent with the company's stated purpose, strategy, and long-term value. In addition, with specificity, the company discloses fixed pay and variable pay, sign-on bonuses, terminational payments, claw backs, and retirement benefits to board members, senior executives, and all other employees.

For the second expanded metric, *progress against strategic milestones*, the company reports the "material strategic economic, environmental, and social milestones expected to be achieved in the following year, such milestones achieved from the previous year, and how those milestones are expected to or have contributed to long-term value."[17] This means the company must focus on the quality of its governing body by disclosing positive and negative "indicators of the board oversight and management's ability to set, guide and execute the company's strategy."[18]

Risk and Opportunity Oversight category contains *integrating risk and opportunity into business process* as the core metric requiring the company to disclose how its risk and opportunity integrate material economic, environmental, and social issues, including climate change and data stewardship. This reporting places the responsibility on the company's board to oversee the management of the risk and opportunity. The expanded metric, *economic, environmental, and social topics in capital*

[16] "Explore the Metrics," *supra*, note 10.
[17] Ibid.
[18] Ibid.

allocation framework, requires a report on how the company's board considers economic, environmental, and social issues when overseeing major capital allocation decisions, inclusive of expenditures, acquisitions, and divestitures, at the company.

In the *Stakeholder Engagement* category, the company discloses *material issues impacting stakeholders* by identifying and listing the topics that are material to key stakeholders and the company, explaining how the topics were identified and how the stakeholders were engaged. This type of disclosure solidifies the relationship between the company and stakeholders.

HOW BIG BANKS RESPONDED TO STAKEHOLDER CAPITALISM METRICS (SCM)

The extensive requirements under the People Pillar, Planet Pillar, Prosperity Pillar, and Principles of Governance Pillar of the Stakeholder Capitalism Metrics approach mean signatory companies must take the reporting of each of the metrics seriously. Implementing policies and programs to meet the requirements for reporting the metrics demands commitments and significant resources. Gathering relevant information and reporting the metrics are complicated tasks and can be costly.

Bank of America is one of the key signatory companies but a look at its website unearths a different picture. Bank of America (BOA) cleverly washed over the People Pillar along with *diversity and inclusion, pay equality, wage level, discrimination and harassment, union,* among other metrics. Instead, BOA replaced all the metrics and rationales under the People Pillar with an explanation that this pillar covers "the extent to which a company's practices support an end to problems such as local poverty and hunger and help ensure that all human beings can fulfill their potential."[19] This replacement suggests that BOA does not care even to pay lip service to the metrics, including *diversity and inclusion*. It suggests that BOA does not care about the pay inequity at the Bank and is not interested in its employees' freedom of association and collective bargaining. Otherwise, BOA should have displayed the People Pillar metrics in full and provided its detailed report on the metrics as required under this pillar.

Again, the Bank's website for the Planet Pillar simply states that under this pillar is "the company's commitment to protecting the planet from degradation," including "sustainable use of natural resources and efforts to help counteract climate change."[20] This statement waters down the importance of the Planet Pillar. It drastically ignores the rigorous requirements of reporting greenhouse gas emissions, and full implementation of TCFD recommendations to achieve net-zero

---

[19] "A New Standard for Measuring Global Sustainability," *supra*, note 8.
[20] Ibid.

emissions, among other metrics and concrete commitments dictated by the Planet Pillar to address climate change.

Likewise, under the Prosperity Pillar, BOA states a company should consider whether its practices support people's ability to live prosperous and fulfilling lives and whether its innovations create both economic and social value for its customers. Here, for instance, BOA ignores the requirements of reporting new hires and turnovers by age group, gender, and other diversity indicators. BOA conveniently fails to touch on the reporting requirement on the economic contribution which details revenue, operating costs, employee wages, and benefits, payments to providers of capital, payments to government, and community investment during each reporting period.

For the Governance Pillar, BOA simply claims that "as stakeholder capitalism evolves, so, too, do the responsibilities of companies' governing bodies" and that leaders must "ensure the company adheres to its stated purposes, behaves ethically and uses its capital responsibly." Most significantly, BOA disregards the governance body composition metric. The metric specifically requires signatory companies to provide the composition of the board and its committees by "competencies relating to economic, environmental, and social topics; executive or non-executive; independence; tenure on the governance body; the number of each individual's other significant positions and commitments, and the nature of the commitments; gender; membership of under-represented social groups; stakeholder representation." By outright ignoring or watering down these metrics, BOA sets a course unbecoming of a leader who has touted the Stakeholder Capitalism Metrics approach for ESG.

To be fair, going beyond BOA's website and reading BOA's ESG report, the Bank's ESG SCM Report contains some meaningful metrics. Bank of America, one of the largest banks in the United States, unfortunately, does not fare better in its reporting of the SCM metrics.

For instance, in its 2021 ESG Performance Data Summary and Global Reporting Initiative Index, BOA made it rather difficult to locate the disclosures. Under the *diversity and inclusion* core metric of the *Dignity and Equality* category under the People Pillar, BOA is required to report a "percentage of employees per employee category, by age group, gender, and other indicators of diversity (e.g., ethnicity)." Searching through BOA's Annual Report for relevant disclosures, however, did not lead to satisfaction. The Annual Report failed to include any numbers "per employee category, by age group, gender, *and* other indicators of diversity" (emphasis added). The Annual Report only provided the percentage of employees per some employee category by gender and race but not by age group. This reporting does not meet the core metric requirement.

Also, under the *absolute number and rate of employment* core metric of the *Employment & Wealth Generation* category under the Prosperity Pillar, the Bank was required to disclose the "total number and rate of new employee hires" and "employee turnover" during the reporting period by age group, gender, or other indicators of diversity and region. BOA mentioned the phrase "new employees hires and turnover" in the *ESG Summary* and cited its *2021 Annual Report on Human Capital Management Update* for new employee hires. Again, the *Annual Report* did not disclose the required metric. The *Annual Report* disclosed by gender the turnover in 2019, 2020, and 2021, but the numbers were not broken down by age group, racial group, or region. There was no report on new hires in compliance with the core metric in the Annual Report's Human Capital Management Update.[21]

On the *pay equality* core metric under the People Pillar, the Bank must report the "ratio of the basic salary and remuneration for each employee category by significant locations of operation for priority areas of equality: women to men, minor to major ethnic groups, and other relevant equality areas" but the Bank responded by referring to its "Equal Pay for Equal Work Section in our 2022 Proxy Statement available on the Bank of America Investor Relations website at www.bankofamerica.com/investor." The 2022 Proxy Statement of 110 pages included a table of contents but the "Equal Pay for Equal Work Section" did not appear in the table. The small section was embedded on page 46 of the Proxy Statement with a conclusory phrase that "compensation received by women was on average more than 99 percent of that received by men, and that compensation received by people of color in the United States was on average more than 99 percent of that received by non-people of color employees." This reporting failed to meet the core metric disclosure asking the signatory company to provide the "ratio of the basic salary and remuneration for each employee category." The conclusory phrase is almost identical to the phrase used by Fifth Third Bank, discussed later in this chapter, on their failure to fully report on the *pay equality* core metric. Like Fifth Third, BOA bragged:

> We conduct rigorous analysis with outside experts to examine individual employee pay before year-end compensation decisions are finalized, adjusting compensation where appropriate. The results of our equal pay for equal work review are disclosed in the Proxy Statement. Our analysis focuses on total compensation and includes geographies where we have significant operations for women and covers the US for people of color.[22]

> We are committed to equal pay for equal work. We maintain robust policies and practices that reinforce equal pay for equal work, including reviews with oversight from our Board and senior leaders.[23]

[21] "Driving Responsible Growth: Now and Going Forward: Annual Report 2021," *Bank of America*, 2022, available at: https://d1io3yogooux5.cloudfront.net/_27ee7ffbb9f26999efcfd04bc46f8514/bankofamerica/db/867/9640/annual_report/BAC_AR21_Full_Report_030122+%281%29.pdf [https://perma.cc/VR9H-25AG] (last accessed September 29, 2023)..

[22] Ibid.

[23] "2022 Proxy Statement," *Bank of America*, March 7, 2022, available at: https://investor.bankofamerica.com/2022-proxy-statement [https://perma.cc/F7YY-4ZDG] (last accessed September 29, 2023).

Without compliance with the reporting requirement under the pay equality core metric, BOA's assertions ring hollow.

BOA, however, reported under the *wage level* core metric, the ratio of CEO's total annual compensation to median total annual compensation of all employees excluding the CEO. BOA's CEO took home $23,739,465 while the median was $102,497, yielding a gap of 232:1 between the CEO compensation and the median compensation.[24] Whether such a gap perpetuates inequality and hinders the company's long-term value creation is up to investors to determine and make any possible meaningful change.

One would expect BOA, the leader in the ESG SCM approach, to truly take the leadership role in fully complying with all the core metrics and reporting them in exact form and substance as required under the Stakeholder Capitalism Metric approach. Further, one may even expect that, as a leader, BOA may go beyond the core metrics and include disclosures on all the expanded metrics. BOA, however, fell short in its reporting.

Another disappointment with BOA is that, despite its leadership role in the ESG SCM approach movement, the bank was not forthcoming in its compliance and took a laissez-faire response with the Stakeholder Capitalism Metric approach. By making the ESG summary index difficult to follow, by making references to its Proxy Statement, by citing other sources, instead of directly providing the specific numbers as required by each of the core metrics, BOA presented itself as a reluctant follower at best, and nonbeliever at worst.

Because BOA did not perform well in its SCM reporting, what would be the expectation of other banks? How did Wells Fargo, the bank that people hate the most, fare in its ESG factors? How did Fifth Third, ComericA, First Republic, among other banks, conduct themselves in SCM reporting? How did Silicon Valley Bank, the bank of the innovation economy, fare?

Wells Fargo, ranked third among the US largest banks by assets, published its ESG report for 2021 which totaled ninety-eight pages. The glossy report did not disclose the numbers, ratios, or percentages required under the core metrics. Wells Fargo ignored the Stakeholder Capitalism Metrics approach. Wells Fargo's CEO Charlie Scharf, nevertheless, crowed that the report "provides a comprehensive picture of the environment, social, and governance (ESG) work underway at Wells Fargo."[25] Wells Fargo's *ESG Report* referenced Wells Fargo's ESG goals and performance data (ESG Data) which is itself a thirty-four-page document, together the two reports and document constituting Wells Fargo's "foundational

---

[24] Ibid.

[25] "Environmental, Social, and Governance (ESG) Report," *Wells Fargo*, September 2022, available at: www08.wellsfargomedia.com/assets/pdf/about/corporate-responsibility/environmental-social-governance-report.pdf [https://perma.cc/G2ZM-5ZW4] (last accessed September 29, 2023).

ESG disclosures" for 2021. Unfortunately, the report fell significantly short of the "comprehensive picture."

For instance, on *composition and diversity* of the board, Wells Fargo stated that its Board of Directors' current composition is "a result of a thoughtful process informed by the Board's own evaluation of its composition and effectiveness, and feedback received from our engagement with shareholders and other stakeholders." Nothing in the report revealed the composition of the board and its committees by competencies relating to ESG topics, such as executive or non-executive, independence, tenure on the governance body, number of each individual's other significant positions and commitments, or the nature of the commitments, gender, membership of under-represented social groups, or stakeholder representation. Finding some supporting data for the Wells Fargo board's composition requires a look at the ESG Data document. On page eight of that document is a chart entitled "board diversity" providing the gender, race, and average tenure of independent director-nominees, executive and independent directors, directors with ESG qualifications, and directors with financial services risk expertise. At Wells Fargo, only one director out of twelve possesses ESG qualifications. Three of the twelve directors are women and diverse. Wells Fargo did not disclose the actual numbers in its ESG Data relating to the composition of its board committees.

Similarly, on *executive compensation*, Wells Fargo asserted in the ESG Report that "strong governance and oversight of executive compensation programs is essential to our long-term success." The ESG Data, however, showed that the CEO's salary in 2019 was $36,288,490 while the median was $69,931 yielding a pay ratio of 550:1. The accompanying footnote explained that the CEO received a one-time award of $28,788,490 in connection with his hire. In 2020, the same CEO received $20,392,046 and the median compensation of Wells Fargo employees was $74,416, generating a pay ratio of 274:1. Though the Wells Fargo Board approved the CEO compensation, these pay ratios are still embarrassingly high because the "wide gap between the CEO compensation and the median reinforces inequality and could impede long-term value creation."[26]

For *pay equality*, Wells Fargo ESG Data issued a blanket statement that its "female employees earn more than ninety-nine cents for every $1 earned by their male peers." There was no disclosure as to the ratio of the basic salary and remuneration for *each employee category* by significant locations of operation for women to men and other relevant equality areas. The conclusory statement from Wells Fargo is similar to the conclusory statement asserted by BOA and Fifth Third. The failure to provide the metrics by these banks may suggest that the actual numbers for each employee category are not favorable to the banks or is a simple oversight.

---

[26] "Explore the Metrics," *supra*, note 10 (providing the *wage level* core metric, *Dignity and Equality* category, under the *People Pillar*).

Moreover, Wells Fargo devoted pages 48–67 of the ESG Report to "Investing in our Employees" without providing the actual metrics for the core and expanded metrics under the *People* and *Prosperity Pillars* of the *Stakeholder Capitalism Metric* approach. The ESG Data, pages 11–22, disclosed very limited data, primarily providing the total gender numbers and ratios of all Wells Fargo employees, numbers of employees self-identified as having disabilities, as LGBTQ, and as veterans, and numbers of employees by gender and racial groups in a list of job categories.

Overall, the "comprehensive picture" of the Wells Fargo ESG Report seems to mean lots of pictures, not metrics. Perhaps this report is another example contributing to Wells Fargo's reputational crisis.

Another bank, Fifth Third, published its *ESG SCM Index* of ten pages and *ESG Report* of 171 pages.[27] The bank's *ESG SCM Index* states that the report is "intended to meet the core metrics and disclosure" as required for a signatory company. That statement is not unsupported by what the bank disclosed. For example, on the "*Pay equality*" core metric under the People Pillar, the Bank must report the "ratio of the basic salary and remuneration for each employee category by significant locations of operation for priority areas of equality: women to men, minor to major ethnic groups, and other relevant equality areas" but the bank did not. The bank responded with a blanket statement that "women are paid more than ninety-nine percent of what men are paid, and minorities are paid more than ninety-nine percent of what non-minorities are paid." The bank did not indicate which employee category and at which locations women are paid more than 99 percent of what men are paid. The bank did not identify which minority or ethnic groups are paid 99 percent of what non-minorities are paid. The bank's response also listed page seventy-eight of the Bank's 2020 *ESG Report* for "additional details." However, that referenced page repeated the same phrase "women are paid more than ninety-nine percent of what men are paid, and minorities are paid more than ninety-nine percent of what non-minorities are paid" without any additional details as claimed. Without additional details or evidence to support the blanket statement, the bank's claim of "fully reporting" the "pay equality" metric is highly suspect.

Likewise, under the *diversity and inclusion* core metric of the *Dignity and Equality* category under the People Pillar, the bank is required to report "percentage of employees per employee category, by age group, gender, and other indicators of diversity (e.g., ethnicity)", but Fifth Third failed miserably in its reporting efforts. The bank's response was "Fifth Third has published demographic diversity data as part of our commitment to inclusion and diversity since our 2016 *Corporate Social*

27 "FifthThird Bancorp 2020 ESG SCM Index," *Fifth Third Bancorp*, June 2021, available at: https://s23.q4cdn.com/252949160/files/doc_downloads/ESG/2021/Final/2020_ESG_SCM_Index.pdf [https://perma.cc/ANC4-4WMW] (last accessed September 29, 2023) and "FifthThird Bancorp 2020 ESG Report," *Fifth Third Bancorp*, June 2021, available at: https://s23.q4cdn.com/252949160/files/doc_downloads/ESG/2021/Final/2020-ESG-Report.pdf [https://perma.cc/L92H-P86P] (last accessed September 29, 2023).

Responsibility Report. In 2020, we expanded our EEO-1 ethnicity categories to improve transparency." The Bank provided no numbers as dictated by the core metric. The bank cited page sixty of its *ESG 2020 Report* for support. Page sixty presented a table by gender and race of executives/senior managers, first/mid-level managers, professionals, and all others. This reporting does not seem to meet the reporting requirements under the core metric that demands information "per employee category, by age group, gender and other indicators of diversity." The bank seemed to not take the core metric seriously.

Another example, under *the absolute number and rate of employment* core metric in the *Employment & Wealth Generation* category under the Prosperity Pillar, Fifth Third was required to disclose the "total number and rate of new employee hires" and "employee turnover" during the reporting period by age group, gender, or other indicators of diversity and region. The bank responded "3,148 total number of new employees in 2020, with 38.8 percent internal hires" and "employee turnover was 13.9 percent in 2020." There was no reporting on age group, gender, and other indicators of diversity among the new hires and employee turnover. The bank referenced pages 70–83 of the ESG Report for further details. Peculiarly, those pages do not contain the information sought by the core metric. Fifth Third either failed to respond to what was being asked or just simply ignored the core metric because there are no consequences for failure to report.

On the *governance body composition* core metric under the *Quality Governing Body* category in the Governance Pillar, Fifth Third must disclose the composition of the board and its committees "by competencies relating to economic, environmental and social topics; executive or non-executive; independence; tenure on the governance body; the number of each individual's other significant positions and commitments, and the nature of the commitments; gender; membership of underrepresented social groups; stakeholder representation," but the bank did not comply in its reporting. Fifth Third merely cited two pages in its 2021 *Proxy Statement* for director nominee overview, director profiles, director skills matrix, and committee composition.

In summary, Fifth Third's reporting efforts did not meet what the Stakeholder Capitalism Metric approach aims to achieve. Moreover, the bank's lengthy *ESG Report* is more or less a glossy advertisement brochure lacking the specific metrics the *People, Planet, Prosperity,* and *Governance Pillars* require in the disclosures. The *ESG Report* is full of pictures and self-congratulatory statements. That is not reporting of core metrics. Fifth Third's shortcomings are troubling because if the Bank is another representative of big banks in the United States, its reporting practices reveal that banks are not taking the SCM approach seriously. One has to wonder why the bank chose to become a signatory member of the ESG SCM movement.

ComericA Bank, operating in the innovation economy, is not so keen on the Stakeholder Capitalism Metric approach. ComericA instead stated in its 2021

Corporate Responsibility Report that it is "proud to present" the Bank's "14th annual corporate responsibility report, which includes a summary of ComericA's progress on key environmental, social governance ESG issues, achievements, and challenges. ComericA provides a long history of proactively addressing ESG matters, and we are looking toward the future with a renewed sense of urgency."[28] By not following the SCM approach, ComericA bank can avoid providing disclosures on core and expanded metrics under the People, Planet, Prosperity, and Governance Pillars with ease.

For example, ComericA stated that at year-end 2021, 65 percent of its employees and 52 percent of its managers are women, and 41 percent of its employees are racial/ethnic minorities. The numbers may be admirable, but they are not reported by employee category for a better understanding of the bank's workforce diversity and inclusion. On page 75, ComericA instead provided the number of women employees who are "officials and managers," "professionals," and "others."

On *governance*, ComericA was silent on the composition of the board and its committee. The *Report* merely stated that there were ten independent directors on the board. The tenure of the directors was absent. Metrics on how many directors possess ESG qualification were not identified. Under *diversity, equity and inclusion*, ComericA reported that 27 percent of its directors are female and/or diverse.

On *pay gap*, ComericA stated "We believe that businesses play a critical role in reducing the national pay gap affecting women and minorities. We are committed to identifying and promoting best practices to reduce bias in hiring, promotion, and compensation decisions." The bank, however, disclosed no metrics relating to the pay gap and CEO pay ratio.

On *pay equity*, ComericA informed that

> Our pay equity initiatives, as part of our broader DEI initiatives, make our company stronger and delivers value to our shareholders. We examine the main components of compensation, like salaries and bonuses by grade level and position to ensure similar positions receive similar pay to the extent other factors can be equalized (e.g., time in position, performance, education). We also consider equitable benefits and look at policies and practices that potentially drive inequities. We have made a corporate-wide decision to prohibit the solicitation of salary history from applicants in all of our markets.

Those are nice self-praising descriptions, but they lack substance; there are no metrics on the ratio of the basic salary and remuneration for each employee category

---

[28] "2021 Corporate Responsibility Report: A Comprehensive Review of Comerica's Environmental, Social and Governance Practices and Progress," ComericA Bank, February 2022, available at: www.comerica.com/content/dam/comerica/en/documents/resources/about/sustainability/comerica-2021-cr-report-final.pdf [https://perma.cc/YVD4-YNC5] (last accessed September 29, 2023).

by significant locations of operation for priority areas of equality between women to men; minor to major ethnic groups; and other relevant equality areas.

Overall, ComericA bank's ESG reporting practices are disappointing. Like many banks, ComericA can talk the big games, including wonderful statements like this: "We strengthened our commitment to driving change and being a part of the solution to eliminate racial inequalities through participation in the CEO Action Race & Equity Fellows Program" and

> In 2021, ComericA established an Office of Corporate Responsibility to serve as a focal point for all of the collaborative ESG efforts across the bank. The Office and its colleagues serve as a corporate catalyst to enhance synergies, develop fresh ideas, standardize reporting, monitor the ESG landscape for best practices, and take note of the resulting benefits to colleagues, customers, communities, and the planet.

Unfortunately, as ComericA does not adopt the SCM approach to report the metrics; all of these statements are just talk.

First Republic Bank, a full-service bank and wealth-management company founded in 1985 in San Francisco, was the twenty-first largest US bank by assets in 2022 before its collapse after SVB's demise in March 2023. First Republic had eighty offices throughout seven states. First Republic proudly featured a commanding eagle as its logo. The eagle faced directly to the right knowing its path and destination. The eagle carried a message: "It is a privilege to serve you."

Indeed, First Republic detailed under its Sustainable and Responsible Investing practice that the relevant team sought to provide "best-in-class investment options and other solutions that are mindful of factors including resource and waste management, carbon emissions policy, opportunities in clean technology, workplace health and safety, employee benefits, factory conditions, product quality and safety, and board diversification."[29] An assumption, here, is the Bank itself was ahead of its own class in both ESG understanding and reporting. The assumption, unfortunately, was disappointingly erroneous upon close inspection.

One thing stood out for First Republic: it had reached carbon neutrality for the first time, as indicated in its 2021 report. The bank claimed that, since its founding, "diversity has been a key competitive advantage" and that women made up 40 percent of the founding executive team. The board currently enjoys 40 percent women and 30 percent people of color as directors. Its total workforce saw 47 percent women and 51 percent people of color. First Republic, however, failed to provide the diversity and inclusion metrics by employee category.

Regarding, *wage levels*, *pay equality*, and *CEO pay ratio*, First Republic did not disclose in the 2021 *Corporate Responsibility Report*. Instead, the *Report* cited the

---

[29] "Sustainable and Responsible Investing," *First Republic*, available at: www.firstrepublic.com/pri vate-wealth-management/features/sustainable-and-responsible-investing [https://perma.cc/V6SU-R8V5] (last accessed September 29, 2023).

Bank's *Proxy Statement* for the compensation. The same *Report* did not provide the specific metrics related to its workforce diversity and inclusion.

Overall, concerning disclosures related to core and expanded metrics under the People, Planet, Prosperity and Governance Pillar, First Republic's disclosures in the 2021 *Corporate Responsibility Report* did not meet the reporting practices under the Stakeholder Capitalism Metric approach. Instead, First Republic, along with all the banks, carefreely used the phrase environmental, social, and governance (ESG) without seriously embracing the rigorous reporting practices.

Silicon Valley Bank released its 2022 *ESG Report* in August 2022 with a total of sixty-six pages. The Report contained mostly narratives under flattering section headings like "Living Our Values: Our ESG Strategy and Goals," "Engaging and Empowering Employees," "Building a Culture of Diversity, Equity, and Inclusion at SVB," "Championing Inclusion in the Innovation Economy," "Supporting Communities Where We Live and Work," "Advancing the Transition to a Sustainable, Low-Carbon World," and "Practicing Responsible Corporate Governance." These self-congratulatory sections soaked in a positive light seem to be the common public relations practices employed by Silicon Valley Bank and most, if not all, banks. The *Report* attached an appendix section where the Bank's disclosures under the Stakeholder Capitalism Metric reside in the very last pages numbered 56–65.

Silicon Valley Bank (SVB) stated that it is "committed to providing our stakehold-ers with meaningful data on our environmental, social and governance (ESG) performance, underscoring our long-standing pledge of transparency and account-ability."[30] The appendix constituted the Bank's second disclosure under the Stakeholder Capitalism Metric approach.

Under the *governance body composition* core metric, SVB responded by referen-cing the "Director Nominees, Selection, Composition and Other Information" and "Biographies of Director Nominees" sections of the Bank's 2022 *Proxy Statement* and mentioned that additional information is on the Bank's "Diversity, equity & inclu-sion webpage." Flipping back to page forty-two of the *Report* on "Board Diversity," the information revealed that there are five women on the board and the current chair is a woman. Regarding racial diversity, there is one director. There is one LGBTQ+ director. On tenure, there are three directors with more than eleven years of service, four directors with six to ten years, and four with five years or less serving on the board. In other words, the appendix falls short on SCM reporting on the *governance body composition* core metric which asks a signatory company to disclose the "composition of the board and its committee by competencies." The appendix

[30] "Environmental, Social, and Governance Report 2022: A Review of Our Corporate Responsibility Practices," *SVB Financial Group*, 2022, available at: www.svb.com/globalassets/library/uploaded files/svb-environmental-social-governance-report-2022.pdf [https://perma.cc/8HRY-PR59] (last accessed September 29, 2023).

did not provide the number of board directors with competencies relating to economic, environmental, and social topics. The Bank's response to this number was a general statement that "With respect to the membership of SVB's Board of Directors, the primary areas of experience, qualifications and attributes we typically seek include, but are not limited to, the following areas related to ESG." Such a general statement does not amount to metric disclosure. Likewise, the metrics relating to the "number of each individual's other significant positions and commitments and the nature of the commitments" and "stakeholder representation" under the governance body composition core metric are missing. Moreover, by referencing the proxy statement and the webpage instead of directly providing the metrics, the Bank conveyed a lack of forthcoming in reporting practices. Unfortunately, SVB's practice for this core metric was similar to the other banks discussed.

On *material issues impacting stakeholders* core metric, SVB responded by referencing "Our ESG Strategy." Following the reference, on page 12 of the *Report*, there is a list of goals and targets, including the goal to increase women in senior leadership roles globally to 43 percent by 2025, increase Black and Hispanic representations in US senior leadership roles to 5 percent and 6 percent, respectively, by 2025, and increase total cumulative spending with diverse suppliers to 8 percent by 2026. The Bank included the goal to achieve 100 percent carbon-neutral operations by 2025 and 100 percent renewable electricity use by 2025, among others. The *material issues impacting stakeholders'* core metric specifically states that the signatory company is to provide "a list of the topics that are material to key stakeholders and the company, how the topics were identified and how the stakeholders were engaged." The Bank's "Our ESG Strategy" does not squarely comply with the disclosure sought under this core metric.

Under the *diversity and inclusion* core metric, which asks for disclosure of the "percentage of employees per employee category, by age group, gender and other indicators of diversity (e.g., ethnicity)," the Bank responded with: "An inclusive workplace expands opportunities for everyone. SVB benefits from a diverse workforce and aims to continue to increase diverse representation at all levels of the company. To see a full breakdown of our workforce demographics, please visit our Diversity, Equity & Inclusion webpage."

Visiting SVB's webpage in 2022 on "Diversity, equity and inclusion," there were the Bank's workforce diversity metrics showing gender and racial breakdown of the total workforce, senior leadership, and board. Silicon Valley Bank simply failed to *provide a percentage of employees per employee category by age group, gender, and ethnicity.*

On *pay equality* core metric, which requests the "ratio of the basic salary and remuneration for each employee category by significant locations of operation for priority areas of equality: women to men, minor to major ethnic groups, and other relevant equality areas," Silicon Valley Bank stated that "since 2018, SVB has engaged an external expert to complete an annual fair-pay analysis to ensure that all employees are paid fairly and there are no discrepancies across gender and race." Where is the ratio by "significant locations of operation"? Silicon Valley Bank did not list any ratio for any of the key offices or locations in the United States. Neither did the Bank list anything for the United States as a whole, nor did it cite any reference or source for its United States operations.

Instead, the Bank touted that it publicly reported the "SVB UK Gender Pay Gap Report on our UK webpage." The Bank could not escape this gender pay gap reporting because the United Kingdom legislation "requires employers with more than 250 staff to publish certain information about the pay gap between men and women." In the UK report, the Bank provided the mean and median averages of the gender pay gap for hourly pay, the mean and median averages of the gender pay gap for bonus pay, the proportion of men and women receiving bonuses, and the proportion of men and women in each quartile of Silicon Valley Bank UK's pay structure. The mean gender pay gap was 9.9 percent, and the median gender pay gap was 23.1 percent. The bonus pay gap was 26.8 percent, and the percentage of men and women receiving a bonus payment was 93.3 percent and 87.3 percent, respectively. These numbers are both unflattering and disappointing for Silicon Valley Bank, the leader, the partner, and the bank of the innovation economy.

Drawing on the UK pay gap report and the failure to provide a pay gap report by significant locations of operation in the United States, SVB's commitment to gender equality was still a long journey to trek. Due to the UK legislation, the public learned about Silicon Valley Bank's pay gap. Without legislation, Silicon Valley Bank would not be that forthcoming. The United States lacks counterpart legislation, and most likely will not have such legislation any time soon. Consequently, the SCM approach adopted by signatory companies provides the only meaningful way for the public to know. Silicon Valley Bank and other banks, however, blatantly either ignored or evaded SCM's pay gap reporting. Their action or inaction may lead to relegating the SCM approach to that of a meaningless global effort on one of the important core metrics.

On the *wage level* core metric, Silicon Valley Bank reported that the ratio of the annual total compensation of our CEO to the median of the annual total compensation of all employees was seventy-nine to one. This ratio is better than the CEO pay ratio at the largest banks.

Regarding *the absolute number and rate of employment* core metric under the *Employment & Wealth Generation* category of the Prosperity Pillar, which requires the "total number and rate of" new employee hires during the reporting period "by age group, gender, and other indicators of diversity and region," Silicon Valley Bank responded that the Bank's "full-time equivalent employees grew by just over forty-seven percent to 6,567 full-time equivalent employees" in 2021. That response, however, failed to comply with the core metric asking for disclosure. Moreover, Silicon Valley Bank again directed readers to "learn more about our workforce demographics, please visit our Diversity, equity & inclusion webpage." Just like the percentage of employees' breakdown, unfortunately, there existed no disclosures specific to the core metric regarding new hires by age group, gender, race, and region. In addition, the same core metric asks for disclosure of the total number and rate of employee turnover during the reporting period by age group, gender, race, and region. SVB replied that the Bank is working on evaluating how to disclose its numbers. Two years had already passed for Silicon Valley Bank to still be working on how to report its employee turnover.

On "financial assistance received from the government: total monetary value of financial assistance received by the organization from any government during the reporting period" under the *Economic Contribution* core metric, the Bank responded by directing the attention to "pages 161 and 162" of its "Form 10-K for more information on our effective tax rate and deferred tax assets and liabilities." The Bank could have easily provided the metrics without forcing the public to find the Bank's Form 10-K and search for the information.

Overall, Silicon Valley Bank did not take the lead in reporting ESG under the Stakeholder Capitalism Metric approach. Like the other largest banks, BOA, Wells Fargo, and Fifth Third, Silicon Valley Bank fell short in the reporting practices in many of the core metrics.

Whether all the largest banks would rectify their conduct by disclosing the metrics in accordance with specificities requested under the SCM approach next year and beyond rests on the leadership commitment. Instead of releasing glossy and feel-good reports, leaders at the banks should provide the metrics regardless of how dismal the revelation of numbers reflects on the current status of the bank in the core metrics. Without the real numbers, the banks continue their own business as usual and disregard their commitments to ESG. Without disclosing the metrics, the banks are not willing to confront their own shortcomings and identify how they will overcome the challenge. Worst of all, if the largest banks continue to ignore reporting the core metrics, thousands of banks can rely on these banks' inaction to justify their own.

ESG AND VENTURE CAPITAL

As more than 5,000 companies committed as signatories to the Stakeholders Capitalism Metrics (SCM) approach representing $6 trillion in assets management, the venture capital industry has been mostly silent. There are more than 2,900 VC firms globally. Only a few publicly vocalized their commitments to sustainability. Diversity and inclusion attract more attention among some VCs.[31] Overall, ESG integration has not gained much traction in the VC industry.

---

[31] Johannes Lenhard and Susan Winterberg, "How Venture Capital Can Join the ESG Revolution," *Stanford Social Innovation Review*, August 26, 2021, available at: https://ssir.org/articles/entry/how_venture_capital_can_join_the_esg_revolution [https://perma.cc/VAU3-J3S2] (last accessed September 29, 2023).

The VC market is divided into 43 percent in North America, 42 percent in Asia, 10 percent in Europe, and 5 percent in the rest of the world. In the investment ecosystem, venture capital plays a pivotal role in creating the next generation of business leaders and key companies worldwide through funding entrepreneurial innovators to identify technological solutions solving pressing needs. In 2020, the total venture capital investments reached $300 billion in 22,000 companies, mostly in the technology sector.[32]

The VC industry, through its transformation in the last decades, is about the competition to create and grow companies for rapid scaling. Leveraging network effects, regardless of the social cost of privacy violation, misinformation, polarization, and mental health problems, VCs push on in their relentless drive to birth unicorns. Along the way, venture capitalists, investors, founders, and entrepreneurs celebrate and condone the mentality of *fake it until you break it, move fast and break things, disruptive,* and *bro culture.* Competition among VC firms for the next unicorn hinders these firms' desire to integrate ESG into their business. In *Evaluating Venture Capital Performance,* Bill Janeway analyzed data and explained the unicorn bubble problem in the VC industry, noting only 10 percent of VC firms outperform the market.[33] Consequently, the investors or Limited Partners (LPs), from university endowments, foundations, and family offices to pension funds are afraid to miss their opportunities for investments in the funds at the marquee VC firms; they avoid demanding the VC firms for ESG integration.

Recently, there are some small movements in the VC ecosystem for ESG incorporation. There are several initiatives to develop a systematic approach to incorporate ESG factors in investment processes. For instance, General Partners from GMG Ventures and Houghton Street Ventures founded VentureESG with the goal of working toward defining relevant ESG issues to venture capital. Similarly, ESG VC developed a forty-eight-question standardized ESG portfolio company questionnaire. ROSE created a framework for individual portfolio companies to adopt for measuring their impact on sustainability outcomes. UN-Principles for Responsible Investment (PRI) provided guidance in *Integrating ESG in Private Equity: A Guide for General Partners.*[34] For diversity, equity, and inclusion, both Diversity VC and Level 20 extend support to venture capital professionals and recruitment guidance to venture capital firms. The National Venture Capital Association also lends its support to Venture Forward, a nonprofit organization with a focus on promoting an inclusive VC industry. These efforts constitute,

---

[32] Peter Dunbar, "Starting Up: Responsible Investment in Venture Capital," *Principles for Responsible Investment,* 2022, available at: www.unpri.org/download?ac=15607 [https://perma .cc/F8HV-ZUDM] (last accessed September 29, 2023).

[33] Bill Janeway, "Evaluating Venture Capital Performance, #3, Venture Capital in the 21st Century," *YouTube,* February 10, 2021, available at: www.youtube.com/watch?v= sTXuopR8M-8&ab_channel=NewEconomicThinking (last accessed September 29, 2023).

[34] Dunbar, *supra,* note 32.

unfortunately, a very small and insignificant step in meaningfully considering, accepting, and integrating ESG factors in VC investment processes.

A survey of 104 venture capital GP respondents who are mainly signatories to the Stakeholder Capitalism Metric approach or members of VentureESG's working groups revealed several challenges to ESG integration in the VC industry.[35]

First, among the VC professionals, there is a perception that ESG issues are immaterial to the VC ecosystem because the investments are in early-stage companies with a high rate of failures. The venture capital business model itself may present a challenge to ESG incorporation because VC firms do not see the need to invest in a dedicated ESG headcount. VCs desire to win and invest in many companies with the hope of catching a mythical unicorn to make up for all the losses. As such, VCs may decline to divert attention from the rapid growth mindset. Also, professionals with ESG experience are few in number.

Second, due to the founder-friendly approach and deference to the management team, GPs are reluctant to exert their influence on portfolio companies. Founders want to focus on running their companies and may not see that their innovation and scaling drive to reach their next milestones impacts ESG. Moreover, the passive investment structure may not be conducive to pressing companies to incorporate ESG factors. When finding investments, ESG due diligence is not a priority for VC firms.

Third, as venture capital portfolios cover a large group of portfolio companies, GPs simply cannot actively engage as board members of all portfolio companies. That can lead to ignoring ESG-related issues such as new employee hires, turnover, and pay gaps because these issues are not within the board's jurisdiction.

Fourth, the VC industry is not client/investor centered as far as information is concerned. Typically, GPs report only fund-level investment performance to LPs. GPs do not report the performance of individual portfolio companies. Moreover, the VC industry lacks transparency; GPs control and guard information from public view. Even at some VC firms where GPs collect ESG data, the GPs don't report them to the LPs. Consequently, internal and external monitoring of ESG data and metrics encounters barriers.[36]

Lastly, ESG oversight responsibility, unfortunately, resides in the province of investors' relations personnel who do not have investment decision-making authority. These professionals can generate glossy but meaningless reports. Real actions require the senior GPs with authority to collaborate, identify relevant ESG metrics, set up tailored resources, and design how to meet their targets.

To address these challenges, the UN-Principles for Responsible Investment (PRI) published a paper, *Starting Up: Responsible Investment in Venture Capital.*[37] PRI articulates six principles for the VC industry to consider:

---

[35] Ibid. (discussing the survey's results and observations).
[36] Ibid., at 27.
[37] Ibid.

1. We will incorporate ESG issues into investment analysis and decision-making processes.
2. We will be active owners and incorporate ESG issues into our ownership policies and practices.
3. We will seek appropriate disclosure on ESG issues by the entities in which we invest.
4. We will promote acceptance and implementation of the Principles within the investment industry.
5. We will work together to enhance our effectiveness in implementing the Principles.
6. We will each report on our activities and progress toward implementing the Principles.

PRI also recommended steps for the VC industry to consider. Driving the PRI principles home in the VC industry requires the top marquee VC firms to buy in. Silicon Valley Bank, the bank of the VC ecosystem, had already issued its ESG report under the PRI Stakeholder Capitalism Metric approach in the last two consecutive reporting periods. The Bank possessed the experience and expertise in compliance and reporting ESG core metrics and expanded metrics under People, Planet, Prosperity, and Governance Pillars. The Bank could lead the ESG integration in the VC industry because the Bank established long-term relationships with the GPs and LPs and nurtured most of their portfolio companies. No other bank in the United States or the world had attained such experience and influence.

* * * * *

The future for ESG integration under the Stakeholders Capitalism Metrics framework was with Silicon Valley Bank to disrupt both the financial and VC industries by reimagining capitalism.[38] But that future ended abruptly on March 10, 2023, for Silicon Valley Bank. ESG became the politically charged word for the Republican politicians who attempt to excite their base in gathering support for the next election cycle.

---

[38] Klaus Schwab, "A Better Economy Is Possible. But We Need to Reimagine Capitalism to Do It," *Time*, October 21, 2020, 9:46 PM EDT, available at: https://time.com/collection/great-reset/5900748/klaus-schwab-capitalism/ (last accessed September 29, 2023) (founder, and executive chairman of the World Economic Forum).

11

SVB's Sudden Death and Lessons Learned from Banking Innovators

Bob Medearis, Roger Smith, and Bill Biggerstaff founded Silicon Valley Bank in 1983. Smith ran the Bank as a startup business in the first decade. Subsequent CEO John Dean restructured the Bank and Ken Wilcox redirected the Bank with a central focus on exclusively serving the tech community. Greg Becker accelerated the Bank, connecting its past to the future. The bank's assets grew at a fast pace during the pandemic. Becker tripled the size of the bank between 2019 and 2022.

SVB had significantly evolved from a commercial bank for startups to a conglomeration of Silicon Valley Bank, SVB Private, SVB Capital, and SVB Securities. SVB perched on the top of thousands of banks as the most influential bank in the United States to serve the innovation economy.[1] Becker led supremely as CEO, but the weight of the future of the Bank rested on the shoulders of the Midwesterner.

Medearis and Smith, two other Midwesterners from Kansas City and Elkhart, Kansas, respectively, embraced California and the State's optimism and opportunities. Like them, Becker arrived in Silicon Valley from the Midwest, specifically from Fort Wayne, Indiana, but a few decades later. He credits his parents, farmers and business owners, for shaping his values, work ethic, and character. He also attributes his ability to appreciate different perspectives to his extensive travel experience. Like Medearis and Smith, he harbored no desire to return to life on the farm in Indiana. Becker explained,[2]

> I grew up on a farm 25 minutes outside of Fort Wayne, Indiana. My parents were very religious. We farmed and my dad ran a company. My parents traveled a lot. I traveled a lot around the United States. My parents traveled internationally, and

---

[1] Mark Calvey, "Silicon Valley Bank Names First Woman as Board Chair," *Business Journal*, April 25, 2022, available at: www.bizjournals.com/triangle/bizwomen/news/latest-news/2022/04/silicon-valley-bank-s-parent-names-new-chair.html?page=all [https://perma.cc/ZEH2-LG6R] (last accessed September 29, 2023).
[2] Interview with Greg Becker April 19, 2022 (on file with the author).

they had a very different perspective than a lot of my contemporaries that I hung out with. I think the combination of those things, values-driven, incredible work ethic, but also seeing things differently from the travel helped shape me.

It's so foreign to me when I go back; it's like I'm there for three days, and I want to leave Indiana.

Becker joined the legions of Midwesterners before him enticed by the promise of the opportunities California offered. Becker loved being part of the innovation economy where discussions of new ideas are daily routines. The young graduate from Indiana University took his job as a banker trainee at SVB in 1993, the year when Smith was ousted by the Board. Becker didn't know much about banks, and he didn't even know the depth of the problems the Bank was facing then. He didn't anticipate that he would have a successful career at the Bank. Becker arrived two months after the Board hired John Dean as the new CEO to turn the Bank around. Few bankers were working at SVB during the turnaround period. That meant new and exciting opportunities for the young Becker. One of the terrific opportunities soon arrived at Becker's desk: Becker was to assist in opening SVB's office in Boulder, Colorado. At the time, he had been at the Bank for only a couple of months. Becker recalled:

> The good news about when I joined SVB in 1993 as a banker trainee, I didn't know enough about the bank, and didn't even know how bad SVB was. I didn't know how much trouble we were actually in before I got here. I joined the bank, and it was great. I mean, one of the advantages of being at the bank at the time was we were small, you got to do a lot of different things. I was 26 years old. I volunteered to travel to Boulder, Colorado, and opened up our office there. I was only 27 years old and had the chance to open an office. I felt incredibly blessed that I was here when I was here. We were going through a challenging time, but I got to do a lot of interesting things. So, the timing, at least for me, literally, could not have been any better.

Becker thrived at SVB. He became a banker who built relationships with VC and private equity firms. With those relationships, Becker led the Venture Capital Group and founded SVB's first funds of funds and first direct equity fund. He was also the chief operating officer and head of commercial banking for SVB. By 2008, the Board installed him as President of Silicon Valley Bank. In 2011, Becker took the helm as the President/CEO, of Silicon Valley Financial Group.

Under Becker's leadership, the Bank grew to a large corporation with more than 8,000 employees in offices across the United States and around the world.[3] Becker held everyone together under SVB's corporate culture which included five core values. The values were percolated through a long process gathering perspectives from employees, clients, and the executive committee. The values described what

---

[3]   Written Testimony before the US Senate Committee on Banking, Housing, and Urban Affairs by Gregory W. Becker, Former CEO, Silicon Valley Bank (May 16, 2023).

SVB was as an institution, whom SVB aspired to be, and what SVB's clients thought of the Company. Becker described:

> Values are things that we have, over time, built. We have five core values. Those aren't values that we, that I woke up one day and said here are the core values of SVB. We brought together, I think, eighty employees from all around the world that were here for a week or two. People who just started [and] people that had been here for thirty years and came from all different roles, were brought together in a three-day session that facilitated a discussion around the values of SVB.

> Then we brought in [our] clients' perspective[s]. Because one thing is we look at our values through our lens. But really what you want to understand is how we show up. How do we show up in the market? It's the combination of those two things [that] have been put together. Then, it went to the executive committee to review. The executive committee then gave feedback on it, and then it went back to that group of people. Then we finalized our corporate values.

SVB's corporate culture, according to Becker, was a combination of two things: corporate values and corporate norms. Becker accorded corporate norms as encompassing how the corporation looks and feels to how employees treat each other. Corporate norms are organic, nurtured, and structured. Becker elaborated:

> Corporate norms are about your dress code, how your offices are set up, your look and feel, and how you engage each other. It's about your responsiveness, emails, and the whole list goes on. And that is [what] you let happen to some extent based on the people you have, but then you also could put guardrails on it to make sure it stays. But then what do you want it to be and how do you operate?

Becker disdained the passive-aggressive and obnoxiously assertive corporate cultures embraced by other companies. To maintain the special SVB culture, Becker followed the approach adopted in the early days by Smith, the first CEO of the Bank. When the Bank was small, employees participated in daily check-in meetings. With the 8,000 employees residing in different time zones, Becker implemented the once-a-week conference call, and everyone dialed in for forty-five minutes. From Asia to Israel, from the east coast to the west coast, employees participated in the weekly meeting. The bankers would provide highlights on clients, recognize practice groups, and emphasize SVB's corporate culture of shared corporate values and corporate norms. Corporate culture had to be alive through the participants who lived and practiced it. Becker recounted those calls:

> In that meeting, we highlight clients and how we've helped clients. We highlight different groups. We would talk about we just launched a new brand Monday morning. So, you have to keep it top of mind. All our events are set up to talk about values and talk about corporate norms. So, you just have to keep that culture highlighted in ways that people feel it and live it. And, it helps to have people who have been here a while that know what it's like to be at the bank.

Running a big bank and financial institution meant hiring many employees who were outsiders. They are not homegrown with SVB's DNA. They are from other banks with different corporate cultures of different values and norms. Becker explained how SVB dedicatedly practiced a path of valuing talents while refusing to tolerate behaviors inconsistent with SVB's culture.

> When you're interviewing somebody from Goldman, somebody from Morgan Stanley, JP [Morgan], or wherever, you want to make sure that you interview for our values. You interview to make sure that they're going to fit into this sort of values and corporate norms that we have. But you also have to have a perspective that if they're good at what they do, you've got to listen to them as well. What you don't tolerate are things that violate your values. You don't tolerate, for example, if somebody is used to the passive-aggressive culture and they were in a meeting and they nodded their head: "Oh yeah, I agree with you." They then walked out of the room and later said to someone who was in the meeting, "Oh my gosh, that was a horrible idea. Can you believe they're going down that path?" You make sure that individual knows that is not an acceptable behavior. At some point, if they keep acting that way, either they will self-select out or you will self-select them out. You just have to be disciplined about that.

Under the Board and Becker's leadership, SVB joined other banks positioning its embrace of Environmental, Social, and Governance (ESG) for the betterment of society and others. SVB insisted that the embrace was consistent with SVB's ecosystem where SVB's bankers, clients, entrepreneurs, and founders have been working for more than four decades in transforming technology and science into useful products and services to serve and improve the world. As Paula Solanes, SVB Senior Portfolio Manager, explained on SVB's website:

> ESG stands for Environmental, Social and Governance – the set of criteria typically used by socially conscious investors, with each element acting as a determining factor to measure an overall ESG rating. *Environment* considers how a company's operations affect climate and the environment. *Social* takes many forms and evaluates how a company acts from a social perspective, including whether it embraces diversity and prioritizes human rights, and whether it partners with companies that do the same. Finally, *Governance* digs into the structure of a company, examining items such as transparent accounting practices and the diversity of its board of directors.

SVB was on its path of integrating ESG. The tech sector was and still is notoriously slow in addressing the lack of diversity and inclusion. Venture capital firms are not backing minorities in technology, Silicon Valley, and innovation centers across the United States. SVB was the banker and financial leader and partner to investors and entrepreneurs in the tech sector, and SVB's actions mattered. Becker seemed to realize the gravity of SVB's stature and impact in influencing the tech sector to practice ESG. Becker vocally acknowledged at a conference in 2022 that venture capitalists are backing more minorities in the tech sector, but the changes are still too slow.[4] He insisted that dramatic change would not occur without limited partners calling on venture capitalists, private equity fund managers, angel investors, and other sources of funding for early-stage companies to shift their priorities.[5] In other words, those who hold the lever of the capital supply must act now by investing and backing minorities in the tech ecosystem throughout the United States. The "Social" and "Governance" in the ESG commitments demanded investors literally put the money where it matters most to diversity and inclusion.

Chastising the tech sector for its extremely slow pace in addressing ESG was one step in the right direction. SVB tried to practice what it preached on diversity and inclusion by funding minorities in tech. SVB believed that it could both make money and practice ESG. Becker emphatically gave an affirmative answer to the question. Becker illustrated how SVB itself had already begun its ESG approach in its investing in first-time fund managers who are Black, Latinx, or female:

> You can make money and do ESG. I'll give you some examples. One is, we, off of our balance sheet, have allocated $10 million per year where we're investing in first-time fund managers that are diverse.

> Currently, we're not ready to take a limited partner's money because we can't look a limited partner in the eyes and say we are nearly as confident as ever that we're going to get the right return on those investments. But we, as an institution, [I] can put our own capital behind it because we have other benefits to it, right? So, we'll do that. And then what we're going to do is, let's say we invest in five, six, seven funds per year over five years, will have twenty-five to thirty-five new funds that then we can pick. With our limited partners, we then actually can say we believe this fund is going to be one of the top funds. And therefore, you can accomplish both.

> So, of the investments we've made, we have made more than five or six so far. They have all been either Black, Latinx, or female-led.

> As we invested over time, we're talking about taking it from $10 million a year to $25 million a year. That'll be something we'll talk about here in the next few weeks. So yeah, you absolutely can.

The future for "a more just, equitable, and sustainable world" was espoused by SVB as the Bank was the most influential bank in the innovation economy. How SVB would shoulder that responsibility to truly make meaningful changes in the tech sector where exclusions of minorities and women continue to reign supremely, where bro culture is celebrated, where wealth accumulations see no bottom, and

---

[4] "SVB's Becker Says Tech Lags on Inclusiveness: Milken Update," *Bloomberg*, May 3, 2022, available at: www.bnnbloomberg.ca/svb-s-becker-says-tech-lags-on-inclusiveness-milken-update-1 .1760518 [https://perma.cc/FX9Y-YNPN] (last accessed September 29, 2023).
[5] Ibid.

where privacy is reserved for the rich tech overlords, was very much not just a "wait and see" but a call to action by Becker.

Becker's words filled with conviction echoed the glass-filled conference room nestled inside the SVB building located in a park-like setting next to powerful VCs whom the Bank had cultivated relationships with for years. His zeal confirmed SVB's stature and influence that would deliver results in reducing the racial and gender disparity in the tech ecosystem. Becker did not show any hint of worries as SVB was about to hold its Board meeting in April 2022 in the same building where a beautiful display of a vintage wine collection prominently occupied the space on the first floor near the conference room, reminding all that SVB banking is all about relationships. Unlike other banks, Becker's SVB had so much cash from deposits from VCs' portfolio companies and the tech lending's loans-to-deposit ratio was always kept low. In the same conference room, Kellogg and Arron Gershenberg wondered whether Becker would stay on as a CEO or move to a new chapter solidifying his legacy. They stepped outside to pose for some pictures. Kellogg had not seen his dream team's Aaron and Greg for a while and his face exuded so much pride and affection toward them. The air outside was simply perfect.

The beautiful Palo Alto air and sunshine in April 2022 betrayed the pending arrival of the crypto winter, resurrecting Mark Twain's well-known remark that the coldest winter he ever spent was a summer in San Francisco.

∗ ∗ ∗ ∗ ∗

THE CASH-RICH TECH WORLD DURING THE PANDEMIC

In early 2022 the tech world was still brimming with cash. There were 900 tech startups, each worth more than $1 billion.[6] Unicorns are supposed to be rare, but tech unicorns in January 2022 appeared everywhere. A few years earlier, say, 2015, only 80 tech unicorns were enjoying the $1 billion mythical status after achieving the threshold valuation. So much cash in the economy, so much cash in the VC ecosystem that a perversion unfolded: reverse fundraising. That is, hot startups don't seek investors for funding; investors seek out and pitch themselves to the startups. Imagine a Friday afternoon, the investors make a pitch to the startup, and by Sunday evening, the deal is sealed. Startup founders termed the reserve fundraising with all the frenzy as "wild." Some explained that the pandemic shutdown and everything-is-virtual meant all aspects of life and business rely on tech, translating new ideas related to tech and more money flow to tech projects. The frenzied world of tech, from artificial intelligence, nuclear technology, electric vehicles, space

---

[6] Erin Griffith, "'It's All Just Wild': Tech Start-Ups Reach a New Peak of Froth, There's More Money and More Bubbly Behavior. Investors Insist It's Rational," *The New York Times*, January 19, 2022.

travel, remote-work software, and telehealth services, to food delivery, saw no limit in growth.

According to Pitchbook, in 2021 alone, US startups raised $330 billion, almost doubling 2020's record of $167 billion.[7] There were more unicorn tech startups minted in 2021 than in the previous five years combined. Crunchbase noted that the median raised by startups in their first round of funding grew 30 percent. On the exit end in IPO, the value shot up to $774 billion, almost tripling the prior year's returns. In January 2022, Miro, a digital whiteboard startup, startled everyone with a valuation of $17.75 billion. Checkout.com, a payment startup, flashed out a valuation of $40 billion. OpenSea, an NFT platform, garnered $13.3 billion in valuation. Investors all vied to get a piece of the action. Andreessen Horowitz, a VC firm, had to please its investors by opening new funds to allow investors to pour in $9 billion. Investors at Khosla Ventures and Kleiner Perkins rushed to fill new funds at $2 billion each.

Investors carry on their sleeves the Fear of Missing Opportunities (FOMO). The pandemic and the abundance of cheap money presented investors and founders with a new purpose and their actions displayed that bravado. That meant startups wanted to accomplish things in a shorter time, the investors wanted the milestones to be reached sooner, and, instead of the normal VC fresh round of funding coming in every 18 months, hot startups got new rounds multiple times a year.[8]

For instance, Daniel Perez, a cofounder of Hinge Health, which provides online physical therapy programs, received unsolicited pitches from investors with research information about Hinge Health to persuade him to take their investment money. The reverse pitch from Tiger Global secured a $300 million funding round together with investments from Coatue Management in January 2021. A few months after that flush round, Perez received new reverse pitches from different investors, and these investors went to the extreme of hiring celebrities like Andrew Kirilenko, of whom Perez is a fan, to send a video to Perez.[9] By October 2021, Hinge Health raised another $600 million in a new round of funding led by Coatue and Tiger Global.

Early 2022 was still filled with optimism. Ambar Bhattacharyya, an investor at Maverick Ventures, told *The New York Times* that funding for startups was still competitive.[10] Phil Libin, a founder of Mmhmm, a video communication provider for remote workers, secured $136 million in funding and yet received calls from interested investors a few times a week, as he told *The New York Times*.

---

[7] "US VC Tops $329B in 2021, Nearly Doubling Previous Record," *PitchBook*, available at: https://pitchbook.com/newsletter/us-vc-tops-329b-in-2021-nearly-doubling-previous-record-sqr (last accessed October 3, 2023).

[8] Erin Griffith, "'This Is Insanity': Start-Ups End Year in a Deal Frenzy. Investors Are Tripping over One Another to Give Hot Start-Ups Money. DoorDash and Airbnb Are Going Public. The Good Times Are Baaack." *The New York Times*, December 7, 2020.

[9] Griffith, "'It's All Just Wild,'" *supra*, note 6 (reporting instances of reverse pitches in the VC ecosystem for hot startups).

[10] Griffith, "This Is Insanity'" *supra*, note 8.

With all of the cash influx in 2020 and 2021, where did VCs and their portfolio companies park their money? Which bank would like to accept all the liabilities holding the mountain of cash? Which bank would accept the cash from startups knowing that the startups would burn cash at unpredictable rates and amounts? Which bank would dare to bank these tech companies with their unique set of unpredictability? Which bank could manage the risks ensuring the bank's investments of the mountain of cash would meet the sudden demands of withdrawals from the startups? No bank. Only SVB tried, but it caused its demise. From China to Israel, the world learned about Silicon Valley Bank and the unprecedented 24-hour bank run in the history of banking when they woke up that fateful morning of Friday, March 10, 2023.

* * * *

TECH DEPOSITS

In 2019, SVB held $60 billion in assets. The rapid growth in the tech economy and the infusion of cash by governments to rescue the COVID-19 pandemic pushed SVB to its own ascent. The high valuation of startups in 2020 and 2021 translated to lots of cash flowing into the Bank as deposits. By the end of December 2022, SVB's assets climbed more than three times in a short three years to reach $209 billion.

A former SVB banker intimated that the bank had to turn away deposits in the past. Having too many deposits presents a unique problem for the Bank. SVB was not created from inception in 1982 to be in the retail banking industry. Medearis wanted a Bank to serve the tech community. Smith's vision of the tech community is nationwide wherever tech entrepreneurs reside and innovate. Subsequent CEOs and Becker elevated SVB to its preeminent stature as the bank for the innovation economy. The assets expanded as SVB closely followed the VC clients to lend and provide banking services to the investors and their portfolio companies.

On the tech lending side, SVB mastered the model to create venture debts. The model worked exceedingly well and SVB never faced loan default problems. Harry Kellogg remarked that VC-backed tech companies have so much money infused from the VCs that they typically don't need to obtain loans. Overall, SVB made few loans in tech lending. Kellogg shared that, for every ten dollars, only three dollars were lent. The common reason for banks' failures is making too many bad loans. A high ratio of loan-to-deposit means less liquidity due to lending out all of the deposits and a low ratio means high liquidity as the Bank has more deposits than loans. SVB's loan-to-deposit ratio was only 41 percent as of December 31, 2022.[11] The loan-to-deposit ratio across the entire US banking industry was above 60 percent, with some banks carrying

---

[11] "Silicon Valley Bank & Safe Cash," *ACap Advisors & Accountants*, available at: www.acapam .com/blog/silicon-valley-bank/ [https://perma.cc/5P9G-AC4Q] (last accessed September 29, 2023).

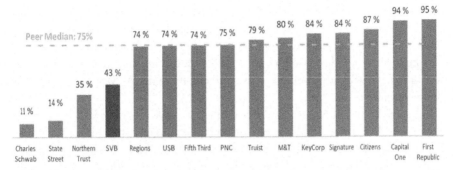

FIGURE 11.1 Loan-to-deposit ratio for SVB and other banks.
Source: SVB Q1 2023 Mid-Quarter Update, https://s201.q4cdn.com/589201576/files/doc_downloads/2023/
03/Q1-2023-Mid-Quarter-Update-vFINAL3-030823.pdf

a ratio significantly higher (see Figure 11.1).[12] Commentators even espouse that "a good ratio is seventy-five percent" for banks.[13] Based on the conventional loan-to-deposit ratio, SVB was a very solid and highly liquid bank.

However, the low loan-to-bank ratio generated a problem for SVB, as with any bank, because banks make money by making more loans versus investing the deposits in securities. Unlike other banks, SVB's clients were all in startup and high-growth tech and could store lots of cash at the bank when they received VC rounds of funding, but they then quickly withdrew lots of cash as they burned through their cash between rounds. Some tech companies, however, don't make it to the next round of financing.

With so much cash from deposits parked by investors and tech companies in the VC ecosystem and with a low loan-to-deposit ratio, SVB faced a unique problem relating to investments of all the extra cash. If SVB locked the cash in boring, longer-term, extremely low-risk investments like US Treasuries and government-sponsored mortgage-backed securities, SVB's financial conditions would be fine as long as the tech clients did not demand all their deposits back at the same time and as long as the Fed interest rate remained the same low rate for a long time. Long-term Treasuries, however, posed a quagmire to the Bank because, when the Fed hiked its interest rates, the value of SVB's long-term Treasuries declined and the Bank suffered massive unrealized losses.

In fact, SVB invested those deposits by holding 55 percent of its assets in fixed-income securities in the US "Treasuries and securities issued by government-sponsored enterprises."[14] And 55 percent of $212 billion in assets, as reported by

---

[12] Ibid.
[13] Ibid.
[14] "Silicon Valley Bank Strategic Actions/Q1 2023 Mid-Quarter Update," SVB, March 8, 2023, available at: https://s201.q4cdn.com/589201576/files/doc_downloads/2023/03/Q1–2023-Mid-Quarter-Update-vFINAL3–030823.pdf [https://perma.cc/6QNM-FLFM] (last accessed September 29, 2023).

the bank for Q1 2023, meant SVB held $116 billion in long-term securities.[15] When the crypto winter hit the summer months of 2022 and unleashed its crypto contagion force and the tech industry contraction throughout 2022 and early 2023, SVB experienced a liquidity crunch due to the unexpected increase in outflows of withdrawals. SVB had to sell all of its Available-For-Sale (AFS) securities to meet the withdrawals.

When SVB sold AFS securities for $21 billion as of March 8, 2023, the yield of the securities sold was only 1.79 percent compared to the significantly higher interest for Treasuries at that time, and the bank suffered a realized loss of $1.8 billion. With the Fed's successive interest rate hikes, SVB faced a very large unrealized loss on the remainder of the long-term investments or Held-To-Maturity (HTM) securities. William Martin, the shorter seller, noted SVB problems caused by long-term securities, interest rate hikes, and tech's fast rates of cash burning, and the problems were indeed in full disclosure. SVB was in a very vulnerable situation, but the problems could be fixed if the Bank raised the capital it needed and if tech clients did not echo rumors without a clear understanding of bank business. In the end, tech bros and clients fed on their own irrational fear and misunderstanding of SVB's interim liquidity problem caused by very safe, long-term investments and the Fed's successive interest hikes to tamper the stubborn inflation.

Playing Monday quarterback after the SVB failure suggests the Bank executives should have addressed the misalignment earlier. Some argued that the Bank should have hedged the interest rates. SVB should have engaged in interest rate swaps. Some claimed that the bank should not put the bulk of the investments in long-term securities. Others asserted that the bank should invest in short-term securities. But all commentators missed the key features of SVB's problem: tech clients function in their own bubbles, park lots of cash and withdraw lots of cash without any predictability, demand online and instant banking services and withdrawals, and feed on their own misunderstanding and fear.

The mountain of cash from tech clients' deposits constituted an undaunting liability to SVB in the age of cell phones, online banking, and instant and constant viral communications among the investors and tech companies in the VC ecosystem.[16] On their way to burning cash at a fast and furious rate in the post-COVID-19 pandemic, the tech community burned down their own bank.

---

[15] Ibid.

[16] Byprarthana Prakash, "One of the World's Richest Men Knows Why Silicon Valley Bank Really Failed: 'People on iPhones'," *Fortune*, March 30, 2023 9:30 AM PDT), available at: https://fortune.com/2023/03/30/blackstone-ceo-steve-schwarzman-svb-iphones-contagion-wont-spread/ [https://perma.cc/JP6X-V49P] (last accessed September 29, 2023).

THE CRYPTO WINTER

The spring of 2022 ended. As usual, summer arrived. But in the summer of 2022, the crypto winter thrashed the summer warmth, hurling the collapse of global crypto platforms, spreading the crypto contagion, burning companies through bankruptcies, and wiping $1.3 trillion off the value of crypto assets from its peak in November 2021.

The early wrath of the crypto winter began in the unraveling of TerraForm Labs in May 2022. The Company's algorithmic stablecoin UST, which was pegged as equal to one dollar, lost its peg and traded for a nickel. The Company's reserve of $1.4 billion disappeared along with the collapse of the peg. Along with the collapse, the Company's governance token LUNA watched its market cap of $30 billion crashing to $680 million. The contagion brought down thousands of investors who poured their cash into projects built on the Terra blockchain.

Do Kwon, the trash-talking CEO of TerraForm Labs, was a crypto fugitive leading a very public life, while both the Korean and US governments went on a manhunt worldwide to capture him.[17] The SEC accused Kwon and his company of orchestrating a multi-billion dollar crypto asset securities fraud scheme involving an algorithmic stablecoin and other crypto securities. Terraform and Kwon raised billions of dollars from investors from 2018 until the scheme's collapse in May 2022. Under the scheme, the defendants created "mAssets," security-based swaps designed to pay returns by mimicking corporate stock prices, and Terra USD (UST) or "algorithmic stablecoin" that supposedly maintained its peg to the US dollar by being interchangeable for defendants' other crypto asset securities, LUNA. According to the SEC, the defendants misled investors about the stability of its UST, and about the hype of high returns for their tokens. The defendants committed fraud by repeating false and misleading statements.

The contagion led by TerraForm Labs spread to other platforms. The Celsius Network, a crypto lending platform, filed for bankruptcy as it faced $1.2 billion in more liabilities than assets. The bankruptcy filing reminded everyone that Celsius had just enjoyed its golden days two months prior with a client base of 1.7 million users and $11.7 billion in assets under management. Perching on top of the commanding height of crypto's glorious time, Celsius issued $8 billion in loans and showered depositors with a popping 17 percent annual yield. All that came to a sudden crash as crypto prices fell quickly back to earth. Celsius shut down on June 12, 2022, while its users watched their assets frozen and investors' investments vanished.

[17] David Yaffe-Bellany, John Yoon, and Karoun Demirjian, "A Crypto Fugitive's Very Public Life While on the Run, Do Kwon, the Founder of the Failed Crypto Company Terraform Labs, Is Facing Charges by the Authorities in Both South Korea and the United States," *The New York Times*, March 24, 2023.

On June 17, 2022, Babel Finance, a crypto lender, informed its customers that it was suspending withdrawals because the lender faced unusual liquidity pressures. On June 27, 2022, three Arrows Capital (3AC), a crypto hedge fund with heavy investments in TerraUSD, faced its own demise in the crypto winter. A few months before its collapse, 3AC managed $10 billion. The hedge fund's death brought down Voyager Digital – a crypto platform for lending, buying, and trading – when 3AC defaulted on a $650 million loan from the lender. On July 5, 2022, Voyager Digital filed for bankruptcy when the lender's holding of crypto assets that were once worth billions of dollars vaporized. Other crypto lenders like Genesis and BlockFi also folded soon after, as all three lenders had extended loans to 3AC. Genesis lent $2.36 billion to 3AC and tried to prolong its existence after the 3AC collapse but soon met its own demise when FTX also collapsed in November 2022. BlockFi faced a similar fate; it became the first large institutional victim of FTX's collapse.

On November 2, 2022, *CoinDesk* published an article stating that Alameda Research's assets of a token created by its sister company FTX were overvalued, igniting a run on FTX, one of the world's largest crypto platforms. A few months back, in February 2022, FTX was the poster child of the Venture Capital, crypto, and political worlds. On February 13, 2022, Americans witnessed the height of FTX during the Superbowl with expensive ads featuring sports figures and celebrities, capturing future investors and raising its profile and the crypto industry. At that time, the Fed announced the coming rate increases. The value of bitcoin tumbled from a peak of $67,802 in November 2021, to $42,259.28 in February 2022. On May 4, 2022, the Fed raised its benchmark rate by a half-percentage point to rein in the rising inflation, drawing the largest increase since 2000. Consequently, the interest rate increases set off the dumping of speculative investments, especially crypto assets. Bitcoin's value went down to $39,780 on the same day the Fed hiked its interest rate.

The run on FTX succumbed the platform to a sudden liquidity crunch. Sam Bankman-Fried, CEO and one of the founders of FTX, reached out to its rival Binance for a rescue on November 8, 2022. Binance agreed to rescue FTX but changed its mind upon informing the world that FTX and its problems were uncontrollable. The news reported that FTX had made loans in billions of dollars in customer assets to fund its sister company Alameda Research. FTX filed for bankruptcy the following day, November 11, 2022.

All of these crypto companies were interconnected in their dealings. They rose and fell together like dominoes, and their schemes cratered along with the cash and crypto assets once held by many investors and users in the United States and worldwide. The crypto winter was hurling its destructive force everywhere, including Silicon Valley and the VC industry.

Sequoia, one of the most successful and revered VC firms in the world and a very important, long-term client of Silicon Valley Bank, was infatuated with FTX's founder.

Sam Bankman-Fried or SBF represented a new breed of founders in the new world of crypto. Instead of Steve Jobs' black turtleneck shirt, SBF choreographed his hair and clothes to project the image of a tech CEO and founder who was too smart to care about conventional looks. With the purposeful hobo genius appearance, SBF set out to dominate the world with his FTX empire. Sequoia believed that SBF would become the world's first trillionaire. A private historian was hired by Sequoia to paint the future trillionaire in the most flattering light, which Sequoia prominently posted on its website until the VC took it down when the FTX empire exploded.[18] Through the hired historian, Sequoia elevated SBF to the same level as Apple's and Google's founders and crafted a myth about SBF as a legend in crypto and that his FTX, "a company that may very well end up creating the dominant all-in-one financial super-app of the future" that could eclipse "the big four of American banking (JPMorgan Chase, Bank of America, Wells Fargo and Citibank)." The article shamelessly praised SBF's effective altruism, embracing that the "best way for him to maximize the good in the world would be to maximize his wealth" and that "he was going to get filthy rich, for charity's sake. All the rest was merely execution risk." Sequoia and other VCs were very impressed with a new model of visionary entrepreneur in SBF.

Alfred Lin, a veteran partner at Sequoia, led the investment in FTX and spent a year-and-a-half building the relationship between Sequoia and SBF. As later reflected by Lin, he failed to see any signs of the many lies of SBF during that time. Lin spoke about VC trust in founders and that trust constitutes the bedrock of the investment in founders and their companies, and that trust was what SBF understood and seized from the VC ecosystem.

Lin proudly led the deal that culminated in a $214 million investment by Sequoia in FTX. According to the hired article, Lin and Michelle Bailhe, a partner at Sequoia, organized a last-minute Zoom meeting between SBF and the partners at Sequoia in July 2022. SBF dazzled everyone with his super-app answer to Lin's question about SBF's long-term vision for FTX: "I want FTX to be a place where you can do anything you want with your next dollar. You can buy bitcoin. You can send money in whatever currency to any friend anywhere in the world. You can buy a banana. You can do anything you want with your money from inside FTX." The Sequoia partners exclaimed "I LOVE THIS FOUNDER," "I am a 10 out of 10," "YES," and gushed with: "We were incredibly impressed. It was one of those your-hair-is-blown-back types of meetings." FTX raised a billion dollars in a Series B round in July 2021, and three months later they received another $420 million from sixty-nine investors in the B-1 round and the company was valued at $25 billion in October 2021.

---

[18] Adam Fisher, "Sam Bankman-Fried Has a Savior Complex: And Maybe You Should Too," *Sequoiacap.com*, September 22, 2022, https://web.archive.org/web/20221109230422; www.sequoiacap.com/article/sam-bankman-fried-spotlight. This feature has been removed from the Sequoiacap.com website.

In 2022, the investors pushed FTX's valuation to $32 billion. Investors were willing to pour in their investments with the understanding that SBF would run his empire with little oversight.[19] The investors praised SBF as a visionary founder in a press release:[20]

Teachers' Innovation Platform (TIP) invests in innovative companies that use technology to help shape new categories. As a global, technology-driven innovator in the financial sector, FTX fits well with our mandate. We look forward to working with FTX's management team in supporting the continued growth of the company.

Olivia Steedman, Senior Managing Director, TIP

Sam Bankman-Fried is a special founder who is ambitious and daring enough to build the future of crypto by establishing FTX as the global exchange with the best overall product offering and leveraging the world's crypto rails to build the future of finance. We are thrilled to partner with FTX on their next phase of growth.

Alfred Lin, General Partner at Sequoia Capital

FTX is forging the way to create a modern financial system. We admire Sam and the FTX team's laser focus on product and user experience which we believe has been core to FTX's success as a leading global crypto exchange. We are thrilled to partner with them as they leverage their underlying infrastructure to expand into broader financial services and become the exchange of everything.

Divesh Makan, Founding Partner at ICONIQ

FTX has that rare combination of a visionary founder, impeccable execution and an exploding market. They also take regulatory compliance and engagement seriously. Our thesis has been and continues to be that only the trusted, regulated exchanges will win in the long run. Ambition, creativity, velocity and rigor make FTX truly unique. We're excited to partner with Sam and the entire FTX team.

Tom Loverro, General Partner at IVP

Lightspeed is excited to double down in FTX's B-1 round. Sam Bankman-Fried and the team are innovators in products with a thoughtful approach to working closely with regulators across 150+ jurisdictions. We believe FTX will continue to be a leader in powering crypto transactions across financial services and consumer businesses.

Amy Wu, General Partner at Lightspeed Venture Partners

Along with Sequoia, other VCs vied their way into the inner sanctum of the FTX empire through their investments. The list includes prominent VCs in the United

[19] Erin Griffith and David Yaffe-Bellany, "Investors Who Put $2 Billion Into FTX Face Scrutiny, Too," *The New York Times*, November 11, 2023.
[20] "FTX Trading Ltd. Closes $420 Million Series B-1 Funding Round: This Financing Round Raises the Company's Valuation to $25 Billion," *prnewswire.com*, October 21, 2021, available at: www.prnewswire.com/news-releases/ftx-trading-ltd-closes-420-million-series-b-1-funding-round-301405473.html [https://perma.cc/6FWQ-YXWT] (last accessed September 29, 2023).

States: NEA, IVP, Iconiq Capital, Third Point Ventures, Tiger Global, Altimeter Capital Management, Lux Capital, Mayfield, Insight Partners, Sequoia Capital, SoftBank, Lightspeed Venture Partners, Ribbit Capital, Temasek Holdings, BlackRock, and Thomas Bravo. Most, if not all, of these investors, were among Silicon Valley Bank's clients. SVB, as always, stood by the investors and their portfolio companies in the last four decades.

When FTX tumbled down, Sequoia wrote its $214 million in SBF's empire as zero. On November 10, 2022, when SBF's empire crashed like a house of cards, Sequoia reported that it had pulled its investment from FTX. It turned out that Sequoia also invested in FTX's rival, Binance.

Sequoia still had a $600 million crypto fund. Alfred Lin later stated in January 2023 that 10 percent of Sequoia's crypto fund had been deployed.

The crypto world burned in 2022 along with many VC investments in that dark, murky world. For Silicon Valley Bank, the crypto winter translated into an increase in withdrawals by the VCs and their portfolio companies.

＊＊＊＊＊

VALUATIONS TUMBLE IN 2022

The year 2022 may be remembered as the year when tech valuations tumbled. This was not good news for Silicon Valley Bank throughout 2022. Significantly lower valuations than previous rounds put tech companies in their own cash crunch and that meant these companies had to withdraw lots of cash and some would soon run out of cash. Also, no new money was coming in from the investors. And if money did flow in, the low valuations yielded little cash. Burn. Everywhere. Take a look at some.

During the COVID-19 pandemic, people wanted their fresh groceries to be delivered to their front doors. Contactless, please. Fresh groceries from suppliers to consumers, no middleman. Checked. Fast deliveries. Checked. Good Eggs, Inc., a San Francisco-based startup was one of the game changers, delivering groceries in the Bay Area in early 2021 and then expanding its footprint to other cities.[21] Investors loved the idea and wrote a big check of $100 million in early 2021.[22] Good Eggs beamed at a post-money valuation in the range of $500 million to $1 billion as of February 3, 2021 in Series D round, according to PrivCo.[23] In total, Good Eggs raised a total of $201.5M in funding over 10 rounds, Seed to Series D, from twenty-seven investors, including Glade Brook Capital Partners and Benchmark. Vaccines

---

[21] Deena Shanker, "Startup Good Eggs Raises $100 Million for Expansion to L.A.," *Bloomberg*, February 3, 2021.

[22] Ibid.

[23] Ibid.

then became widely available and few people wanted groceries delivered, and Good Eggs stared at a 94 percent write-down of its valuation. The company accepted a $7 million investment at a $22 million valuation.

Stripe, a known payments startup and darling in the tech world backed by VCs, was not immune from valuation cuts. In November 2022, the fintech startup laid off 14 percent of its workforce of 8,000 workers and reduced its internal valuation of the company.[24] Joining Stripe, Instacart lowered its internal valuation from $39 billion to $24 billion in March 2022, and then again to $13 billion in October 2022. These late-stage startups missed their revenue targets, and investors did not like that.[25] The median pre-money late-stage valuation fell 29 percent from Q1 to Q3 in 2022, according to a PitchBook report. Cooley, one of tech's leading law firms, reported that in Q4 2022 the bleeding continued, with downward trends in deal count, invested capital, and pre-money valuations based on the firm's own data.[26]

> We have witnessed the downward trend in amounts raised during 2022 across all stages of financing, but the decline is most significant in mid- to late-stage deals. Series D and later deals have seen a 78% drop, from $10.5 billion in Q4 2021 to just $2.3 billion in Q4 2022. The drop in amount raised in Series C deals was even more significant at just over 87%, from $3 billion in Q4 2021 to $377 million in Q4 2022. The 2022 drop was nearly 74% for Series B deals (from $5.3 billion to $1.4 billion), just under 58% for Series A deals (from $3.5 billion to $1.5 billion) and just over 38% for seed deals (from $932 million to $576 million). While the percentage decline in amount raised for Series D and later deals during the full year of 2022 is consistent with that seen in the first three quarters of 2022, the decline increased meaningfully for Series C deals and earlier between the first three quarters – where the decline was 64% for Series C, 61% for Series B, 50% for Series A and only 9% for seed deals – versus the full year.

Soon, Cooley reduced the hiring of new lawyers as tech work was drying up. Tech layoffs dominated headlines.

Outside the tech industry, other startups suffered a similar fate. Tonal, the strength training home fitness company with the backing of celebrity athletes and superstars, was valued at $1.6 billion after a $250 million Series E funding round in 2021. The company reached its height of $1.9 billion in valuation in September 2022 but soon fell to a devastating new valuation as the company sought new funding.

[24] Natasha Mascarenhas, "Stripe's Internal Valuation Gets Cut to $63 Billion," *TechCrunch*, January 11, 2023.

[25] Marina Temkin, "More Cuts in Late-Stage Valuations Loom, as Startups Miss Revenue Targets," *Pitchbook.com*, November 9, 2022, available at: https://pitchbook.com/news/articles/valuations-409a-cuts-instacart-forecast [https://perma.cc/C2AG-ZXVN] (last accessed September 29, 2023).

[26] "Q4 2022 Venture Financing Report – Downward Trends Continue in Deal Count, Invested Capital and Pre-Money Valuations, Up Rounds Drop to Less Than 80% of All Deals," *Cooley.com*, January 27, 2023, available at: www.cooley.com/news/insight/2023/2023-01-27-venture-financing-report-q4-2022 [https://perma.cc/Q97K-CJA2] (last accessed September 29, 2023)..

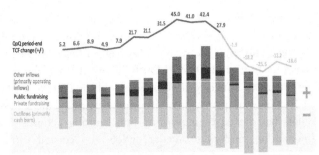

FIGURE 11.2 SVB's elevated client cash burn pressuring balance of fund flows.
Source: SVB Q1 2023 Mid-Quarter Update, https://s201.q4cdn.com/589201576/files/doc_downloads/2023/03/Q1-2023-Mid-Quarter-Update-vFINAL3-030823.pdf

The valuation came at less than $500 million by March 1, 2023.[27] Real estate in Silicon Valley, which witnessed skyrocketing prices, had cooled down significantly. DeLeon Realty sold more than $1 billion in homes in 2021 in Silicon Valley but experienced a tough time in early 2023. Cash, the ultimate dry powder of Silicon Valley, seemed to evaporate quicker than it arrived.

While valuations crashed down to earth for tech clients, the cash in deposits at SVB faced waves of withdrawals as clients burned through money twice as quickly as pre-2021 levels. Figure 11.2 shows a gyrating graph of SVB's elevated client cash burn pressuring balance of fund flows in its filing on March 8, 2023.

SVB was still hopeful that the VC investments would hold up to $120–$140 billion in 2023, and that a good chunk of that infusion would come to SVB to withstand the elevated client cash burn bleeding the Bank – if the Bank could survive that long.

* * * * *

DEATH BY $142 BILLION CUTS

SVB watched its tech clients increase their withdrawals of the deposits they had parked at the Bank. Tech clients burned their mountain of cash much faster than SVB had anticipated in 2022. Tech deposits, just like all deposits with banks, were not insured beyond the FDIC limit of $250,000. Banks, SVB included, typically don't leave the bulk of cash deposits at hand for withdrawals. But the increase in the withdrawals might pose a cash shortage problem to SVB.

At least at the end of 2022, however, the withdrawals did not alarm the regulators because they still issued a satisfactory rating believing in the bank's safety and

[27] Shawn Johnson, "Athlete Investors Can't Save Tonal's Falling $500M Valuation," *BusinessNews*, March 1, 2023.

soundness.[28] Not until January 2023 did the regulators flag that the bank was at risk of a possible cash shortage.[29] Around this time, short seller William Martin of Raging Venture in the market also flagged the bank's cash shortage problem and began to short on its stock.[30] On February 21, 2023, the *Financial Times*, following the American Banker's earlier article published on November 7, 2022,[31] wrote about SVB's financial quarry, noted its profit squeeze by the tech downturn, and the short sellers had flexed their scrutiny into shorting action.[32] *The Financial Post, The Information*, and other media outlets also carried similar stories on February 22, 2023.

The regulators, two weeks after SVB's collapse, blamed SVB executives for their failure to manage the Bank's interest rate and liquidity risk which caused the Bank to suffer a devastating and unexpected bank run by their tech depositors in 24 hours. The tripling in assets size came back to haunt the Bank. The massive mountain of cash deposits parked at the bank came back to haunt the Bank. With the significant deposit growth, the bank prudently invested the money in longer-term securities to capture yield and secure profits. What SVB invested in is what other banks typically do with their deposits. In normal times, what and how SVB invested was and still is the boring and safe investments by a typical commercial bank. But the pandemic and post-pandemic macroeconomics were not normal times.

To cope with COVID-19, the Federal Reserve cut the interest rate by −0.50 percentage points on March 3, 2020, and thirteen days later, on March 16, 2020, the Fed slashed a huge −1.00 percentage point at two unscheduled emergency meetings in March 2020. These cuts sat on top of the three prior rate reductions that had occurred on August 1, 2019, September 19, 2019, and October 31, 2019, each by −0.25 percentage points. The economy then became overheated and, in late 2021, the Fed announced that it would increase the interest rate. The Fed aggressively addressed inflation by raising interest rates seven times in 2022, totaling a whopping 4.75 percentage points in one year. Inflation then hit 6 percent in February 2023, prompting the Fed to raise interest again on February 1, 2023, and March 3, 2023, by

---

[28] "Composite Ratings Definition List," *FDIC*, available at: www.fdic.gov/regulations/examin ations/ratings/ [https://perma.cc/GVF2–8U2E] (last accessed September 29, 2023); Jeanna Smialek and Emily Flitter, "Fed Vice Chair Calls Silicon Valley Bank a 'Textbook Case of Mismanagement,'" *The New York Times*, March 27, 2023.

[29] John Foley, "Fed's Self-Scrutiny Starts Off on the Wrong Foot," *Reuters*, March. 22, 2023.

[30] Yun Li, "The Investor Who Famously Shorted Silicon Valley Bank in January on What's to Come in the Crisis," *CNBC*, March 16, 2023; Isabelle Lee and Bloomberg, "For Nearly 2 Months, a Short Seller was Warning on Twitter that Silicon Valley Bank was About to Blow Up. 'It was sitting there in plain sight.,'" *Fortune*, March 10, 2023, available at: https://fortune .com/2023/03/10/silicon-valley-bank-svb-short-seller-william-martin-twitter-2-months/ [https:// perma.cc/3624-3KSR] (last accessed September 29, 2023). See also "Silicon Valley Bank Profit Squeeze in Tech Downturn Attracts Short Sellers," *Financial Times*, February 21, 2023.

[31] Allissa Kline, "SVB Financial Squeezed by Tech Economy Downturn," *American Banker*, November 7, 2022.

[32] "Silicon Valley Bank Profit Squeeze," *supra*, note 30.

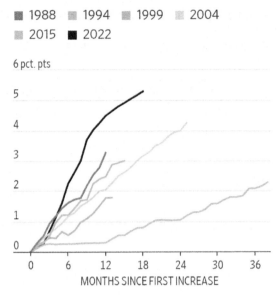

■ 1988 ■ 1994 ■ 1999 ■ 2004
■ 2015 ■ 2022

FIGURE 11.3 Cumulative change in federal-funds rate since start of initial rate increase.
Sources: Wall Street Journal & Federal Reserve, www.wsj.com/livecoverage/stock-market-today-dow-jones-08-22-2023/card/2-vs-3-the-debate-over-the-fed-s-inflation-target-tYIBiGcGqyBjp4BnaD50

0.25 percentage points each time.[33] In other words, the Fed raised rates in nine consecutive meetings in its efforts to rapidly reduce liquidity in the financial markets and control high inflation. From the Fed funds rate hovering around 0 percent in March 2022, the rate jumped to 4.75 percent in February 2023. In March 2023, the Fed funds rate was 4.75–5 percent.[34]

One thing was clear: The Fed was doing too much, too fast, and all at once, echoing the chaos in the movie in which Michelle Yeoh captured her Oscar.[35] Unlike the happy ending in *Everything Everywhere All at Once*, the Fed inflicted irreversible pain on SVB (Figure 11.3).

SVB's investments in long-term (10 years) securities which included Treasury bonds and mortgage-backed securities backfired. As the interest rates climbed up at a punishingly quick pace in a short time, SVB stared at its mounting losses on the investments. The Fed knew about the economic conditions SVB and other banks faced while holding the HTM and AFS securities: enormous amounts of unrealized losses on these investments. Figure 11.4, from the FDIC, illustrates the pain inflicted by interest rate hikes.[36]

---

[33] James Royal, "Biggest Winners and Losers from the Fed's Interest Rate Hike," *BankRate*, March 22, 2023.

[34] Brian O'Connell, "Understanding the Federal Funds Rate," *Forbes*, March 22, 2023.

[35] Jeff Sommer, "The Fed Is Doing Too Much, All at Once," *The New York Times*, March 31, 2023, available at: https://nyti.ms/3m1ieoL (last accessed September 29, 2023).

[36] Martin J. Gruenberg's Statement on Recent Bank Failures and the Federal Regulatory Response before the Committee on Banking, Housing, and Urban Affairs, United States Senate, March 28,

Unrealized Gains (Losses) on Investment Securities

FIGURE 11.4 Unrealized gains (losses) on investment securities experienced by banks. FDIC Chairman Gruenberg admitted that the data, demonstrated here, shows "elevated level of unrealized losses on investment securities due to high market interest rates." Remarks by FDIC Chairman Martin Gruenberg on the Fourth Quarter 2022 Quarterly Banking Profile, www.fdic.gov/news/speeches/2023/spfeb2823.html

As noted, William Martin, a short seller of Raging Venture, also stared at the same data of unrealized losses and SVB's earnings reports. Martin sent out his tweets, about the SVB's eminent blow-up, on January 18, 2023: "Investors have rightfully been fixated on $SIVB's large exposure to the stressed venture world, with the stock down a lot. However, dig just a little deeper, and you will find a much bigger set of problems at $SIVB." Martin explained that at first he suspected that he would find a weakness in SVB's loan portfolio to tech startups but he soon realized that SVB's fixed-income investments were the culprit of exposing the Bank to massive unrealized losses in the bond market. Martin saw that, on the one hand, SVB's clients withdrawing their deposits rapidly, and, on the other hand, the tech startup funding had been drying up while the startups themselves were burning cash at a higher pace as they could not raise fresh funding; together, the situation was set up for shorting the Bank's stock. Martin did just that.[37] Martin sent out a total of ten tweets

2023, available at: www.banking.senate.gov/imo/media/doc/Gruenberg%20Testimony%203-28-23 .pdf [https://perma.cc/EU9C-BV9Y] (last accessed September 29, 2023).

[37] Lee and Bloomberg, *supra*, note 30.

with images from the Bank's earnings reports illustrating a fuller picture of the Bank in distress.

The overstressed Bank was in plain sight but the regulators and the Bank addressed the problems in typical ways: the bank examiners issued six "matters requiring attention" in November 2021 but these did not amount to a serious concern.

In fact, the Bank was without a chief risk officer as of April 2022 but that warranted only three findings from the regulators relating to ineffective board oversight, risk management weaknesses, and the Bank's internal audit function. In other words, business continued as usual at the Bank in the first half of 2022. By the summer of 2022, the regulators lowered the Bank's management rating to "not well managed" and they subjected the Bank to growth restrictions. This showed that the regulators exhibited no specific concern about the Bank's interest rate risk profile at that time. Not until October 2022 did the regulators first raise concerns with the Bank's senior executives about the Bank's interest rate risk profile and, in November 2022, the regulators issued a supervisory finding on interest rate risk management to the Bank. Understandably, the regulators did not see any interest rate risk problems to discern in early 2022 because the Fed funds rate was around 0 percent in March 2022. The Federal Reserve, however, tried to taper down inflation by successively raising interest rates seven times during 2022, and the Fed's action caused the Bank to overstress. The supervisors finally sought the overstress as they delivered the supervisory finding on interest rate risk management to the Bank in 2022. In hindsight, their finding came too late. The finding sent the Bank into searching for ways to address the problem while the Fed continued to raise the interest rate by another 0.25 percentage point on February 1, 2023, and then again on March 3, 2023, by the same percentage point, exacerbating the Bank's interest rate risk profile and financial condition.

The Federal Reserve's Board of Governors finally received a briefing from staff in mid-February 2023 about the impact of rising interest rates on some banks' financial conditions. That was the first time the Fed learned in broad strokes about how their interest rate hikes impacted some banks, including Silicon Valley Bank. Even then, neither the Fed nor their staff was overly concerned about the fate of Silicon Valley Bank because the Fed's staff assured the big bosses that they were actively engaged with Silicon Valley Bank. In fact, Michael S. Barr, Vice Chair, FDIC, did not know about Silicon Valley Bank until the bank run on March 9.[38]

Martin J. Gruenberg, Chairman, and Barr, both of FDIC, appeared at the first federal hearing dated March 29, 2023, on the bank collapse, and took turns to accuse

---

[38] Michael S. Barr's Statement to the Committee on Financial Services, US House of Representatives, on March 29, 2023, available at: https://docs.house.gov/meetings/BA/BA00/20230329/115605/HHRG-118-BA00-Wstate-BarrM-20230329.pdf [https://perma.cc/SQF2-J8QC] (last accessed September 29, 2023).

SVB executives of waiting too long to address the Bank's financial conditions. Barr stated that the SVB's failure was a "textbook case of mismanagement." Sadly, if it were indeed a textbook case, the regulators should have prevented the collapse. The long hearing revealed that the regulators had neither the understanding nor the tools in place to monitor a bank like SVB that was "too tech to fail." Finger-pointing and blame games dominated the hearing.

Perhaps SVB believed that the VCs would return to the high rate of investments, high valuations would come back, plenty of cash would be available, and the Fed would not increase the interest rate. Perhaps SVB believed that all of its tech bros in the VC ecosystem would stand by its side because it had been the one and only truly tech community's bank for them in the last four decades. Perhaps not. But Becker tried too late.

In the last week of February 2023, on the 27th, the fate of Silicon Valley Bank was sealed. Silicon Valley Bank received the bad news from the credit rating agency Moody's that it was considering a double-downgrade of the Bank. Silicon Valley Bank reached out to the venerable Goldman Sachs investment bankers to raise capital and talked to private equity firms, including General Atlantic, for capital infusion, but the efforts yielded a plan of raising $2.25 billion via issuing shares for sale, including $500 million from General Atlantic.

SVB faced its fate by composing its own requiem through an announcement that all immediately and later criticized as the worst public relations communication in the history of banking, in addition to the ill-timing of the release of the announcement on the same day the Silvergate Bank announced that it would self-liquidate, a nice word for the bank's death. On that fateful date, Wednesday, March 8, 2023, after the market close, SVB announced that it realized a $1.8 billion loss in the sale of its available-for-sale (AFS) long-term securities in order to raise liquidity. SVB sold $21 billion worth of securities at an after-tax loss of $1.8 billion to remedy its liquidity problem. The announcement was a huge surprise to many in the tech industry. In the same announcement, the Bank also stated that it planned to raise capital during the following week. That meant the Bank was broadcasting to the world that it was still in a deep liquidity problem.

Perhaps the Bank should get a little credit for being honest, but the tech bros did not care much for that honesty. Becker urged the VC clients to "stay calm" and keep their deposits in the Bank during the Thursday, March 9, 2023, conference call. Becker explained that the Bank has "ample liquidity" and was in a "strong capital position." Becker's message, however, fell on deaf ears; the Bank's VC clients decided to abandon him and SVB.

Becker was no longer in control of his cathedral. The tech bros were in charge.[39] For instance, the executives at Founders Fund implored their investors to get their

---

[39] Elizabeth Spiers, "I Was an S.V.B. Client. I Blame the Venture Capitalists," *The New York Times*, March 16, 2023, available at: https://nyti.ms/3YLWA5q (last accessed September 29, 2023).

cash out of SVB and put the money into bigger banks and informed the public on the morning of Thursday, March 9, 2023, that they had already drained all of its SVB accounts.[40] They believed that they were doing the right thing. After all, tech companies could do no wrong, and tech bros were always in charge, not a bank! Tech bro Peter Thiel is a founding partner of Founders Fund, an $11 billion venture capital fund. Union Square Ventures and Coatue Management also advised their portfolio companies to withdraw their money from the Bank. SVB's top ten accounts parked $13 billion in deposits at the Bank. Most tech deposits at SVB were above $250,000. With cell phones in hand, tech talked and amplified tech's own hysteria of extracting their cash out of the Bank. Unlike a typical commercial bank where you must physically go to the bank, or some banks insist that you have to call first to make sure your bank would have money available, to withdraw a limited amount of your money, Silicon Valley Bank allowed you to withdraw all your money with ease and with a swipe of your finger.

Moody's released its downgrade. S&P followed with its own downgrade on SVB on Thursday, March 9, 2023. Short sellers and the rest of the market were ready to end the Bank. The planned share sale would not cure the Bank's vulnerability as Martin had exposed in his tweets in January 2023. The Bank's share price which had been dropping throughout 2022, sank 60 percent further on that Thursday.[41] Together, the short sellers made $500 million from the SVB collapse.[42]

All the tech bros and their investors, all the VCs and their portfolio companies, and all the tech companies that had accounts at the bank, through the echo chamber of social media, learned about the bank's vulnerability. Every tech company is for itself. The bank run began and tech drained $42 billion or a quarter of all SVB's deposits in one day – Thursday, March 9, 2023.

In denial, the Bank hosted venture capitalist Bill Reichert, Pegasus Tech Ventures, who presented "How to Pitch Your WOW? Investors" for about fifty people on its last night as a bank on Thursday, March 9, 2023. Mike McEvoy, CEO of OmniLayers, shared with *The Verge* that the vibe was eerie, and people looked subdued. Roger Sanford, CEO of Scare Health, stated that "Everyone was in denial. The band played on."[43] But only a few were still believing in the band.

[40] Dan Primack, "The Week That Killed Silicon Valley Bank," AXIOS, March 14, 2023, available at: www.axios.com/2023/03/14/week-that-killed-silicon-valley-bank [https://perma.cc/87JL-695E] (last accessed September 29, 2023).

[41] Erin Griffith and Rob Copeland, "Silicon Valley Bank's Financial Stability Worries Investors," *The New York Times*, March. 9, 2023.

[42] Breanna Bradham, "Short Sellers Make $500 Million on SVB's Demise. Collecting Won't Be Easy," *Bloomberg*, March 10, 2023 12:39 PM PST, available at: www.bloomberg.com/news/articles/2023-03-10/shorts-make-500-million-on-svb-demise-collecting-won-t-be-easy [https://perma.cc/J8QS-9SR6] (last accessed September 29, 2023).

[43] Nadiya Ivanenko, "The Technology Industry Developed So Quickly That It Broke SVB: Its Most Prestigious Bank," *Mezha Media*, March 13, 2023, available at: https://mezha.media/en/2023/03/13/the-technology-industry-developed-so-quickly-that-it-broke-svb-its-most-prestigious-bank/ [https://perma.cc/94WV-QEST] (last accessed September 29, 2023).

Market-to-market losses and uninsured deposit runs were gathering strength outside the subdued gathering.[44]

On Friday, March 10, 2023, the Bank executives contacted the Fed and informed it of the unthinkable news that an additional $100 billion withdrawal from the bank's tech clients had been scheduled.[45] The Bank must be shut down. The Bank's sudden death was inflicted with $142 billion cuts. The total withdrawals of $142 billion represented a staggering 81 percent of SVB's $175 billion in deposits as of year-end 2022. The long-treasured VC ecosystem and tech community of relationships, as the bank run demonstrated, amounted to empty words. Harry Kellogg could only scream in anguish as he witnessed the evaporation of the relationships that he helped build for decades. The world, according to Becker, came to a tragic end when bands of tech brothers abandoned their own tech community's bank. The cell phone, social media, and tech echo chamber swirled powerful forces of herd mentality to ignite the second largest bank run in US history, as the largest run on Washington Mutual bank during the 2008 financial crisis. SVB, with $212 billion in customer assets, created a system for their tech clients to easily park their deposits and initiate withdrawals, but that same system of tech-friendly-and-cell-phone-banking-at-your-command buried SVB alive.

The $142 billion cuts killed SVB, along with the beloved memories nursed by Robert Medearis, Roger Smith, and Bill Biggerstaff. Perhaps Smith's epitaph would be changed to read: "It was a good run." Of course, the pun was not intended.

* * * * *

TOO TECH TO FAIL

On Thursday, March 9, 2023, early morning, Alexander Torrenegra, who was a depositor at SVB for his two companies and his own personal banking, was in one chat with more than 200 tech founders in Silicon Valley and questions about SVB began to circulate. An hour later, at 10:00 a.m., some founders in the chat suggested getting money out of SVB because there were "only upside" and "no downside."[46]

VC firms in the United States and abroad fed on the whispered rumor of SVB's imminent bank run began their own campaign of broadcasting and amplifying the

---

[44] Erica Xuewei Jiang, Gregor Matvos, Tomasz Piskorski, and Amit Seru, "Monetary Tightening and U.S. Bank Fragility in 2023: Mark-to-Market Losses and Uninsured Depositor Runs?" Working Paper 31048, National Bureau of Economic Research, March 2023, www.nber.org/papers/w31048 [https://perma.cc/T3PP-27NZ] (last accessed September 29, 2023).

[45] Hugh Son, "SVB Customers Tried to Withdraw Nearly All the Bank's Deposits over Two Days, Fed's Barr Testifies," March 28, 2023 1:44 PM EDT, available at: www.cnbc.com/2023/03/28/svb-customers-tried-to-pull-nearly-all-deposits-in-two-days-barr-says.html [https://perma.cc/6297-9WC8] (last accessed September 29, 2023).

[46] Spiers, *supra*, note 398.

fear by urging all of their portfolio companies to move their funds out of SVB immediately. Pear VC, an early-stage VC firm based in San Francisco, sent an email to all of its portfolio companies to withdraw their money from SVB. Hoxton Ventures, a London-based VC firm, advised founders to withdraw their money in amounts equivalent to two months' worth of their burn from SVB.[47]

Bloomberg sent out an article that Peter Thiel's Founders Fund had advised their portfolio companies to pull money from Silicon Valley Bank due to concerns about SVB's financial stability.[48] According to the article, Founders Fund told the portfolio companies that there was no downside to taking all the money out. Seeking Alpha reported that venture capitalists themselves were moving their money out of SVB because they were afraid of a bank run.[49] *The LA Times* also ran an article credited to *Bloomberg* that Peter Thiel's Founders Fund and other VC firms had already urged their founders to take their money out of SVB.[50] Jenny Fielding, Managing Partner of The Fund, which invests in early-stage startups, shared that a "good deal of panic" was unfolding.[51]

Indeed, Garry Tan, CEO of Y Combinator, issued a warning to all of its startups, spreading the fear about SVB solvency risk:

> We have no specific knowledge of what's happening at SVB. But anytime you hear problems of solvency in any bank, and it can be deemed credible, you should take it seriously and prioritize the interests of your startup by not exposing yourself to more than $250K of exposure there. Your startup dies when you run out of money for whatever reason.[52]

When the commander on top of the pyramid instructs the followers to run, you run. If the commanders warn of your death if you don't run, you run and run as fast as you can. Tan and other VCs were the commanders and all portfolio companies and startups in their networks quickly followed in line, like sheep. Likewise, Tribe Capital, an apt name for a VC firm, did not want to fall behind, instructing the startups to follow suit by moving their cash out of SVB.[53]

[47] Ryan Browne and Hugh Son, "VCs Urge Startups to Withdraw Funds from SVB," *CNBC*, March 10, 2023.

[48] Katie Roof and Gillian Tan, "Peter Thiel's Founders Fund Tells Companies to Pull Money from Silion Valley Bank," *Bloomberg*, March 9, 2023.

[49] Jessica Kuruthukulangara, "VC Firms Pull Funds out of Silicon Valley Bank, CEO Asks Clients to Stay Calm," *Seeking Alpha*, March 9, 2023 6:47 PM ET, available at: https://seekingalpha.com/news/3946296-vc-firms-pull-funds-out-of-silicon-valley-bank-ceo-asks-clients-to-stay-calm-report [https://perma.cc/C9ZK-7XHF] (last accessed September 29, 2023).

[50] Hannah Miller, Gillian Tan, and Sarah McBride, "Silicon Valley Banks Tells Clients to 'Stay Calm' As Shares Sink," *Los Angeles Times*, March 9, 2023.

[51] Ibid.

[52] Ibid.

[53] Ibid.

In the fateful conference call, as reported by *The Information* at noon Pacific Time, Becker informed the VCs that "calls started coming and started the panic."[54] SVB broadcasted a higher-than-expected, double-digit percentage decline in deposits for 2023, eclipsing the decline that already took place in 2022.[55] Becker was still bullish; he asserted that SVB has "ample liquidity to support our clients with one exception: If everyone is telling each other SVB is in trouble, that would be a challenge."[56]

Becker told the tech bros to "stay calm" but they did not like to be told and, as tech bros, they love a challenge. He begged them "to support us just like we supported you during the challenging times." Tech bros did not like the begging as they are known to prefer hubris, arrogance, and the breaking-without-asking mentality. Tech bros were not interested in saving nor publicly extending support to SVB.[57]

The VCs and their portfolios created a stampede of online-deposit flight, a modern bank run. They drained $42 billion out of Silicon Valley Bank. After the market close on the Thursday, Silicon Valley Bank shares plunged 60 percent after Becker's infamous statement and SVB's disclosures about the Bank's plan to raise $2.25 billion to meet its liquidity needs.[58]

In premarket trading on the morning of Friday, March 10, 2023, Silicon Valley Bank shares tumbled another 60 percent.[59] The tech bros and founders scheduled $100 billion more for their withdrawals on top of the $42 billion they had just drained from SVB the day before.[60]

It turned out that Thursday evening of March 9, the FDIC was informed by the federal regulator, the Federal Reserve, of the deposit run at SVB, the Bank's subsequent funding debacle, and the liquidity demand problems. FDIC worked with the California Department of Financial Protection and Innovation (CADFPI), the charter authority of SVB, in an effort for a resolution. A couple of hours later, learning about the $100 billion scheduled outflows, the CADFPI appointed the FDIC as the receiver and SVB's life ended at 11:15 a.m. EST.

The tech baby cry exploded. When tech could not move their money out, they began crying in chorus. On March 10, the crypto firm Circle revealed that $3.3

---

[54] Erin Woo, Amir Efrati, Lauren Tara LaCapra, Michael Roddan, Kate Clark, and Kaya Yurieff, "Silicon Valley Bank CEO Tells VC Clients to 'Stay Calm,'" The Information, March 9, 2023 12:02 PM PST.

[55] Liz Hoffman and Reed Albergotti, "Some VC Firms Are Urging Founders to Pull Money from Troubled Silicon Valley Bank," SEMAFOR, March 10, 2023; SVB Financial Group Form 8-K, March. 8, 2023; Silicon Valley Bank Strategic Actions/Q1 2023 Mid-Quarter Update, March 8, 2023.

[56] Kuruthukulangara, *supra*, note 49.

[57] Hoffman and Albergotti, *supra*, note 55.

[58] Kuruthukulangara, *supra*, note 49.

[59] Browne and Son, *supra*, note 47.

[60] Son, *supra*, note 45; Ben Eisen, "SVB Expected $100 Billion in Outflows on Day It Was Seized, Fed's Barr Says," Wall Street Journal, March 28, 2023.

billion of its $40 billion reserves were hoarded in Silicon Valley Bank. Circle, the principal operator of USD stablecoin, touting itself as "the leading dollar digital currency powering always-on internet-native commerce and payments with a circulation greater than $33 billion and over $1.3 trillion in-on-chain transactions," in November 2021 to launch a VC fund for early stage crypto startups.[61] Circle investors included Wall Street's bold names, asset manager BlackRock Inc., Fidelity Management and hedge fund firm Marshall Wace.[62] Flushed with enthusiastic interests in crypto, the fund, even without a predetermined total fund amount, was reported to already deployed initial capital on blockchain projects to support its mission "to raise global economic prosperity through the frictionless exchange of financial value."[63] With $3.3 billion stuck at the collapsed SVB, crypto investors scrambled to cash out over $2 billion worth of USDC within 24 hours, causing Circle's USDC stablecoin to break as the dollar-pegged coin fell below 87 cents.[64] Circle attempted to transfer its $3.3 billion out of SVB on Thursday but no settlements occurred before the Fed shut down the bank. Another crypto firm with money parked at Silicon Valley Bank is BlockFi, a crypto lender which filed for bankruptcy in November as part of the FTX contagion, with $227 million at Silicon Valley Bank.[65] Crypto firms took to traditional and social media crying about the skies falling because their billions were unprotected by the FDIC.

Lost in the louder tech cries were the stories about tech startups unable to meet their payrolls because their funds were stuck in accounts at Silicon Valley Bank.[66] Media outlets quickly focused on the payroll problem. For many tech companies, the next pay period was a few days away, and tech and news media reports put pressure on the regulators to allow depositors to gain access to their funds.[67] Startup

[61] "Circle Launches 'Circle Impact' to Improve Financial Inclusion, Digital Financial Literacy and Humanitarian Response via Digital Currency," *CISION*, available at: www.prnewswire.com/news-releases/circle-launches-circle-impact-to-improve-financial-inclusion-digital-financial-literacy-and-humanitarian-response-via-digital-currency-301426062.html (last accessed October 3, 2023); Brandy Betz, "Circle Launches Venture Capital Fund for Early Stage Blockchain Projects," *CoinDesk*, November 9, 2021.

[62] Vicky Ge Huang, Hannah Miao, and Caitlin Ostroff, "Circle's USDC Stable Breaks Peg with $3.3 Billion Stuck at Silicon Valley Bank," *Wall Street Journal*, March 11, 2023.

[63] Betz, *supra*, note 61.

[64] Huang et al., *supra*, note 62.

[65] Becky Yerak, "Bankrupt BlockFi Has $227 Million in Unprotected Funds at Silicon Valley Bank," *Wall Street Journal*, March 10, 2023.

[66] "Companies Scramble to Meet Payroll, Pay Bills after SVB's Collapse," *CNBC*, March 10, 2023; "Tech Startup Leaders Concerned About Making Payroll," *GeekWire*, March 10, 2023; Megan Hernbroth and Michael Flaherty, "Startups Fear Delayed Payrolls amid Silicon Valley Bank's Collapse," *AXIOS*, March 10, 2023.

[67] Dan Primack, "This Weekend Is Everything for Silicon Valley Bank and Its Customers," *AXIOS*, March 10, 2023; Greg Bensinger, Anna Tong, Krystal Hu, and Jeffrey Dastin, "SVB Shutdown Sends Shockwaves through Silicon Valley as CEOs Race to Make Payroll," *Reuters*, March 12, 2023; Hannah Miller, Katie Roof, and Priya Anand, "Startups Are Worried Paying Employees after SVB," *Bloomberg*, March 10, 2023.

founders expressed their worries about whether they were able to keep paying their employees, and whether their companies would survive.[68]

Tech idealists have long preached their disdain for government. They view the government as an innovation nuisance interfering with tech ideas and executions. When college students ask the government for loan forgiveness, tech bros decried such a bailout. But when tech billions were exposed and unprotected under the FDIC's limit of $250,000 for deposits, tech libertarians demanded a complete bailout.[69] With social media megaphones, they predicted an economic apocalypse if every dollar in all deposits was not back in the pockets of tech bros and their portfolio companies. The billionaire investor Bill Ackman ranted on Twitter Blue on March 11, 2023, and his long 649-word tweet garnered 14.6 million views.

Another billionaire investor, Mark Cuban, vented his frustration with the "too low" $250,000 FDIC guarantee. The Federal Reserve, according to Cuban, must completely rescue tech by purchasing all of SVB's assets and liabilities. Some tech libertarians were vocal as they sent their tweets in all caps warning of a stampede for cash by Americans at local banks across the United States.[70]

The tech industry also dialed up their lobbying power. Representative Eric Swalwell, a California Democrat, tweeted out on Friday, March 10, 2023, that "We must make sure all deposits exceeding the FDIC $250k are honored. Banking is about confidence. If depositors lose confidence in the safety of their deposits over 250k then we are in trouble." Congressman Ro Khanna, Democrat, who represented the California District where Silicon Valley Bank was headquartered, sprang into action as calls came demanding protection for tech's massive and uninsured deposits. On the "Face the Nation" show on CBS, Khanna portrayed the depositors as "payroll companies," "climate startups," "startups that are helping cure cancer," "companies in the wine industry," "companies that are dealing with AI and defense to keep us ahead of China," and "50,000 of them employing Americans across the country" who "just had their money in a bank."[71] Khanna called on the Biden Administration to take "decisive action" on Silicon Valley Bank's collapse.

Decisive action was what the government did in rescuing tech and all of their billions in deposits. To protect insured depositors, the FDIC created the Deposit Insurance National Bank (DINB) to provide insured depositors with access to their

[68] Dara Kerr, "Startups 'On Pins and Needles' until Their Funds Clear from Silicon Valley Bank," *National Public Radio*, March 13, 2023.

[69] Sara Morrison, "What Happens to Silicon Valley without Silicon Valley Bank?," VOX, March 16, 2023.

[70] @jason, *Twitter*, March 11, 2023, available at: https://twitter.com/Jason/status/1634771851514900480 (last accessed September 29, 2023); Edward Ongweso Jr., "The Incredible Tantrum Venture Capitalists Threw over Silicon Valley Bank," *Slate*, March 13, 2023.

[71] "Face the Nation Transcript: Rep. Ro Khanna on 'Face the Nation'," *CBS News*, March 12, 2023 12:18 PM, available at: www.cbsnews.com/news/ro-khanna-face-the-nation-transcript-03-12-2023/ [https://perma.cc/BV7M-WLWA] (last accessed September 29, 2023).

funds.[72] On Sunday, March 12, 2023, the FDIC announced that all uninsured depositors can obtain an advance dividend against their claims for the uninsured amounts when DINB was scheduled to reopen on Monday, March 13, 2023.[73] In fact, the Department of the Treasury, Federal Reserve, and FDIC released a Joint Statement that the FDIC could use emergency systemic risk authorities under the Federal Deposit Insurance Act (FDI Act) to fully protect all depositors. All of their deposits in the amount of hundreds of billion would be fine. The government swiftly rescued tech.

The regulators assured the public that any losses to the FDIC's Deposit Insurance Fund as a result of rescuing tech customers of Silicon Valley Bank would be repaid by "a special assessment on banks as required by law." The tech rescue cost to the FDIC insurance fund was estimated at over $20 billion.

Many others, politicians and ordinary people, were unhappy with the government's rescue of tech companies as uninsured depositors. Some were baffled by the online tantrums of tech investors who caused the SVB crisis, shifted the blame thereafter, and demanded rescue.[74] Others observed tech hypocrisy for a government bailout.[75]

With a bold face, a group of more than 5,000 tech CEOs and founders vocalized their righteousness that they "are not asking for a bank bailout" because they only wanted the uninsured billions back to them. Tech commander, Garry Tan, CEO of Y Combinator, led the herd again, this time with a letter to Secretary Janet Yellen, FDIC Chairman Martin J. Gruenberg, US Senator Sherrod Brown, and US Congressman & Chairman Patrick McHenry:

> We, the undersigned, are deeply concerned about the rapid failure of Silicon Valley Bank, a leading financial institution that has played a vital role in supporting the technology industry in the United States. We are not asking for a bailout for the bank equity holders or its management; we are asking you to save innovation in the American economy.

[72] FDIC Press Release, FDIC Creates a Deposit Insurance National Bank of Santa Clara to Protect Insured Depositors of Silicon Valley Bank, Santa Clara, California, March 10, 2023, available at: www.fdic.gov/news/press-releases/2023/pr23016.html [https://perma.cc/9GB2-CHRQ] (last accessed September 29, 2023).

[73] FDIC Press Release, Joint Statement by the Department of the Treasury, Federal Reserve, and FDIC, March 12, 2023, available at: www.fdic.gov/news/press-releases/2023/pr23017.html [https://perma.cc/89YH-RL2K] (last accessed September 29, 2023).

[74] Ongweso, *supra*, note 70.

[75] Niccolo Caldararo, "How SVB Rescue Shows the Hypocrisy of Tech Economy," *Financial Times*, March 30, 2023; John Naughton: "The SVB Debacle Has Exposed the Hypocrisy of Silicon Valley," *Mutual Fund Observer*, March 18, 2023; "The Tech Industry's Latest Reckoning: Should It be Blamed for SVB's Failure? The Need for Emergency Government Action Was the Latest Black Eye for an Industry Whose Reputation has Taken Repeated Punches in the Past Few Years," *NBC News*, March 15, 2023; Michael Hiltzik, "Silicon Valley Libertarians' Hypocrisy over SVB Bailout," *Los Angeles Times*, March 12, 2023; Erin Griffith and Mike Isaac, "After Bank Debacle, Silicon Valley Reckons with Its Image," *The New York Times*, March 13, 2023.

We ask for relief and attention to an immediate critical impact on small businesses, startups, and their employees who are depositors at the bank. According to the NVCA, Silicon Valley Bank has over 37,000 small businesses with more than $250,000 in deposits. These balances are now unavailable to them, and without further intervention, according to the FDIC website, may be inaccessible for months to years.

In the Y Combinator community, one-third of startups with exposure to SVB used SVB as their sole bank account. As a result, they will fail to have the cash to run payroll in the next 30 days. By that measure, we can estimate that payroll-related furlough or shutdown will impact more than 10,000 small businesses and startups. If the average small business or startup employs 10 workers, this will have an immediate effect of furlough, layoff, or shut down, affecting over 100,000 jobs in the most vibrant sector of innovation in our economy.

Silicon Valley Bank's failure has a real risk of systemic contagion. Its collapse has already instilled fear among founders and management teams to look for safer havens for their remaining cash, which can trigger a bank run on every other smaller bank.

If we allow this to happen, it will immediately impact the US technology industry and US competitiveness worldwide and ultimately set back US competitiveness by a decade or more, while the rest of the world races forward.

We have a simple ask:
- Small business depositors at Silicon Valley Bank should be made whole. Regulators need to conduct a backstop of depositors. We are not asking for a bank bailout.
- Longer term, Congress should work to restore stronger regulatory oversight and capital requirements for regional banks, and any malfeasance or mismanagement on the part of SVB executives leading to this failure should be investigated.

This requires swift and decisive action in order to prevent further shockwaves through the economy that could lead to financial crisis and layoffs of more than 100,000 workers. We must protect US competitiveness in the world.

Thank you for your attention to this important matter.

Sincerely,

Garry Tan, CEO & President Y Combinator

Mr. Tan, who a few days earlier had participated in spreading the rumor about the SVB solvency crisis and the urgency of deposit flights or facing death, fetched signatures of more than 5,000 tech CEOS and founders, representing 400,000 employees.[76] The tech letter was supported by the billionaire hedge-fund Bill Ackman's tweet that "this was not a bailout" on Sunday, March 12, 2023. The

---

[76] "Sign Our Petition: Thousands of Startups and Hundreds of Thousands of Startup Jobs Are at Risk," Garry Tan, CEO & President Y Combinator, available at: https://docs.google.com/forms/

White House avoided the word "bailout" to quell down anger expressed in different quarters.[77] When tech bros speak, regulators and politicians listen. They surely did.

The federal regulators announced that $175 billion in tech deposits would be backstopped by the federal government. The FDIC insurance cap of $250,000 was removed for tech. There was no doubt, it was a bailout for the VC firms and tech companies. Furthermore, the federal regulators essentially provided a new kind of insurance on interest-rate risk for banks. The government bailout implied that future banks facing liquidity problems stemming from interest-rate risks investments could look to the government again for rescue.

* * * * *

The FDIC created Silicon Valley Bridge Bank, N.A. on March 13, 2023, after being the receiver of the former SVB by the California Department of Financial Protection and Innovation. The Silicon Valley Bridge Bank resumed the SVB's banking operations while the FDIC gained some time to stabilize the chaos and find a buyer for some of SVB's assets.

As of March 10, 2023, SVB had around $167 billion in total assets and approximately $119 billion in total deposits. The FDIC placed the SVB on the auction block, severing different assets for different suitors while the parent company of SVB filed for bankruptcy on March 17, 2023. Finally, a buyer emerged. First Citizens Bank, a bank with about $100 billion in assets, headquartered in North Carolina, bought SVB's deposits and loans from the FDIC in a deal announced by the regulators late on Sunday night, March 26, 2023. On the following Monday, the name Silicon Valley Bank or SVB was gone as SVB's seventeen branches opened as First Citizens Bank. First Citizens got itself a deal of the year by paying only $16.5 billion for SVB's assets of $72 billion. First Citizens also assumed Silicon Valley Bank's $56 billion in deposits. The FDIC also agreed to share losses with First Citizens for SVB's loan portfolio. The FDIC held on to $90 billion worth of SVB's assets and securities in receivership. The FDIC estimated that the SVB's collapse would cost the FDIC Insurance Fund $20 billion.[78]

Far from the tech innovation epicenter of Silicon Valley, First Citizens is based in Raleigh, N.C. with its roots in serving agricultural customers in 1898 in Johnston County. Not until the 1970s did First Citizens open branches across North Carolina

---

d/e/1FAIpQLSdo_oJOGdaXSDs-WaAXzzEy_tR7akOF7GBTfTb-r-MeotrNPQ/viewform?usp=
sf_link (last accessed September 29, 2023)

[77] Bobby Allyn, "The White House Is Avoiding One Word When It Comes to Silicon Valley Bank: Bailout," *National Public Radio*, March 14, 2023.

[78] FDIC Press Release, First-Citizens Bank & Trust Company, Raleigh, NC, to Assume All Deposits and Loans of Silicon Valley Bridge Bank, N.A., From the FDIC," March 26, 2023, available at: www.fdic.gov/news/press-releases/2023/pr23023.html [https://perma.cc/7WEJ-L5QE] (last accessed September 29, 2023); Elliot Smith, "First Citizens Shares Soar 50% after the Bank Buys a Large Chunk of Failed Silicon Valley Bank," *CNBC*, March 27, 2023.

and moved its headquarters from Smithfield to Raleigh with assets of over $1 billion. In 1994, First Citizens ventured outside of North Carolina to open a branch in West Virginia. In 1957, R. P. Holding, the founder of First Citizens passed away and left the management of the bank to his three sons. In 2009, Frank B. Holding, Jr. was elected Chairman of First Citizens. Along with his sister, Hope Holding Bryant, the third generation of the Holding family controls the bank.

By 2022, First Citizens had 500 branches in 22 states. The acquisition of the deeply discounted but prized SVB's assets pushed First Citizens' shares up 50 percent on Monday, 27, 2023. First Citizens immediately recalculated its assets, adding SVB's assets at the whole price instead of the discounted price, and updated on its website that First Citizens now has $218 billion in assets. With the acquisition at a deep discount, First Citizens jumped from being the thirtieth to the fourteenth largest bank based on assets overnight.[79] How First Citizens would serve tech entrepreneurs is a challenge to be discovered very shortly. Some investors wondered about the logic of the deal.[80]

* * * *

TOO WOKE TO FAIL?

In the wake of SVB's collapse, the immediate response from Republicans was that the Bank was too woke. Florida Governor Ron DeSantis framed his talking points around SVB being too focused on policies around diversity and ESG. With the government's bailout plan for SVB's depositors of VCs and tech companies, US Republican Senator Josh Hawley labeled Silicon Valley Bank as "too woke to fail."[81] Hawley insisted that the federal government bailed out SVB because the Bank was woke, the Bank invested in climate change startups that received financial backing from powerful people. Hawley also tweeted that SVB failed because it was "funding woke garbage ('climate change solutions') rather than actual banking and now a

---

[79] Federal Reserve Statistical Release: Large Commercial Banks, March 31, 2023, available at: www.federalreserve.gov/releases/lbr/current/ [https://perma.cc/M6PS-PHAN] (last accessed September 29, 2023) (ranking of banks as of March 31, 2022).

[80] Joel Rosenblatt, "First Citizens Sues HSBC for Stealing SVB Staff, Secrets," *Bloomberg*, May 22, 2023 ("First Citizens Bank & Trust Co. sued HSBC Holdings Plc for allegedly raiding dozens of employees from Silicon Valley Bank in a scheme dubbed "Project Colony" as First Citizens was taking over the failed California lender."); DanielWiessner, "First Citizens Sues HSBC for Hiring Away Silicon Valley Bank Staff," *Reuters*, May 22, 2023; Dan Ennis, "First Citizens Sues HSBC over the Departure of 42 SVB Bankers," *Banking Dive*, May 23, 2023 ("First Citizens Bank sued HSBC on Monday, claiming the British lender poached more than forty bankers from the failed Silicon Valley Bank so it could gain access to SVB's confidential, proprietary, and trade secret information about tech and healthcare clients.").

[81] Sahil Kapur, "Josh Hawley Labels Silicon Valley Bank 'Too Woke to Fail'," *NBC News*, March 16, 2023.

handout from taxpayers to save them." Simply, there was no evidence to support the assertion that banking and lending to climate tech startups and embracing the ESG disclosure framework caused the bank to fail.

On gender and racial diversity, SVB's collapse laid bare a void in the tech ecosystem for women, Black founders, and immigrant entrepreneurs. News media reckoned that minority founders would hurt the most.[82] Black entrepreneurs are historically excluded from the VC industry; Black founders receive a pittance of 2 percent of all VC dollars. The reality is harsh for Black female founders; they see less than 1 percent of all VC dollars.[83] In dollars, Black founders raised $264 million out of the total $33.6 billion in venture capital.[84] In 2022, venture capital for Black founders sank 45 percent.[85] The SVB collapse further shrunk funding opportunities for Black entrepreneurs.

Inclusion and diversity in the funding, again, took a back seat because the VC industry has always invested in white men. Many investors continue to consider investing in Black entrepreneurs as a riskier bet.[86] After George Floyd was murdered by the police and unrest exploded across the countries, some tech titans and VC firms turned their philanthropic attention to believing that investing in Black founders and Black-led startups are good market-based investments after all. That led to a change in 2021, Black founders and Black-led startups witnessed historic gains in securing VC funding.[87] All that attention immediately frizzled during tech contraction in 2022 before the SVB shutdown.

For startup founders who were never members of the tech bros circles, the loss of SVB was agony.[88] Isa Watson, founder and CEO of Squad, a voice-only social messaging app, shared with CNBC her observations that many of the Black founders like her reacted differently than the white founders; they were more distraught over SVB's collapse because SVB was known to support founders from diverse

[82] Ellen McGirt, "Silicon Valley Bank's Collapse Is a Blow to Black Founders and Immigrant Entrepreneurs," *Fortune*, March 21, 2023; Kat Stafford, Claire Savage, and the Associated Press, "Silicon Valley Bank Collapse Means Startup Founders of Color Lose One of Their Biggest Financial Havens," *Fortune*, March 24, 2023; Dominic-Madori Davis, "'Trust Is a Hard Thing to Earn': SVB's Closure Could Disproportionately Affect Black Founders," *TechCrunch*, March 15, 2023 ("The social impact of Silicon Valley Bank was 'unparalleled'.").

[83] Cheyenne DeVon, "'It Was Agony': Why SVB's Collapse Is Especially Hard as a Black Founder, says CEO," *CNBC*, March 24, 2023.

[84] Kori Hale, "What Silicon Valley Bank Collapse Means for Black Entrepreneurs," *Forbes*, March 14, 2023.

[85] Gabrielle Fonrouge, "Venture Capital for Black Entrepreneurs Plummeted 45% in 2022, Data Shows," *CNBC*, February 2, 2023.

[86] Ibid.

[87] "Former Microsoft CEO Steve Ballmer Invests $400 Million to Support Black Entrepreneurs," *CNBC*, October 21, 2022 9:14 AM EDT, available at: www.cnbc.com/video/2022/10/21/former-microsoft-ceo-steve-ballmer-invests-400-million-to-support-black-entrepreneurs.html (last accessed September 29, 2023).

[88] Stafford et al., *supra*, note 82.

backgrounds.[89] Watson recounted how SVB went "above and beyond" typical banking services in an industry that is traditionally hostile to Blacks. SVB connected Black founders to investors by ensuring "the front-row seats at industry events" enabling Watson to meet with investors and arranging for her to be "in front of users in her company's target demographic."[90]

Joey Womack, cofounder of the Atlanta Black Tech, Kelly Burton, CEO of the Black Innovation Alliance, Sherrel Dorsey, the founder of the Black tech-focused research firm The Plug, and many other tech entrepreneurs noted that SVB's failure would translate into a decrease in support for the Black tech ecosystem across the United States.[91]

Indeed, SVB was a major supporter across the Black entrepreneurial ecosystem; the Bank was known among Black founders for partnering with Black VC to create the inaugural State of Black Venture report which surveyed Black entrepreneurs and gathered the data "to set a baseline" against future progress toward equitable representations. Both SVB and BLCK VC shared the belief that what gets measured gets improved.[92] Which bank will now fund the State of Black report going forward? Most likely, no one.

On the other side of the Atlantic, in London, remember the good old days, SVB hosted Black founders at a breakfast meeting of networking and panel discussions with Q&A on venture debt? SVB brought black founders to the table to meet other founders, bankers, and lawyers from Wilson Sonsini, providing opportunities to learn and discuss how to finance startups' growth.[93]

In the wake of SVB's collapse, Reign Venture canceled its Black Founder ecosystems networking events at SXSW because SVB was its major financial backer. VC+Include, an organization founded to support the pipeline of BIPOC fund managers voiced its concerns about the immediate and future funding and challenges of Black founders.

For female founders, the SVB collapse hit them quite hard. No other bank had stepped up in the last forty years to address the funding gap for women in tech. SVB

[89] DeVon, *supra*, note 83.
[90] Ibid.
[91] J. J. McCorvey, "Black Founders Who Banked with SVB Fear Backsliding on Hard-Won Gains," *NBC News*, March 16, 2023, 4:00 AM PDT, available at: www.nbcnews.com/business/business-news/black-entrepreneurs-used-silicon-valley-bank-fear-broader-fallout-rcna75133 [https://perma.cc/8VVB-9ED2] (last accessed September 29, 2023) ("Silicon Valley Bank earned mostly good reviews from entrepreneurs of color who recalled strained alliances with the financial industry. The collapse has struck some as a potentially lasting setback.").
[92] "State of Black Venture," *BLCK Venture*, 2022, 2023, available at: www.blckvc.org/state-black-venture-2022 [https://perma.cc/FDM7-JKUN] (last accessed September 29, 2023).
[93] "SVB & Google For Startups Black Founders Fund Present Venture Debt & US Expansion," *SVB*, September 13, 2022, available at: https://events.svb.com/svbandgoogleforstartupsblackfoundersfund (last accessed September 29, 2023).

was the only bank that had started to address the gender disparity.[94] The Bank became bullish about helping female entrepreneurs.[95] SVB collected the data and saw that only 7 percent of total VC dollars went to companies with female founders in 2019. The Bank believed that the lack of female VCs or general partners influences funding decisions. SVB knew its power within the tech ecosystem, used that power, and articulated a bold plan to bring more dollars to female founders. Here is what Lorraine Monick, SVB Private Bank, explained a year before the collapse:

> First of all, core values recognize the importance of embracing diverse perspectives. One of our core values is we embrace diverse perspectives. Second, SVB has initiated comprehensive reporting to transparently share the industry's current state of the participation of women founders and investors as is noted in the Women in the US Technology Leadership Report. Third, SVB is transparent with our own success of diversity inclusion and we also disclose our workforce gender and race and ethnicity data publicly on our website. We aim to be transparent, and clear, and our reporting aims to accommodate various country laws, including privacy. Fourth, SVB gives all of its employees opportunities to be involved in our many initiatives aimed at supporting women and founders and other underrepresented communities.[96]

> We are a founding partner and investor in the board list, which connects diverse executives with global board opportunities. We're a founding partner of All Raise, which has a goal of increasing VC funding for women founders to 25% of total VC investments in five years. As a final example, for the last 20 years, SVB has been a partner in Ostia, which works to increase investment in women-led startups.

Liz Giorgi, a cofounder of Soona, a virtual photoshoot company, experienced rejection from two dozen banks but SVB welcomed her as a client.[97] Female founders told news media how SVB had assisted them and raised concerns that the funding doors once opened by SVB would now close on female entrepreneurs again.

Whether First Citizens will recognize women and Black entrepreneurs as first citizens is a wait-and-see story. Whether First Citizens will serve as the connector to link women and Black entrepreneurs to investors is unknown at the moment. Hopefully, the investors do not return to business-as-usual of all-things-white-men. Investors should not ignore studies that have established that diversity enhances innovation. The innovation economy dictated by tech bros, unfortunately, will continue to be hostile to women and Black entrepreneurs.

SVB's death ended a meaningful ESG embrace by a tech bank.

[94] Kelsey Butler, "SVB Helped Close the Funding Gap for Women and Minority Founders," *Bloomberg*, March 16, 2023.

[95] Shannon Saccocia and Lorraine Monick, "How Female Founders Rise to the Challenge," *SVB*, March 21, 2022, available at: www.svb.com/private-bank/insights/wealth-insights/how-female-founders-rise-to-the-challenge [https://perma.cc/A7AK-S6SE] (last accessed September 29, 2023).

[96] Ibid.

[97] Ibid.

A NEW SEASON?

Two weeks after the SVB collapse, reports about the chillier reception tech startups received from investors surfaced. Many investors decided to pull back their money further in addition to the tech funding retrenchment in 2022. Some investors reoriented their focus on their existing startups and declined to jump on potential deals. Founders cried that no new checks were coming from investors.[98] Other investors, however, found new opportunities in the hyped artificial intelligence and generative AI, and money found almost no boundaries in the hype.

Open AI released GPT-4. The new artificial intelligence program aced the bar exam and AP tests. News and reports about the wonders and destructions of AI dominated headlines. Everywhere and everyone and AI were on at full speed. Google rolled out Bard but failed. Microsoft giggled. A Google top researcher in AI resigned after learning Bard was trained on stolen data from ChatGPT. The race for AI intensified and so did the money thrown by investors searching for AI projects to fund. Investors' FOMO – Fear of Missing Out – was back in full force but only in the AI space.[99]

For instance, a new startup, Mobius AI, with four former Google AI researchers formed a new AI company that could generate its own photos and videos. News reported that Andreessen Horowitz and Index Ventures rushed in with a funding offer, and the startup of one week old was valued in the neighborhood of $100 million. Other investors heard about the startup and didn't want to miss out so they begged for an opportunity to fund Mobius. Anything with generative AI attracted investors' attention, and valuations for such AI startups rocketed again, and incredulously climbed beyond 2021's valuations for startups.

Take Dust, yes, that is the name of a new startup founded by two of OpenAI's former employees, who have already received funding offers. Media reported that, after the SVB collapse, Dust rejected a generous funding offer from Coatue, the same VC firm where tech bros urged their portfolio companies to abandon Silicon Valley Bank. What does Dust possess or what is Dust? Dust aims "to build AI tools that improve white-collar workers' productivity" or a euphemism that cynics may say is to dismantle white-collar jobs.[100] Dust secured a $5 million funding round led by none other than Sequoia Capital, which bestowed Dust a valuation of $30–$40 million. Dust was courted by investors who came with valuations twice the amount Dust decided to accept from Sequoia.

[98] Erin Griffith, "Silicon Valley Bank's Collapse Chills Start-Up Funding," *The New York Times*, March 27, 2023.

[99] Erin Griffith and Cade Metz, "'Let 1,000 Flowers Bloom': A.I. Funding Frenzy Escalates," *The New York Times*, March 14, 2023.

[100] Krystal Hu and Jeffrey Dastin, "Venture Capitalists Race to Land Next AI Deal on Big Tech's Turf," *Reuters*, March 24, 2023.

OpenAI could not hold on to its employees. Each tech man, yes, often man, is for himself. Former employees of OpenAI propped up Perplexity AI. The company enjoyed a valuation of $150 million from a deal led by NEA with money from Google and Meta handing Perplexity an amount of $20–$25 million. Opportunistic investors reign the day. Benchmark-backed LangChain. OpenAI raised $13 billion from Microsoft. Anthropic, another AI startup raised $300 million in early 2023. Salesforce announced in the week of the SVB collapse that it created a $250 million fund in generative AI startups.

VCs are in open season for AI deals descending on Big Tech's space. Deals are reportedly closed in days instead of weeks. The tech bros are always in charge, again. The mantra of "disruption is inevitable" is back on top, as Konstantine Buhler, a Sequoia Capital partner who led the Dust deal preached.[101] The tech bros are telling everyone that AI is the new internet.[102] The investors have lavished $5.9 billion on AI early-stage companies since 2022. Founders pitched everything and everywhere AI. Fifty of YCombinator's 218 companies are working on generative AI. Welcome back to the herd mentality of tech. AI is the new season now, the bright spot for the retrenched and depressed VC market.

Where will these startups park their fresh cash from the VCs? Which bank will touch those deposits knowing that these startups will burn the cash so fast? Which bank will make a loan to a startup without profit? Which bank will bank startups who may also burn themselves down so soon thereafter? Which bank will happily become the new bank of tech when the tech bros are still the lords and commanders with cell phones in hand and social media for amplification?

In this new season of reckoning and learning about SVB's history and place within the tech ecosystem, the regulators should leave tech lending alone. The business model created by SVB is a safe and sound banking practice. The low ratio loans to deposit employed by SVB should continue to provide significant comfort to the regulators about tech lending. Of course, the tech lending model is dependent on the support of the VCs themselves, and the VCs know that they always need a bank with a strong understanding of the tech ecosystem to serve them and their portfolio companies. Whoever emerges as the new bank or banks to serve the innovators, whether in Silicon Valley or innovation centers across the United States, should gather the VCs to speak to the regulators. The regulators should take time to learn about the VC industry and different types of VCs and associated risks. Tech lending will not work if the VCs who back a tech company decided to walk away, exposing the lenders to enormous risks. Evaluating the quality of the VCs is part of the equation that the regulators must comprehend.

SVB built intensive personal relationships with all the VCs throughout its history and leveraged the relationships into insider knowledge in carving the tech lending

---

[101] Ibid.
[102] Ibid.

practices. New banks in tech lending will face an uphill climb to build VC relationships because the bankers must go to tech for business instead of sitting in the offices waiting for tech investors and founders to walk through the door. New banks should learn from what SVB has demonstrated: that traditional banking practices fail to serve tech. New banks should learn that to serve tech the bankers must be the lubricants that bring different stakeholders in tech together. That means the conference inside the bank belongs to startup clients who need the space to hold a meeting when the tech CEOs and founders make a request. That means the bank does not close at 5:00 p.m. because the bankers would convene various workshops and gathering events for founders, influencers, mentors, investors, lawyers, accountants, and other stakeholders in the tech ecosystem during the evening hours. That means the bankers deeply plant themselves into the fabric of the tech ecosystem. That means the bankers are the cheerleaders, the counselors, the confidants, and the connectors to nurture startups – many of which, without the support, would wither.

The regulators must understand tech funding in order to truly comprehend the deposit side. Very few tech companies receive VC backing. That means the VCs themselves have in their arsenal methods of valuating and selecting tech companies to fund. Top-tier VCs are sophisticated investors. Competition in the VC space is fierce and FOMO is real. Investors who put their money in VC funds come from a wide range of sources and many different countries. As the tech industry has occupied a large segment of the economy, tech investments are sensitive to the macroeconomy. The regulators should learn about the investors' side.

Consequently, regulating a bank with a strong focus on serving tech startups dictates the regulators to be concerned not just about size. The regulators must anticipate how interest rate hikes by the Federal Reserve severely impact banks' investments in long-term Treasuries and bonds, particularly for banks catering to the tech industry. The regulators must realize that, in the race to be the first mover with the first idea in the marketplace, startups are very risky because they can burn cash faster than they have stated to the investors. The bank, unfortunately, does not possess this insider information at the speed of Twitter (or X) to address the quickly percolated problem. Insisting startups place their accounts at the bank so the bank can monitor the spending is a prudent practice but that alone is not sufficient. The bank still lacks intelligence about the cash burn rates at a particular startup. The bank still lacks intelligence on whether the investors are planning to walk away or decline to infuse the startup with new funding.

If the investors decline to participate in the new round, no new cash will come in, and the deposit associated with that startup will face both fast outflow and little-to-zero inflow. The huge deposit is almost gone in a short period of time in the startup's existence, meaning, the fast withdrawals of the deposit at the bank. This poses a real risk to the bank on its liquidity. That means the regulators must focus on the bank's mitigation of risks relating to startups' unpredictable withdrawals as their burn rate can quickly change and as investors change their minds refusing to infuse new funding. Whether regulators would require a larger reserve, a new diversified approach to investments by the bank of the deposits, a cap on how much a bank should accept in tech deposits, a new insurance system for banks accepting tech deposits, and a more frequent examination of the banks operating in the tech ecosystem. All of these may cause an increase in the cost of banking and lending to tech startups. This may mean that having an account at the bank for a startup's operating expenses will cost the startup. But all of the new cost increase is significantly less than facing another destructive bank run.

Social media risks are an extreme risk to banking tech startups. Regulators must factor in this newly realized type of risk in banking. The wildfire analogy is no longer apt in the age of social media communications of echo chambers and amplifications. Tech clients are gossipy, and as SVB's failure demonstrated, tech clients are smart but severely lack an understanding of how banks invest deposits and how banks are regulated, and they can spread rumors in their echo chambers, chatgroups, emails, Twitter (X), and other social media outlets. When the rumors spread, banks face insurmountable tasks of controlling their own narratives of rational reason.

Social media risks can destroy the long-term relationships the new bank creates with the VC ecosystem when the investors themselves participate in inciting and amplifying a possible bank run because of the investors' own lack of understanding about the banking system. The new bank cannot rely on their clients of VC investors to control the rumors or the exposure to social media risks.

The regulators in the tech banking space, working with banks, should meet with VCs to educate them on how banks work and how regulations govern the safety and soundness of banks, help them see that the VC-mindset and understanding of risks are inapplicable to banks, and that social media risks of misinformation harm banks, and government rescue of a bank for the tech industry, regardless of how tech billionaires could spin their narratives, angering the public.

In the end, everyone hates banks, along now with having a new dislike and distrust toward the tech industry. Banking innovators in Silicon Valley, innovation centers and beyond the US boundaries is a challenge that SVB founders identified and embraced but eventually failed in a tragic death. It is now up to the tech industry to take on its own challenge of tackling the challenge without SVB. Tech bros love challenges, and they now have to build a bank to replace the one that they burned down within 24 hours. Until then the American public continues to hate banks.

Made in the USA
Las Vegas, NV
17 February 2024

85912546R00164